ACCOUNTING PRINCIPLES
for midmanagement

Dale L. Flesher
and
Tonya K. Flesher

ACCOUNTING PRINCIPLES
for midmanagement

Dale L. Flesher
and Tonya K. Flesher

DELMAR PUBLISHERS

LIBRARY OF CONGRESS CATALOG CARD NUMBER: 78-62620
ISBN 0-8273-1628-3

Printed in the United States of America
Published simultaneously in Canada by
Delmar Publishers, A Division of
Van Nostrand Reinhold, Ltd.

DELMAR PUBLISHERS • ALBANY, NEW YORK 12205
A DIVISION OF LITTON EDUCATIONAL PUBLISHING, INC.

Preface

ACCOUNTING PRINCIPLES FOR MIDMANAGEMENT is a general presentation designed to meet the needs of the non-accountant in business. The text develops fundamental accounting principles and applications needed by midmanagers whose career goals do not require the rigor of the traditional accounting presentation, as well as by those who wish to continue on to more advanced accounting courses.

Comprehensive in scope, ACCOUNTING PRINCIPLES FOR MIDMANAGEMENT develops the accounting process from initial journal entries to financial statements for selected service, merchandising, and manufacturing firms. Topical areas, including accounting for assets, specialized systems for increasing efficiency, payroll accounting, and income taxes are treated in depth. Where relevant to the needs of the midmanager, more advanced topics such as partnership and corporation accounting, financial statement analysis, budgeting, and auditing are presented.

In addition to specific learning objectives and a fully developed glossary of accounting terms, functional examples and illustrations are interwoven throughout the text presentation to enhance student interest and improve comprehension. Review sections complete each chapter, thereby reinforcing basic concept development, while exercises and problems provide the necessary practice of basic skills.

The WORKBOOK AND PRACTICE SET to accompany ACCOUNTING PRINCIPLES FOR MIDMANAGEMENT provides all required ancillary materials at a cost lower than any comparable publication. The WORKBOOK AND PRACTICE SET is directly correlated with the text and includes the forms necessary for the completion of the text problems, plus an answer checklist for student use. Developed to be functional and in keeping with modern accounting practice, the WORKBOOK AND PRACTICE SET addresses the student need for a review of accounting principles and applications through the recording of frequently encountered business transactions.

Completing the learning package, the Instructor's Guide reflects the flexibility and practical emphasis of the text and ancillary items. In addition to complete answers to all exercises and problems in the text, it also includes major objectives and lesson suggestions for each chapter, additional resources for use in presenting various topics, a pretest, and additional test questions for each chapter.

The authors of the text, Dale L. Flesher and Tonya K. Flesher, are equally experienced in education and accounting practice. Both are certified public accountants and are currently teaching accounting at the University of Mississippi.

Dale Flesher received a BS in Business Education/Economics and an MA in Accounting from Ball State University, and a PhD in Accounting from the University of Cincinnati. He also holds a Certificate in Management Accounting and was awarded the Certificate of Distinguished Performance for his exceptional score on the exam for this certificate. Dale has held teaching positions at several universities and has both industrial and public accounting experience. He is the author of *Operations Auditing in Hospitals.*

Tonya Flesher received a BS from Ball State University and earned her MA in Accounting at Appalachian State University. She received her PhD in Accounting from the University of Mississippi. In addition to several teaching positions, Tonya has been employed as an auditor for the Internal Revenue Service and has experience in public accounting. Both authors have written articles for accounting journals, and are members of various national accounting associations.

Dr. Lawrence L. Kogut, author of the WORKBOOK AND PRACTICE SET, lends additional expertise to the learning package. He received a DBA in Accounting/Business from Indiana Northern University, and is presently serving as Professor of Accounting and Chairman of the Business Administration Department at Hillsborough Community College in Tampa, Florida. Dr. Kogut also has had accounting experience in his own firm and as a consultant for a division of the Office of Equal Opportunity (OEO).

Contents

SECTION 1

Introduction to the Accounting Process

1
The Importance of Accounting

OBJECTIVES

After studying this chapter, the student will be able to:

- Describe the uses of accounting records.
- Explain the purpose of accounting records.
- Explain what an accountant does.
- Identify the three parties who are interested in accounting records, and how they use accounting information.
- List the three basic types of accountants and explain how they differ.
- Identify the two major accounting examinations.

WHAT IS ACCOUNTING?

Accounting is defined as the art of recording and summarizing business transactions and their effects on a business firm. A *business transaction* is an exchange of property or services. Thus, the purpose of accounting is to record changes caused by a firm's buying and selling properties or services. The following are examples of business transactions:

- Buying a truck for cash.
- Buying a truck on credit.
- Selling a typewriter for cash.
- Selling a typewriter on credit.
- Trading a cow for a horse.
- Investing money in a business.
- Paying the secretary a weekly salary.
- Paying for an ad in the newspaper.
- Paying the monthly rent.

Accounting has also been defined as the language of business. In its role as a language, accounting is a method of communication used to explain the actions of a business. Like all languages, accounting has certain words and symbols which have special meaning to those who use it.

For those who know the language, accounting records can answer many questions about a firm. For example:

- What property does the firm own?
- How much debt is owed and to whom?
- Are there any customers who are behind in paying the firm?
- How much profit did the firm earn?
- Is too much merchandise being kept on hand?
- Is anything being stolen from the firm?
- Should selling prices of goods be changed?
- How much cash is needed to run the firm?
- How much money is due in taxes?
- Can the firm borrow money?
- Should the firm try to get a short-term loan or a long-term loan?

Some people confuse accounting with *bookkeeping.* Actually, bookkeeping is a part of accounting: it is the routine clerical job of recording transactions. The bookkeeper records the transactions as they occur. The accountant's work begins where that of the bookkeeper ends. Thus, the accountant summarizes and interprets the records prepared by the bookkeeper. It can be said that bookkeeping is the preliminary stage of accounting. Once the skills of bookkeeping are mastered, a person is ready to learn accounting.

THE HISTORY OF ACCOUNTING

As a field of study, accounting has existed for as long as people have needed to keep records. Some of the earliest accounting records were carved into stone by people who lived in caves. Many early Biblical records are also examples of accounting documents. In fact, some of the Dead Sea Scrolls were originally intended as accounting records. Biblical accounting often dealt with lists of animals brought to be sacrificed at the temple, rather than amounts of money.

Fig. 1-1. An accountant summarizes and interprets the financial records of a firm and often makes suggestions that lead to more profitable operation.

Although accountants have always been important to the people they served, the Industrial Revolution made accounting and accountants even more necessary. During this period, businesses grew both in size and complexity. Owners were unable to oversee all aspects of these larger businesses. Thus, detailed accounting records became important as an aid in management.

Accounting has continued to grow as a professional field and as a business necessity. While one accountant can usually keep all of the records for a small firm, today's large firms employ thousands of accountants. Regardless of the size of the accounting task, the information supplied by accountants is basically the same.

WHO NEEDS ACCOUNTING INFORMATION?

Several groups of people use accounting information for various purposes. Three important users of the accounting records of a firm are:

- The owners of the business.
- Its creditors and suppliers.
- The government.

The owners of the business. The owners need accounting records in order to determine whether or not the firm is earning a profit. If the firm is not profitable, the owner may be able to learn the reason by looking at accounting records. Accounting records also help owners to decide whether or not to expand the firm, hire more employees, or buy additional merchandise.

Creditors and suppliers. *Creditors* are those to whom a firm owes money. Creditors and suppliers use accounting information to decide whether a firm will be able to pay its debts on time and should be given credit. If a firm does not have accurate and complete accounting records, it may not be able to borrow money. In fact, most banks will not lend money to a firm until the firm's financial records have been examined.

The government. Both the state and federal governments require that firms keep accounting records for tax purposes. Since firms pay taxes based upon the income they earn, it is necessary to keep accurate records that show this information. The lack of good records causes the most tax difficulties for small firms. A firm that has poor accounting records may have problems with the Internal Revenue Service (IRS). Although the IRS does not prescribe the type of records to be kept, it does require that the owner keep permanent books of account. Records must be available for inspection by IRS officers.

WHO KEEPS THE BOOKS?

Once an accounting system has been set up, the question is: "Who will keep the books?" There are several possible answers to this question. The least expensive answer is for the owner or owners to keep the books themselves. This method can save the small firm a great deal of money, since most accountants are quite highly paid. The accounting records for a small, new firm are usually simple; thus, it is easy for an owner with some accounting knowledge to keep adequate records.

If the owner of a firm does not have the time or knowledge to keep the records, a professional accountant may be hired. Two types of professional accountants are available to a firm. The first type is called a public accountant. *Public accountants* are those who offer their services to the public for a fee in the same way a lawyer does. A public accountant may work for one company one day, and then work for someone else the next day. In fact, one public accountant may work for several firms each day. The cost of hiring a public accountant may be quite high, but the professional advice received can often increase the firm's profits, and thus more than cover the cost of the service.

The second type of accountant is a private accountant, figure 1-2. Private accountants are also called industrial accountants or management accountants. A *private accountant* works for only one firm. If a firm hires a private accountant, that accountant will work only for that firm. It is usually less costly per hour to hire a private accountant than a public accountant. Some small firms find the best solution is to hire a part-time private accountant.

A third type of accountant that should be mentioned at this time is the *governmental accountant.* Although a business firm cannot hire a governmental accountant, the firm may, at times, work with governmental accountants. The Internal Revenue Service is one of the largest employers of governmental accountants. Most firms come in contact with IRS accountants at some time. Other government employers of accountants include state and county governments, the Securities and Exchange Commission (SEC), and the Federal Bureau of Investigation (FBI).

Fig. 1-2. These two private accountants are trying to decide upon the best tax strategy for their firm.

LICENSING AND PROFESSIONAL EXAMINATIONS IN ACCOUNTING

All states license certified public accountants (CPAs) just as they do doctors and lawyers. A *certified public accountant* is one who has accounting experience and has passed a difficult two and one-half day examination. The examination has four parts: Accounting Theory, Accounting Practice, Auditing, and Business Law. All four parts must be passed before a person can be a CPA. The exam is prepared and graded by the *American Institute of Certified Public Accountants* (AICPA). It is given twice a year (May and November) in every state. Licensing maintains high professional standards in the accounting profession. Those who have proven themselves by passing the difficult CPA exam are the most highly paid accountants.

Many states also license public accountants who are not CPAs. Although state laws vary, most states will grant a license to a public accountant (PA) only after one or more parts of the CPA exam have been passed.

Although states do not license private accountants, there is an exam that private accountants can take to demonstrate their abilities. The *Certificate in Management Accounting* or CMA is a two and one-half day exam given twice a year (June and December). It is designed to measure the skills needed in private accounting.

The requirements for taking the CPA exam vary from state to state. Therefore, interested persons should check the requirements of the state where they reside. Some states require a four-year degree with a major in accounting and from one to three years of public accounting experience before a person may take the exam. Others permit students to take the exam within ninety days of their expected graduation. Then, after the experience requirement is met, the license is issued.

Before sitting for the CMA exam, a person must have had at least twenty-four semester hours (or thirty-six quarter hours) of college accounting courses.

Any person who is planning to become a professional accountant should plan to take one (or both) of these exams upon graduation from college.

SUMMARY

Accounting is the language of business. It is used to record and summarize business transactions. The major purpose of accounting is to determine whether or not a firm is successful in making a profit. It has been found that there is a high correlation between the quality of accounting records kept by a firm and its financial success. Complete and accurate records are essential for use in preparing federal and state income tax returns. Creditors and banks may also desire to see the accounting records of a firm in order to estimate the firm's financial reliability.

There are three types of accountants: public accountants, private accountants, and governmental accountants. If the owners of small firms do not keep the accounting records themselves, they must hire either a public or private accountant.

The best qualified accountants are those who have passed at least part of an accounting examination. The two major examinations are:

the CPA (Certified Public Accountant) exam and the CMA (Certificate in Management Accounting) exam.

Accounting communicates the results of business transactions to the people who need to know such information. Accounting records show the owner or manager how the business is doing financially. With this knowledge, the owner or manager is able to make adjustments that result in maximum profitability for the firm. Thus, accounting is a language for expressing business information which can then be used as a management tool.

REVIEW

1. Define accounting.
2. Define a business transaction.
3. Give five examples of business transactions.
4. In general, what does an accountant do? How does this compare with the duties of a bookkeeper?
5. List three groups of people that use accounting information.
6. Why would a banker want to look at a small firm's accounting records?
7. Why does the government require firms to keep accurate accounting records?
8. What are the three basic types of accountants?
9. Which two types of accountants can be hired by a private firm?
10. What are the two major accounting examinations and how often are they given?
11. The passage of which accounting exam leads to licensing by a state government?

2
The Accounting Equation

OBJECTIVES

After studying this chapter, the student will be able to:

- Define assets, liabilities, and owner's equity.
- Describe the basic accounting equation.
- Show the effects of transactions upon the basic accounting equation.

EXPLANATION OF THE BASIC ACCOUNTING EQUATION

The phrase *double entry accounting* is often used to describe the records kept by business firms. The word *double* means that two different types of records are kept. The two types of items for which records are kept are: (1) properties and (2) rights to properties. Properties owned are usually called assets. Property rights are normally called equities. Since assets must be equal to equities in those assets, the basic accounting equation is sometimes written as:

ASSETS = EQUITIES

Assets

Assets are the properties owned by a firm. For example, cash, land, vehicles, buildings, and equipment are all assets. Assets are things that a firm owns that have value. They are the resources of a firm. Thus, one goal of accounting is to keep a record of the assets owned by a firm.

Equities

The term *equities* means the rights or claims to assets. There are two types of equities. One type is the owner's equity in his or her own business. It is sometimes called the *owner's net worth.* The second type is the equity of outsiders who do not own the firm, but who have some claim to its assets due to business transactions with the firm. This type of equity is called a liability. A *liability* is defined as the equity of someone who has lent money to the firm or sold goods to the firm on credit. It is sometimes called a *debt.*

The people to whom a firm owes money are known as *creditors.* Creditors have a right to some of the firm's assets until the debts are paid. Thus, it is said that creditors have a right to (or an equity in) some of the firm's assets. If creditors do not have rights to all of the assets of a firm, the owner has a right to the remaining assets.

Since there are really two types of equities, it is more accurate to write the basic accounting equation as:

ASSETS = LIABILITIES + OWNER'S EQUITY

Memorize this equation, and remember that it must always be balanced. In other words, the two sides must be equal in value. The total assets of the firm are listed on the left side. The listing of liabilities and owner's equity, which shows who has the rights to the assets, appears on the right side. If an amount is added or deducted from one side of the equation, it must also be added to or deducted from the other side so that the two sides remain equal (balanced). This expanded equation is preferred for legal reasons since creditors have first claim on assets if a firm goes out of business.

USING THE BASIC ACCOUNTING EQUATION

The following examples demonstrate the effect of various business transactions on the basic accounting equation.

Suppose that Jim Fox starts a new law firm with an investment of $1,000 in cash. This can be represented by the accounting equation as follows:

ASSETS	=	LIABILITIES	+	OWNER'S EQUITY
Cash, $1,000	=	0	+	$1,000

Jim then borrows $500 from the bank. The equation expresses this transaction in the following way:

ASSETS	=	LIABILITIES	+	OWNER'S EQUITY
Cash		Payable to Bank		
$1,000	=	0	+	$1,000
+ 500	=	500		
1,500	=	500	+	1,000

Because Jim has acquired $500 additional assets, $500 is added to the left side of the equation. However, since the $500 is owed to the bank, it must also be recorded as a liability on the right side of the equation. Using this procedure, the two sides of the equation remain balanced (equal to each other). The last equation shows an accountant that Jim's firm has total assets of $1,500 – of which the bank has the first right to $500. Jim has a right to only $1,000 of the assets.

To operate his business, Jim needs a typewriter. He buys a typewriter for $100 cash. The equation now appears as shown in figure 2-1.

The $100 is subtracted from Jim's cash assets but is added to his property assets. Hence, the total on the left side of the equation remains the same, and the equation is still in balance. Jim's total assets of $1,500 ($1,400 cash and a typewriter worth $100) are equal to the total liabilities plus owner's equity of $1,500.

Next, Jim finds it necessary to buy $250 worth of office supplies on credit from a local store. The basic equation after this transaction

ASSETS		=	LIABILITIES	+ OWNER'S EQUITY
Cash	+ **Typewriter**	=	Payable to Bank	
$1,000		=		$1,000
+ 500		=	$500	
1,500		=	500	1,000
- 100	+100	=		
1,400	**100**	=	**500**	**1,000**

Fig. 2-1. The basic accounting equation after purchase of a typewriter.

ASSETS			=	LIABILITIES		+ OWNER'S EQUITY
Cash	+ Typewriter	+ **Office Supplies**	=	Payable to Bank	+ **Accounts Payable**	
$1,000			=			$1,000
+ 500			=	$500		
1,500			=	500		1,000
- 100	+100		=			
1,400	100		=	500		1,000
		+250	=		+250	
1,400	**100**	**250**		**500**	**250**	**1,000**

Fig. 2-2. The basic accounting equation after purchase of office supplies on credit.

is shown in figure 2-2. The $250 worth of office supplies is added to the asset side of the equation. This also creates a new liability for Jim's firm as shown on the right side of the equation. It is added to the right side of the equation as *accounts payable.*

Note that the equation is still in balance. Assets total $1,750. Creditors' rights to those assets total $750. The owner still has an equity of $1,000.

The owner's equity in the firm will increase if the owner invests some additional assets in the company. Jim decides to invest a truck worth $4,000. The equation reflects this investment as shown in figure 2-3. The assets now total $5,750 and the owner's equity in those assets has increased to $5,000. Outsiders (creditors) still have a right to $750 of the assets.

ASSETS				=	LIABILITIES		+ OWNER'S EQUITY
Cash	+ Typewriter	+ Office Supplies	+ **Truck**	=	Payable to Bank	+ Accounts Payable	
$1,000				=			$1,000
+ 500				=	$500		
1,500				=	500		1,000
- 100	+100			=			
1,400	100			=	500		1,000
		+250		=		+250	
1,400	100	250		=	500	250	1,000
			+4,000	=			+4,000
1,400	**100**	**250**	**4,000**	=	**500**	**250**	**5,000**

Fig. 2-3. The basic accounting equation after investment of a truck by the owner.

ASSETS				= LIABILITIES		+	OWNER'S EQUITY
Cash	+ Typewriter	+ Office Supplies	+ Truck	= Payable to Bank	+ Accounts Payable		
$1,000				=			$1,000
+ 500				= $500			
1,500				= 500			1,000
- 100	+100			=			
1,400	100			= 500			1,000
		+250			+250		
1,400	100	250		= 500	250		1,000
			+4,000	=			+4,000
1,400	100	250	4,000	= 500	250		5,000
- 250				=	-250		
1,150	100	250	4,000	= 500	0		5,000

Fig. 2-4. The basic accounting equation after payment of accounts payable.

Jim now decides to use some of the firm's cash to pay off the liability to the office supply store ($250). The changes in the equation resulting from this transaction are illustrated by figure 2-4. Note that although the assets decreased to $5,500, the owner's equity did not change.

INCREASE IN OWNER'S EQUITY

There are two ways the owner's equity in a firm can increase. One way, as shown in the example of Jim's firm, is for the owner to invest personal assets (cash and truck) in the business. The second way in which owner's equity is increased is by performance of a service for a fee. This is referred to as *earning a revenue.* A *revenue* is defined as an increase in owner's equity resulting from the performance of a service or a sale of something. When a firm earns a revenue, an asset is increased and the owner's equity in the assets is also increased. Revenue from services may be received in one of two forms: as cash, or as an account receivable.

Cash

A firm may perform a service for which cash is received. For example, if Jim's firm performed a service for which $300 was received, the accounting equation would change as shown in figure 2-5. The asset, cash, is increased by $300. Since no other asset is affected, the total of all assets (the left side of the equation) is increased by $300. To balance the equation, the right side of the equation (liabilities and owner's equity) must also be increased by $300. Since there is no type of liability involved, the entry must be made under the owner's equity column.

Account Receivable

Suppose a firm performs a service for another customer who buys for credit instead of paying cash. The work is completed and the

ASSETS				=	LIABILITIES		+ OWNER'S EQUITY
Cash	+ Typewriter	+ Office Supplies	+ Truck	=	Payable to Bank	+ Accounts Payable	
$1,000				=			$1,000
+ 500				=	$500		
1,500				=	500		1,000
- 100	+100			=			
1,400	100			=	500		1,000
		+250		=		+250	
1,400	100	250		=	500	250	1,000
			+4,000	=			+4,000
1,400	100	250	4,000	=	500	250	5,000
- 250				=		-250	
1,150	100	250	4,000	=	500	0	5,000
+ 300				=			+ 300
1,450	**100**	**250**	**4,000**	=	**500**	**0**	**5,300**

Fig. 2-5. The basic accounting equation after receiving cash from earning a revenue.

customer promises to pay within thirty days. In this instance, the firm also earns a revenue. However, cash is not the asset that is affected since no cash has been received. Instead, an asset called an *account receivable* is increased. Note that a firm does not have to receive cash in order to earn a revenue. The revenue is earned when the work is performed.

Jim's firm performs a service for a customer and extends the customer credit for $1,050. Figure 2-6 shows the equation after recording a $1,050 revenue which will not be collected for thirty days.

ASSETS					=	LIABILITIES		+ OWNER'S EQUITY
Cash	+ Typewriter	+ Office Supplies	+ Truck	+ **Accounts Receivable**	=	Payable to Bank	+ Accounts Payable	
$1,000					=			$1,000
+ 500					=	$500		
1,500					=	500		1,000
- 100	+100				=			
1,400	100				=	500		1,000
		+250			=		+250	
1,400	100	250			=	500	250	1,000
			+4,000		=			+4,000
1,400	100	250	4,000		=	500	250	5,000
- 250					=		-250	
1,150	100	250	4,000		=	500	0	5,000
+ 300					=			+ 300
1,450	100	250	4,000		=	500	0	5,300
				+1,050	=			+1,050
1,450	**100**	**250**	**4,000**	**1,050**	=	**500**		**6,350**

Fig. 2-6. The basic accounting equation after acquiring an account receivable.

ASSETS					=	LIABILITIES		+ OWNER'S EQUITY
Cash	+ Typewriter	+ Office Supplies	+ Truck	+ Accounts Receivable	=	Payable to Bank	+ Accounts Payable	
$1,000					=			$1,000
+ 500					=	$500		
1,500					=	500		1,000
- 100	+100				=			
1,400	100				=	500		1,000
		+250			=		+250	
1,400	100	250			=	500	250	1,000
			+4,000		=			+4,000
1,400	100	250	4,000		=	500	250	5,000
- 250					=		-250	
1,150	100	250	4,000		=	500	0	5,000
+ 300					=			+ 300
1,450	100	250	4,000		=	500	0	5,300
				+1,050	=			+1,050
1,450	100	250	4,000	1,050	=	500		6,350
+ 525				- 525	=			
1,975	**100**	**250**	**4,000**	**525**	=	**500**		**6,350**

Fig. 2-7. The basic accounting equation after collecting partial payment of an account receivable.

As an asset, the account receivable is equally valuable as cash. Although it cannot be spent immediately, it represents the right to collect cash in the future.

RECORDING REVENUES

The last illustration points out a basic rule of accounting: record revenues when the work is performed. Do not wait until the cash is collected. The most important event in earning a revenue is the performance of the work. Thus, as soon as the work is completed, an asset has been earned. That asset will either be cash or accounts receivable (the right to receive cash in the future).

When the charge customer pays, no revenue is recorded. Figure 2-7 shows how the equation would be changed if the customer in figure 2-6 who was charged $1,050 paid half of the amount owed ($525). Since this payment is only a trade of one asset for another (an account receivable for cash), there is no change in total assets. Therefore, since total assets do not change, the right side of the equation does not change.

The firm earns and records the revenue when the work is performed. The collection has no effect on the owner's equity. The increase in assets has already been recorded.

DECREASE IN OWNER'S EQUITY

When people go into business, their main objective is to earn revenues and thus increase their owner's equity. Of course, it is also possible for the owner's equity in a firm to decrease. There are two ways in which the owner's equity can become smaller: withdrawal of assets and incurring expenses.

ASSETS						= LIABILITIES		+ OWNER'S EQUITY
Cash	+ Typewriter	+ Office Supplies	+ Truck	+ Accounts Receivable	=	Payable to Bank	+ Accounts Payable	
$1,000					=			$1,000
+ 500					=	$500		
1,500					=	500		1,000
- 100	+100				=			
1,400	100				=	500		1,000
		+250			=		+250	
1,400	100	250			=	500	250	1,000
			+4,000		=			+4,000
1,400	100	250	4,000		=	500	250	5,000
- 250					=		-250	
1,150	100	250	4,000		=	500	0	5,000
+ 300					=			+ 300
1,450	100	250	4,000		=	500	0	5,300
				+1,050	=			+1,050
1,450	100	250	4,000	1,050	=	500		6,350
+ 525				- 525	=			
1,975	100	250	4,000	525	=	500		6,350
- 200	-100				=			- 300
1,775	0	250	4,000	525	=	500		6,050

Fig. 2-8. The basic accounting equation after the withdrawal of assets by the owner.

Withdrawal of Assets

The owner may decide to withdraw assets from the business. This is just the opposite of investing in the firm. Using the previously discussed firm as an example, assume that the owner, Jim Fox, withdraws \$200 cash and the typewriter from the firm. Since the assets are for personal use, and not for business use, they must be removed from the firm's records. Figure 2-8 shows how the basic equation is affected.

Since the asset side is decreased by \$300 (cash, \$200, and typewriter, \$100), the right side of the equation must also be decreased by \$300. There are no outsiders involved. Therefore, liabilities are not changed. Thus, the owner's equity is the only column on the right side of the equation that can be changed. Note that the equation is still in balance. Total assets are \$6,550 and liabilities plus owner's equity are \$6,550.

Incurring Expenses

The owner's equity also decreases when the firm incurs an expense. An *expense* is the opposite of a revenue; it arises when cash is paid out but no other asset is received. For instance, assume that Jim Fox hires a secretary at a salary of \$100 per week. At the end of the week he pays the secretary \$100. This transaction would appear as shown in figure 2-9.

Since cash is the only asset affected, the total change on the left side of the equation is a \$100 decrease. Thus, something on the right side will also have to decrease by $100. It is the owner's equity in the firm's assets that decreases. Other examples of expenses include advertising, electric utility bills, rent, repairs, and telephone bills.

Note that every transaction affects one or more elements of the basic equation. The equation is important because it allows for double entry accounting. *Double entry accounting* refers to the process of keeping a record both of assets and of who has rights to the assets.

It is also important to note that our accounting system is a *cost-based system.* In other words, assets are always recorded at their cost even though they might be worth more than their cost. Called the *cost principle of accounting,* this principle states that all transactions must be recorded at cost.

SUMMARY

The basic accounting equation is:

ASSETS = LIABILITIES + OWNER'S EQUITY

This equation must always be in balance. Assets are the items that a firm owns. Liabilities are the debts that the firm owes. Those people to whom the debts are owed are known as creditors. Owner's equity is the owner's right to assets in his or her own business. The owner's equity is made up of assets not owed to creditors.

Owner's equity may increase or decrease. There are two ways for the owner's equity in a firm to increase. First, the owner may invest personal assets in the firm. Second, the firm may earn revenues for performing services. There are also two ways in which owner's equity

ASSETS					=	LIABILITIES		+ OWNER'S EQUITY
Cash	+ Typewriter	+ Office Supplies	+ Truck	+ Accounts Receivable	=	Payable to Bank	+ Accounts Payable	
$1,000					=			$1,000
+ 500					=	$500		
1,500					=	500		1,000
- 100	+100				=			
1,400	100				=	500		1,000
		+250			=		+250	
1,400	100	250			=	500	250	1,000
			+4,000		=			+4,000
1,400	100	250	4,000		=	500	250	5,000
- 250					=		-250	
1,150	100	250	4,000		=	500	0	5,000
+ 300					=			+ 300
1,450	100	250	4,000		=	500	0	5,300
				+1,050	=			+1,050
1,450	100	250	4,000	1,050	=	500		6,350
+ 525				- 525	=			
1,975	100	250	4,000	525	=	500		6,350
- 200	-100				=			- 300
1,775	0	250	4,000	525	=	500		6,050
- 100					=			- 100
1,675		**250**	**4,000**	**525**	=	**500**		**5,950**

Fig. 2-9. The basic accounting equation after paying an expense.

in a firm may decrease. One way is for the owner to withdraw some assets from the firm for personal use. The second way is for the firm to incur expenses. An expense is incurred when cash is paid out and no other asset is received in return.

Familiarity with the basic accounting equation is necessary before undertaking the more technical aspects of bookkeeping and accounting.

REVIEW

1. Write the basic accounting equation.
2. What is an asset?
3. List five examples of assets.
4. What is a liability?
5. What are the two ways in which the owner's equity may increase?
6. What are the two ways in which the owner's equity may decrease?
7. When an owner puts money into a business it is called an investment. What is it called when the owner takes money out of the business?

EXERCISES

1. If the assets of a firm are $8,000 and the liabilities are $2,000, how much is the owner's equity?
2. If the assets of a firm are $3,200 and the owner's equity is $3,000, how much are the liabilities?
3. If a firm has liabilities of $4,200 and owner's equity of $1,000, what are its total assets?
4. A new firm completed the following three transactions.
   (1) The owner invested $3,000 in the firm.
   (2) The firm borrowed $1,000 from the bank.
   (3) The firm bought a $3,000 truck, paying $1,500 down and agreeing to pay the rest over the next twelve months.
   a. After the third transaction, what are the total assets of the firm?
   b. After the third transaction, what are the total liabilities of the firm?
   c. After the third transaction, what is the owner's equity in the firm?

PROBLEMS

1. Record the following transactions in an expanded accounting equation as illustrated in this chapter. Calculate the total of each column after every transaction.
   a. Ann Benjamin invested $2,000 in a new real estate business.
   b. The firm bought a new car for $3,000. Since she was short of cash, Ann paid only $500 down. The rest is to be paid at a later time.
   c. Ann bought a typewriter for the office on credit, $140.
   d. The firm placed an advertisement in the newspaper at a cost of $30.
   e. The monthly telephone bill of $20 was paid.

f. Ann sold a house for a customer and the firm received a $400 commission.
g. The firm paid for the typewriter purchased in transaction *c*.
h. Ann withdrew $200 from the business for her personal use.

2. Record the following transactions in an expanded accounting equation as illustrated in this chapter. Calculate the total of each column after every transaction.
   a. Bob Pelsak started a new law firm by investing $8,000 in cash.
   b. The firm bought a law library consisting of 600 books. The books cost $5,000 and were paid for in cash.
   c. Bob bought a typewriter for the office at a cost of $300. The firm paid $100 down and will pay the rest at the end of the month.
   d. Bob did legal work for a client and received $200 in cash.
   e. Bob did legal work for his client, Al Smith. Al promised to pay the $450 fee in a few weeks.
   f. The monthly telephone bill of $25 was paid.
   g. Bob hired a secretary and paid her $100 as her first week's salary.
   h. The firm made a partial payment of $50 on the typewriter bought in transaction *c*.
   i. Al Smith paid half of what he owed for the legal work done in transaction *e*.
   j. The firm paid $62 for the first month's electric bill.
   k. Bob withdrew $150 to buy his wife a present.

3. Toby Green established a new delivery business which he named Fast Delivery Service. During a short period the firm completed these business transactions:
   a. Sold a personal investment in Ford Motor Company stock for $1,615 and deposited $1,500 of the proceeds in a checking account opened at the bank in the name of the firm.
   b. Paid $180 for rent of office space for three months in advance.
   c. Paid $800 for a used motorcycle for delivering packages.
   d. Bought an office desk and chair from Office Supply Company for $200 in cash.
   e. Bought $50 worth of office supplies from Office Supply Company on credit.
   f. Paid $25 for a newspaper advertisement announcing the new business.
   g. Delivered packages for the Ames Store and collected $50 cash for the service performed.
   h. Delivered packages for the Everything Shop on credit, $25.
   i. Toby took from home a typewriter having a $75 fair market value for permanent use in the business.
   j. Collected the $25 owed by the Everything Shop for delivering packages in transaction *h*.
   k. Paid Office Supply Company $50 for the Office supplies purchased in transaction *e*.
   l. Toby wrote a $10 check on the business bank account to pay the electric bill for his personal residence.

A. Arrange the following asset, liability, and owner equity titles in an equation like that shown in figure 2-6: Cash, Accounts Receivable, Prepaid Rent, Office Supplies, Office Equipment, Delivery Equipment, Accounts Payable, and Toby Green Equity.

B. Show by additions and subtractions the effects of each transaction on the assets, liabilities, and owner's equity of Fast Delivery Service. Show new totals for all items after each transaction.

3 Journalizing and Posting Accounting Transactions

OBJECTIVES After studying this chapter, the student will be able to:

- State the rules of debit and credit for all accounts.
- Record transactions in journal entry form.
- Post to the accounts in the ledger.
- Use a chart of accounts.

THE ACCOUNT

In chapter 2, business transactions were recorded using the accounting equation. Pluses and minuses were used to show increases and decreases in the columns. However, this method becomes too complicated if there are many transactions to record. A better way to show increases and decreases is to record each type of transaction separately. This is done by setting up an account for each type of transaction.

An *account* is a place where transactions are summarized. Each asset, liability, and owner equity item has a separate account. The increases and decreases in each item are recorded on the page designated for that item. Many pages of paper are necessary to record all the accounts of a firm. These pages may be bound in a book like a notebook called a ledger. A *ledger* is defined as a group of related accounts.

Like any other book, the ledger has a table of contents. The table of contents for a ledger is called a chart of accounts. The *chart of accounts* is a list of all account titles and their assigned numbers. The accounts in the ledger are placed in the following order: assets, liabilities, owner's equity account, drawing account, revenues, and expenses. The numbering follows this same order. Using this system, the account numbers for assets start with 1, liabilities with 2, owner's equity with 3, revenues with 4, and expenses with 5. For example, the chart of accounts for the law firm owned by Jim Fox shown in chapter 2 might look like the one in figure 3-1.

The simple form for an account is the *T-account*, so called because it is shaped like the letter *T*. A T-account has three parts: a title, a left side, and a right side. It looks like this:

Title of Account	
left side	right side

	Chart of Accounts
111	Cash
112	Accounts Receivable
113	Office Supplies
121	Typewriter
125	Truck
211	Notes Payable
212	Accounts Payable
311	Jim Fox, Capital
312	Jim Fox, Drawing
411	Revenue from Fees Earned
531	Salary Expense

Fig. 3-1. Chart of accounts for the Jim Fox Law Firm.

Use of accounts is a clearer, much more convenient way to record transactions than the use of the columns shown in chapter 2. When all amounts are written in the same column, it is easy to confuse the increases and decreases. With an account, the increases and decreases are written on different sides of the page.

Debit and Credit

Accountants call the left-hand side the *debit side*. The right-hand side is called the *credit side*. Debit and credit are often abbreviated as *Dr.* and *Cr.* Thus, the T-account can be shown as:

Title of Account	
debit (Dr.)	credit (Cr.)

To debit an account means to write a number on the left-hand side of the account. To credit an account means to write a number on the right-hand side of the account. In accounting, these two words do not have the negative and positive connotations often given them in popular usage. They merely indicate an entry on the left or right side of the account. It is sometimes said that an account has a *debit balance*. This means that the amounts on the debit side are greater than those on the credit side. A *credit balance* means that the sum of the credits is greater than the sum of the debits.

T-ACCOUNTS AND THE ACCOUNTING EQUATION

The use of the T-account with the accounting equation is shown in figure 3-2. As has been stated, a separate account is set up for each asset, liability, and owner's equity item. Increases and decreases in each item are recorded as indicated under the T-accounts for each item.

ASSETS		=	LIABILITIES		+	OWNER'S EQUITY	
Debit increases.	Credit decreases.		Debit decreases.	Credit increases.		Debit decreases.	Credit increases.

Fig. 3-2 The rules of debit and credit for the accounting equation.

In learning the rules of debit and credit, it is helpful to think of the accounting equation as a mirror. One side of the equation reflects the other. Thus, like a mirror image, one side is the reverse of the other. In other words, the rules for asset accounts and the rules for liability and owner's equity accounts are just the opposite.

An account that usually has a debit balance, such as an asset, is said to have a *normal debit balance.* An account that usually has a credit balance is said to have a *normal credit balance.* For example, liabilities and revenues have normal credit balances.

Use of T-Accounts with the Expanded Equation

Using the double-entry system, an expense of operating the firm, such as rent or advertising, is recorded as a decrease in cash (a credit to cash) and a decrease in owner's equity (a debit to owner's equity). However, if all expenses were recorded in one owner's equity account, it would be almost impossible to learn the amount of each type of expense. For example, assume that rent expense and advertising expense were both debited to the same owner's equity account. If, at a later time, someone wanted to know how much the rent expense had been, there would be no way to tell. For this reason, firms do not use just one owner's equity account. Instead, they use a different owner's equity account for each different type of expense. For example, in the situation just described, separate expense accounts would be set up for rent and advertising.

Expense accounts always have a debit balance since they are really just temporary owner's equity accounts. They are used only to record decreases in owner's equity. Since decreases in owner's equity are recorded with debits, then expenses must be recorded with debits.

Two other types of temporary owner's equity accounts are commonly used. One type of account is used to record revenues. Since a revenue is an increase in owner's equity (a credit), revenue accounts always have a credit balance. Revenues increase owner's equity. Therefore, the rules for revenue accounts are the same as for owner's equity accounts.

The *drawing account* is another type of temporary owner's equity account. This account is used to record withdrawals of assets from the firm by the owner. The drawing account shows decreases in owner's equity. When recording transactions, the drawing account is treated just the opposite of the owner's equity account. In other words, increases are debited and decreases are credited.

When the basic accounting equation is expanded to include accounts for expenses, revenues, and owner's drawing, the rules for recording transactions are summarized as shown in figure 3-3.

ASSETS		= LIABILITIES		+ OWNER'S EQUITY		- Owner's Drawing		+ Revenues		- Expenses	
Debit increases.	Credit decreases.	Debit decreases.	Credit increases.	Debit decreases.	Credit increases.	Debit increases.	Credit decreases.	Debit decreases.	Credit increases.	Debit increases.	Credit decreases.

Fig. 3-3. The rules of debit and credit for the expanded equation.

RECORDING TRANSACTIONS USING T-ACCOUNTS AND THE RULES OF DEBIT AND CREDIT

All transactions can be recorded using the accounting equation and the rules of debit and credit. Note that the equation must always be balanced. This means that for each transaction the sum of the debits must always equal the sum of the credits. This is one of the main rules of double-entry bookkeeping or accounting.

With the rules of debit and credit in mind, the transactions in chapter 2 can now be recorded in T-accounts.

A. Jim Fox starts a new law firm with an investment of $1,000 in cash, figure 3-4(a). This transaction increases cash, which is an asset. It also increases the owner's equity. The owner's equity in the firm is represented by an account for capital in the owner's name. Following the rules shown in figure 3-2, to increase Cash, debit the Cash account for $1,000. To increase the owner's equity account, credit the account for $1,000. The T-accounts should be visualized as part of the accounting equation: ASSETS = LIABILITIES + OWNER'S EQUITY. Thus far, only the accounts for assets and owner's equity are being considered. Note that these items are on opposite sides of the accounting equation and, because the

Cash	
(a) *1,000*	

Jim Fox, Capital	
	(a) *1,000*

Fig. 3-4(a).

B. The firm borrows $500 from the bank by signing a note. This transaction increases cash and increases liabilities by creating a note payable. It requires a debit (increase) to Cash and a credit (increase) to Notes Payable, figure 3-4(b).

Cash	
1,000	
(b) *500*	

Notes Payable	
	(b) *500*

Fig. 3-4(b).

C. The firm purchases a typewriter for $100 in cash. A typewriter is a thing of value and is thus an asset. In this transaction, one asset account (Typewriter) will be increased while another (Cash) will be decreased. This is simply an exchange of one asset for another. Figure 3-4(c) illustrates how this is recorded in the two accounts.

Cash	
1,000	(c) *100*
500	

Typewriter	
(c) *100*	

Fig. 3-4(c).

D. The firm buys $250 of office supplies on credit from a local store. This will increase the asset, Office Supplies, and it will increase liabilities. The liability account to be used is called Accounts Payable. (The Notes Payable account is used only when a formal legal document, called a *note*, has been signed for the debt.) In this case, the supplies were purchased on open account and no note was signed. Figure 3-4(d) shows the two accounts that were affected. Note that both accounts were increased.

Office Supplies

(d) 250	

Accounts Payable

	(d) 250

Fig. 3-4(d).

E. Jim Fox invests a truck worth $4,000 in the firm. This transaction causes an increase in assets (recorded as a debit to the Truck account) and an increase in owner's equity (a credit to Jim Fox, Capital). Figure 3-4(e) shows the two accounts after the entry has been recorded.

Truck

(e) 4,000	

Jim Fox, Capital

	1,000
	(e) 4,000

Fig. 3-4(e).

F. The firm uses cash to pay off the liability of $250 to the office supply store. This causes a decrease in Cash (a credit to the Cash account) and a decrease in Accounts Payable (a debit to this account), figure 3-4(f).

Cash

1,000	100
500	(f) 250

Accounts Payable

(f) 250	250

Fig. 3-4(f).

G. The firm performs a service for a client and receives $300 in cash. This is a revenue which results in an increase in assets. Thus, the Cash account is debited and Revenue is credited as shown in figure 3-4(g).

Cash

1,000	100
500	250
(g) 300	

Revenue From Fees Earned

	(g) 300

Fig. 3-4(g).

H. The firm performs a service for a client on credit for $1,050. This is also a revenue, but the asset to be increased is Accounts Receivable.

Accounts Receivable is debited and Revenue is credited as shown in figure 3-4(h).

Accounts Receivable	
(h) 1,050	

Revenue From Fees Earned	
	300
	(h) 1,050

Fig. 3-4(h).

I. The credit customer pays half of his bill with $525 in cash. This is an exchange of one asset for another. Cash is increased and Accounts Receivable is decreased. Figure 3-4(i) shows how the entry would be recorded in the two accounts.

Cash	
1,000	100
500	250
300	
(i) 525	

Accounts Receivable	
1,050	(i) 525

Fig. 3-4(i).

J. Jim Fox, the owner, withdraws $200 in cash and the typewriter. This decreases assets and owner's equity. The separate owner's equity account described earlier, the Drawing account, is used to record this transaction. Since withdrawals represent a decrease in owner's equity, they are debited to the drawing account. Thus, the $300 is debited as shown in figure 3-4(j). The typewriter and cash accounts are also affected by this transaction. The typewriter asset is decreased and is, therefore, credited to that account. Cash is also decreased, so the $200 is entered on the credit side of the account. These entries balance the accounting equation.

Cash	
1,000	100
500	250
300	(j) 200
525	

Typewriter	
100	(j) 100

Jim Fox, Drawing	
(j) 300	

Fig. 3-4(j).

K. Jim hires a secretary and pays her a salary of $100 for the first week. This represents an expense of the firm and thus decreases the Cash account. It is recorded as shown in figure 3-4(k).

Cash	
1,000	100
500	250
300	200
525	(k) 100

Salary Expense	
(k) 100	

Fig. 3-4(k).

THE GENERAL JOURNAL

In the preceding example, all transactions were recorded only in the accounts. Since each account has a separate page in the ledger, it is not possible to examine the whole transaction at a glance. The debit for a transaction is entered on one page while the credit is shown on another. This makes it difficult to discover an error or survey the records to see the general trend in the business. To provide a place where all transactions can be recorded together, a type of diary is kept of the firm's activities. This diary, or record, is called a *journal.* Since every transaction is recorded first in the journal and then in the ledger, the journal is called *the book of original entry.*

Each transaction is recorded separately in a journal entry. The process of making journal entries is called *journalizing.* The basic type of journal is called a *general journal.* A partial page from a journal is shown in figure 3-5. It has two money columns which are used for debit and credit amounts.

Making Journal Entries

The following steps are necessary in making a journal entry.

1. **Enter the date.** The year is written at the top of the date column. The month is written below it in the same space. The month and year need not be repeated as long as they remain the same. The day of the transaction is entered in the second column under the *Date* heading.
2. **Enter the name of the account to be debited.** The name of the debited account is written on the same line as the date under the column titled *Account Titles and Explanation.* The name begins at the left margin of the column.
3. **Enter the amount to be debited** in the debit column after the account title.
4. **Enter the name of the account to be credited** on the next line, indented about one inch from the left margin.
5. **Enter the amount to be credited** in the credit column on the same line as the title of the account.

GENERAL JOURNAL Page

Date		Account Titles and Explanation	Post. Ref.	Debit	Credit

Fig. 3-5. Sample page from a general journal.

6. **Enter a brief explanation.** On the line after the title of the credited account, an explanation of the transaction may be written. It is indented about one-half inch from the left margin of the Account Titles section.

Figure 3-6 illustrates the correct journal entries for each of the transactions of the Jim Fox Law Firm described earlier in the chapter. In actual accounting practice, these entries would be made before the transactions were recorded in the ledger. The first entry is explained as follows:

> Jim Fox starts a new law firm with an investment of $1,000 in cash on May 1, 1980. The entry required is a debit to Cash and a credit to Jim Fox, Capital. Note the entry made in figure 3-6.

All transactions for the firm have been entered in the journal using the same basic procedure. The dates have been made up to complete the illustration. The letters on the left refer to the T-accounts explained earlier in the chapter. Re-read the explanation of each transaction (A-K) and study the journal entry made in figure 3-6.

A journal entry with more than one debit or credit is called a *compound entry.* Entry J on May 21 is a compound entry. Note that the debits are shown before the credits. In any journal entry the sum of the debits must be equal to the sum of the credits.

POSTING TO THE GENERAL LEDGER

After transactions are entered in the journal, they must be recorded in the ledger. The ledger which contains all of the accounts for a firm is called a *general ledger. Posting* is the process of transferring the information from the journal to the ledger. The accounts in the ledger are arranged in the order shown in the chart of accounts. (See figure 3-1.)

Usually, at the end of the day, all entries for that day are posted from the journal to the ledger. Accounts in the ledger are basically the same as the T-accounts described earlier, except that they usually have an extra column in which a running balance is shown for each account. The balance of an account is the difference between the debits and the credits. A ledger account for Cash might look like the one shown in figure 3-7.

Although ledger accounts have an explanation column, it is rarely used. It exists only for historical reasons. Five hundred years ago, most firms did not use a journal. Thus, explanations had to be recorded in the accounts. Today, if someone needs an explanation, it is available in the journal.

Steps in Posting

To post an entry from the journal to the ledger, complete the following steps. Do them first for the debit part of the entry and then for the credit part:

1. **Write the date** of the transaction in the date column of the proper account.

	Date		Account Titles and Explanation	Post. Ref.	Debit	Credit
	1980					
a	*May*	*1*	*Cash*		*1000 00*	
			Jim Fox, Capital			*1000 00*
			"To record the investment by owner."			
b		*2*	*Cash*		*500 00*	
			Notes Payable			*500 00*
			"To record a loan from the bank."			
c		*3*	*Typewriter*		*100 00*	
			Cash			*100 00*
			Bought a typewriter.			
d		*3*	*Office Supplies*		*250 00*	
			Accounts Payable			*250 00*
			Bought office supplies on account.			
e		*5*	*Truck*		*4000 00*	
			Jim Fox, Capital			*4000 00*
			Owner invested truck in firm.			
f		*6*	*Accounts Payable*		*250 00*	
			Cash			*250 00*
			To record payment on account.			
g		*7*	*Cash*		*300 00*	
			Revenue from Fees Earned			*300 00*
			Received payment from client.			
h		*8*	*Accounts Receivable*		*1050 00*	
			Revenue from Fees Earned			*1050 00*
			Performed services for client on account.			
i		*15*	*Cash*		*525 00*	
			Accounts Receivable			*525 00*
			Client paid on his account.			
j		*21*	*Jim Fox, Drawing*		*300 00*	
			Cash			*200 00*
			Typewriter			*100 00*
			Owner withdrew assets.			
k		*31*	*Salary Expense*		*100 00*	
			Cash			*100 00*
			Paid the secretary's salary.			

GENERAL JOURNAL — Page *1*

Fig. 3-6. Journal entries for the Jim Fox Law Firm.

Cash Acct. No. *111*

Date		Explanation	Post. Ref.	Debit	Credit	Balance
1980 May	1		J.1	1000 00		1000 00

Fig. 3-7. Sample page from a ledger showing a balance column account for cash.

2. **Record the amount** in the proper debit or credit column.
3. **Copy the page number of the journal** in the Posting Reference column of the ledger account.
4. **Write the ledger account number in the Posting Reference column** of the journal. These two posting references act as cross references. The last step in posting is always entering the numbers in the Posting Reference column. Using this procedure, it is easy to see what posting has already been done if the posting process is interrupted for some reason. Putting the posting reference numbers (account numbers) in the journal insures that no entry will accidently be posted twice.

   For example, the first journal entry for Jim Fox would be posted as shown in figure 3-8. Starting with the debit entry, the items are entered as numbered. The numbers correspond with the steps given for posting. The same steps are then repeated for the credit entry.

The remaining entries for the Jim Fox firm should be posted in the same manner. When posting is completed, all posting references should be filled in. The journal and ledger are shown in their completed form in figure 3-9 and figure 3-10.

SUMMARY

The first step in the accounting process is to record the transactions in the journal, which is called the book of original entry. A journal serves as a diary of all the activities of a firm. A journal entry is a record of one transaction. In a journal entry, the date of the transaction and the accounts to be debited and credited are shown. The debit and credit follow the rules of debit and credit and the accounting equation. In any journal entry, the sum of the debits must equal the sum of the credits.

The second step in the accounting process is posting to the ledger accounts. Posting means to transfer the information from the journal to the ledger accounts. The ledger is the group (or book) of accounts for a firm. An account is a separate page used to record one type of transaction such as increases and decreases in cash. The accounts in the ledger are listed in the order of assets, liabilities, owner's equity, drawing,

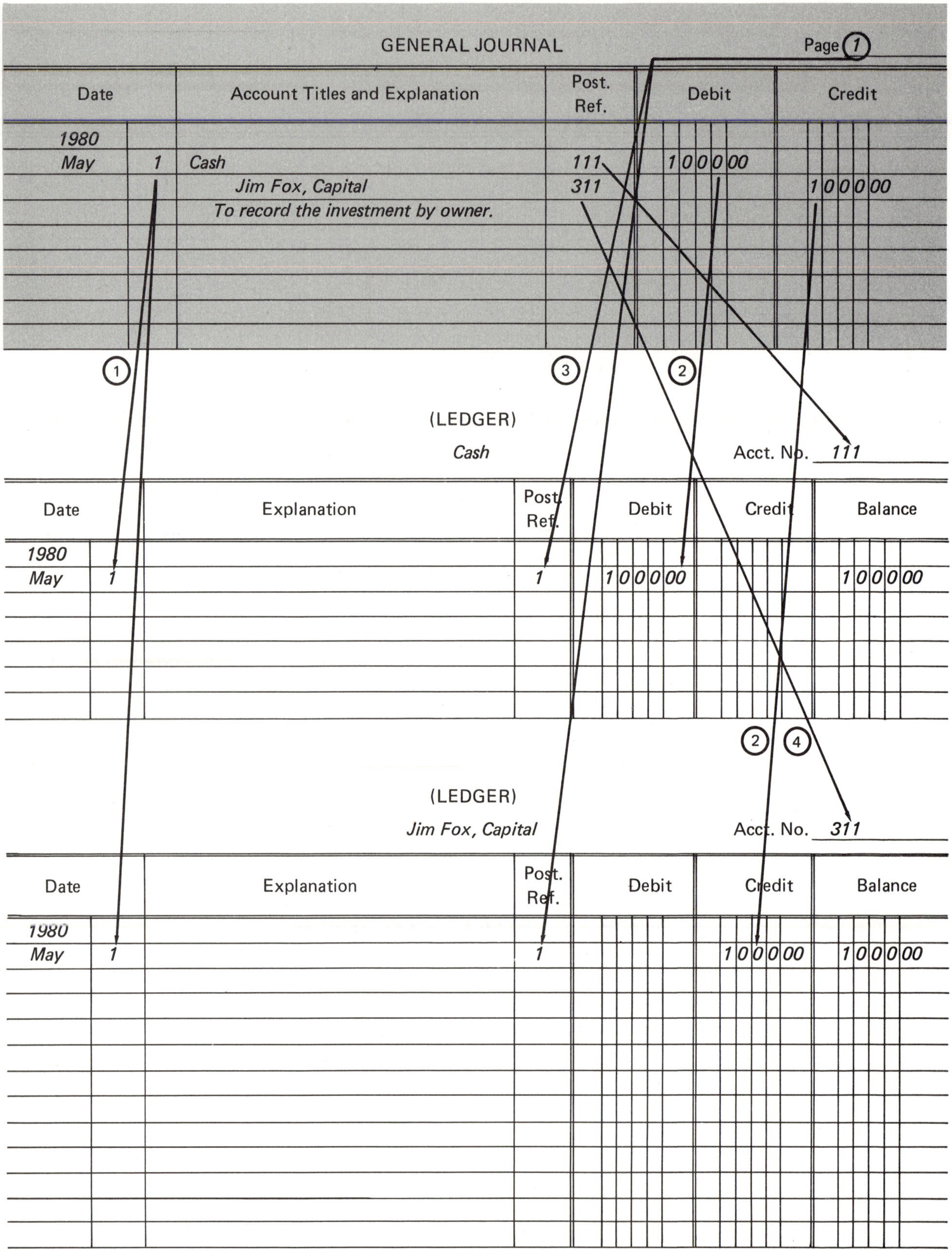

Fig. 3-8. Posting procedure for a journal entry.

GENERAL JOURNAL

Page 1

	Date		Account Titles and Explanation	Post. Ref.	Debit	Credit
	1980					
a	May	1	Cash	111	100000	
			Jim Fox, Capital	311		100000
			To record the investment by owner.			
b		2	Cash	111	50000	
			Notes Payable	211		50000
			To record a loan from the bank.			
c		3	Typewriter	121	10000	
			Cash	111		10000
			Bought a typewriter.			
d		3	Office Supplies	113	25000	
			Accounts Payable	212		25000
			Bought office supplies on account.			
e		5	Truck	125	400000	
			Jim Fox, Capital	311		400000
			Owner invested truck in firm.			
f		6	Accounts Payable	212	25000	
			Cash	111		25000
			To record payment on account.			
g		7	Cash	111	30000	
			Revenue from Fees Earned	411		30000
			Received payment from client.			
h		8	Accounts Receivable	112	105000	
			Revenue from Fees Earned	411		105000
			Performed services for client on account.			
i		15	Cash	111	52500	
			Accounts Receivable	112		52500
			Client paid on his account.			
j		21	Jim Fox, Drawing	312	30000	
			Cash	111		20000
			Typewriter	121		10000
			Owner withdrew assets.			
k		31	Salary Expense	531	10000	
			Cash	111		10000
			Paid the secretary's salary.			

Fig. 3-9. General journal after posting has been completed.

Cash Acct. No. *111*

Date		Explanation	Post. Ref.	Debit	Credit	Balance
1980						
May	*1*		*1*	*1 000 00*		*1 000 00*
	2		*1*	*500 00*		*1 500 00*
	3		*1*		*100 00*	*1 400 00*
	6		*1*		*250 00*	*1 150 00*
	7		*1*	*300 00*		*1 450 00*
	15		*1*	*525 00*		*1 975 00*
	21		*1*		*200 00*	*1 775 00*
	31		*1*		*100 00*	*1 675 00*

Accounts Receivable Acct. No. *112*

Date		Explanation	Post. Ref.	Debit	Credit	Balance
1980						
May	*8*		*1*	*1 050 00*		*1 050 00*
	15		*1*		*525 00*	*525 00*

Office Supplies Acct. No. *113*

Date		Explanation	Post. Ref.	Debit	Credit	Balance
1980						
May	*3*		*1*	*250 00*		*250 00*

Typewriter Acct. No. *121*

Date		Explanation	Post. Ref.	Debit	Credit	Balance
1980						
May	*3*		*1*	*100 00*		*100 00*
	21		*1*		*100 00*	*–0–*

Truck Acct. No. *125*

Date		Explanation	Post. Ref.	Debit	Credit	Balance
1980						
May	*5*		*1*	*4 000 00*		*4 000 00*

Fig. 3-10 Ledger accounts after posting has been completed.

Notes Payable Acct. No. *211*

Date		Explanation	Post. Ref.	Debit	Credit	Balance
1980						
May	2		1		500.00	500.00

Accounts Payable Acct. No. *212*

Date		Explanation	Post. Ref.	Debit	Credit	Balance
1980						
May	3		1		250.00	250.00
	6		1	250.00		-0-

Jim Fox, Capital Acct. No. *311*

Date		Explanation	Post. Ref.	Debit	Credit	Balance
1980						
May	1		1		1000.00	1000.00
	5		1		4000.00	5000.00

Jim Fox, Drawing Acct. No. *312*

Date		Explanation	Post. Ref.	Debit	Credit	Balance
1980						
May	11		1	300.00		300.00

Revenue From Fees Earned Acct. No. *411*

Date		Explanation	Post. Ref.	Debit	Credit	Balance
1980						
May	7		1		300.00	300.00
	8		1		1050.00	1350.00

Salary Expense Acct. No. *531*

Date		Explanation	Post. Ref.	Debit	Credit	Balance
1980						
May	31		1	100.00		100.00

Fig. 3-10. Continued.

revenues, and expenses. The chart of accounts serves as a table of contents to the ledger.

The rules of debit and credit show how increases and decreases should be recorded in the accounts. Debit means the left side of an account and credit means the right side. The debits must always equal the credits so that the accounting equation stays in balance. The rules of debit and credit as used with the accounting equation are summarized in figure 3-3. These rules must be memorized by the student of accounting.

REVIEW

1. What is a journal?
2. What is a ledger?
3. Where are transactions first recorded, in the journal or in the ledger?
4. What is a compound entry?
5. What does debit mean?
6. What does credit mean?
7. What record is called the book of original entry?
8. State the rules of debit and credit for asset accounts.
9. State the rules of debit and credit for liability accounts.
10. State the rules of debit and credit for owner equity accounts.
11. Is the debit or credit written first when recording transactions in a journal?
12. How far should credits be indented in a journal?
13. What is recorded in the Explanation column of an account?
14. What is recorded in the Posting Reference column of a journal?
15. What is recorded in the Posting Reference column of an account?

EXERCISES

1. Record the following transactions in a journal. Use the current year.

   June 1: Joe Swartz invested $4,000 in a new furniture business.
   2: The firm bought a delivery truck for $1,000 cash and a $2,500 note payable.
   6: Joe paid the secretary a week's wages of $100.
   7: Joe withdrew $50 for personal use.

2. Increases and decreases in various types of accounts are described in the following list. On a separate sheet of paper, set up two columns as shown to the right of the transactions. For each transaction, indicate whether the change in the account would be recorded as a debit or as a credit, and whether the normal balance of the account is a debit or credit.

	Recorded as a:	Normal Balance is:
a. Increase in Professional Fees	________	________
b. Decrease in Cash	________	________
c. Increase in J. Barnes, Capital	________	________
d. Increase in Notes Payable	________	________
e. Increase in Prepaid Insurance	________	________
f. Increase in Supplies Expense	________	________
g. Increase in Accounts Receivable	________	________
h. Decrease in Advertising Expense	________	________
i. Increase in J. Barnes, Drawing	________	________
j. Decrease in Accounts Payable	________	________

3. Select the number assigned to the account as listed in column B that would be debited and credited in journalizing each of the following transactions.

	Column A Debit	Column A Credit	Column B
a. Edna Stone invested cash in the business	_____	_____	1. Cash
			2. Accounts Receivable
b. Purchased office equipment for cash	_____	_____	3. Supplies
c. Withdrew cash for personal use	_____	_____	4. Land
			5. Building
d. Collected Accounts Receivable	_____	_____	6. Office Equipment
e. Purchased supplies on account	_____	_____	7. Accounts Payable
f. Purchased land and building, paying cash down and issuing note for balance	_____	_____	8. Notes Payable
			9. Edna Stone, Capital
			10. Edna Stone, Withdrawals
g. Paid accounts payable for supplies purchased	_____	_____	

PROBLEMS

1. James Martinez started a new firm on May 1 of the current year. The firm has the following chart of accounts:

110 Cash	210 Accounts Payable
120 Accounts Receivable	220 Notes Payable
125 Prepaid Insurance	310 James Martinez, Capital
126 Office Supplies	320 James Martinez, Drawing
130 Truck	411 Revenues from Fees
140 Office Equipment	510 Advertising Expense
	520 Wage Expense
	530 Rent Expense

The firm had the following transactions during the first three weeks of May. Record the transactions in general journal form.

May 1: James Martinez invested $3,000 in cash and a truck worth $3,500 in the new firm.
2: Placed an advertisement in the newspaper, $20.
3: Performed work for Ned Small for which $270 was received.
5: Performed work for Beverly Johnson. Beverly promised to pay the $140 fee in about ten days.
6: Paid $60 for a one-year fire insurance policy.
7: Bought a typewriter on credit, $160.
10: Borrowed $4,000 from the bank for which a note was signed.
14: Paid $40 as partial payment on the typewriter bought on May 7.
15: Paid secretary's wage, $110.
16: Withdrew $200 for personal use.
17: Beverly Johnson paid the $140 she owed for the work on May 5.
19: Bought office supplies, $230.
20: Performed work for Beverly Johnson on account, $720.
21: James Martinez took $300 to pay the monthly rent on his personal home.

2. Post the journal entries in Problem 1 to the proper ledger accounts.

3. Bill Brown began a new business on June 1 of the current year. His firm has the following chart of accounts:

110 Cash	310 Bill Brown, Capital
120 Accounts Receivable	320 Bill Brown, Drawing
130 Shop Supplies	410 Revenues Earned
140 Tools	510 Advertising Expense
150 Truck	520 Rent Expense
210 Accounts Payable	530 Wage Expense
220 Notes Payable	

Record each of the firm's transactions in general journal form and then post to the ledger accounts.

June 1: Invested $600 in cash and $1,200 worth of tools in a new carpentry business.
1: Paid a month's rent on the shop building, $150.
2: Bought shop supplies for cash, $100.
3: Placed an ad in the local newspaper, $25.
4: Performed work for Ann Haynes on credit, $60.
5: Bought shop supplies on credit, $130.
8: Hired an assistant and agreed to pay him $100 per week.
9: Performed work for First National Bank and received $230 cash.
10: Bought a used truck for $1,600. Of this amount, $300 was paid in cash and the rest was financed by a note to First National Bank.

June 11: Ann Haynes paid the $60 she owed for the June 4 work.
12: Paid the assistant his first week's wages, $100.
12: Withdrew $80 in cash and $10 worth of shop supplies for personal use.
15: Bought shop supplies for cash, $13.

4. Following is a list of account names with each name preceded by an identifying number, and several transactions completed by Frieda Mullins, a lawyer. Indicate the accounts debited and credited in recording the transactions by selecting the correct account identifying numbers. An example is provided.

1. Accounts Payable
2. Accounts Receivable
3. Frieda Mullins, Capital
4. Frieda Mullins, Drawing
5. Cash
6. Law Library
7. Office Equipment
8. Office Supplies
9. Prepaid Insurance
10. Pure Oil Company
11. Rent Expense
12. Revenue from Legal Fees
13. Salaries Expense
14. Utilities Expense

Transaction	Debit	Credit
EXAMPLE: Frieda Mullins began the practice of law by investing cash and a legal library.	*5, 6*	*3*
1. Paid the premium on a one-year public liability insurance policy.		
2. Bought office equipment and office supplies on credit from Third Company.		
3. Completed legal work for Scott and immediately collected cash for the work done.		
4. Returned for credit a portion of the office supplies purchased in Transaction 2.		
5. Did legal work for Pure Oil Company on credit.		
6. Paid Third Company the balance due for the equipment and supplies bought in Transaction 2.		
7. Paid the secretary's salary.		
8. Received the electric bill and issued a check for its payment.		
9. Frieda brought from home a personally owned typewriter for permanent use in the law firm.		
10. She wrote a check on the law firm bank account in payment of the rent on her personal apartment.		
11. Collected the amount owed by Pure Oil Company.		
12. Paid the monthly rent.		
13. Bought an adding machine for the office on credit.		
14. Bought some law books for the library for cash.		
15. Paid for the adding machine bought in Transaction 13.		

4

Preparing the Trial Balance

OBJECTIVES After studying this chapter, the student will be able to:

- Foot and find the balance of accounts.
- Prepare a trial balance.
- Use a procedure to locate errors.
- Explain why a trial balance is prepared.

FOOTING AND FINDING THE BALANCE OF AN ACCOUNT

Once posting is completed, the next step is to find the balance of the accounts. The *balance* is the difference between the debits and the credits. Accounts often have a column in which a running balance can be shown. However, to find the balance when T-accounts are used, the clerk must add up the debits, add up the credits, and find the difference between these two totals. As each side of the T-account is added, the sums are written in small figures with a pencil. These small figures are called *footings.* The act of adding up each side of the T-account is called *footing.* The balance is the difference between the two footings.

Figure 4-1 illustrates the use of footings in the T-account for cash used as an example in figure 3-10. The balance is shown on the side of the account that has the larger total. It is indicated by writing *balance* next to the number or by circling the number to show that it is a balance and not an entry. The balance in the Cash account is a $1,675 debit balance because the debits are greater than the credits. This balance is the same as the figure in the balance column of the Cash account in the ledger in figure 3-10.

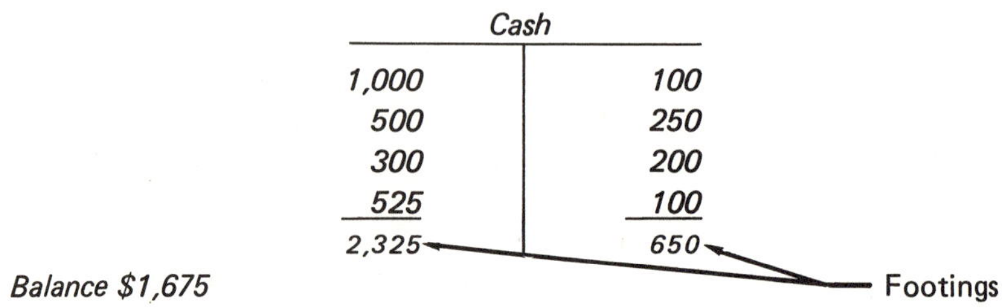

Fig. 4-1. Footings and balances for a T-account for cash.

ASSETS	=	LIABILITIES	+	OWNER'S EQUITY	-	Owner's Drawing	+	Revenues	-	Expenses
Debit increases. | Credit decreases.		Debit decreases. | Credit increases.		Debit decreases. | Credit increases.		Debit increases. | Credit decreases.		Debit decreases. | Credit increases.		Debit increases. | Credit decreases.
Normal Debit Balance		Normal Credit Balance		Normal Credit Balance		Normal Debit Balance		Normal Credit Balance		Normal Debit Balance

Fig. 4-2. The accounting equation showing normal balances.

The Normal Balance

When footing, it is usually found that the column in which increases are recorded has the larger total. Thus, the *normal* (or usual) balance of the account is on the plus side of the account (side on which increases are recorded). The side on which increases are recorded varies with the rules of debit and credit as applied to the account. Figure 4-2 shows the normal balances for the basic accounts as derived from the accounting equation and the rules of debit and credit. In general, if increases are debited to an account, it will have a normal debit balance, and if increases are credited to the account, it will have a normal credit balance.

It is assumed that the balance of an account is the normal balance unless otherwise indicated. Thus, in ledger accounts with a running balance column, the balance need not be labeled debit or credit since it is assumed that the balance is the normal balance for that type of account. In an unusual case where the balance is not normal, the balance should be circled or written in red.

Refer back to the accounts in chapter 3. Note whether the balance of each account is a debit or credit.

TRIAL BALANCE

After posting is completed and the balances for all accounts are known, it is helpful to see that the debits in the ledger equal the credits. The ledger is in balance if the debit balances of accounts equal the credit balances. Accountants do a trial balance for their own benefit to see whether or not the ledger is in balance. The *trial balance* is a list of all account balances. It is a work paper for the accountant; the public does not see it. The name of the work paper shows its purpose – to do a *trial* run to see if the ledger balances.

The trial balance form has a heading showing what it is and two columns. The debit balances of accounts are listed in the debit column and the credit balances in the credit column. A trial balance for the ledger shown in chapter 3 would resemble figure 4-3. Note that only the balances of the accounts are listed. This trial balance proves that the debits equal the credits for the law firm at this point. Double underlines placed under the totals show that the two columns are equal.

PROCEDURE FOR FINDING ERRORS

A balanced trial balance proves that the debits are equal to the credits. It does *not* prove that no mistakes have been made in journalizing or posting. If a whole entry is left out, the debits will still be equal to

Jim Fox Law Firm Trial Balance May 31, 1980		
Cash	$1,675	
Accounts Receivable	525	
Office Supplies	250	
Truck	4,000	
Notes Payable		$ 500
Jim Fox, Capital		5,000
Jim Fox, Drawing	300	
Revenue from Fees		1,350
Salary Expense	100	
	$6,850	$6,850

Fig. 4-3. A trial balance for the Jim Fox Law Firm.

the credits. Also, if a debit is posted to the wrong account or a credit amount is credited to the wrong account, the debits and credits will still be the same. For instance, if $100 is credited to Accounts Payable in the journal entry but the $100 is posted to Notes Payable, then the trial balance will still be in balance even though a mistake has been made. In addition, if a wrong amount is placed on both sides of the entry, the error will not be shown by a trial balance. Thus, not all types of errors will show up in a trial balance.

If a trial balance does not balance, an error has been made and must be found. To find an error it may help to repeat the following steps until the mistake is found:

1. Add the trial balance columns.
2. Check the posting to see that all numbers were posted correctly.
3. Add the balances of the ledger accounts.
4. Check the journal to be sure that the debits equal the credits in each entry.

Accountants also use the following procedures to provide clues as to the type of error that has been made. First, find the difference between the debits and credits in the trial balance columns. If the difference can be divided evenly by two, this is a clue that a debit was listed as a credit or vice versa. Then look for an amount that is one-half the difference. Also, look for an amount that is exactly the difference in case only half of the entry was posted.

If the difference between debits and credits is evenly divisible by nine, the error may be a transposition or a slide. A *transposition error* is one in which the numbers are switched around during the writing of the number. For instance, the amount should be $3,675, but it is written $3,657. Note that the difference between $3,675 and $3,657 is $18 which may be evenly divided by nine. A *slide* is an error in placement of the decimal point. An example of a slide is writing $1,567 instead of $156.70. The difference between the two numbers is $1,410.30 which may be evenly divided by nine.

SUMMARY

After journalizing and posting, the accounts are footed and the balance of each of the accounts is found. Footing is the process of totaling the debit and credit columns for each account. The difference between the footings is the *balance.* Normally, the balance of an account is found on the plus (or increases) side as is shown in the accounting equation. Accountants must know the normal balances of all accounts.

The next step in the process is to do a trial balance to see that the debits are the same as the credits. The trial balance is a work paper for the benefit of the accountant. If the trial balance does not balance, an error has been made and the mistake must be found.

The entire accounting process from the transaction through the preparation of the trial balance is summarized in figure 4-4.

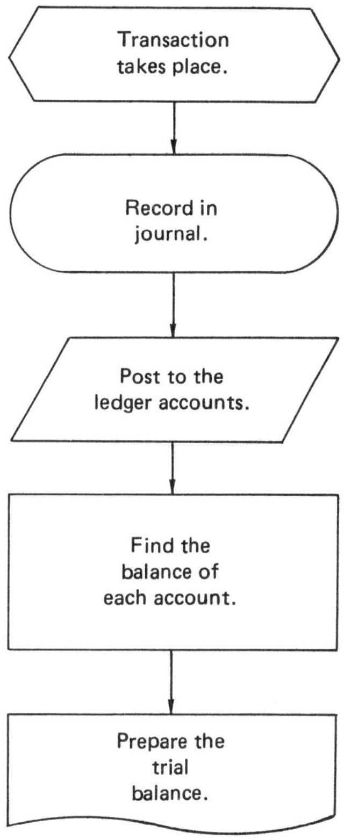

Fig. 4-4 Summary of the accounting process from the transaction through the trial balance.

REVIEW

1. What is footing?
2. What is the normal balance of the Cash account?
3. What is the normal balance of Accounts Payable?
4. What is the normal balance of a revenue account?
5. Why is a trial balance prepared?
6. Does a balanced trial balance prove that all of the accounts are correct?
7. What types of errors are not revealed by a trial balance?
8. What is a transposition error?
9. What is a slide?

EXERCISES

1. Several errors were made in recording transactions of the Burns Company during the past month. For each error tell
   (1) whether the error would be caught when doing the trial balance.
   (2) the amount the trial balance would be out of balance.
   (3) the side of the trial balance that would have the larger total because of the error.
   a. A $55 debit to cash was debited to Accounts Receivable.
   b. A $30 credit to cash was credited to Accounts Payable.
   c. A $300 debit to equipment was recorded in the account as a $30 debit.
   d. A $220 debit to Accounts Payable was credited to Accounts Payable.
   e. An $88 debit to Cash was not posted.

2. Pam Beck began a new business with the following transactions. Record the transactions in a journal, post to T-accounts, and prepare a trial balance.

   March 1: Pam invested $600 in the firm.
   2: The firm bought some office supplies on credit, $50.
   3: The first month's rent was paid, $150.
   8: Received $40 from a customer for work performed this day.
   15: Did work for a customer. Customer will pay $75 in thirty days.
   31: Pam withdrew $50 for her personal use.

3. The following account balances are for the Venturi Company. All are normal balances. Use the accounts and their balances to prepare a trial balance dated May 31 of the current year. (*Note:* To increase your skill, the accounts are listed in alphabetical order instead of in the regular chart of accounts order.)

Accounts Payable	$ 190
Accounts Receivable	300
Advertising Expense	40
Bill Venturi, Capital	1,820
Bill Venturi, Drawing	100
Cash	230
Notes Payable	1,000
Prepaid Insurance	120
Rent Expense	150
Revenue from Fees	800
Supplies	240
Telephone Expense	30
Truck	2,400
Wage Expense	200

4. Following are the accounts for the First Company. Determine the balance of each account and prepare a trial balance. The trial balance should be dated May 31 of the current year.

Cash	
1,000	500
130	80
30	50
500	100
	10
	90

Accounts Receivable	
50	30
90	

Truck	
4,000	

Accounts Payable	
	20

Notes Payable	
100	3,500

Steven Turner, Capital	
	1,000
	500

Steven Turner, Drawing	
50	

Revenue from Fees	
	50
	130
	90

Rent Expense	
80	

Wages Expense	
90	

Advertising Expense	
20	

Telephone Expense	
10	

PROBLEMS

1. Record the following transactions in general journal form, post to the ledger accounts, and then prepare a trial balance.

June 1: Larry Bruno invested $2,000 in a new business.
2: The business bought a typewriter for $150 cash.
3: Bought a new $2,800 truck, paying half in cash and signing a note for the remainder, $1,400.
4: Purchased supplies on account, $700.
5: Lent $100 to friend. He agreed to pay back the loan next week.
8: Larry took out $30 for a gift for his wife.
9: Received $210 for work performed.

2. On June 1, 19–, Joanna Rees, CPA, opened a new office. The following transactions were completed during June. Journalize the transactions, post to the ledger accounts, and then prepare a trial balance.

a. June 1: Invested $8,000 cash and $3,000 worth of office equipment in the firm.
b. 1: Paid $200 rent for the month.
c. 2: Paid $500 for office supplies.
d. 5: Paid the secretary a salary of $200.
e. 9: Collected fees amounting to $6,000.
f. 10: Bought a $7,000 automobile on credit. (A note was signed.)
g. 15: Paid $1,000 on notes payable.
h. 16: Withdrew $250 cash for personal use.
i. 18: Paid $300 for gasoline and oil for the automobile.
j. 19: Received a bill for $30 from the Electric Company.
k. 24: Paid the $30 bill for electricity received in j.
l. 25: Purchased $600 worth of additional office equipment on account.
m. 26: Paid $120 for fire insurance.
n. 28: Paid $900 cash for a reference library.
o. 30: Paid $200 to a secretary for salary.

3. The ledger accounts for the Town House Restaurant are given below. Using whatever information is needed, prepare a trial balance. The trial balance is as of March 31 of the current year.

Cash	
15,000	720
3,200	1,280
262	618
	500
	150

Accounts Receivable	
3,462	1,620
	976

Land	
8,000	

Building	
17,000	

Furniture	
1,225	300

Accounts Payable	
650	2,960
280	17,000

Capital	
	22,843

Revenue	
	262

Salary Expense	
150	

4. Ann Barnes' CPA firm had the following trial balance on January 1 of the current year:

Cash	$3,000	
Accounts Receivable	850	
Supplies	200	
Equipment	2,000	
Accounts Payable		$ 100
Ann Barnes, Capital		5,950
	$6,050	$6,050

During January the firm had the following transactions:

January 2:	Received $50 from a customer on account.
4:	Bought additional supplies on credit, $40.
5:	Did work on credit for Jane Jones, $380.
8:	Paid $90 on accounts payable.
10:	Paid monthly utility bill, $20.
12:	Ann Barnes took out $400 for personal use.
15:	Paid the secretary's salary, $300.
19:	Bought additional equipment for cash, $1,000.
22:	Received $380 payment from Jane Jones for the January 5 work.
24:	Received $230 for work performed for a client.
29:	Paid monthly rent of $200.
31:	Paid secretary's salary, $300.

---

a. Record the beginning trial balance directly in the ledger accounts.
b. Record the transactions for the month in the journal.
c. Post the journal entries to the ledger accounts.
d. Prepare a trial balance.

5
The Income Statement

OBJECTIVES After studying this chapter, the student will be able to:

- Name the two basic financial statements of a firm.
- Prepare an income statement.
- Explain the source of the data on an income statement.
- Explain the matching principle of accounting.
- Identify other revenues and other expenses.

Financial statements are the final product of the accounting process. They are the means of communication for accountants. The most important financial statements are the income statement and the balance sheet. These statements provide valuable information about the firm to interested parties. The income statement is discussed here; the balance sheet is the topic of chapter 6.

THE INCOME STATEMENT

The income statement is the first statement to be prepared. An *income statement* shows the revenues, expenses, and the net income or net loss for a specific period of time. It measures the progress or gain that a firm has made during that length of time. In other words, it tells whether or not the firm has achieved a profit.

The period of time covered by an income statement is called a *fiscal period.* A fiscal period may be any period of time. However, income statements usually cover a month, a quarter of a year, or a year. A *fiscal year* is any twelve consecutive months. For example, the fiscal year may begin and end in April or August rather than with the calender year in January.

The income statement consists of four basic sections: the heading, revenues, expenses, and net income.

Heading

All financial statements begin with an appropriate heading that includes the:

- Name of the firm.
- Name of the statement.
- Date of the statement.

Revenues and Expenses

As explained in chapter 2, revenues are the assets received by the firm in exchange for goods or services. Normally, the asset received is either cash or an account receivable. A firm records the revenue when the sale is made or when a service is performed. Expenses are the assets that a firm spends to earn its revenues. If more assets are received than are spent, then the firm has earned a *net income*. On the other hand, if the firm uses up more assets than it takes in, this is known as a *net loss*.

To show the revenues earned during the period and the expenses used in earning those revenues on the same income statement, accountants follow the matching principle. The *matching principle* requires that all revenues and the expenses incurred in earning those revenues be shown on a financial statement for a certain period. In other words, the revenues are *matched* with the expenses for each fiscal period for which an income statement is prepared. Revenues are listed first, and then the corresponding expenses.

The income statement for the Jim Fox Law Firm considered in chapters 2, 3, and 4 is prepared as shown in figure 5-1 by listing the total of all of the revenue and expense account balances. Each of the account balances is obtained from the trial balance. To see how the balances were transferred from the trial balance to the income statement, compare the income statement shown here with the trial balance shown in figure 4-3.

In this firm the revenue account is called *Revenue from Fees Earned*. Other firms might use different account titles depending on the type of firm. For example, a store might use the title *Sales*. A bank would show *Revenue from Interest,* while the owner of an apartment building would list *Rent Revenue*.

Net Income

On the income statement, the net income or loss of a firm is equal to the revenues minus the expenses. Net income or loss is shown below the expense and revenue entries on the statement. Note that in figure 5-1 the revenues are greater than the expenses. Thus, there is a net income.

Jim Fox Law Firm
Income Statement
For Month Ended May 31, 1980

Revenues:	
Revenue from Fees Earned	$1,350
Expenses:	
Salary Expense	100
Net Income	$1,250

Fig. 5-1. Income statement for the Jim Fox Law Firm.

OTHER REVENUE AND OTHER EXPENSES

In addition to the basic entries on the income statement shown in figure 5-1, two other types of information may also be given: other revenues and other expenses.

Other Revenues

The revenue section of the income statement is used for the revenues from normal operations. In other words, it shows only the revenues from the firm's regular business activities. At times, a firm may earn revenue from sources other than those related to its main operation. For example, if a firm puts cash in a savings account at the bank and earns interest on that money, this is not a revenue from its normal operations. Revenue of this kind is known as *other revenue.* Other revenue is shown separately on a firm's income statement. Examples of titles of other revenue accounts are *Gain on Sale of Assets* and *Rent Revenue* (when renting is not the main activity of the firm). If a law firm earns extra income by renting out part of its building, the rent revenue would be shown in the Other Revenue section of the income statement. If a firm sells its old truck at a gain, this too would be listed under Other Revenue.

Other Expenses

The phrase *other expenses* means those expenses that do not result from the main operations of the firm. Interest expense is an example of an expense that is not related to the earning of revenues. Another example is a loss on the sale of assets. Other expenses should be shown separately at the bottom of the income statement.

EXAMPLE OF AN INCOME STATEMENT

An example of a more detailed and complex income statement is shown in figure 5-2. Note that the revenues and expenses from normal

Ace Company
Income Statement
For Year Ended June 30, 1980

Revenues:		
Sales		$31,000
Expenses:		
Rent Expense	$12,000	
Delivery Expense	8,000	
Insurance Expense	600	
Salary Expense	9,000	
Supplies Expense	500	
Miscellaneous Expense	100	
Total Expenses		30,200
Income From Operations:		$ 800
Other Revenues:		
Gain on Sale of Equipment	1,000	
Interest on Savings Account	80	1,080
		$ 1,880
Other Expenses:		
Interest Expense		2,000
Net Loss		$ (120)

Fig. 5-2 Example of an income statement.

operations are shown first. Subtracting normal expenses from normal revenues gives the income from operations. Next, the Other Revenues are added to the Income from Operations. Other Expenses are then deducted giving (in this case) a net loss.

The Ace Company has sustained a net loss. Net loss is enclosed in parentheses so that it will not be mistaken for net gain.

SUMMARY

Financial statements are the end result of the accounting process. The two main financial statements are the income statement and the balance sheet. The first statement prepared, the income statement, indicates the progress made by a firm by showing the revenues and expenses over a specific period of time. Revenues are the assets received in exchange for selling goods or services to customers. Expenses are the assets given up in earning those revenues. The matching principle of accounting calls for matching of the revenues and expenses sustained within the same time period. Revenues minus expenses equal net income or net loss. Other revenues and other expenses are shown separately on the income statement because they do not result directly from the main operation of the firm.

It is important to note that the income statement covers a specific period of time, not just a single date. The heading shows the length of the period and the last day of the period. Most firms prepare income statements for monthly, quarterly, or yearly time periods.

REVIEW

1. What are the two main types of financial statements?
2. What types of accounts appear on the income statement?
3. Explain the matching principle of accounting.
4. Why are other revenues and other expenses shown in a separate section of the income statement?
5. Give examples of other revenues and other expenses.
6. If total expenses are greater than total revenues, what is the difference called?
7. What is a fiscal year?
8. What three types of information appear in the heading of an income statement?
9. What is the most convenient source from which to obtain the balances for the total of each account that appears on the income statement?

EXERCISES

1. The income statements for four different firms are shown below. Some of the account balances and totals have been omitted and

letters substituted for the amounts. Determine the omitted amounts.

Revenue from Commissions	$3,600	$ C	$ E	$2,900
Operating Expenses:				
Rent Expense	400	650	100	400
Wage Expense	700	330	200	265
Advertising Expense	600	D	F	300
Total Expenses	A	1,100	580	G
Net Income (Loss)	$ B	$(210)	$1,000	$ H

2. The following is the trial balance for Aide Company. Prepare an income statement for the month of March.

Aide Company
Trial Balance
March 31, 19–

Cash	$ 170	
Accounts Receivable	440	
Truck	3,000	
Accounts Payable		$ 400
George Aide, Capital		2,940
George Aide, Drawing	250	
Revenue From Fees		2,000
Rent Expense	450	
Wage Expense	500	
Utility Expense	330	
Interest Expense	200	
	$5,340	$5,340

3. Using the information given in the trial balance for exercise 3 in chapter 4, prepare an income statement for the month of January.

4. Using the accounts in exercise 4 of chapter 4, prepare an income statement for the month of May.

5. Following are the income statements for four different firms. Letters have been substituted for some of the account balances. Determine the omitted amounts.

Revenue from Fees	$2,000	$ D	$ G	$3,300
Operating Expenses:				
Rent Expense	300	E	730	500
Wage Expense	400	80	450	100
Delivery Expense	500	240	900	300
Total Expenses	A	320	H	J
Income from Operations	B	F	1,250	K
Other Revenues:				
Interest Revenue	130	100	I	110
Other Expenses:				
Interest Expense	200	180	800	330
Net Income (Loss)	$ C	$ 500	$ 600	$ L

PROBLEMS

1. Record the following transactions in a journal, post to the ledger accounts, and then prepare a trial balance and an income statement. The transactions are for the month of June.

   June 1: Doug Cord invested $10,000 in the Cord Company.
   2: A building was bought for $3,000 cash and a $7,000 note payable.
   3: Paid $45 for a newspaper advertisement.
   4: A truck was purchased for $4,000 cash.
   5: Bought office supplies on account, $180.
   6: Performed work for a customer on credit, $790.
   17: Accounts payable of $32 were paid.
   18: Performed work for a customer and received $900 cash.
   27: Collected one half of the money for the work done on June 6.
   29: Paid secretary's wages of $200.
   30: Paid monthly rent of $150.

2. Given the following account balances for the Corina Company, prepare the annual trial balance and income statement for the firm. The fiscal year ends December 31. The accounts are listed alphabetically to increase your skill in deciding whether accounts have debit or credit balances.

Accounts Payable	$ 212
Accounts Receivable	1,835
Advertising Expense	195
Cash	2,303
Alice Corina, Capital	788
Alice Corina, Drawing	5,500
Equipment	12,300
Interest Expense	240
Interest Revenue	153
Notes Payable	1,000
Rent Expense	1,200
Revenue from Services	29,100
Wage Expense	7,680

3. The Ming Company has the following account balances at the end of the current year. Prepare a trial balance from the accounts and then do the income statement.

Cash	$ 2,000
Accounts Receivable	10,000
Store Supplies	1,000
Equipment	20,000
L. Ming, Capital	17,550
Revenue From Fees	50,000
Advertising Expense	29,000
Wage Expense	3,000
Rent Expense	1,400
Insurance Expense	750
Interest Revenue	150
Interest Expense	550

4. The Hen Service Company is operated by June Van Dusen. The firm began the current year with the following account balances:

Cash	$3,000	
Supplies	120	
Equipment	2,400	
June Van Dusen, Capital		$5,520
	$5,520	$5,520

The firm completed the following transactions during January:

January 3: Bought more supplies, $200, on credit.
4: Paid for an advertisement in the newspaper, $15.
5: Received $720 from a customer for work performed.
8: Paid rent for the month, $250.
10: Paid monthly utility bill, $17.
15: Received $600 from a customer for work performed.
16: Did work for a customer on account, $320.
17: Paid for a newspaper advertisement, $30.
22: Received $160 as half payment from the customer for whom work was performed on January 16.
29: Paid secretary's wages, $500.

---

a. Record the beginning balances in the ledger accounts.
b. Journalize the transactions for the month.
c. Post the journal entries to the accounts.
d. Prepare a trial balance.
e. Prepare an income statement.

6
The Balance Sheet

OBJECTIVES After studying this chapter, the student will be able to:

- Classify balance sheet accounts.
- List the order of accounts within classifications.
- Prepare a classified balance sheet.
- Use the account form and the report form of balance sheet.
- Prepare a statement of owner's equity.

The *balance sheet* shows the financial position of a firm at a given time. It is sometimes called a *statement of financial position.* The balances in the asset, liability, and owner's equity accounts are shown on the balance sheet. Thus, the balance sheet shows what is owned (assets), what is owed (liabilities), and what a firm is worth (owner's equity). The balance sheet follows the basic accounting equation:

ASSETS = LIABILITIES + OWNER'S EQUITY

The income statement, as described in chapter 4, shows whether a business achieved or failed to achieve a profit over a specific period of time. The balance sheet, on the other hand, shows the financial position of a company on a particular date. Thus, the income statement may be compared to a movie of the firm as it progresses, while a balance sheet is like a photograph of the way a firm looks at any given moment.

PREPARING A BALANCE SHEET

When preparing a balance sheet, the balances of the asset, liability, and owner's equity accounts are listed using the format shown in figure 6-1. Recall the effect of revenues and expenses on owner's equity:

ASSETS = LIABILITIES + OWNER'S EQUITY + Revenues - Expenses

Thus, if revenues are greater than expenses, resulting in a net income, the owner's equity is increased. If expenses are greater than revenues (a net loss), then owner's equity is decreased. The accounting equation may also be written as follows:

ASSETS = LIABILITIES + OWNER'S EQUITY + NET INCOME - NET LOSS

Jim Fox Law Firm
Balance Sheet
May 31, 1980

ASSETS:		LIABILITIES:		
Cash	$1,675	Notes Payable	$ 500	
Accounts Receivable	525	Total Liabilities		$ 500
Office Supplies	250	OWNER'S EQUITY:		
Truck	4,000	Jim Fox, Capital	5,000	
		Add: Net Income	1,250	
			6,250	
		Less: Drawing	300	
		Total Owner's Equity		5,950
		Total Liabilities &		
Total Assets	$6,450	Owner's Equity		$6,450

Fig. 6-1. Balance sheet for the Jim Fox Law Firm.

Thus, the income statement must be prepared before the balance sheet to learn the effect of the net income or net loss on the owner's equity.

In the example of the Jim Fox Law Firm in chapter 5, the net income was $1,250. This amount is added to the owner's equity account on the balance sheet. (See figure 6-1.) Note that in the balance sheet, assets equal liabilities plus owner's equity (the basic accounting equation). Also, look at the owner's equity section on figure 6-1, and note that net income is added to the owner's equity. The owner's withdrawals are deducted to find the owner's final capital balance.

Each account on a trial balance will appear on one of the two financial statements of a firm. Figure 6-2 shows how the trial balance of the Jim Fox Law Firm (figure 4-3) was used to prepare the income statement (figure 5-1) and the balance sheet (figure 6-1).

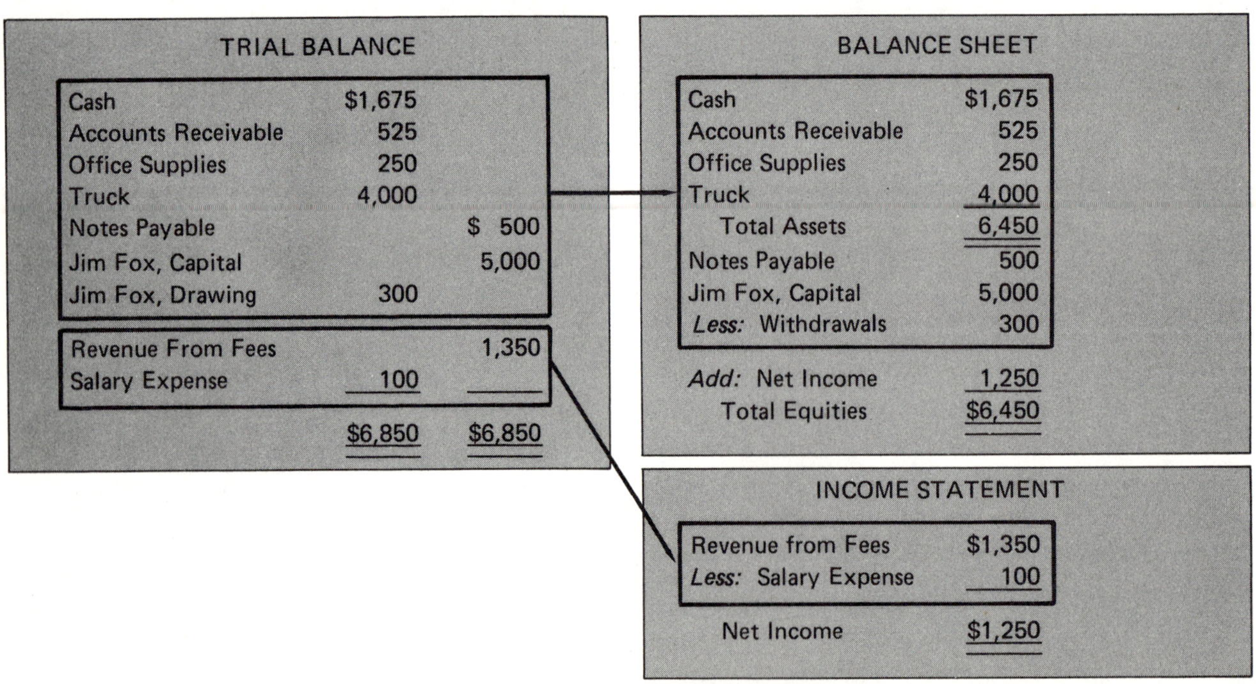

Fig. 6-2. The trial balance is used in preparing both the income statement and the balance sheet.

Statement of Owner's Equity

The details of the changes in the owner's equity may be shown on the balance sheet as in figure 6-1, or in a separate statement. If a separate form is used, it is called a *statement of owner's equity.* It is used to summarize the changes in the capital account. Changes in owner's equity may be caused by

- an additional investment by the owner,
- withdrawals by the owner, and/or
- net income or net loss.

To prepare a statement of owner's equity, start with the initial balance. This is the balance that was in the capital account at the beginning of the period. Next, show any changes that have taken place (additional investments or withdrawals). A statement of owner's equity prepared for the Jim Fox Law Firm is shown in figure 6-3. Note that when a statement of owner's equity is included with a balance sheet, only the final balance of the Capital account (in this case $5,950) is included on the balance sheet. Thus, Net Income and Drawing, as seen on figure 6-1, are omitted when a separate statement is used for owner's equity, figure 6-4.

As shown in figure 6-3, Jim Fox's firm had an increase in capital or net gain in the period described on the statement. If a firm has a

Jim Fox Law Firm
Statement of Owner's Equity
For Month Ended May 31, 1980

Jim Fox, Capital, May 1, 1980		$1,000
Additional Investment		4,000
Total Investment		5,000
Add: Net Income for May	$1,250	
Less: Withdrawals for May	300	
Increase in Capital		950
Jim Fox, Capital, May 31, 1980		$5,950

Fig. 6-3. Statement of owner's equity for the Jim Fox Law Firm.

Jim Fox Law Firm
Balance Sheet
May 31, 1980

ASSETS:		LIABILITIES:		
Cash	$1,675	Notes Payable	$ 500	
Accounts Receivable	525	Total Liabilities		$ 500
Office Supplies	250	OWNER'S EQUITY:		
Truck	4,000	Jim Fox, Capital		5,950
		Total Liabilities &		
Total Assets	$6,450	Owner's Equity		$6,450

Fig. 6-4. Balance sheet to be used with a separate statement of owner's equity.

Albreti Company Statement of Owner's Equity For Year Ended June 30, 1980		
Maria Albreti, Capital, July 1, 1979		$10,000
Additional Investment, May 5, 1980		2,000
Total Investment		12,000
Less:		
Net Loss for the Year	$ 20	
Withdrawals for the Year	1,850	
Decrease in Capital		1,870
Maria Albreti, Capital, June 30, 1980		$10,130

Fig. 6-5. A statement of owner's equity.

net loss for the period, it is shown as in figure 6-5. The statement of owner's equity acts as a bridge or connection between the income statement and the balance sheet. In other words, the income is computed on the income statement. It is then added to the beginning capital balance on the statement of owner's equity. Thus, it becomes part of ending capital on the balance sheet.

THE CLASSIFIED BALANCE SHEET

As a firm expands, new accounts are needed and the balance sheet grows larger. At this point, it becomes helpful to group, or classify, the accounts by type on the balance sheet. It is then referred to as a *classified balance sheet.* A classified balance sheet for Albreti Company is shown in figure 6-6. Note the classification of accounts used on this balance sheet. Each of the groups is described in the following section.

Current Assets

Current assets are cash assets or those that can be turned into cash or used up within a short period of time (usually less than one year). Current assets are listed in the order of their liquidity. *Liquidity* means the ease of conversion into cash. Hence, cash is always listed first and then notes receivable, accounts receivable, and merchandise inventory. A *note receivable* is a signed promissory note from a customer. An *account receivable* is the amount to be collected from a customer on *open account* (an account for a service which has not been fully paid for). *Merchandise inventory* is an asset that a firm plans to sell to its customers. The firm hopes that this inventory will be sold to customers in the near future and thus turned into cash. Supplies and prepaid insurance are also considered current assets since they will be used up or will expire within a year.

Investments

Investments are assets that are not used in the operation of the firm and are to be held for more than one year. Investments in stocks and bonds are included in this group of accounts.

Albreti Company
Balance Sheet
June 30, 1980

ASSETS:			
Current Assets:			
Cash	$ 356		
Notes Receivable	1,100		
Accounts Receivable	9,325		
Merchandise Inventory	31,697		
Supplies	215		
Prepaid Insurance	286		
Total Current Assets			$42,979
Investments:			
Investment in Stock of X Company			150
Plant and Equipment:			
Land		$ 3,000	
Building	21,000		
Less: Accumulated Depreciation	8,600	12,400	
Equipment	7,050		
Less: Accumulated Depreciation	2,800	4,250	
Total Plant and Equipment			19,650
Intangible Assets:			
Patent			250
Other Assets:			
Plant Assets Held for Future Sale			900
Total Assets			$63,929
LIABILITIES:			
Current Liabilities:			
Notes Payable		9,000	
Accounts Payable		29,800	
Wages Payable		1,879	
Unearned Rent		1,120	
Total Current Liabilities			$41,799
Long-term Liabilities:			
Mortgage Payable			12,000
Total Liabilities			$53,799
OWNER'S EQUITY:			
Maria Albroti, Capital			10,130
Total Liabilities and Owner's Equity			$63,929

Fig. 6-6. A classified balance sheet in report form.

Plant and Equipment

Plant and equipment are assets that will be used for more than one year in the operation of the firm. They may also be called *plant assets* or *fixed assets.* Examples of plant and equipment assets include furniture, vehicles, buildings, and land.

Intangible Assets

An *intangible asset* is an asset that has no physical existence, but that has value to the firm. This value must last for more than one year. For example, a patent, a license issued by the federal government that gives an inventor the exclusive right to produce an invention for seventeen years, is an intangible asset. Although a patent does not exist physically, it does have a value to the firm which lasts for several years. Another kind of intangible asset is a copyright. A copyright, also issued by the federal government, gives a firm the sole right to publish something for a certain period of time.

Other Assets

Other assets include any asset that does not fit elsewhere on the statement. In figure 6-6, the account entitled Plant Assets Held for Future Sale has been placed in Other Assets. Plant Assets Held for Future Sale cannot be included under plant and equipment because they are not being used in the firm. Since these assets will not fit into any other group, they are shown as other assets.

Current Liabilities

Current liabilities are debts that are to be paid from the current assets of the firm within a short time (usually within less than one year). These debts are listed in the order in which they have to be paid. The debt that comes due first is shown at the top. *Notes payable* are promissory notes issued to creditors. *Accounts payable* are debts due on open account. *Wages payable* represents pay that is owed to the firm's employees. *Unearned rent* is rent which has been received but not yet earned.

Long-term Liabilities

Long-term liabilities are debts that do not have to be paid for a long time (usually for more than one year). Examples include *mortgage payable, long-term notes payable,* and *bonds payable.*

Owner's Equity

Note that the details of the capital account may be found in the statement of owner's equity as seen in figure 6-5. Thus, only the final balance is shown on the balance sheet.

FORM USED IN PREPARING A BALANCE SHEET

Two forms may be used in preparing a balance sheet. One is the *account form.* Here, assets are shown on the left and liabilities and owner's equity appear on the right. In other words, the account form parallels the accounting equation (Assets = Liabilities + Owner's Equity). The balance sheet in figure 6-1 uses the account form.

The second possible form is the *report form.* In this form, the assets, liabilities, and owner's equity are placed in vertical order on the page as follows:

ASSETS
=
LIABILITIES
+
OWNER'S EQUITY

Figure 6-6 is an example of the report form.

Figure 6-6 also shows some other rules used in writing financial statements. First, place dollar signs at the top of each column and with each total. Second, use single lines under numbers that are to be added or subtracted and use double lines under final figures. Note the double lines under Total Assets and under Total Liabilities and Owner's Equity. Since the double-underlined numbers match, it may be concluded that the balance sheet balances.

SUMMARY

A balance sheet shows the financial position of a firm at a particular time. The balance sheet shows what is owned (assets), what is owed (liabilities), and what a firm is worth (owner's equity). Owner's equity may be changed by (1) additional investments by the owner; (2) withdrawals by the owner; and (3) net income or net loss. These changes in owner's equity may be shown on the balance sheet or on a separate statement which is called a statement of owner's equity.

The accounts on the balance sheet are classified into groups. The assets are divided into five groups. Listed in order of liquidity, they are

- current assets,
- investments,
- plant and equipment,
- intangible assets, and
- other assets.

Liabilities are either current or long term. Current liabilities are listed in the order of their due date. A balance sheet may be prepared using either the report form or the account form.

Figure 6-7 summarizes the entire accounting process as studied so far.

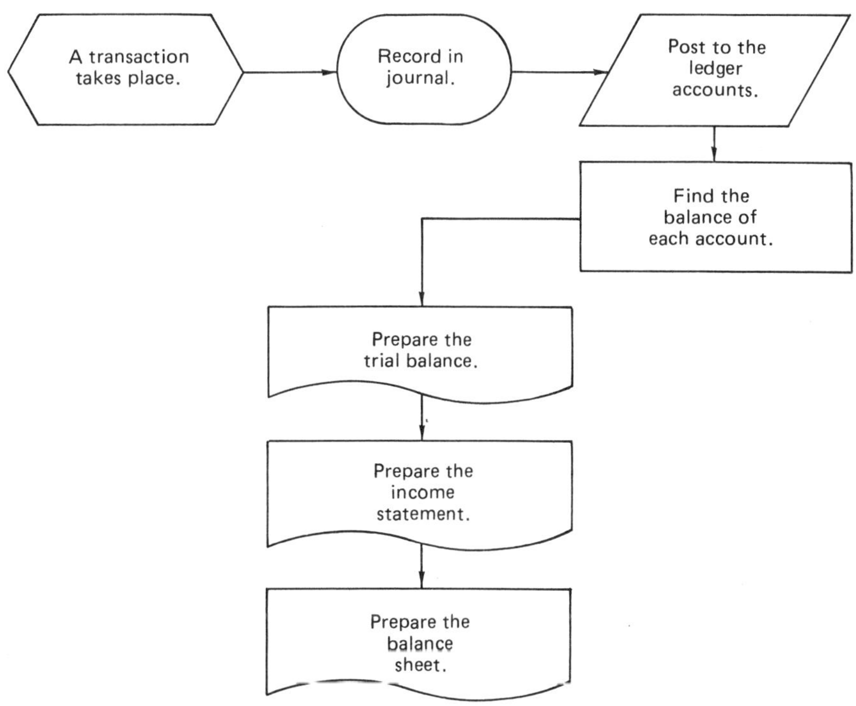

Fig. 6-7. Summary of the accounting process from the transaction through the preparation of the balance sheet.

REVIEW

1. What accounts appear on a balance sheet?
2. List the five classifications of assets.
3. List the classifications for liabilities.
4. What determines the order in which assets are listed within a category?
5. Is it necessary to have a separate statement of owner's equity?
6. Give at least five examples of current assets.
7. What does *current* mean when talking about current assets or current liabilities?
8. Give at least three examples of plant assets.
9. Give examples of intangible assets.
10. What is the difference between the account form and the report form of the balance sheet?
11. Which of the two major financial statements is prepared first?
12. On which financial statement does the drawing account appear?
13. Listed below are the steps of the accounting cycle listed in random order. Which step would be performed first? Which step would be performed third?
    A. Prepare the income statement.
    B. Journalize transactions.
    C. Prepare the trial balance.
    D. Prepare the balance sheet.
    E. Post to the ledger.

EXERCISES

1. Indicate whether each of the following accounts belongs on the income statement (I) or the balance sheet (B).

    1. Cash
    2. Revenue from Sales
    3. Insurance Expense
    4. Prepaid Insurance
    5. Accounts Payable
    6. Salaries Expense
    7. Building
    8. Supplies Expense
    9. Tim Cox, Capital
    10. Accounts Receivable
    11. Tim Cox, Drawing
    12. Miscellaneous Expense
    13. Interest Expense
    14. Interest Revenue
    15. Patents

2. Prepare a statement of owner's equity using the following information:

Jennifer Hall, Capital	
	7,000

Jennifer Hall, Drawing	
3,000	

Net Income for the year = $10,000.

3. For each of the accounts numbered 1–20 indicate the proper classification on the balance sheet by writing the letter of one of the account types in the following list.

A. Current Assets
B. Investments
C. Plant and Equipment
D. Intangible Assets
E. Other Assets
F. Current Liabilities
G. Long-term Liabilities
H. Owner's Equity

1. Wages Payable
2. Store Supplies
3. Patents
4. Merchandise Inventory
5. Delivery Truck
6. Accounts Receivable
7. Investment in BD Corporation Stock
8. Store Equipment
9. Cash
10. Prepaid Insurance
11. Accounts Payable
12. Notes Receivable
13. Prepaid Taxes
14. Notes Payable
15. Land
16. Taxes Payable
17. Mortgage Payable
18. Building
19. Copyright
20. Unearned Rent

4. Bench, Rose, and Kluzewski each own their own firm. Given below is the owner's equity section of their balance sheets for the year just ended. Some of the data is omitted. Fill in the missing information.

	Bench	Rose	Kluzewski
Capital, January 1	$10,887	$22,222	$
Net Income or (Loss)	10,850	7,120	(3,370)
Withdrawals	8,650		6,000
Capital, December 31		8,620	16,540

PROBLEMS

1. From the following list select the term that is most closely related to each of the statements 1–17. Write the letter on a separate sheet of paper.

A. Accounts Receivable
B. Accounts Payable
C. Asset
D. Balance Sheet
E. Capital
F. Cash
G. Credit
H. Current Assets
I. Current Liabilities
J. Debit
K. Income Statement
L. Intangibles
M. Journal
N. Ledger
O. Liabilities
P. Long-term Liabilities
Q. Posting
R. Plant Assets
S. Revenue
T. Slide
U. Supplies Used
V. Transposition
W. Trial Balance

1. Accidentally posting $123.10 instead of $1,231.00.
2. A patent would be shown in this section of the financial statements.

3. The equity of the owner of a firm.
4. Liabilities that will be due in a relatively short time.
5. Assets of a relatively permanent nature used in the operation of the firm.
6. A way of determining if the debits and credits in a firm's accounts are equal.
7. Transfer of debits and credits from a preliminary record to the ledger.
8. The equity of the creditors of a firm.
9. A summary report of the revenues and expenses of a firm for a specific period of time.
10. A preliminary record of transactions or the book of original entry.
11. Assets that are expected to be turned into cash within a year or less.
12. Something owned that has a monetary value.
13. Liabilities that are due in ten years.
14. A group of accounts.
15. The financial statement that is similar to a photograph of the firm.
16. The first asset to be listed on a balance sheet.
17. An expense account.

2. Following are the Pedreski Company's December 31 assets and equities. Prepare the firm's December 31 balance sheet for the current year, using a form that employs all appropriate headings and subheadings, and uses correct account order and layout.

Accounts Payable	$ 2,500
Accounts Receivable	1,503
Cash	4,079
Furniture	1,883
Income Taxes Payable	1,635
Land	875
Buildings	9,092
Store Supplies	549
Mortgage Payable (Due 1989)	298
Notes Payable (Due 1990)	?
Prepaid Rent	205
Patents	70
Property Taxes Payable	770
Oscar Pedreski, Capital	10,200

(The amount for Notes Payable is omitted and must be calculated.)

3. The following trial balance is for the Home Real Estate Agency. The firm prepares its financial statements once a year. The owner made no additional investments during the year shown.

Home Real Estate Agency
Trial Balance
December 31, 19–

Account	Debit	Credit
Cash	$ 279	
Accounts Receivable	1,805	
Office Supplies	190	
Prepaid Insurance	230	
Equipment	2,400	
Building	25,000	
Land	5,000	
Accounts Payable		$ 903
Mortgage Payable		18,590
Louise Small, Capital		1,508
Louise Small, Drawing	6,000	
Revenue from Commissions		46,100
Advertising Expense	8,330	
Rent Expense	5,600	
Wages Expense	8,340	
Utility Expense	1,132	
Auto Expense	2,795	
	$67,101	$67,101

a. Prepare an income statement for the year.
b. Prepare a classified balance sheet using the correct form.

4. The following are the account balances as of December 31 for the Holmes Company. The firm prepares its financial statements once a year. The owner made no additional investments during the year described.

Cash	$ 305
Accounts Receivable	990
Shop Supplies	640
Prepaid Insurance	110
Land	6,500
Building	23,500
Equipment	4,965
Accounts Payable	337
Mortgage Payable	12,240
Note Payable – Due in two years	5,000
Wayne Holmes, Capital	27,010
Wayne Holmes, Drawing	6,000
Revenue from Services	32,307
Interest Revenue	100
Interest Expense	230
Advertising Expense	6,100
Telephone Expense	1,809
Rent Expense	6,000
Wage Expense	19,845

a. Prepare a trial balance for the firm.
b. Prepare an income statement using the correct form.
c. Prepare a balance sheet in the correct form.

5. You are given the following accounts for the Kome Company. Prepare a balance sheet from them. The accounts are shown as of December 31 of the current year. Your balance sheet should be classified and in the proper form.

Cash

Balance	16,250	Dec. 31	720
Dec. 31	3,200	31	2,930
31	262		

Accounts Receivable

Balance	3,462	Dec. 31	1,620
		31	976
		31	30

Land

Balance	8,000		

Building

Balance	17,000		

Furniture

Balance	1,225	Dec. 31	300

Accounts Payable

Dec. 31	650	Balance	2,960
31	280	Dec. 31	17,250

Capital

		Balance	22,893

Revenue

		Dec. 31	262
		31	618

Salary Expense

Dec. 31	150		

Rent Expense

Dec. 31	50		

Advertising Expense

Dec. 31	30		

7 Adjusting Entries

OBJECTIVES After studying this chapter, the student will be able to:

- Explain the reason for making adjusting entries.
- Identify the four types of situations in which adjusting entries are necessary.
- Journalize and post adjusting entries.
- Recognize mixed accounts.
- Prepare the adjusted trial balance.
- Perform the steps in the accounting cycle through the preparation of the two financial statements.

THE NEED FOR ADJUSTING ENTRIES

Journal entries are designed to show the effects of various transactions on the financial position of the firm. However, it is not practical to keep the accounts in such a way that they show all of the daily changes in the firm's financial state. Therefore, to achieve an accurate end-of-the-period statement, some accounts must be adjusted to reflect items not recorded in the transaction entries. Entries made for this purpose are called *adjusting entries* and are made on the last day of the financial period.

For example, the assets represented by the items purchased for use in the operation of a business are gradually used up. However, it is not possible to show the decrease which takes place in these assets on a day-to-day basis. Thus, the accounts for these items do not show the correct value during the accounting period. Instead, the value of the assets not used up in the period are calculated upon completion of that period. Adjusting entries make possible the preparation of correct financial statements as of the end of each period.

Adjusting entries allow accountants to use the matching principle even when transactions involve items that apply to more than one financial period. Remember, when using the matching principle, all revenues shown on the financial statement for the period must be matched with the expenses incurred in earning those revenues. Without adjusting entries, the picture given by the financial statement would be inaccurate.

When to Make Adjusting Entries

Four types of situations call for adjusting entries. They are made when:

- Costs that have been recorded must be *allocated* (divided) between two or more accounting periods.
- Revenues that have been recorded must be allocated over two or more periods.
- Unrecorded expenses must be shown in the accounts.
- Unrecorded revenues must be shown in the accounts.

ALLOCATION OF RECORDED COSTS

The first use of adjusting entries is for recorded costs that must be divided between two or more accounting periods. Such costs result in mixed accounts. A *mixed account* is an account consisting of expired cost and unexpired cost. The *expired cost* is the part of the cost that has been used up during the period. The *unexpired cost* is the part that has not been used up and is still an asset. For example, the inventory or stock remaining at the end of the period is an unexpired cost.

Prepaid Expenses

One kind of mixed account results from prepaid expenses. *Prepaid expenses* are payments made in advance. Initially, prepaid expenses are debited to asset accounts. Insurance, supplies, and rent are examples of items that are paid for in advance and are then used up or expire. At the end of the period, the part of the payment that has expired or been used up must be tranferred from the asset account to an expense account. An adjusting entry is used for this transfer. Adjusting entries are recorded in the journal. They are then posted to the ledger accounts.

As shown on the trial balance, prepaid expenses (assets) are *overstated.* This means that the amount listed on the trial balance is greater than the amount actually in the account. This occurs because no adjustment has yet been made for assets which have been used up or have expired during the period. If not adjusted, these assets will also be overstated on the balance sheet. Failure to make the proper adjustments before preparing the income statement also results in an inaccurate picture of the firm's status. Without the proper adjustments, expenses are shown as less than they really were and income is shown as greater than it really was for the period.

Prepaid Rent. For example, assume that rent is paid for a year in advance at the rate of $100 per month. The $1,200 prepayment is debited to an asset account called *Prepaid Rent.* At the end of the first month, the asset is not worth $1,200 because one month's rent has been used up. Thus, the asset account is now a mixed account. An adjusting entry should be made to move one month's rent from the asset account to an expense account. The entries are handled as follows:

Entry at Time of Payment

Prepaid Rent	1,200	
Cash		1,200
To record payment of one year's rent in advance.		

Adjusting Entry at End of First Month

Rent Expense	100	
Prepaid Rent		100
To record rent expense for the month.		

After the adjusting entry has been posted, the balance in the asset account, Prepaid Rent, will be $1,100. This balance equals the value of eleven months rent paid in advance at the rate of $100 per month. Thus, the assets will be stated correctly on the balance sheet and Rent Expense will be correct on the income statement for the first month.

The adjusting entry is made at the end of each month. At the end of the year when the prepaid rent is used up, the balance in the Prepaid Rent account is zero. The asset no longer has any value. The expense is placed in the proper accounting periods by monthly adjustment entries and is matched against the revenues for each of the months.

Supplies. When a firm buys store supplies, an asset account is debited for their cost. This is proper since an asset is being increased. However, even though some store supplies are used up every day, usually, no entry is made to show the decrease in the asset. This is taken care of with an adjusting entry at the end of the period.

Assume that a firm buys $200 worth of store supplies during its first month of business. This initial entry is recorded as follows:

Entry at Time of Purchase

Store Supplies	200	
Cash		200
To record purchase of store supplies.		

On the trial balance at the end of the month, the Store Supplies account shows a $200 balance. However, this is probably incorrect since some of the store supplies have been used up. At this time, it is necessary to count the actual value of store supplies still on hand. A count shows that only $70 worth of store supplies are on hand. The following adjusting entry is made:

Adjusting Entry

Store Supplies Expense	130	
Store Supplies		130
To adjust the store supplies account.		

Since only $70 worth of office supplies remain, it is assumed that the remainder ($200 – $70 = $130) has been used up.

Prepaid Insurance. A similar situation occurs when a firm buys an insurance policy. For example, if a firm buys a one-year fire insurance policy at a cost of $180, the following entry is made:

Entry at Time of Purchase

Prepaid Insurance	180	
Cash		180
To record purchase of a one-year policy.		

After one month has passed, the policy is only good for eleven more months. Therefore, the asset account, Prepaid Insurance, should have a balance equal to an eleven-month policy. Since one month's worth of the policy has been used up, that part of the cost is transferred to an expense account. If one-twelfth of the policy has expired, one-twelfth of the cost, or $15, should be transferred. The adjusting entry after the first month is:

Adjusting Entry

Insurance Expense	15	
Prepaid Insurance		15
To record one month's expense.		

Thus, the balance sheet at the end of the first month will show an asset in the Prepaid Insurance account of $165.

Depreciation of Fixed Assets

When a firm buys a truck, an asset account is debited for the cost. However, since all vehicles wear out, the truck will not remain an asset forever. At some future time the truck will have almost no value. This decrease in the worth of the truck must be shown in the accounts.

For example, a firm buys a truck for $6,000. The truck is expected to last for ten years. In the accounting procedure, it is assumed that at the end of ten years the truck will no longer have any value (will represent zero amount of assets). Therefore, from the time the truck is bought, until the end of ten years, the firm will have an expense of $6,000. It would not be correct to charge the whole $6,000 to any one year since the truck will be used in ten separate years. The best method is to allocate some of the $6,000 to each of the ten years. The $6,000 divided by ten years equals $600 per year. Thus, the truck is said to *depreciate* (decrease in value) $600 each year or $50 each month ($600 ÷ 12 = $50). This $50 expense is recorded in an expense account each month. At the end of the first month the following adjusting entry would be made:

Adjusting Entry

Depreciation Expense	50	
Accumulated Depreciation – Truck		50
To record depreciation for one month.		

Note that a new account has been started to record the credit – an account called *Accumulated Depreciation – Truck.* It might have been assumed that the fixed asset account, Truck, would be credited. However, this would be a violation of the cost principle. The most efficient way to record the depreciation while following the cost principle is to credit a contra account. A *contra account* is an account which when used with another account can be subtracted to produce the correct value for the first account. The word *contra* as used here means *offset,* or in terms of the T-account, an entry on the other side of the account. The new account, Accumulated Depreciation – Truck, appears on the balance sheet in the asset section with an entry as follows for the first month:

Truck	$6,000	
Less Accumulated Depreciation – Truck	50	
Book Value of Truck		$5,950

Only the $5,950 will be added in with the other assets. Since the account Accumulated Depreciation – Truck appears in the asset section, it is called a contra-asset account. The phrase *book value* as used in the above illustration means the value of an asset according to the firm's books. It is equal to cost minus accumulated depreciation.

The contra account is used instead of the Truck account to record the depreciation because depreciation is simply an estimate. No one can be sure that the truck will last exactly ten years. It may last longer; it may not last as long. The contra account indicates that the amount is only an estimate of the decline in the truck's worth.

Adjusting entries for depreciation expense must be made for all fixed assets that will someday be worthless. These include equipment, machinery, and buildings. Land is the only fixed asset that is not depreciated. Land, unlike other fixed assets, does not wear out. Thus, no entry is made to show the depreciation of land.

ALLOCATION OF RECORDED REVENUES

The second category of adjusting entries deals with revenue that is received before it is earned. Such revenue is called *unearned* revenue or *deferred* revenue. As the revenue is received, the amounts are credited to a liability account. As services are performed or goods delivered, the unearned revenue is transferred to a revenue account by an adjusting entry.

For example, a firm that sells magazine subscriptions receives revenues before they are earned. If a year's subscription is paid for, the publisher has an obligation to send the subscriber a magazine regularly. The revenue is not earned until the magazine is sent out. The following entries would be made to record the receipt of $24,000 in payments for yearly subscriptions to a monthly magazine:

At Receipt of Subscriptions

Cash	24,000	
Unearned Subscriptions		24,000
To record the receipt of payments for subscriptions.		

Adjusting Entry at End of First Month

Unearned Subscriptions	2,000	
Subscriptions Earned		2,000
To recognize revenue earned during the month.		

Notice that when payment was received, a liability account, Unearned Subscriptions, was credited. At the end of the first month when one issue had been sent out to all subscribers, one-twelfth of the liability was transferred to a revenue account, Subscriptions Earned. Now the balance sheet will show a liability for eleven month's of subscriptions, or $22,000. At the end of each month, the same adjusting entry is made. Thus, revenue for each month is correctly stated.

UNRECORDED EXPENSES

The third category of adjustments is *unrecorded expenses.* These expenses are liabilities incurred within a period which have not yet been paid. They are called *accrued expenses.* Accrued expenses must be recorded in the proper accounting period with an adjusting entry. In the adjusting entry, a debit should be made to an expense account and a credit to a liability account. Wages and interest are examples of unrecorded expenses.

Wages. As an example, consider a firm that pays wages of $5,000 per week to its employees. Assume that the accounting period ends on a Wednesday and the employees are paid on Friday. The employees have worked three days this week: Monday, Tuesday, and Wednesday. The pay for these three days is an expense of the current accounting period. However, the employees will not be paid until Friday for that work. An adjusting entry is needed if the wages are to be recorded in the proper period. The pay rate is $1,000 per day ($5,000 divided by five days). Thus, $3,000 for the three days of work is an unrecorded expense. An adjusting entry is needed to record the expense in the proper accounting period. The entry would be:

Adjusting Entry

Wages Expense	3,000	
Wages Payable		3,000
To record wages earned but not yet paid.		

On Friday (next period) when the wages are paid, the entry should be:

Adjusting Entry

Wages Payable	3,000	
Wages Expense	2,000	
Cash		5,000
To record payment of weekly wages.		

Note that the payment on Friday is for two items. These two items are the last period's liability for wages and the wage expense for the first two days of the new period. Thus, the proper expense of $2,000 is recorded for the two days that the employees worked in the new period.

UNRECORDED REVENUES

The last group of adjusting entries is unrecorded revenues. Unrecorded revenues are revenues which have been earned but not yet received. The adjusting entry needed is a debit to an asset account and a credit to a revenue account. The purpose of the adjusting entry is to record the accrued revenues in the proper time period. In this way, the revenue appears on the income statement at the time that it is earned.

Interest Revenue. For example, assume that a firm makes a one-year loan of $1,000 with a 6% interest rate. In other words, the $1,000 loan is to be paid back after one year along with the interest for a year at 6%. The amount to be paid back will thus be $1,060 ($1,000 plus $60 interest).

Interest rates are normally stated on an annual basis. The procedure for computing interest is as follows: Interest is equal to principal (amount of the loan) × interest rate × time. In this case, interest equals $1,000 (principal) × 6% (rate) × one year (time), or $60.

By the end of one month, a month's interest is earned. The interest will not be received until the loan is paid off at the end of the year. However, the interest has been earned and is shown as a revenue for each month of the year. Each month, interest of $5 is earned ($60 divided by twelve months). The $5 is recorded as an asset, a receivable from the debtor, and as a revenue. The adjusting entry is:

Adjusting Entry

	Debit	Credit
Interest Receivable	5	
Interest Revenue		5
To record interest for one month on a $1,000 loan.		

ADJUSTED TRIAL BALANCE

All of the adjusting entries should be posted to the ledger accounts from the journal. The next step is to prepare an *adjusted trial balance.* The adjusted trial balance is completed in the same manner as the trial balance discussed in chapter 4. The balances of all of the accounts should be listed to check the equality of the debits and credits. The purpose of the adjusted trial balance is to check that the sum of the debits still equals the sum of the credits after the adjusting entries have been made. The adjusted trial balance tests the correctness of the posting of the adjusting entries. Once this test is met the financial statements can be accurately prepared.

SUMMARY

Adjusting entries may be thought of as corrections. They are necessary to correct those accounts that are inaccurate due to the passage of time. The accounting principle which is most closely related to adjusting entries is the matching principle. The matching principle emphasizes the fact that revenues and expenses should be recorded in the period to which they apply. Adjusting entries are often needed to match revenues and expenses to the proper accounting period.

There are four types of situations that call for adjusting entries:

- Allocation of recorded expenses to the correct period.
- Allocation of recorded revenues to the correct period.
- Recording expenses that are not already on the books.
- Recording revenues that are not already on the books.

In all cases, the accountant must analyze the accounts and determine what must be done to make them correct. Once the adjusting entries are completed, the adjusted trial balance is prepared. The balance sheet and income statement are then prepared based on the figures on the adjusted trial balance.

REVIEW

1. Why is it necessary to make adjusting entries?
2. What is a mixed account?
3. What are the four situations in which there is a need for adjusting entries?
4. Which is prepared first, the trial balance, the adjusted trial balance, or the financial statements?
5. Which is prepared last, the trial balance, the adjusted trial balance, or the financial statements?

EXERCISES

1. During the first month of business, a firm paid $100 for store supplies and debited that amount to an asset account. Supplies worth $30 were on hand at the end of the month. What adjusting entry is necessary at the end of the month?
2. A firm pays its employees wages of $500 per week every Friday for a five-day work week. Financial statements are prepared at the end of each month.
   a. What adjusting entry must be made if December 31 falls on a Tuesday?
   b. What adjusting entry must be made if December 31 falls on a Thursday?
3. A firm borrows $1,000 on May 1 for one year. The interest rate is 12%. What adjusting entry should be made at the end of May?
4. A bank lends $5,000 to a customer on May 1 for one year. The interest rate is 6%. What adjusting entry should the bank make at the end of May?
5. A firm began the year with a balance of $400 in its store supplies account. During the year the firm bought $975 worth of supplies and these were all debited to the Store Supplies account. During the year, no credits were entered in the Store Supplies account. However, an inventory of store supplies showed that there were only $50 worth remaining. What adjusting entry should be made on December 31?

PROBLEMS

1. The firm of Slade Sales prepares its financial statements once a year on December 31. Use the following information to make the adjusting entries that must be made before preparing the balance sheet and income statement as of December 31, 1980.
   a. A three-year fire insurance policy was paid for on June 1, 1980. An asset account, Prepaid Insurance, was debited on that date for the total cost, $450.
   b. The asset account, Store Supplies, has a debit balance of $4,120 on December 31. An inventory count shows that only $180 worth of store supplies are on hand in the storeroom.
   c. The sum of $10,000 was loaned to Al Smith on May 1, 1980. Smith has promised to pay back the loan plus interest at 6% on May 1, 1981. The only entry that has been made is a $10,000 debit to Notes Receivable and a $10,000 credit to Cash.

d. The firm of Slade Sales pays its yearly rent in advance every November 1. On November 1, 1980, the account Prepaid Rent was debited and Cash was credited to record the $12,000 rent for the period through October 31, 1981.

e. Slade Sales bought a new truck on March 31, 1980, at a cost of $5,000. The new truck should have a useful life of ten years.

f. On December 1, 1980, Slade Sales borrowed $1,000 from the First State Bank. Though interest on the loan is 8% per year, no interest has yet been recorded on the books. The loan is due to be paid on March 1, 1981.

g. Slade Sales needs extra warehouse space during the months of December and January. Therefore, a spare room has been rented in a nearby house. Even though Slade Sales has used the room since December 1 and plans to use the room though the month of January, the rent of $75 per month has not yet been paid.

2. The Hill Company borrowed $3,000 from the local bank on June 1 of the current year. The loan is to be paid back with interest on March 1 of next year. The bank gave the firm $3,000, and the owner signed a note payable for $3,100. (The note included both the principal of the loan plus the interest.) The firm made the following entry on June 1:

Cash	3,000	
Prepaid Interest	100	
Notes Payable		3,100

a. What adjusting entry should be made on June 30 if the firm prepares its financial statements each month?

b. What adjusting entry should be made on December 31 if the firm prepares its financial statements only at year end instead of each month?

3. The Ace Book and Magazine Publishing Company began publishing a monthly, *Ace Magazine*, in June of this year. The firm sold one-year subscriptions to the new magazine at a price of $10 per year. When cash was collected, Cash was debited and a liability account, Unearned Subscriptions, was credited. Subscribers receive their first issue of the new magazine in the month after the cash for the subscription is recorded. For example, if the firm receives the cash in May, the subscribers will not get their first issue until June. Seven issues of Ace Magazine were published in the first year of business. The following amounts of cash were received each month for the one-year subscriptions.

May	$14,000
June	12,000
July	15,000
August	9,000
September	12,000
October	9,000
November	6,000
December	18,000

a. How much subscriptions revenue should be shown on the income statement prepared for the month of May?
b. What adjusting entry should be made on June 30 if the firm prepares its financial statements every month?
c. What would be the amount of liability that would be shown on the balance sheet prepared as of the end of the year?
d. What adjusting entry would be made on December 31 if the firm prepared its financial statements only once a year instead of monthly?

4. The Stein firm has prepared the following trial balance as of the end of the month of June. The firm prepares statements for each month.

Cash	$ 1,000	
Prepaid Insurance	330	
Accounts Receivable	6,000	
Supplies	300	
Equipment	6,000	
Accumulated Depreciation – Equipment		$ 3,000
Building	10,000	
Accumulated Depreciation – Building		3,500
Accounts Payable		5,000
Stein – Capital		9,930
Revenue from Fees		6,000
Wages Expense	2,200	
Advertising Expense	1,100	
Rent Expense	500	
	$27,430	$27,430

The data needed to prepare the adjusting entries are as follows:

(1) The insurance policy was bought several months ago. The cost is $10 per month.

(2) The value of the supplies that are on hand at the end of June is $80.

(3) The equipment depreciates $100 per month.

(4) The building depreciates at the rate of $600 per year.

(5) The firm pays its employees on Fridays only. Since the last day of June was a Tuesday, the firm has accrued wages for two days of $110 ($55 per day).

---

a. Prepare the adjusting entries.
b. Prepare an adjusted trial balance.
c. Prepare an income statement for the month of June.
d. Prepare a balance sheet as of June 30.

8
The Work Sheet

OBJECTIVES After studying this chapter, the student will be able to:

- Complete a work sheet.
- Prepare an income statement and balance sheet directly from the work sheet.
- Journalize the adjusting entries from the adjustments columns.

THE WORK SHEET

To be of value, the financial statements of a firm must be prepared as soon as possible after the end of the accounting period. The accounting tool developed to make this preparation easier and more efficient is called a *work sheet.* The work sheet:

- Shows the effects of adjusting the accounts.
- Allows the accounts to be sorted according to their use on either the balance sheet or income statement.
- Helps in calculating and proving the accuracy of the net income.

It also eliminates the use of a separate sheet for the trial balance since the trial balance is written directly on the work sheet in the trial balance columns. The work sheet is prepared solely for the benefit of the

	Trial Balance		Adjustments		Adjusted Trial Balance		Income Statement		Balance Sheet	
	Dr.	Cr.	Dr.	Cr.	Dr.	Cr.	Dr.	Cr.	Dr.	Cr.
Account Titles	Assets				Assets				Assets	
		Accumulated Depreciation				Accumulated Depreciation				Accumulated Depreciation
		Liabilities				Liabilities				Liabilities
		Owner's Equity				Owner's Equity				Owner's Equity
	Drawing				Drawing				Drawing	
		Revenues				Revenues		Revenues		
	Expenses				Expenses		Expenses			
							Net Income			Net Income

Fig. 8-1. Basic format of the work sheet indicating the placement of entries from various accounts. Broken lines indicate that the amounts are carried across and entered in columns to the right of the original entry.

accountant. Therefore, pencil can be used rather than ink, and corrections can be made neatly and easily.

As shown in figure 8-1, there are five sets of columns on the work sheet. They are used as follows.

Trial Balance. The first set of columns is labeled *Trial Balance.* Under debit and credit in this column, the accountant copies the unadjusted balances from the ledger accounts. The trial balance is thus prepared in these columns instead of on a separate sheet of paper. Figure 8-2 shows the unadjusted trial balance for the accounts of the Bob East Firm as entered on the work sheet.

Adjustments. The second column is labeled *Adjustments.* The debits and credits under Adjustments show proposed adjusting entries. Two adjusting entries are needed for the Bob East Firm as seen in figure 8-3. Depreciation of $100 on the equipment is recorded. Also, one-third of the prepaid rent has been used up. These two adjustments are shown in the adjustments columns of the work sheet and are labeled adjustments (a) and (b). The key letters help the accountant keep track of related debits and credits (the amounts debited and credited in one entry) so that he or she can more easily enter them in the journal and post them to the ledger. This is especially important when a firm has many adjusting entries to make. Figures in the Adjustments columns are now totaled to check that the totals match.

Also note that adjustments have been made to accounts that were not listed under Account Titles (the first column) in the trial balance. Thus, these account titles are now added to the work sheet.

Bob East Firm
Work Sheet
For Month Ended March 31, 1980

Account Titles	Trial Balance		Adjustments		Adjusted Trial Balance		Income Statement		Balance Sheet	
	Dr.	Cr.	Dr.	Cr.	Dr.	Cr.	Dr.	Cr.	Dr.	Cr.
Cash	*1,062*									
Accounts Receivable	*585*									
Supplies	*750*									
Prepaid Rent	*600*									
Equipment	*6,000*									
Accounts Payable		*1,400*								
Bob East, Capital		*6,300*								
Bob East, Drawing	*500*									
Sales		*2,540*								
Salary Expense	*743*									
	10,240	*10,240*								

Fig. 8-2. Work sheet with the trial balance filled in.

Bob East Firm
Work Sheet
For Month Ended March 31, 1980

Account Titles	Trial Balance Dr.	Trial Balance Cr.	Adjustments Dr.	Adjustments Cr.	Adjusted Trial Balance Dr.	Adjusted Trial Balance Cr.	Income Statement Dr.	Income Statement Cr.	Balance Sheet Dr.	Balance Sheet Cr.
Cash	1,062									
Accounts Receivable	585									
Supplies	750									
Prepaid Rent	600			(b) 200						
Equipment	6,000									
Accounts Payable		1,400								
Bob East, Capital		6,300								
Bob East, Drawing	500									
Sales		2,540								
Salary Expense	743									
	10,240	10,240								
Depreciation Expense			(a) 100							
Accum. Deprec. – Equip.				(a) 100						
Rent Expense			(b) 200							
			300	300						

Fig. 8-3. Work sheet with adjustments.

Bob East Firm
Work Sheet
For Month Ended March 31, 1980

Account Titles	Trial Balance Dr.	Trial Balance Cr.	Adjustments Dr.	Adjustments Cr.	Adjusted Trial Balance Dr.	Adjusted Trial Balance Cr.	Income Statement Dr.	Income Statement Cr.	Balance Sheet Dr.	Balance Sheet Cr.
Cash	1,062				1,062					
Accounts Receivable	585				585					
Supplies	750				750					
Prepaid Rent	600			(b) 200	400					
Equipment	6,000				6,000					
Accounts Payable		1,400				1,400				
Bob East, Capital		6,300				6,300				
Bob East Drawing	500				500					
Sales		2,540				2,540				
Salary Expense	743				743					
	10,240	10,240								
Depreciation Expense			(a) 100		100					
Accum. Deprec. – Equip.				(a) 100		100				
Rent Expense			(b) 200		200					
			300	300	10,340	10,340				

Fig. 8-4. Work sheet with adjusted trial balance.

Step III

Adjusted Trial Balance. The third column is the *Adjusted Trial Balance.* The amounts for this column are found by adding (or subtracting) the amounts in the first two columns for each account. For example, in figure 8-4 Prepaid Rent has a debit balance of $600 in the Trial Balance column and a credit of $200 in the Adjustments column. In the Adjusted Trial Balance, then, $200 is subtracted from $600 and $400 becomes the new Balance of Prepaid Rent in the Adjusted Trial Balance column. This process is called *crossfooting* and reflects the effect of the adjusting entries.

After an adjusted trial balance amount is computed for each of the accounts, the Adjusted Trial Balance columns are added to assure that the debits and credits are equal.

Sorting the accounts for use on the Income Statement and Balance Sheet. The final step is to sort the accounts in the Adjusted Trial Balance into one of the remaining four columns (the debit or credit columns of either the income statement or balance sheet).

The first question to consider in sorting is whether the account appears on the income statement or the balance sheet. The next question is whether the account has a debit or a credit balance.

In answering the first question, remember that revenues and expenses appear on the income statement and assets, liabilities, and owner's equity items are listed on the balance sheet. Secondly, those amounts which are debits remain debits and those which are credits remain credits. The amounts for the Bob East Firm are shown in the proper columns in figure 8-5.

After the amounts for all accounts are entered under either the balance sheet or income statement columns, the credit and debit sides of the Income Statement column are totaled. This gives the net income or net loss. (If the credit column total exceeds the debit column total, the difference is a net income. If the debit column total exceeds the credit column total, the difference is a net loss.) In figure 8-5 the Bob East Firm has a net income of $1,497 ($2,540 - $1,043 = $1,497). In order to make the income statement columns balance, the net income figure must be added to the debit side. Remember that if there is a net income, the revenues (credits) are greater than the expenses (debits). Therefore, to make the columns balance, an equal amount must be added to the debit column to make it agree with the credit column.

Note in figure 8-5 that the title *Net Loss* or *Net Income* is entered in the Account Titles column. Thus, this amount is labeled on the work sheet.

After the net income is determined in the Income Statement columns, it is added to the total of the Balance Sheet credit column. The reasoning behind this procedure is that net income has the effect of increasing owner's equity and thus must appear on the balance sheet. Note that up to this point all accounts except Capital have been updated to reflect end-of-the-period balances. By adding the net income to the credit column of the Balance Sheet, the capital account is, in

Bob East Firm
Work Sheet
For Month Ended March 31, 1980

Account Titles	Trial Balance		Adjustments		Adjusted Trial Balance		Income Statement		Balance Sheet	
	Dr.	Cr.	Dr.	Cr.	Dr.	Cr.	Dr.	Cr.	Dr.	Cr.
Cash	*1,062*				*1,062*				*1,062*	
Accounts Receivable	*585*				*585*				*585*	
Supplies	*750*				*750*				*750*	
Prepaid Rent	*600*			*(b) 200*	*400*				*400*	
Equipment	*6,000*				*6,000*				*6,000*	
Accounts Payable		*1,400*				*1,400*				*1,400*
Bob East, Capital		*6,300*				*6,300*				*6,300*
Bob East, Drawing	*500*				*500*				*500*	
Sales		*2,540*				*2,540*		*2,540*		
Salary Expense	*743*				*743*		*743*			
	10,240	*10,240*								
Depreciation Expense			*(a) 100*		*100*		*100*			
Accum. Deprec. – Equip.				*(a) 100*		*100*				*100*
Rent Expense			*(b) 200*		*200*		*200*			
			300	*300*	*10,340*	*10,340*	*1,043*	*2,540*		
							1,497			*1,497*
Net Income							*2,540*	*2,540*	*9,297*	*9,297*

Fig. 8-5. Completed work sheet.

Income Statement		Balance Sheet	
Dr.	Cr.	Dr.	Cr.
Expenses	Revenues	Assets	Liabilities Owner's Equity
Net Income	Net Loss	Net Loss	Net Income

Fig. 8-6. The last two sets of work sheet columns.

effect, also brought up to date and assets once again equal liabilities and owner's equity. Figure 8-6 summarizes the income statement and balance sheet columns of the work sheet.

If there had been a net loss, expenses would have been greater than revenues. In this case, the amount of the net loss must be added to the credit column of the income statement for the columns to balance. Also, a net loss decreases owner's equity, so the net loss is also added to the debit column of the balance sheet to show the effect of reducing the owner's capital. (Refer to figure 8-6.)

PREPARING THE FINANCIAL STATEMENTS

When the work sheet is completed, the financial statements are prepared. To prepare the financial statements, copy the amounts from the Income Statement and Balance Sheet columns into the proper form.

Bob East Firm Income Statement For Month Ended March 31, 1980		
Revenue:		
Sales		$2,540
Expenses:		
Salary Expense	$743	
Depreciation Expense	100	
Rent Expense	200	
Total Expenses		1,043
Net Income		$1,497

Fig. 8-7. Income statement for the Bob East Firm.

Bob East Firm Balance Sheet March 31, 1980		
ASSETS:		
Cash		$1,062
Accounts Receivable		585
Supplies		750
Prepaid Rent		400
Equipment	$6,000	
Less: Accumulated Depreciation	100	5,900
Total Assets		$8,697
LIABILITIES:		
Accounts Payable		$1,400
OWNER'S EQUITY:		
Bob East, Capital	$6,300	
Add: Net Income for March	1,497	
	$7,797	
Less: Bob East, Drawing	500	
Bob East, Capital, March 31, 1980		7,297
Total Liabilities and Owner's Equity		$8,697

Fig. 8-8. Balance sheet for the Bob East Firm.

The Income Statement of the Bob East Firm is prepared as shown in figure 8-7. Note that all data needed to make up the income statement is shown in the Income Statement columns of the work sheet. Thus, the work sheet is the source used to make up the statement. Similarly, the balance sheet is drawn up from the work sheet as seen in figure 8-8.

JOURNALIZING THE ADJUSTING ENTRIES

Since the work sheet is only a work paper and not an accounting record, the adjustments on the work sheet must be shown in the journal and the ledger. Entries should be made in the journal and posted to the ledger showing the adjustments on the work sheet.

The adjusting entries for the Bob East Firm are made as shown in figure 8-9.

Next, these entries are posted to the accounts in the ledger. Figure 8-10 shows the ledger accounts after the adjusting entries have been posted.

GENERAL JOURNAL

Page 5

Date		Account Titles and Explanation	Post. Ref.	Debit	Credit
1980					
March	31	Depreciation Expense		100 00	
		Accumulated Depreciation – Equipment			100 00
		To record depreciation on the equipment			
		for the month.			
	31	Rent Expense		200 00	
		Prepaid Rent			200 00

Fig. 8-9. Formal adjusting entries for the Bob East Firm as made in the journal.

Prepaid Rent Acct. No. 117

Date		Explanation	Post. Ref.	Debit	Credit	Balance
1980						
Mar.	1		2	600 00		600 00
	31	Adjusting	5		200 00	400 00

Accumulated Depreciation – Equipment Acct. No. 121A

Date		Explanation	Post. Ref.	Debit	Credit	Balance
1980						
Mar.	31	Adjusting	5		100 00	100 00

Rent Expense Acct. No. 535

Date		Explanation	Post. Ref.	Debit	Credit	Balance
1980						
Mar.	31	Adjusting	5	200 00		200 00

Depreciation Expense Acct. No. 538

Date		Explanation	Post. Ref.	Debit	Credit	Balance
1980						
Mar.	31	Adjusting	5	100 00		100 00

Fig. 8-10. Account balances after the adjusting entries have been posted.

SUMMARY

The steps in the accounting process are:

- Record the transactions in the journal.
- Post the journal entries to the ledger accounts.
- Prepare the work sheet.
- Prepare the financial statements from the work sheet.
- Journalize and post the adjusting entries from the adjustments columns of the work sheet.

The work sheet is a tool used by the accountant to show end-of-the-period adjustments and to sort the accounts as they will appear on the income statement and balance sheet. Once the work sheet has been prepared, the accountant knows the amount of the net income and can prepare the financial statements by copying the items from the work sheet to the formal financial statements. Next, the adjusting entries are journalized and posted.

REVIEW

1. Why is a work sheet prepared?
2. Who sees the work sheet?
3. Name the five sets or pairs of columns that appear on a work sheet.
4. In which column of a work sheet does revenue appear?
5. In which columns of a work sheet does a net income appear?
6. In which columns of a work sheet would a net loss appear?
7. Is it necessary to record adjusting entries in the journal if they are shown on the work sheet?
8. Are adjusting entries shown on the work sheet posted to the ledger accounts? If so, when does this take place?
9. In what order are the account titles listed on the work sheet?
10. What is indicated when the work sheet income statement debit column is greater than the income statement credit column?

EXERCISES

1. For this exercise, the last four columns of a work sheet are identified by letter as follows:

Income Statement		Balance Sheet	
(A) Debit	(B) Credit	(C) Debit	(D) Credit

Indicate the column in which each of the following accounts should be entered.

1. Cash
2. Office Supplies
3. Land
4. Taxes Payable
5. Revenue from Commissions
6. Interest Revenue
7. Building
8. Accounts Receivable
9. Interest Expense
10. James Denny, Capital
11. James Denny, Drawing
12. Accumulated Depreciation
13. Depreciation Expense
14. Freight Expense
15. Prepaid Insurance
16. Mortgage Payable

2. Indicate the effect of the described errors on the various elements of a company's financial statements. Use the following code:

O – amount is overstated
U – amount is understated
N – no effect

	Total Revenues	Total Expenses	Net Income	Total Assets	Total Liabilities	Owner's Equity
Example: Failed to record accrued wages	*N*	*U*	*O*	*N*	*U*	*O*
1. Prepaid insurance, an asset account, was not adjusted at end of year to record portion expired.						
2. Interest on bank loan payable was not accrued at year end.						
3. Failed to accrue interest earned on note receivable.						
4. Failed to record depreciation on truck.						
5. Repair expense was erroneously charged to building account.						

3. Given the following account balances, prepare a work sheet.

Cash, $4,400
Accounts Receivable, $1,650
Building, $2,400
Accumulated Depreciation, $600
Accounts payable, $3,620
Capital, $5,690
Drawing, $900
Revenue from Fees, $1,800
Salary Expense, $620
Delivery Expense, $280
Rent Expense, $500
Utility Expense, $960

Note: The depreciation on the building for the year was $100. There were $50 worth of accrued salaries at the end of the year.

4. Prepare a work sheet from the following information. The trial balance shows the following amounts.

Cash	$13,000
Accounts Receivable	3,000
Supplies	1,000
Equipment	6,000
Accounts Payable	3,000
S. L. Lang, Capital	20,500
S. L. Lang, Drawing	6,000
Revenue	75,300
Wage Expense	47,800
Supplies Expense	0
Other Expenses	20,000
Rent Expense	2,000

Supplies used during the period totaled $400.
Depreciation expense for the period was $300.

PROBLEMS

1. The following are all of the account balances of the Pete Walsh Laundromat at December 31, and data needed to prepare year-end adjustments.

Cash	$ 1,198
Laundry Supplies	1,965
Prepaid Insurance	574
Laundry Equipment	22,700
Accumulated Depreciation	5,600
Accounts Payable	315
Walsh, Capital	13,006
Walsh, Drawing	6,120
Laundry Revenue	23,820
Wages Expense	7,335
Rent Expense	1,320
Utilities Expense	1,025
Miscellaneous Expense	504

Inventory of laundry supplies at December 31 = $210
Insurance premiums expired during the year = $305
Depreciation on equipment during the year = $1,810
Wages accrued but not paid at December 31 = $77

a. Using this information, prepare a work sheet.
b. Prepare the income statement and balance sheet.

2. Complete the following work sheet. To test your skills in sorting the accounts to the proper columns, the accounts are not listed in the proper order. Additional facts: Depreciation on the equipment, $150; Accrued wages, $86.

West Company
Work Sheet
For Month Ended May 31, 19–

Account Titles	Trial Balance		Adjustments		Adjusted Trial Balance		Income Statement		Balance Sheet	
	Dr.	Cr.	Dr.	Cr.	Dr.	Cr.	Dr.	Cr.	Dr.	Cr.
Fees Earned		*3,000*								
Accounts Receivable	*5,600*									
Utilities Expense	*85*									
Supplies	*230*									
Faye West, Capital		*11,000*								
Cash	*4,000*									
Miscellaneous Expense	*25*									
Equipment	*3,100*									
Faye West, Drawing	*1,200*									
Accounts Payable		*650*								
Accumulated Depreciation		*450*								
Salary Expense	*650*									
Rent Expense	*210*									
	15,100	*15,100*								

(3) Al South set up a new firm on May 1. He used the following chart of accounts.

101	Cash	401	Revenue from Fees Earned
111	Accounts Receivable	503	Telephone Expense
115	Supplies	504	Depreciation Expense
141	Equipment	516	Rent Expense
141A	Accumulated Deprec.	517	Advertising Expense
201	Accounts Payable	521	Supplies Expense
301	Al South, Capital	531	Salary Expense
302	Al South, Drawing	535	Repair Expense

He engaged in the following transactions.

May 1: Invested $4,000 in cash in the firm.
3: Paid rent for month, $75.
6: Purchased equipment costing $400 by paying $200 in cash and putting the balance on credit.
7: Sold services for the first week of $200; of this amount, $125 was received in cash and the rest on credit.
10: Paid $15 for advertising in the local newspaper.
12: Bought supplies for $40 cash.
14: Sold services for second week of $300; of this amount, $200 was paid in cash and the rest on credit.
17: Collected $125 from customers on their accounts.
23: Paid salaries in cash of $100.
25: Paid for repairs on equipment of $15.

May 28: Withdrew $50 in cash for personal use.
29: Paid $10 telephone bill.
30: Bought supplies on credit, $16.
31: Sold services for week of $500. Received $300 in cash and the rest was placed on credit.

a. Journalize the above transaction using the account titles in the chart of accounts and proper journal entry form.
b. Post the entries to the ledger accounts.
c. Complete a work sheet using the following data:
   Depreciation on the equipment for the month, $80
   Supplies used during the month, $20
   Accrued salaries, $100
d. Prepare an income statement and balance sheet.
e. Journalize and post adjusting entries.

4. The following is an adjusted trial balance as of December 31 of the current year for the Fifth Avenue Club, a firm owned by Veronica Lorenzo. Prepare an income statement and balance sheet in proper form, including headings for each statement.

	Debit	Credit
Cash	$ 17,420	$
Accounts Receivable	18,275	
Store and Office Supplies	1,815	
Prepaid Insurance	910	
Store Equipment	22,800	
Accumulated Depreciation – Store Equipment		13,680
Office Equipment	18,500	
Accumulated Depreciation – Office Equipment		11,100
Building	184,000	
Accumulated Depreciation – Building		20,160
Land	18,000	
Notes Payable		15,000
Accounts Payable		28,275
Mortgage Payable		68,400
Veronica Lorenzo, Capital, January 1		39,285
Veronica Lorenzo, Drawing	10,400	
Revenues		204,180
Sales Salaries	42,400	
Advertising Expense	25,190	
Supplies Expense	2,360	
Depreciation Expense – Store Equipment	2,280	
Office Salaries	16,750	
Depreciation Expense – Office Equipment	1,850	
Depreciation Expense – Building	2,100	
Taxes Expense	5,340	
Insurance Expense	4,185	
Miscellaneous Expense	930	
Interest Expense	4,575	
	$400,080	$400,080

9
Closing Entries

OBJECTIVES

After studying this chapter, the student will be able to:

- Explain the two reasons for making closing entries.
- Journalize and post closing entries.
- Identify and demonstrate the eight steps of the accounting cycle.

REASONS FOR CLOSING ENTRIES

The income statement shows a firm's revenues and expenses for a specific period of time. Revenue and expense accounts store the facts for that accounting period. Once the period ends, and the work sheet and statements are completed, these facts are no longer needed. Thus, at the end of each period, the revenue and expense accounts are cleared out (given a zero balance) so that new facts for the next period may be entered. *Closing entries* are the device used by accountants to clear out or *close* expense, revenue, and drawing accounts.

A second reason for making closing entries is to show the changes in owner's equity that have taken place during the accounting period. Revenue, expense, and drawing accounts are merely temporary accounts whose balances must be transferred to the owner's equity account at the end of each period. The relationship between these accounts may be seen by reviewing the accounting equation.

ASSETS = LIABILITIES + OWNER'S EQUITY
+ Revenues
– Expenses
– Drawing

At the end of each period, the balances of the temporary accounts are transferred to the owner's equity account. Assets, liabilities, and owner's equity accounts are permanent accounts and are never closed. These permanent accounts are sometimes called *real accounts.* Their balances are carried over to the next period. The temporary accounts, on the other hand, have a zero balance at the start of each new period.

Closing entries are necessary to clear out the balances in the temporary accounts by transferring these balances to owner's equity.

Closing an account means making the balance of that account equal to zero.

THE CLOSING PROCESS

A special account is used in the closing process. This account, called the *Income Summary account,* is used only at the end of the accounting period to close out the temporary accounts and to summarize income. It is said that the revenue and expense accounts are closed to the Income Summary account. This means that their balances are transferred to the Income Summary account. After this has been done, the balance in the Income Summary account should be equal to the net income or net loss for the period.

To complete the closing process the accountant must perform the following steps.

- Close revenue accounts to Income Summary.
- Close expense accounts to Income Summary.
- Close Income Summary account balance to the owner's Capital account.
- Close the owner's Drawing account to the Capital account.

The example used to illustrate the closing process is based on the work sheet for the Bob East Firm which appears in figure 8-5. Referring to that figure, study the explanation of the four closing steps given here. T-accounts are used to show the effect of the closing entries.

Close revenue accounts to Income Summary. The revenue account is shown in the Income Statement credit column of the work sheet as Sales with a balance of $2,540. To close out a credit balance of $2,540 to zero, a debit of $2,540 must be made in the Sales account. The corresponding credit is entered in the Income Summary account as follows:

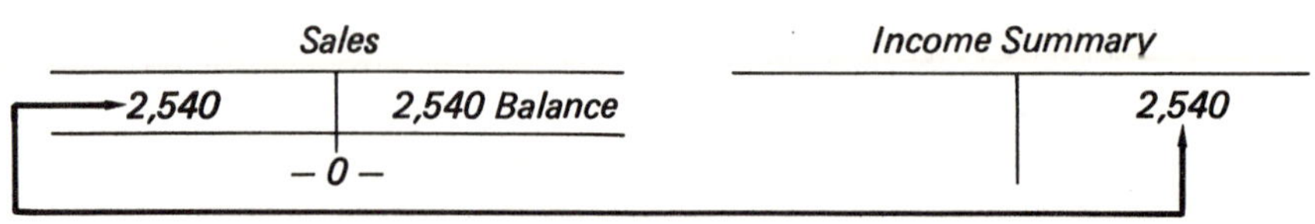

This entry transfers the balance from the Sales account to the Income Summary account. It also gives the revenue account a zero balance. The revenue account is now clear and ready to start the next month. Thus, old amounts are not confused with new amounts.

Close the expense accounts to the Income Summary. The expense accounts are found on the debit side of the Income Statement columns of the work sheet. These accounts have debit balances. Thus, to close them, the accounts must be credited. The corresponding debit is made to Income Summary. The expenses from the work sheet in figure 8-5 and their balances are handled as follows:

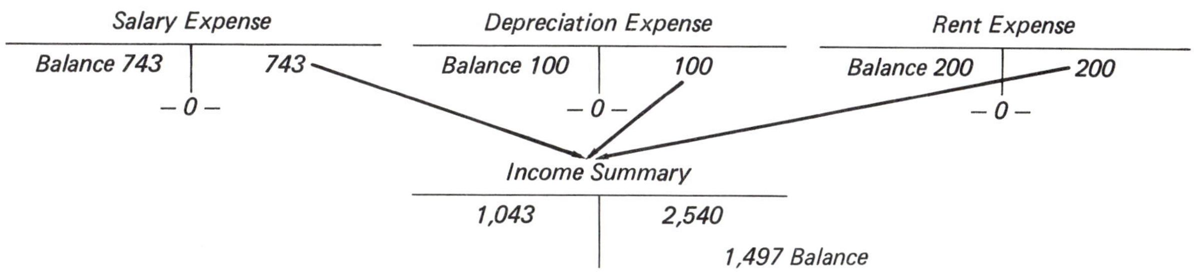

This entry transfers the balances of the expense accounts to Income Summary. Note that one entry is made showing the total of the three expense account balances. Like the revenue accounts, the expense accounts now have zero balances and are clear for the next month. Note that the debit to Income Summary of $1,043 is the same as the work sheet's income statement debit column total. This is one way of checking to be sure the entry is correct. Since all revenues and expenses have been transferred to Income Summary, the balance of the Income Summary account should be the same as the net income for the period. A check with the work sheet shows that the net income was $1,497, which is the balance of Income Summary. Agreement of the two balances is a checkpoint for accuracy.

Close the Income Summary account balance to the owner's Capital account. The Income Summary account is used to close out the revenue and expense accounts and summarize income. At this point, the Income Summary account has served its purpose and is closed. Since the balance in Income Summary is equal to net income, and net income increases owner's equity, Income Summary is closed out to the owner's Capital account. In other words, the Income Summary account is debited and the owner's Capital account credited as follows:

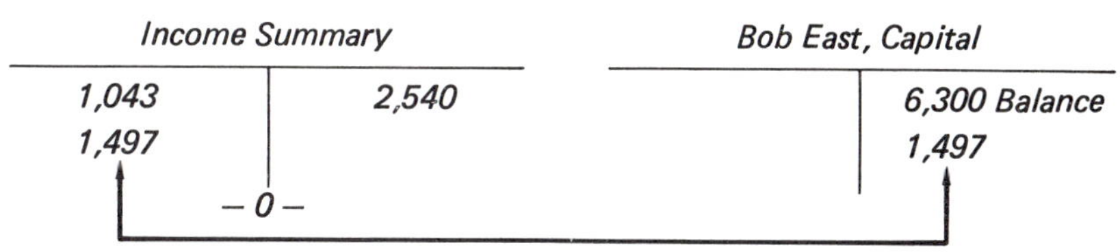

This entry transfers the net income to the Capital account. A net income is credited to Capital because it increases capital. However, a net loss would be debited to the Capital account because it decreases capital.

Close the owner's Drawing account to the Capital account. The Drawing account is used to show the owner's withdrawals for one accounting period, and thus, is closed to start the new period. Withdrawals are a deduction from the owner's capital so the Drawing account is closed to the Capital account. The Drawing account for Bob East as shown in the Balance Sheet columns of figure 8-5 has a debit balance of $500. Thus, Drawing will be credited and the Capital account will be debited in the closing entry.

Bob East, Drawing	
Balance 500	*500*
– 0 –	

Bob East, Capital	
500	*6,300*
	1,497
	7,297 Balance

The final balance in the Bob East, Capital account of $7,297 is the same as the balance shown on the balance sheet for Capital. The closing process is now complete since all revenues, expenses and drawing accounts have a zero balance, and the Capital account shows the effects of the net income and withdrawals for the period.

JOURNALIZING AND POSTING CLOSING ENTRIES

The closing process was shown above in T-accounts. However, the closing entries must be made in the journal and posted to the ledger. The four journal entries for the Bob East Firm are shown in figure 9-1. These entries are then posted to the ledger.

POST-CLOSING TRIAL BALANCE

After the closing entries have been posted, it is wise to check that the ledger is in balance to start the new period. The equality of the debits and credits is checked by preparing a trial balance. The trial balance is a list of the balances of all accounts in the ledger. The only

GENERAL JOURNAL

Date		Account Titles and Explanation	Post. Ref.	Debit	Credit
1980					
March	*31*	*Sales*		*2540 00*	
		Income Summary			*2540 00*
		To close the revenue account.			
	31	*Income Summary*		*1043 00*	
		Salary Expense			*743 00*
		Depreciation Expense			*100 00*
		Rent Expense			*200 00*
		To close the expense accounts.			
	31	*Income Summary*		*1497 00*	
		Bob East, Capital			*1497 00*
		To close net income to capital.			
	31	*Bob East, Capital*		*500 00*	
		Bob East, Drawing			*500 00*
		To close withdrawals to capital.			

Fig. 9-1. The closing entries for the Bob East Firm.

Bob East Firm
Post-closing Trial Balance
March 31, 1980

Cash	$1,062	
Accounts Receivable	585	
Supplies	750	
Prepaid Rent	400	
Equipment	6,000	
Accumulated Depreciation		$ 100
Accounts Payable		1,400
Bob East, Capital		7,297
	$8,797	$8,797

Fig. 9-2. Post-closing trial balance for the Bob East Firm.

accounts with balances that have not been closed are the real accounts (the balance sheet accounts). Therefore, only the assets, liabilities and owner's equity accounts are shown on the post-closing trial balance. The post-closing trial balance for the Bob East Firm is shown in figure 9-2.

SUMMARY

Closing entries are made (1) to cause the temporary accounts to have a zero balance at the start of the new accounting period, and (2) to show the changes in the owner's equity accounts. The following four steps are necessary to complete the closing process.

- Close revenue accounts to Income Summary.
- Close expense accounts to Income Summary.
- Close Income Summary account balance to the owner's Capital account.
- Close the owner's Drawing account to the Capital account.

The Income Statement column totals of the work sheet can be used as check figures for the first two closing entries. The net income or loss is the check figure for the third closing entry.

After all closing entries have been recorded in the journal and posted to the ledger, a post-closing trial balance is prepared. The post-closing trial balance is a final check that the ledger is in balance and ready for the new accounting period. Only real accounts are shown on the post-closing trial balance.

THE ACCOUNTING CYCLE REVIEWED

The accounting cycle, as discussed in chapters 3 through 9, is completed in its entirety in each accounting period. When step 8 is completed, the cycle then repeats itself in the next accounting period. The steps in the accounting cycle are summarized as follows:

1. Record transactions in the journal.
2. Post these journal entries to the ledger accounts.
3. Prepare the work sheet.
4. Prepare the income statement directly from the work sheet.
5. Prepare the balance sheet directly from the work sheet.
6. Journalize and post the adjusting entries from the adjustment columns of the work sheet.
7. Journalize and post closing entries.
8. Prepare post-closing trial balance.

REVIEW

1. What are the two reasons for making closing entries?
2. What accounts are closed out at the end of each period?
3. On which financial statement does Income Summary appear?
4. What are real accounts?
5. Give five examples of real accounts.
6. Are closing entries made before or after the adjusting entries?
7. What are the four types of closing entries?
8. If a firm has a net loss, will Income Summary be debited or credited in the third closing entry?
9. To what account is Income Summary closed out?
10. To what account is the owner's Drawing account closed out?
11. Would it ever be possible for a firm to have only three closing entries? Why or why not?
12. Why is a post-closing trial balance prepared?
13. List the eight steps in the accounting cycle.

EXERCISES

1. A firm has one revenue account, Revenue from Commissions, with a balance of $3,220. Show the journal entry necessary to close out the revenue account.
2. A firm has three expense accounts with balances: Rent Expense, $350; Wage Expense, $500; and Depreciation Expense, $210. Give the journal closing entry for the three expense accounts.

3. A firm has a net income of $4,200 for the year. The owner withdraws $3,000. Give the last two closing entries as shown in the journal for this firm.

4. The following shows the income statement and balance sheet columns from a firm's work sheet. Use the information in the columns to make the firm's four closing entries.

	Debit	Credit	Debit	Credit
Cash			50	
Accounts Receivable			150	
Equipment			800	
Accumulated Depreciation				160
George Schultz, Capital				905
George Schultz, Drawing			105	
Revenue from Fees		1,000		
Interest Revenue		20		
Wage Expense	600			
Rent Expense	300			
Depreciation Expense	80			
	980	1,020	1,105	1,065
	40			40
	1,020	1,020	1,105	1,105

5. The following represent the income statement and balance sheet columns from a firm's work sheet. Use the information given to make the firm's four closing entries and prepare a post-closing trial balance dated March 31 of the current year.

	Debit	Credit	Debit	Credit
Cash			183	
Accounts Receivable			910	
Office Supplies			180	
Land			1,000	
Building			7,000	
Accumulated Depreciation				600
Accounts Payable				238
Mortgage Payable				3,900
Susan Jack, Capital				5,000
Susan Jack, Drawing			180	
Revenue from Commissions		3,650		
Wage Expense	2,110			
Supplies Expense	275			
Rent Expense	1,200			
Depreciation Expense	250			
Interest Expense	100			
	3,935	3,650	9,453	9,738
		285	285	
	3,935	3,935	9,738	9,738

Post Closing Trial Bal
#9,272

PROBLEMS

1. From the following trial balance and supplementary data,
   a. Prepare a work sheet for the year ended December 31, 1981.
   b. Prepare a classified income statement for the year ended December 31, 1981.
   c. Prepare a classified balance sheet as of December 31, 1981.
   d. Journalize the December 31, 1981, adjusting entries.
   e. Journalize the December 31, 1981, closing entries.
   f. Prepare a post-closing trial balance.

Balie Company
December 31, 1981 Trial Balance

Debits	Credits	
$ 18,160	$	Cash
36,260		Accounts Receivable
5,000		Notes Receivable, current
650		Store Supplies
22,000		Store Equipment
	4,400	Accumulated Depreciation – Store Equip.
	19,750	Accounts Payable
	6,000	Notes Payable, current
	95,490	Frederick Balie, Capital
	95,100	Revenue from Commissions
	200	Interest Income
100		Interest Expense
1,960		Delivery Expense
34,600		Salesmen's Salaries and Commissions
19,500		Advertising
740		Store Supplies Expense
2,470		General Office Expense
1,200		Fire Insurance Expense, selling div.
20,200		Office Salaries
40,000		Administrative Salaries
2,500		Legal and Auditing Expenses
1,200		Telephone and Telegraph, admin. div.
12,000		Rent Expense, store
2,400		Rent Expense, office
$220,940	$220,940	Totals

Supplementary data as of December 31, 1981:

(1) Fire insurance unexpired, $250
(2) Store supplies on hand, $475
(3) Prepaid rent expense (store only), $2,000
(4) Depreciate the store equipment $2,200 each year.
(5) Accrued salesmen's salaries and commissions, $1,000
(6) Accrued office salaries, $500

2. The firm of Leslie Brown and Company began the month of May with the following account balances:

	Debit	Credit
Cash	$ 3,250	$
Accounts Receivable	1,270	
Office Supplies	115	
Land	2,000	
Building	12,500	
Accumulated Depreciation		2,500
Accounts Payable		271
Mortgage Payable		5,000
Leslie Brown, Capital		11,364
	$19,135	$19,135

(These balances should be entered in the accounts.)

During the month of May the firm completed the following transactions:

May 1: Collected $200 of accounts receivable.
2: Received $315 from a customer for work performed.
3: Bought office supplies on credit, $295.
4: Paid for a newspaper advertisement, $30.
5: Paid $75 to have the office doors repaired.
8: Paid $180 of accounts payable.
9: Did work for customer on account, $700.
10: Paid monthly rent for May, $500.
11: Leslie Brown withdrew $325 to buy a new coat.
12: Bought a one year fire insurance policy, $240. Coverage is to begin May 16.
15: Paid secretary's wages, $325.
16: Collected $175 of accounts receivable.
17: Sold $10 worth of office supplies to the Boy Scouts for cash.
18: Paid for a newspaper advertisement, $35.
19: Received $1,600 from a customer for work performed.
22: Did work for a customer on credit, $199.
23: Bought a new truck for $5,000. Paid $1,000 in cash and signed a ninety-day note for the balance.
24: Paid accounts payable of $39.
25: Leslie Brown withdrew $20 worth of office supplies to take home for personal use.
26: Paid the monthly utility bill, $58.
29: Paid the rent for the month of June, $500.
30: Paid the secretary's wages, $325.

The following data is needed for the adjusting entries:

(1) One-half of a month's insurance coverage has expired.
(2) A physical count shows $13 worth of office supplies on hand.
(3) Depreciation for the month was: Building, $50; Truck, $10.
(4) Accrued interest on the mortgage was $50.
(5) Accrued interest on the note payable was $11.

a. Journalize the entries for the month of May.
b. Post to the ledger accounts.
c. Prepare a work sheet.
d. Prepare an income statement for the month of May.
e. Prepare a balance sheet.
f. Journalize and post the adjusting entries.
g. Journalize and post the closing entries.
h. Prepare a post-closing trial balance.

SECTION 2

Accounting for Merchandising Concerns

10
Purchases and Sales of Merchandise

OBJECTIVES After studying this chapter, the student will be able to:

- List the accounts used in a merchandising firm.
- Record sales and sales returns and allowances.
- Describe sales and purchase discounts and how they are recorded.
- Record purchases and purchase returns and allowances.
- Record freight charges.
- Explain freight and credit terms.

The accounts and procedures studied thus far are typical of firms that perform a service for the public. Another type of firm, a *merchandising firm,* sells goods or merchandise. The transactions involved in this type of business are somewhat different from those which occur in a service business and require different types of accounts. Two types of accounts used by merchandising firms are the *Sales account,* used to record items sold to customers, and the *Purchases account,* used to record merchandise purchased by the firm for sale to its customers.

THE SALES ACCOUNT

The Sales account is a revenue account with a normal credit balance. It is used to record both the sale of items for cash and the sale of merchandise on credit. Since Sales is a revenue account, an increase is shown by a credit to this account. In recording a sale, the debit is made to an asset account – either Cash or Accounts Receivable. The Cash account is used when recording a cash sale; Accounts Receivable is used for credit sales.

For example, at the end of the day the cash register at the Downtown Boutique showed that sales of $200 had been made for cash. The entry to show these cash sales is:

Cash	200	
Sales		200
To record the cash sales for the day.		

The credit sales for the day at the same shop were $100. This fact is recorded in the following entry:

Accounts Receivable	100	
Sales		100
To record sales on credit for the day.		

The balance in the Sales account is now $300, the amount of total sales for the day.

Sales Returns and Allowances

Most stores allow a customer to return unsatisfactory goods or will reduce the customer's bill if the goods are damaged. Since sales returns indicate customer dissatisfaction, all firms want to record the amount of merchandise returned. Therefore, to inform the management of the frequency of such problems, sales returns and allowances are recorded in a separate account. This account, called *Sales Returns and Allowances,* is deducted from Sales on the income statement. Thus, this account is a contra-revenue account and has a normal debit balance which is opposite that of Sales. The account Sales Returns and Allowances is increased by entering a debit. The credit is made to Cash if the money is refunded to the customer or to Accounts Receivable if the customer's account is reduced.

The seller may notify the customer of the refund allowance by sending a credit memorandum. A credit memorandum might look like the one shown in figure 10-1. The credit memorandum tells the customer that the store has credited or reduced his account. The entry to record the credit memorandum shown in figure 10-1 would be:

Sales Returns and Allowances	12.50	
Accounts Receivable		12.50
To record credit memorandum #67.		

Alpha Company
1 Pace Street
Harris, Maine 28795

No.	67
Date	May 5, 1980
Invoice No.	67543
To	Jones Firm 5 First Street Theresa, Maine

Your account has been credited for:

CREDIT MEMORANDUM

Quantity	Catalog No.	Description	Unit Price	Total
10	595	Hooks	1.25	12.50

Fig. 10-1 Example of a credit memorandum.

Sales Discounts

In order to encourage customers to pay their accounts quickly, a firm may offer a reduction in the original price as a reward for prompt payment. This reward to the customer is called a *cash discount.* When discounts are offered, they are made part of the credit terms and appear on the invoice. The *credit terms* show when payment is due. The cash discount period is also shown. For example, credit terms may be written, 2/10, n/30. The *n/30* means that the net payment is due within 30 days. The *n* stands for *net.* The *2/10* means that the customer may deduct 2% if the bill is paid within ten days after the invoice date. The ten-day period is called the *discount period.* If the bill is not paid within the ten days, the customer must pay the full amount within thirty days after the invoice date. The seller calls this cash discount a *sales discount.*

A separate account is used to record sales discounts. The account *Sales Discounts* is deducted from Sales on the income statement and has a normal debit balance (or the opposite balance of the Sales account). It is a contra-revenue account. At the time of the sale the firm does not know whether or not the customer will pay within the discount period and take the discount. Hence, sales discounts cannot be recorded until the customer pays.

For example, a firm sells $300 worth of goods to a customer on May 11 with credit terms of 1/10, EOM, n/60. (EOM means *end of the month.*) These credit terms mean that the seller offers a 1% discount if the bill is paid within ten days after the end of the month. The entire bill must be paid within sixty days after the invoice date. If the buyer pays before June 10, he may deduct 1% of $300 or $3 and only pay $297 to settle the account. If the customer does not pay within the discount period, he must pay the full $300 by July 10. The entry to record the sale is:

May 11	Accounts Receivable	300.00	
	Sales		300.00
	Sold merchandise on credit, terms 1/10, EOM, n/60.		

Note that the sales discount has been ignored in making the initial entry.

Assume that the customer pays his bill on June 10 and takes the discount. The entry to record the receipt of payment is:

June 10	Cash	297.00	
	Sales Discounts	3.00	
	Accounts Receivable		300.00
	Received payment for May 11 sale less the discount.		

When these entries are posted, the accounts will appear as follows:

Cash		*Accounts Receivable*		*Sales*		*Sales Discounts*	
June 10 297		*May 11 300*	*June 10 300*		*May 11 300*	*June 10 3*	
		–0–					

Note that Accounts Receivable has a zero balance because the customer's account has been settled in full and he owes nothing. If the customer had not paid within the discount period, the entry to record payment would be a debit to Cash for $300 and a credit to Accounts Receivable for $300.

THE PURCHASES ACCOUNT

The Purchases account is used to record merchandise bought for resale. Merchandise may be bought for cash or on credit. For example, if the Knit Company buys $55 dollars worth of ski hats for resale, the entry is:

Purchases	55	
Cash		55
Purchased merchandise.		

If $90 worth of goods for resale are bought on credit, the entry is:

Purchases	90	
Accounts Payable		90
Purchased merchandise for credit, terms 1/10, n/60.		

The Purchases account is classified as a cost account. A *cost account* is like an expense account. It is closed to Income Summary with all other expense accounts. Purchases is increased by debiting the account and has a normal debit balance. The balance in Purchases shows the total cost of all goods bought for resale during the period.

Note that the Purchases account includes only merchandise which is bought for resale. Anything purchased which is not for resale is recorded in another expense account or an asset account. Thus, a typewriter bought by a store which sells office equipment will be shown in the Purchases account because the typewriter will be resold. On the other hand, a typewriter bought by a pet store will be recorded in an asset account, such as Office Equipment, because it will be used in the office and not resold.

Purchase Returns and Allowances

When a firm discovers that merchandise purchased is damaged or unsatisfactory, it may return the merchandise to the seller or seek a reduction in *(allowance on)* the price paid for the goods. The account involved in recording transactions of this nature is called *Purchase Returns and Allowances.* Even though a firm does not pay for goods that it returns, certain costs are involved. For example, goods must be inspected, repacked, and freighted back to the seller. Thus, purchase returns should be kept at a minimum. A separate account is necessary to allow management to keep a record of the amount of merchandise returned.

The Purchase Returns and Allowances account has the opposite balance of the Purchases account – a credit balance. It is a contra account to Purchases. When goods which have been purchased are returned or an allowance is made on the account, Purchase Returns and Allowances is credited and either Cash or Accounts Payable is debited. The buyer sends the seller a debit memorandum to notify him or her of the adjustment for the unsatisfactory goods. A debit memorandum is sent because the buyer debits Accounts Payable. The form for a debit memorandum is basically the same as that for the credit memorandum shown in figure 10-1.

To illustrate a transaction involving returned goods, assume that the $90 worth of goods bought on credit by the Knit Company mentioned earlier is found to be defective. The Knit Company decides to return the goods. It then sends a debit memorandum to the seller for $90 and makes this entry:

	Debit	Credit
Accounts Payable	90	
Purchase Returns and Allowances		90
Returned defective merchandise.		

Note that a memorandum is issued anytime that Accounts Payable or Accounts Receivable is changed and no invoice or check is involved. (An *invoice* is a list of items that are being purchased and the price of each.) If the firm that is making the return debits Accounts Payable, a debit memo is sent out. If the firm whose goods have been returned writes the notice and credits Accounts Receivable, a credit memo is sent. Thus, whatever is done to Accounts Payable or Accounts Receivable determines the name of the memo that is issued. It is the action of the issuer that determines the name of the memo.

Purchase Discounts

As has been noted, the Purchases account records all merchandise bought for resale. Some of this merchandise may be subject to a discount if payment is made within the discount period granted by the seller. If the buyer obtains the discount, it is shown as a credit in an account called *Purchase Discounts.* Purchase Discounts is deducted from Purchases on the income statement and has a normal credit balance. It is a contra-cost account.

For example, on June 2 the Jocelin Company purchases goods for resale for $100 on account with credit terms of 2/10, n/30. This means that the Jocelin Company may deduct 2% from the price if it pays its bill within ten days. However, if it does not pay the bill within ten days, the full $100 must be paid within thirty days of the invoice date. The entry to record the purchase is:

	Debit	Credit
Purchases	100.00	
Accounts Payable		100.00
Purchased merchandise on credit, terms 2/10, n/30.		

If the bill is paid on June 10, only $98 will be paid and recorded as follows:

		Debit	Credit
June 10	Accounts Payable	100.00	
	Cash		98.00
	Purchase Discounts		2.00
	Paid for June 2 purchase less the discount.		

This entry gives the Accounts Payable account a zero balance; the account has been settled in full. If the account is not paid within the discount period and the full $100 must be paid, the entry will show a debit to Accounts Payable and a credit to Cash for $100.

Freight Charges

When merchandise is shipped, freight costs are incurred. The terms of the invoice usually state whether the buyer or the seller must pay these costs.

If the terms are *FOB (free on board) destination,* this means that the goods are shipped *free on board* (without charge) to their destination. In this case, the seller pays for the cost of shipping the merchandise to the customer.

If, on the other hand, the terms are *FOB shipping point,* the seller will load the goods free on board the carrier at the shipping point. However, the buyer must pay the freight charges from there to the destination. When the buyer must pay the freight charges, these charges may be debited to the Purchases account or a separate account may be used.

More information is provided for management when a separate account called *Freight-in* or *Transportation-in* is used. The balance of this account is added to Purchases on the income statement. Thus, Freight-in is a cost account. For example, goods are bought for $500 plus freight charges of $35 on account. The entry to record this is:

Purchases	500	
Freight-in	35	
Accounts Payable		535
Purchased merchandise on account.		

One additional account that appears on the books of a merchandising firm is *Merchandise Inventory.* This account is unique in that it appears on both financial statements. Merchandise Inventory, showing the goods on hand at the end of a period, appears on the balance sheet as a current asset. The beginning-of-the-period merchandise inventory appears on the income statement as a cost. Merchandise Inventory is discussed in more detail in the next chapter.

SUMMARY

Merchandising firms, companies that sell goods, have a need for different types of accounts than those used by the service firms. Accounts are needed to record items sold and items purchased for sale. Separate accounts are used to record any returns of merchandise, either by the firm or its customers. Additional accounts are used when recording purchase or sales discounts. The relationship between the merchandising firm's accounts and the basic accounting equation is shown in figure 10-2.

From this equation it is seen that the accounts in brackets are deducted from the accounts of which they are a part. Thus, Sales Returns and Allowances and Sales Discounts are deducted from Sales.

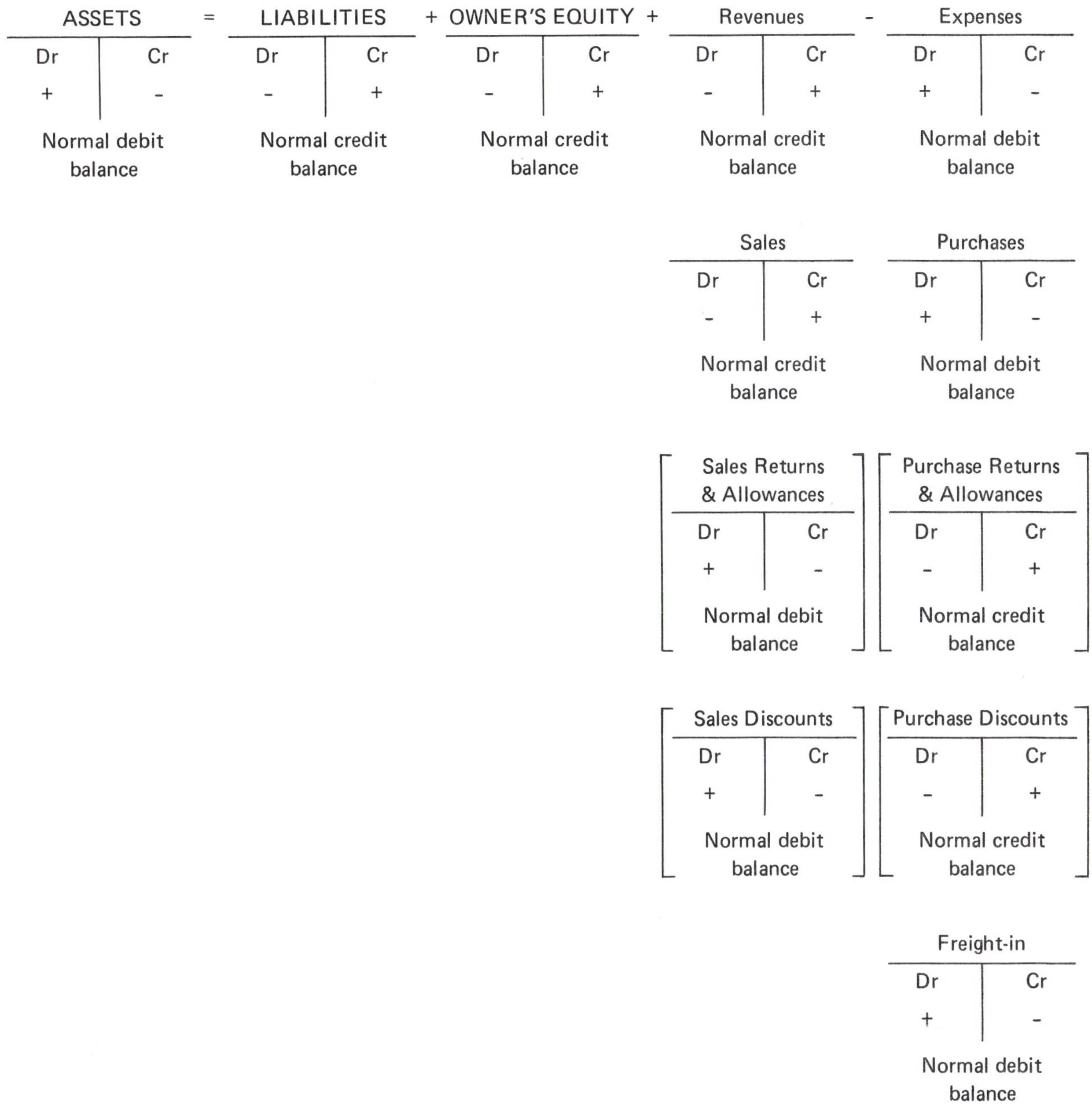

Fig. 10-2. The relationship between merchandising accounts and the accounting equation. [*Note:* A plus sign (+) under the debit column (Dr) indicates that increases are to be debited to that account; a minus sign (-) in the credit column (Cr) indicates that decreases are credited to the account and vice versa.]

The rules of debit and credit of the accounts in brackets are just the opposite of the accounts from which they are deducted. Hence, Sales Returns and Allowances and Sales Discounts have normal debit balances while Sales has a normal credit balance.

As shown by the diagram, Purchase Returns and Allowances and Purchases Discounts are deducted from Purchases. Thus, Purchase Returns and Allowances and Purchase Discounts have normal credit balances while Purchases has a normal debit balance.

All of the special merchandising accounts are closed out to the Income Summary account at the end of the period.

REVIEW

1. List seven accounts that would be used by a merchandising firm, but would not be used by a service firm.
2. Why does a firm use a separate account for sales returns?
3. Why do firms use a separate account for purchase returns?
4. If a firm buys goods on March 1 with terms of 2/10, n/60, what is the last day of the credit period?
5. If a firm buys goods on March 1 with terms of 2/10, n/60, what is the last day of the discount period?
6. Why do firms give cash discounts?
7. Why do firms take cash discounts when they are offered?
8. What type of account is Purchase Returns and Allowances?
9. What type of account is Sales Discounts?
10. What is the normal balance of Purchases?
11. What is the normal balance of Purchase Discounts?
12. Who pays the freight charges if freight terms are FOB destination?

EXERCISES

1. Give the journal entries for the following transactions.

   May 1: Bought merchandise on credit, $390, terms 2/10, n/30.
   11: Paid for the merchandise purchased on May 1.

2. Give the journal entries for the following transactions.

   June 11: Bought merchandise for cash, $200.
   13: Returned $27 of the above merchandise and received a refund, $27.

3. Give the journal entries for the following transactions.

   June 8: Sold merchandise on credit, $650, terms 2/10, n/30.
   18: Received payment for the same merchandise.

4. Give the journal entries for the following transactions.

   May 6: Sold merchandise on credit to Alpha Company, $700, terms 2/10, n/60.
   9: Received debit memo and returned merchandise from Ace Company, $100.
   16: Received check from Alpha Company for amount due.

5. Give the journal entries for the following transactions.

   May 20: Purchased merchandise on credit $1,800, terms 2/10, n/30.
   20: Paid trucking company $72 for delivery of the same goods.
   30: Paid for the goods purchased May 20.

PROBLEMS

1. Give the journal entries for the following transactions completed by the Old Fort Pet Store. All of the firm's credit sales of merchandise are made on terms of 2/10, n/30.

May 1: Purchased merchandise on credit, $800, terms 1/10, n/60.
1: Paid freight charges on the merchandise purchased on May 1, $17.
2: Sold merchandise on credit, $250.
2: Paid trucking company to deliver same merchandise to the customer, $25.
3: Sold merchandise for cash, $28.
4: Purchased merchandise on credit, $600, terms 1/10, n/60.
5: Returned a portion of the May 4 purchase, $100.
9: Paid for the May 1 purchase.
11: Received payment for the May 2 sale.
12: Bought office supplies on credit, $180.
13: Returned a portion of the office supplies along with a debit memo, $20.
14: Paid for the May 4 purchase less the return and discount.
17: Bought a new delivery truck on note, $4,500.
18: Sold office supplies to the Boy Scouts for cash, $5.
19: Sold merchandise on credit, $505.

2. Give the journal entries for the following transactions completed by the Stout Company. All of the firm's credit sales of merchandise are made on terms of 2/10, n/30.

March 1: Purchased merchandise on credit, $7,200, terms 2/10, n/60.
2: Returned $300 of the goods purchased May 1.
3: Sold merchandise on credit, $2,200.
4: Bought office supplies on credit, $85, terms 2/10, n/20.
5: Received debit memorandum from customer and return of some of the goods sold on March 3, $400.
8: Purchased merchandise on credit, $1,700; terms n/30.
9: Paid freight on March 8 purchase, $60.
10: Paid for March 1 purchase less the return and discount.
13: Received payment for May 3 sale less the return and discount.
15: Purchased merchandise for cash, $330.
17: Returned a portion of the goods purchased March 15 and received a refund, $20.

11 Determining the Cost of Goods Sold

OBJECTIVES

After studying this chapter, the student will be able to:

- Determine the cost of goods sold in a periodic inventory system.
- Prepare a classified income statement.
- Distinguish between periodic and perpetual inventory systems.

This chapter deals with the way in which the special accounts used by merchandising firms are handled when determining the cost of goods sold and preparing the income statement.

FINDING THE COST OF GOODS SOLD

On the income statement of a service firm, the net income is equal to revenues less expenses. A merchandising firm has another expense, or cost, to consider – the cost of the goods which have been sold. To show this cost, a *Cost of Goods Sold* section must be added to the income statement. The net income of a merchandising firm is determined as follows:

	Sales
-	Cost of Goods Sold
	Gross Profit
-	Operating Expenses
	Net Income

For example, a firm puts an advertisement in the newspaper to sell its truck for $1,000. The advertisement costs $5. The firm paid $800 for the truck. If it sells the truck for $1,000, the net income is determined as follows:

Sales	$1,000
Cost of Goods Sold	- 800
Gross Profit	200
Operating Expenses	- 5
Net Income	$ 195

The firm's gross profit was $200, but its expenses reduced the net income to $195. *Gross profit* is the difference between the price paid for an item and the price for which it is sold. Gross profit is the profit before expenses. *Net income* is the final figure which results after expenses are subtracted from gross profit.

For a firm which sells many items, the cost of goods sold is determined using the following process.

	Beginning Merchandise Inventory
+	Net Purchases
	Cost of Goods Available for Sale
-	Ending Merchandise Inventory
	Cost of Goods Sold

The term, *merchandise inventory* refers to the goods on hand which are to be sold. (*Inventory* is defined as the goods on hand at a certain date.) Thus, *beginning merchandise inventory* shows the value of the goods on hand at the start of a period. The *ending merchandise inventory* represents the value of the goods on hand at the end of a period. The ending inventory of one period becomes the beginning inventory of the next period. If the accounting period ends on May 31 and the ending inventory is $10,000, the inventory is still $10,000 on the next day (June 1) which is the beginning of the new period. The ending inventory amount is shown on the balance sheet as a current asset.

The Cost of Goods Sold section of the income statement can be thought of in a simplified form as follows:

	Goods on hand at the start of the period
Plus	Amount purchased during the period
Equals	Total amount of goods that could have been sold
Minus	Amount of goods remaining at the end of the period
Equals	The cost of the goods that were sold

In other words, there are two options for the goods available; either they are sold, or they are not sold. The amount not sold, when subtracted from the total goods on hand, gives the amount sold.

The above simplified form can be illustrated with the accounts introduced in chapter 10. When preparing the Cost of Goods Sold section of the income statement, net purchases are added to the beginning inventory and then subtracted from the ending merchandise inventory. *Net purchases* are total purchases plus freight-in and less purchase discounts and purchase returns and allowances. Thus, the cost of goods sold may be shown as follows:

Beginning Merchandise Inventory			XX
Purchases		XX	
Add: Freight-in		X	
Delivered Cost of Purchases		XX	
Less: Purchase Returns & Allowances	X		
Purchase Discounts	X	X	
Net Purchases			XX
Cost of Goods Available for Sale			XXX
Less: Ending Merchandise Inventory			XX
Cost of Goods Sold			XX

Sales				$15,000
Cost of Goods Sold:				
Beginning Merchandise Inventory			$1,000	
Purchases		$5,000		
Add: Freight-in		200		
Delivered Cost of Purchases		5,200		
Less: Purchase Discounts	$300			
Purchase Returns	100	400		
Net Purchases			4,800	
Cost of Goods Available for Sale			5,800	
Less: Ending Merchandise Inventory			2,000	
Cost of Goods Sold				3,800
Gross Profit				$11,200

Fig. 11-1. The Cost of Goods Sold section of an income statement.

As an example of a Cost of Goods Sold section of an income statement, consider a firm with the following account balances and an ending inventory of $2,000.

Sales	$15,000
Purchases	5,000
Purchase Discounts	300
Purchase Returns and Allowances	100
Freight-in	200
Beginning Merchandise Inventory	1,000

The gross profit would be calculated as shown in figure 11-1. Remember, gross profit is the difference between sales (the amount for which goods are sold) and the cost of goods sold.

CLASSIFIED INCOME STATEMENT FOR A MERCHANDISING FIRM

Larger firms of all types use a classified income statement. A *classified income statement* is one in which costs and revenues are grouped together by classes. A classified income statement for a merchandising firm is illustrated in figure 11-2. Read the following explanation while studying the illustration.

The income statement begins with Revenue from Sales. The balance in the Sales account is stated, and Sales Returns and Allowances and Sales Discounts are subtracted from total sales to obtain the *net sales.*

The next section is the Cost of Goods Sold. Cost of Goods Sold is found as described earlier.

The third part is Gross Profit on Sales. This is found by subtracting Cost of Goods Sold from Net Sales.

The Operating Expenses are listed next. *Operating expenses* are the expenses of doing business. On a classified income statement, the operating expenses are divided into two groups: Selling Expenses and General Expenses. *Selling Expenses* are the expenses directly related to the sale of goods. Selling Expenses include such things as salaries of the sales force, rent or depreciation on the store building, advertising, delivery expense, and store supplies. All other expenses fall under the

Right-Price Department Store
Income Statement
For Year Ended May 31, 1981

Revenue From Sales:				
Sales			$100,000	
Less: Sales Returns & Allowances		$ 1,700		
Sales Discounts		500	2,200	
Net Sales				$97,800
Cost of Goods Sold:				
Merchandise Inventory, June 1, 1980			35,000	
Purchases		85,000		
Add: Freight-in		200		
Delivered Cost of Purchases		85,200		
Less: Purchase Returns	$1,000			
Purchase Discounts	1,500	2,500		
Net Purchases			82,700	
Cost of Goods Available for Sale			117,700	
Less: Merchandise Inventory, May 31, 1981			20,000	
Cost of Goods Sold				97,700
Gross Profit				$ 100
Operating Expenses:				
Selling Expenses:				
Sales Salaries		1,300		
Advertising Expense		300		
Depreciation Expense – Store		500		
Store Supplies Expense		300		
Total Selling Expenses			2,400	
General Expenses:				
Office Salaries		2,800		
Depreciation Expense – Office		300		
Telephone Expense		200		
Total General Expenses			3,300	
Total Operating Expenses				5,700
Loss from Operations				(5,600)
Other Income:				
Interest Income		200		
Other Expenses:				
Interest Expense		1,100		(900)
Net Loss				$(6,500)

Fig. 11-2. A classified income statement for a merchandising firm.

heading of *General Expenses* because they are connected with the general operation of the firm.

If an expense is related to both selling and to the firm in general, the expense should be divided between the two groups of expenses. For example, if half of the building is used as a store where the sales are made and the other half is used as the office for the firm, then half of the rent expense or depreciation on the building is shown as a Selling Expense. The rest is shown as a General Expense.

Income or Loss from Operations is the next line of the income statement. Gross profit minus operating expenses equals the Income or Loss from Operations. This figure is important; it shows the results of the regular or routine business activities. The firm's financial status is judged mainly on the basis of this amount.

Other Income is shown next, in a separate section. Other Income is shown separately because it is revenue from sources other than Sales or the regular activity of the firm. Other Income can also be called *nonoperating income.* Examples include income from interest, rents, dividends, and gains from the sale of fixed assets.

Other Expenses are also shown separately. Included here are expenses that were not incurred in the regular activity of making sales. Other Expenses are nonoperating expenses, such as interest expense or a loss from the sale of assets.

The last line of the income statement gives the Net Income or the Net Loss.

PERIODIC AND PERPETUAL INVENTORY SYSTEMS

Merchandising firms have two ways in which to keep track of the cost of goods sold. One way, and the way which has been described in this chapter, is to take inventory periodically. When the *periodic inventory system* is used, an actual physical count of the stock of goods on hand is taken at the end of the accounting period (periodically) to find the amount of the ending inventory. In the periodic system, only the revenue is recorded each time a sale is made. No transactions are recorded in the Merchandise Inventory account. The Merchandise Inventory balance at the beginning of the period remains undisturbed until the end of the period. The only entries to Merchandise Inventory are the closing entries. Closing entries for this account are discussed in chapter 12. The periodic inventory system, which makes use of the Cost of Goods Sold section of the income statement for recording information, is used in this text. However, a brief explanation of the second type of inventory system is included here.

The second method for keeping track of goods sold is the perpetual inventory system. In the *perpetual inventory system,* a running inventory is kept so that the firm will know the amount of goods on hand at all times. This continuous record is kept by making entries for all transactions showing the cost of things purchased and sold. Purchases and sales are recorded in the Merchandise Inventory account at cost. There are no Purchases or Purchase Returns and Allowance accounts. Instead, the Merchandise Inventory account is kept perpetually correct.

Figure 11-3 shows the accounts used for purchases and sales of merchandise with a perpetual method of inventory. Since a purchase is an increase in an asset (merchandise), it is debited to the asset account, Merchandise Inventory. A sale is a decrease in merchandise, thus Merchandise Inventory is credited (decreased) for a sale. The Cost of Goods Sold account always has a debit balance because it represents a cost of doing business.

Merchandise Inventory	
Purchases of Goods	Sales of Goods (at cost)

Cost of Goods Sold	
Sales of Goods (at cost)	

Sales	
	Sales of Goods (at selling price)

Fig. 11-3. Accounts used in a perpetual inventory system.

The balance of the Merchandise Inventory account is the stock of goods currently on hand. However, a physical inventory should be taken at least once a year to test the accuracy of this record.

When a perpetual inventory is used, the balance of the Cost of Goods Sold account is used in place of the Cost of Goods Sold section on the income statement. This is because the one account covers all of the information contained in the Cost of Goods Sold section of a periodic inventory system.

For example, assume that a firm buys goods for $200 and sells half of them for $300. The entries under a perpetual inventory system would be:

Merchandise Inventory	200	
Cash		200
Bought goods for resale.		
Cash	300	
Sales		300
To record sale of goods.		
Cost of Goods Sold	100	
Merchandise Inventory		100
To record the cost of the goods sold.		

The balance in Merchandise Inventory is $100 which is the amount of the stock of goods on hand. The perpetual inventory system is more time-consuming than the periodic. Thus the periodic system is more commonly used.

SUMMARY

On a classified income statement of a merchandising firm, net income is determined by the following calculations:

Net Sales* - Cost of Goods Sold = Gross Profit

Gross Profit - Operating Expenses (Selling and General) = Income from Operations

Income from Operations + Other Income - Other Expenses = Net Income (or Loss)

(*Net Sales is equal to Sales less Sales Returns and Allowances and Sales Discounts.)

Cost of Goods Sold is found as follows:

Beginning Merchandise Inventory			XX
Purchases		XX	
Add: Freight-in		X	
Delivered Cost of Purchases		XX	
Less: Purchase Returns &			
Allowances	X		
Purchase Discounts	X	X	
Net Purchases			XX
Cost of Goods Available for Sale			XXX
Less: Ending Merchandise			
Inventory			XX
Cost of Goods Sold			XX

With a periodic inventory system, the ending inventory is found by taking a physical count of goods on hand at the end of the period. A perpetual inventory is a running record of the inventory as shown by the balance of the Merchandise Inventory account. The Merchandise Inventory account is debited when goods are bought and credited when goods are sold.

The periodic inventory system is used for all merchandising firms discussed in this text. To prepare for further discussion of merchandise accounting, memorize the contents of the Cost of Goods Sold section of the income statement.

REVIEW

1. Give two examples of items that would appear under Other Expenses.
2. Give three examples of items that would appear under Other Revenues.
3. Distinguish between a periodic and a perpetual inventory system.
4. How is ending inventory found in a periodic system?
5. How is ending inventory found in a perpetual system?
6. Define gross profit.
7. What is the bottom line on an income statement called?
8. Is the bottom line the most important line on an income statement?
9. What is a classified income statement?
10. If a firm sells its goods for more than it paid for them, will it always have a net income? Why?

EXERCISES

1. Shown below are the data from four different income statements. Some of the amounts have been omitted. Determine the missing figures.

Sales	200,000		9,000	75,000
Beginning Inventory	12,000		1,000	22,000
Purchases		30,000	8,000	
Ending Inventory	18,000	18,000		1,000
Cost of Goods Sold	14,000	20,000		
Gross Profit		55,000	2,000	
Expenses	180,000		3,000	5,000
Net Income (Loss)		18,000		4,000

2. Given the following account balances determine:
   a. What is Sales?
   b. What is Freight-in?

Beginning Inventory	$20,000
Purchases	52,000
Purchase Returns	11,500
Ending Inventory	18,000
Cost of Goods Sold	53,330
Gross Profit	50,000

3. The following account balances are taken from the Era Company's May 31, 1981, adjusted trial balance. Use the accounts to prepare an income statement. The ending inventory on May 31, 1981, was $750.

Era Company
Adjusted Trial Balance
For Month Ended May 31, 1981

Merchandise Inventory	$ 550	
Sales		$4,200
Sales Returns & Allowances	155	
Sales Discounts	60	
Purchases	2,600	
Purchases Discounts		225
Freight-in	20	
Salaries Expense	350	
Rent Expense	175	
Utilities Expense	80	

4. Given the following adjusted trial balance, prepare an income statement. The ending inventory was $1,100.

Fame Company
Adjusted Trial Balance
For Month Ended July 31, 19–

Cash	$ 675	
Accounts Receivable	450	
Office Supplies	55	
Merchandise Inventory	500	
Automobile	3,000	
Accumulated Depreciation		$ 45
Accounts Payable		355
John White, Capital		2,950
John White, Drawing	200	
Sales		7,790
Sales Discounts	125	
Purchases	5,600	
Purchase Returns		250
Freight-in	20	
Salaries Expense	450	
Rent Expense	230	
Telephone Expense	85	
	$11,390	$11,390

PROBLEMS

1. The following account balances are taken from the Fresh-fruit Company's December 31, 1981, adjusted trial balance. Use the accounts to prepare a classified income statement for the firm. The ending inventory on December 31, 1981, was $1,100.

Merchandise Inventory	$ 1,000	
Sales		$78,865
Sales Returns & Allowances	695	
Sales Discounts	470	
Purchases	51,345	
Purchase Returns & Allowances		715
Purchase Discounts		530
Freight-in	745	
Sales Salaries Expense	8,125	
Advertising Expense	860	
Office Salaries Expense	6,585	
Telephone Expense	120	
Gas, Oil, and Repairs	860	
Rent Expense – Office	4,300	

2. Given the following account balances taken from the Gibin Company's December 31, 1981, adjusted trial balance, prepare a classified income statement. The ending inventory on December 31, 1981, was $1,655.

Account	Debit	Credit
Merchandise Inventory	$ 1,200	
Sales		$68,475
Sales Returns & Allowances	675	
Sales Discounts	280	
Purchases	38,115	
Purchase Returns & Allowances		465
Purchase Discounts		225
Freight-in	540	
Sales Salaries Expense	10,800	
Rent Expense – Selling	4,685	
Advertising Expense	775	
Office Salaries Expense	3,570	
Rent Expense – Office	550	
Depreciation Expense – Auto	675	
Depreciation Expense – Office Equip.	250	
Utilities Expense	375	

3. Given the following adjusted trial balance, prepare an income statement. The ending inventory was $1,875.

Penn Company
Adjusted Trial Balance
For Year Ended December 31, 1981

Account	Debit	Credit
Cash	$ 1,600	
Merchandise Inventory	8,505	
Store Supplies	775	
Office Supplies	490	
Prepaid Insurance	565	
Store Equipment	6,390	
Accumulated Depreciation – Store Equipment		$ 2,235
Office Equipment	9,100	
Accumulated Depreciation – Office Equipment		3,570
Accounts Payable		2,965
Sara Penuci, Capital		20,945
Sara Penuci, Drawing	4,790	
Sales		62,865
Sales Returns & Allowances	675	
Sales Discounts	860	
Purchases	33,715	
Purchase Returns & Allowances		985
Purchase Discounts		305
Freight-in	695	
Salaries Expense	21,900	
Rent Expense	3,125	
Depreciation Expense – Store	200	
Depreciation Expense – Office	485	
	$93,870	$93,870

4. Given the following adjusted trial balance, prepare a classified income statement and a classified balance sheet. The ending inventory was $1,350.

Barnes Company
Adjusted Trial Balance
For Month Ended June 30, 1980

Account	Debit	Credit
Cash	$ 1,865	
Merchandise Inventory	13,130	
Store Supplies	745	
Office Supplies	250	
Prepaid Rent	890	
Automobile	3,250	
Accumulated Depreciation – Auto		$ 55
Office Equipment	1,155	
Accumulated Depreciation – Office Equipment		275
Accounts Payable		4,180
Salaries Payable		150
Doug Barnes, Capital		22,445
Doug Barnes, Drawing	5,000	
Sales		72,135
Sales Returns & Allowances	685	
Sales Discounts	820	
Purchases	48,615	
Purchase Returns & Allowances		705
Purchase Discounts		1,245
Freight-in	1,195	
Sales Salaries Expense	14,125	
Office Salaries Expense	2,900	
Rent Expense	5,135	
Utilities Expense	430	
Depreciation Expense – Auto	600	
Depreciation Expense – Office	400	
	$101,190	$101,190

12
Effect of Inventories on Work Sheet and Closing Entries

OBJECTIVES

After studying this chapter, the student will be able to:

- Prepare a work sheet for a merchandising firm.
- Make the closing entries for a merchandising firm.

The procedure for completing the work sheet and closing entries is the same for merchandising firms as it is for the service firms discussed in chapters 8 and 9. The only difference is in handling the accounts related to the special needs of the merchandising firm. The procedure for handling the merchandising accounts when preparing the work sheet and closing the accounts is discussed in this chapter.

THE WORK SHEET FOR A MERCHANDISING FIRM

Standard Entries

The best way to learn how to prepare a work sheet is to study an example. Figure 12-1, page 118, shows a completed work sheet for the merchandising firm called the Right-Price Department Store. (Three of the columns have been shaded to point out the steps in the completion process.) The trial balance for the firm is entered in the first two work sheet columns. Note that the debit and credit columns are in balance.

The only adjustment needed is to show depreciation on the firm's building. Half of the building is used as a store; the other half is used as an office. Thus, the depreciation expense is divided between the selling and general expenses. This adjustment is shown in the adjustments columns of the work sheet in figure 12-1. It results in the adjusted trial balance shown in the second shaded column in figure 12-1.

The work sheet is completed by sorting the adjusted balances. Each balance is placed in either the Income Statement or Balance Sheet column, depending upon the statement on which the account should appear.

Merchandising Entries

The merchandising accounts appear in boldface on the work sheet. Note the treatment of Merchandise Inventory. Recall that the beginning

Right-Price Department Store
Work Sheet
For Year Ended May 31, 1981

Account Titles	Trial Balance		Adjustments		Adjusted Trial Balance		Income Statement		Balance Sheet	
	Dr.	Cr.	Dr.	Cr.	Dr.	Cr.	Dr.	Cr.	Dr.	Cr.
Cash	5,000				5,000				5,000	
Accounts Receivable	17,500				17,500				17,500	
Merchandise Inventory	35,000				35,000		35,000	20,000	20,000	
Building	50,000				50,000				50,000	
Accounts Payable		25,000				25,000				25,000
Mertz, Capital		75,000				75,000				75,000
Mertz, Drawing	2,000				2,000				2,000	
Sales		100,000				100,000		100,000		
Sales Discounts	500				500		500			
Sales Returns & Allow.	1,700				1,700		1,700			
Interest Income		200				200		200		
Purchases	85,000				85,000		85,000			
Purchase Discounts		1,500				1,500		1,500		
Purchase Returns & Allow.		1,000				1,000		1,000		
Freight-in	200				200		200			
Sales Salaries Expense	1,300				1,300		1,300			
Advertising Expense	300				300		300			
Store Supplies Expense	300				300		300			
Office Salaries Expense	2,800				2,800		2,800			
Interest Expense	1,100				1,100		1,100			
	202,700	202,700								
Deprec. Expense – Office			500		500		500			
Deprec. Expense – Store			500		500		500			
Accumulated Deprec.				1,000		1,000				1,000
			1,000	1,000	203,700	203,700	129,200	122,700		
Net Loss								6,500	6,500	
							129,200	129,200	101,000	101,000

Fig. 12-1. Completed work sheet for a merchandising firm.

inventory amount appears on the income statement and that the ending inventory is shown as a deduction on the income statement and as an asset on the balance sheet. Before closing entries are posted, the balance in the Merchandise Inventory account ($35,000) is the beginning inventory amount. This is the figure which appears in the trial balance column. It is also listed in the Income Statement debit column.

The ending inventory does not appear in any account before closing entries are posted. It is found by taking a physical count of items not sold. This ending amount ($20,000) is entered on the work sheet in both the Income Statement and Balance Sheet columns. It is shown as a deduction from costs on the income statement and, thus, is placed in the credit column. The ending inventory amount must be shown in the Income Statement columns so that the difference between the Income Statement columns equals net income or loss. The ending inventory amount is entered on the balance sheet as an asset. Thus it is shown as a debit in the Balance Sheet column. Note that ending inventory is the only figure shown on both statements (and in both sets of columns).

Since Sales is a revenue account, it appears in the income statement credit column just as did the revenue account of a service firm. Sales Discounts and Sales Returns and Allowances are simply contra accounts to Sales. Thus, these two accounts will be shown opposite Sales in the Income Statement debit column.

Purchases and Freight-in are *cost accounts;* they are like expenses. Thus, as expenses, they are placed in the Income Statement debit column. Purchase Discounts and Purchase Returns and Allowances are contra accounts to Purchases. Thus, they appear on the same financial statement as Purchases, but they have a credit balance. Purchase Discounts and Purchase Returns and Allowances are entered on the credit side of the Income Statement column on the work sheet.

FINANCIAL STATEMENTS AND ADJUSTING ENTRIES OF A MERCHANDISING FIRM

The financial statements are prepared as usual from the information on the work sheet. The income statement information is taken from the Income Statement columns. The income statement for the Right-Price Department Store is shown in figure 11-2 of chapter 11. Look back, and compare the income statement to the work sheet.

The balance sheet for the Right-Price store is shown in figure 12-2. Note the location of Merchandise Inventory under the Assets section.

Right-Price Department Store
Balance Sheet
May 31, 1981

ASSETS:			
Current Assets:			
Cash		$ 5,000	
Accounts Receivable		17,500	
Merchandise Inventory		20,000	
Total Current Assets			$42,500
Plant and Equipment:			
Building		$50,000	
Less: Accumulated Depreciation		1,000	49,000
Total Assets			$91,500
LIABILITIES:			
Current Liabilities:			
Accounts Payable			$25,000
OWNER'S EQUITY:			
Mertz, Capital, June 1, 1980		$75,000	
Less: Net Loss for the Year	$6,500		
Withdrawals	2,000	8,500	
Mertz, Capital, May 31, 1981			66,500
Total Liabilities and Owner's Equity			$91,500

Fig. 12-2. A balance sheet for the Right-Price Department Store.

The adjusting entries for a merchandising firm are the same as for a service firm. The adjusting entry for the Right-Price store as shown on the work sheet in figure 12-1 is entered in the general journal as follows and then posted to the ledger:

1981 May	31	Depreciation Expense – Office	500	
		Depreciation Expense – Store	500	
		Accumulated Depreciation		1,000
		To record depreciation expense.		

CLOSING ENTRIES FOR A MERCHANDISING FIRM

The data for the closing entries comes from the Income Statement columns of the work sheet. All the amounts in the debit column are

GENERAL JOURNAL

Date		Account Titles and Explanation	Post. Ref.	Debit	Credit
1981					
May	*31*	*Income Summary*		*129200 00*	
		Merchandise Inventory			*35000 00*
		Sales Discounts			*500 00*
		Sales Returns and Allowances			*1700 00*
		Purchases			*85000 00*
		Freight-in			*200 00*
		Sales Salaries Expense			*1300 00*
		Advertising Expense			*300 00*
		Store Supplies Expense			*300 00*
		Office Salaries Expense			*2800 00*
		Interest Expense			*1100 00*
		Depreciation Expense — Office			*500 00*
		Depreciation Expense — Store			*500 00*
		To close the beginning inventory and temporary accounts with debit balances.			
	31	*Merchandise Inventory*		*20000 00*	
		Sales		*100000 00*	
		Interest Income		*200 00*	
		Purchase Discounts		*1500 00*	
		Purchase Returns and Allowances		*1000 00*	
		Income Summary			*122700 00*
		To close temporary accounts with credit balances and to put the ending inventory into the account.			
	31	*Mertz, Capital*		*6500 00*	
		Income Summary			*6500 00*
		To close net loss to capital.			
	31	*Mertz, Capital*		*2000 00*	
		Mertz, Drawing			*2000 00*
		To close the Drawing account.			

Fig. 12-3. Closing entries for the Right-Price Department Store.

Merchandise Inventory Acct. No.______

Date		Explanation	Post. Ref.	Debit	Credit	Balance
1980						
May	*31*			*3500000*		*3500000*

Fig. 12-4. Merchandise inventory account before the closing entries are made.

Merchandise Inventory Acct. No.______

Date		Explanation	Post. Ref.	Debit	Credit	Balance
1980						
May	*31*			*3500000*		*3500000*
1981						
May	*31*				*3500000*	*-0-*

Fig. 12-5. Merchandise inventory account after the first closing entry.

Merchandise Inventory Acct. No.______

Date		Explanation	Post. Ref.	Debit	Credit	Balance
1980						
May	*31*			*3500000*		*3500000*
1981						
May	*31*				*3500000*	*-0-*
	31			*2000000*		*2000000*

Fig. 12-6. Merchandise inventory account after the second closing entry.

closed by crediting those accounts and debiting Income Summary for the column total. Study the work sheet in figure 12-1 and the corresponding closing entries which are shown in figure 12-3.

Note the way in which the merchandise inventory is treated in the closing entries. Before the closing entries are posted, the balance in the Merchandise Inventory account is the amount of the beginning inventory. For example, the Merchandise Inventory account for the Right-Price store would appear as shown in figure 12-4.

After the first of the closing entries is posted, the account has a zero balance since the old inventory has been closed out. Figure 12-5 shows the closed account.

When the second closing entry has been posted, the balance is the amount of the ending inventory. This balance becomes the beginning inventory for the next month, figure 12-6.

SUMMARY

The work sheet and the closing entries are basically the same for a merchandising firm as for a service firm, with the exception of several special accounts. The ending inventory of merchandise is shown on both the income statement and the balance sheet. Thus, it is the only amount shown in both statement columns on the work sheet. The beginning inventory is closed out and the ending inventory is added to the account when the closing entries are made.

REVIEW

1. To which of the last four columns of a work sheet would each of the following accounts be extended?

   a. Sales
   b. Purchases
   c. Sales Discounts
   d. Sales Returns and Allowances
   e. Freight-in
   f. Merchandise Inventory
   g. Tim Jones, Drawing
   h. Purchase Discounts
   i. Purchase Returns and Allowances
   j. Accumulated Depreciation – Building

2. If a firm uses a perpetual inventory system, where does the account Cost of Goods Sold appear on the work sheet?

3. What effect do the closing entries have on the Merchandise Inventory account?

4. Which entries are recorded in the journal first – the closing entries or the adjusting entries?

5. After the adjusting entries are posted, which amount appears in the Merchandise Inventory account – the beginning or the ending inventory?

6. What amount is obtained if the *cost of goods sold* is subtracted from *revenue*?

7. What work sheet totals can be used to check the accuracy of the closing entries?

EXERCISES

1. The following balances are from the income statement columns of a work sheet that was prepared for Fox and Company as of March 31.

	Debit	Credit
Merchandise Inventory	$ 600	$ 800
Sales		5,000
Sales Returns & Allowances	170	
Sales Discounts	95	
Purchases	2,400	
Purchase Returns & Allowances		100
Purchase Discounts		46
Freight-in	112	
Wage Expense	400	
Rent Expense	210	
	3,987	5,946
	1,959	
	5,946	5,946

a. Use the above data to prepare an income statement for the month of March.

b. Record the firm's closing entries. (There were no withdrawals during the month.)

2. The last four columns of a work sheet have been assigned the code letters A, B, C, and D as follows:

Income Statement		Balance Sheet	
Debit	Credit	Debit	Credit
A	B	C	D

Using these code letters, state to which columns of the work sheet each of the following accounts would be extended. For example, the Cash account would be noted with the letter *C*, indicating that it is extended to the debit column of the balance sheet.

1. Accounts Receivable
2. Sales
3. Merchandise Inventory (Beginning)
4. Accumulated Depreciation
5. Equipment
6. Depreciation Expense
7. Sales Discounts
8. Purchases
9. Wages Payable
10. Merchandise Inventory (Ending)
11. Sales Returns and Allowances
12. Purchase Discounts
13. Purchase Returns and Allowances
14. Freight-in
15. Delivery Expense
16. Tom Stone, Drawing
17. Interest Revenue
18. Tom Stone, Capital
19. Office Supplies
20. Prepaid Rent

PROBLEMS

1. Prepare a work sheet for the SL Company from the data given below. The trial balance shows the following amounts for the year ended December 31.

Cash	$ 3,000
Accounts Receivable	3,000
Merchandise Inventory	12,000
Supplies	1,000
Equipment	9,000
Accounts Payable	3,000
SL Capital	20,500
SL Drawing	16,000
Sales	93,700
Purchases	53,200
Supplies Expense	0
Other Expenses	20,000

The ending merchandise inventory was $14,500.
Supplies used during the period totaled $400.
Depreciation expense for the period was $300.

2. Use the work sheet completed in Problem 1 to prepare the following:
   a. an income statement.
   b. a balance sheet.
   c. the adjusting entries.
   d. the closing entries.

3. The following accounts form the trial balance of the Watch Fob Company for the year ended December 31.

Cash	$ 195
Merchandise Inventory	1,750
Automobile	2,500
Accumulated Depreciation	400
Accounts Payable	100
Lena Barr, Capital	455
Lena Barr, Drawing	1,200
Sales	20,000
Sales Discounts	190
Sales Returns	840
Purchases	8,000
Freight-in	470
Purchase Discounts	150
Purchase Returns	115
Rent Expense	1,200
Wage Expense	4,800
Interest Expense	75

Additional Information:

(1) An inventory showed $3,000 worth of merchandise on hand on December 31.

(2) Depreciation expense for the year was $400.

Use the above data to prepare the following:
a. work sheet.
b. income statement.
c. balance sheet.
d. the formal adjusting entries.
e. the formal closing entries.

4. The following are the account balances for the firm of James and Company as of December 31.

Cash	$ 700
Accounts Receivable	425
Office Supplies	100
Merchandise Inventory	455
Equipment	4,000
Accumulated Depreciation	1,045
Accounts Payable	350
Dick Crane, Capital	2,955
Dick Crane, Drawing	300
Sales	7,800
Sales Discounts	25
Sales Returns & Allowances	10
Purchases	5,500
Purchase Discounts	100
Purchase Returns	250
Freight-in	20
Wage Expense	400
Rent Expense	430
Advertising Expense	135

Additional information:

(1) An inventory showed $80 worth of office supplies on hand at the end of the year.
(2) An inventory showed $600 worth of merchandise inventory on hand at the year end.
(3) Depreciation expense for the year was $100.

Use the above data to:

a. Prepare a work sheet for the firm.
b. Prepare an income statement for the firm.
c. Prepare a balance sheet for the firm.
d. Record the adjusting entries.
e. Record the closing entries.

5. The following adjusted trial balance accounts were taken from the records of the Hopp Company as of December 31.

Accounts Payable	$ 9,200
Accounts Receivable	16,500
Accrued Taxes Payable	1,600
Accumulated Depreciation	5,500
Cash	2,800
Hopp, Capital	40,000
Depreciation Expense	1,100
Delivery Expense	4,400
Equipment	34,000
Insurance Expense	800
Interest Revenue	740
Merchandise Inventory	21,000

Purchases	82,000
Rent Expense	9,200
Sales	167,860
Sales Returns & Allowances	7,300
Sales Salaries Expense	42,600
Taxes Expense	3,200

Prepare closing entries at the end of the year. The year-end merchandise inventory was $10,000.

13 Inventory Valuation Methods

OBJECTIVES

After studying this chapter, the student will be able to:

- Discuss the importance of inventory valuation as related to the financial statements.
- Value inventories by four different methods.
- Explain the lower-of-cost-or-market rule.
- Use the gross profit method to estimate inventory.

INVENTORY VALUATION AND THE FINANCIAL STATEMENTS

Merchandise inventory is the stock of goods held for resale. As mentioned in previous chapters, that inventory must be counted and valued at the end of each period. This is done by determining the original cost of all inventory items on hand at the balance sheet date. Inventory is the only item which appears on both the balance sheet and the income statement. Merchandise inventory is classified as a current asset on the balance sheet and is also found in the Cost of Goods Sold section of the income statement. Thus, a mistake made in determining the ending merchandise inventory figure results in incorrect amounts on both of the financial statements. This makes both of the financial statements wrong. In addition, because the ending inventory of one period becomes the beginning inventory of the next period, the income statement for the next period will also be incorrect. Therefore, extreme care must be taken in finding the value of a firm's inventory.

The following examples illustrate the effect of inventory valuation on the accuracy of the financial statements. Example A is an income statement for Sports Incorporated, a sporting goods firm.

To demonstrate the effect of an error, suppose that the ending inventory for that year had been incorrectly computed as \$80,000 instead of \$90,000. This error would result in a decrease in net income of \$10,000 as shown in Example B.

Thus, it is apparent that if the ending inventory is understated or decreased, net income is understated or decreased by the same amount. Ending inventory and net income are directly proportional. If ending inventory is overstated, net income will be overstated. To further prove

Example A: Year 1 (with correct inventory)

Revenue:		
Net Sales		$200,000
Cost of Goods Sold:		
Beginning Merchandise Inventory	$ 80,000	
Purchases	100,000	
Goods Available for Sale	$180,000	
Less: Ending Merchandise Inventory	90,000	
Cost of Goods Sold		90,000
Gross Profit		$110,000
Expenses		80,000
Net Income		$ 30,000

Example B: Year 1 (with error in inventory)

Revenue:		
Net Sales		$200,000
Cost of Goods Sold:		
Beginning Merchandise Inventory	$ 80,000	
Purchases	100,000	
Goods Available for Sale	$180,000	
Less: Ending Merchandise Inventory	**80,000**	
Cost of Goods Sold		100,000
Gross Profit		$100,000
Expenses		80,000
Net Income		**$ 20,000**

this relationship, substitute an ending inventory of $100,000 in the preceding example. Net income will then be $40,000, or an overstatement of $10,000.

To examine the effects of the error on the second year's statements, recall that the ending inventory of one year becomes the beginning inventory of the next year. If the correct ending inventory of $90,000 is used as the beginning inventory for Year 2, the income statement for the second year will appear as follows:

Year 2 (with correct inventory)

Revenue:		
Net Sales		$170,000
Cost of Goods Sold:		
Beginning Merchandise Inventory	$ 90,000	
Purchases	70,000	
Goods Available for Sale	$160,000	
Less: Ending Merchandise Inventory	80,000	
Cost of Goods Sold		80,000
Gross Profit		$ 90,000
Expenses		70,000
Net Income		$ 20,000

However, if the incorrect ending inventory of $80,000 for the first year becomes the beginning inventory for the second year, the following income statement will result.

Year 2 (with error in inventory)		
Revenue:		
Net Sales		$170,000
Cost of Goods Sold:		
Beginning Merchandise Inventory	$ 80,000	
Purchases	70,000	
Goods Available for Sale	$150,000	
Less: Ending Merchandise Inventory	80,000	
Cost of Goods Sold		70,000
Gross Profit		$100,000
Expenses		70,000
Net Income		$ 30,000

Note that beginning inventory and net income are inversely related. In other words, if the beginning inventory is understated, the net income is overstated. It follows, then, that if beginning inventory is overstated or increased, net income will be understated. To prove this relationship, substitute a beginning inventory of $100,000 in the last example. Net income will then be $10,000, or an understatement of $10,000.

Now consider the effect that the errors related in these examples have on the balance sheet for Sporting Incorporated. The effects can be summarized as follows:

- When the ending inventory is understated in the first year, assets and capital are also understated. Assets are understated because Merchandise Inventory should be 90,000 but is shown as 80,000. Capital is understated because the net income is understated.

- When net income is overstated in the second year, capital and assets are correctly stated. Assets are correct because a new inventory count has been made. Capital is correct because the overstatement of income in the second year offsets the understatement of the first year.

It is clear that an error in the inventory figure has far-reaching effects on both the balance sheets and income statements for two different years. Note, however, that the two incorrect net income figures will offset each other so that by the end of the second year, the assets and capital will be corrected.

FINDING THE COST OF THE INVENTORY

A physical count of the number of units is necessary to determine the ending inventory. After the number of units is known, the next step is to determine the cost of those units. A problem may arise if identical units have been purchased at different prices at different times. This is shown in the following example from the records of the In-Town Company. (The symbol, @, stands for the word *at*.)

Beginning Inventory		3 units @ $3	= $ 9
Purchases:	March 1	4 units @ $4	= $16
	November 1	3 units @ $5	= $15
Goods Available for Sale		10 units	= $40

Sales: 6 units @ $8 = $48

Ending Inventory = 4 units

The firm had ten units available for sale and six were sold. Thus, four units are left in the ending inventory. The question is: What cost should be assigned to these four units? Should they be valued at three, four, or five dollars each?

There are four possible methods of determining the value of the units in this example. They are:

- Specific identification.
- Weighted average.
- First-in, first-out (FIFO).
- Last-in, first-out (LIFO).

Specific Identification

In some cases, it may be possible to keep track of all the units and know exactly how much each one cost. When using this method, some type of tag, mark, or number is placed on each unit so that the cost can be looked up in the records. Hence, the name of the method is *specific identification.*

In the In-Town Company example, suppose that the units are marked so that the four left over can be identified as follows: one unit came from the beginning inventory; one unit was purchased on March 1; and two units were purchased on November 1. Thus, the ending inventory cost is: 1 unit @ $3 = $3; 1 unit @ $4 = $4; and 2 units @ $5 = $10, for a total cost of $17. Using this amount for the ending inventory, the gross profit for the year is determined as follows:

Sales		$48
Cost of Goods Sold:		
Beginning Inventory	$ 9	
Purchases	31	
Goods Available for Sale	$40	
Less: Ending Inventory	17	
Cost of Goods Sold		23
Gross Profit		**$25**

It is costly and difficult to use the specific identification method if many items are sold or the items are small. Thus, specific identification is used most often by firms which sell large items in small quantities, such as cars or furs.

Weighted Average

Another method of valuing inventories is to find the *weighted average cost* per unit.

$$\text{Weighted average cost per unit} = \frac{\text{cost of goods available for sale}}{\text{number of units available}}$$

For example, the weighted average cost per unit can be calculated as follows:

$$\text{Weighted average cost per unit} = \frac{\$40}{10 \text{ units}}$$
$$= \$4 \text{ per unit}$$

Using this method, the ending inventory consists of four units at an average cost of $4 per unit or a total of $16. Using this amount, gross profit for the year would be determined as follows:

Sales		$48
Cost of Goods Sold:		
Beginning Inventory	$ 9	
Purchases	31	
Goods Available for Sale	$40	
Less: Ending Inventory	16	
Cost of Goods Sold		24
Gross Profit		**$24**

This method works well for a firm such as an oil company or a firm that sells any liquid. Since separate purchases are usually mixed together and cannot be identified, it makes sense to average the costs.

First-in, First-out Method (FIFO)

The *first-in, first-out method (FIFO)* makes the assumption that the first units *in,* or purchased, are the first units *out,* or sold. Thus, the units left over in the ending inventory are the last ones purchased, or the newest. In the In-Town example, it is assumed that the ending inventory is made up of the newest units or the last ones purchased. In this case, the three newest units are the ones purchased on November 1 at a cost of $5 each, or a total of $15. The next newest unit is one of those purchased on March 1 at a cost of $4. Thus the total cost of the four newest units is $19. This is the cost of the ending inventory under the FIFO method. It would result in the following gross profit:

Sales		$48
Cost of Goods Sold:		
Beginning Inventory	$ 9	
Purchases	31	
Goods Available for Sale	$40	
Less: Ending Inventory	19	
Cost of Goods Sold		21
Gross Profit		**$27**

The physical flow of perishable goods follows this method. Thus fruit, meat, or dairy products are arranged in stores so that the oldest items are sold first and the newest are placed at the back of the shelf to be sold later.

Last-in, First-out Method (LIFO)

The *last-in, first-out* or *LIFO method* follows the reasoning that the last units in are the first ones out, or sold. Thus, the units left over in the ending inventory are assumed to be the first or oldest units. In the In-Town example, the ending inventory using the LIFO method would be made up of the four oldest units. The three oldest units are the ones in the beginning inventory which cost $3 each for a total cost of $9. The next oldest unit is one of those purchased on March 1 at a cost of $4. So, the ending inventory under LIFO has a cost of $13 and the gross profit is determined as follows:

Sales		$48
Cost of Goods Sold:		
Beginning Inventory	$ 9	
Purchases	31	
Goods Available for Sale	$40	
Less: Ending Inventory	13	
Cost of Goods Sold		27
Gross Profit		$21

The physical flow of any nonperishable natural resource such as coal might correspond with the LIFO method. For example, coal is usually stacked in piles. The first coal to be sold comes from the top of the pile where the newest coal is. The coal left over at the bottom of the pile is the oldest.

Selection of Method

As can be seen from the example, different inventory methods may result in different gross profit totals and, consequently, different net income figures. Several factors are important when selecting a method for valuing inventory.

- The specific identification method exactly matches costs with revenues. However, it may be very costly and time consuming.
- On the income statement, FIFO matches old costs with current sales. On the balance sheet, it shows the ending inventory at the most recent cost.
- The LIFO method matches current costs with current revenues but, on the balance sheet, it shows the ending inventory at old costs.

Thus, one consideration in selection is whether more emphasis is placed on the balance sheet or the income statement. FIFO results in the more reliable balance sheet; LIFO gives the more accurate income statement. The weighted average method represents a middle road between (or an average of) FIFO and LIFO. However, record keeping for this method may be costly.

Fig. 13-1. All merchandising firms must choose some method of valuing inventory. What would be the best method for these construction materials?

The income tax effects are also considered, particularly in a period of rising prices. During a period of inflation, LIFO results in a lower net income than FIFO because LIFO matches the current high costs with the current revenues. In the example in this chapter the prices of goods were on the increase. The gross profit was $21 under the LIFO method whereas it was $27 under the FIFO method. This means that the income tax liability will be less under LIFO than under FIFO during a period of rising prices. (The income tax liability for the weighted average method will fall somewhere between that for FIFO and LIFO.) Thus, there are tax advantages in using LIFO during a time of inflation.

A third consideration might be the desire of a firm to match its inventory valuation method with its physical flow of goods. For example, a dairy products firm may want to use the FIFO method since its oldest goods are always sold first. However, it is not essential that the inventory method match the physical flow of goods, and some firms may not consider this factor important in their choice of methods.

All of the methods are currently in use. FIFO and LIFO are the two most commonly used methods. Once a method is chosen, the firm should not change back and forth among methods. The *consistency principle of accounting* requires that a firm use the same practices and methods from year to year so that the financial statements are uniform and comparable. This principle does not prohibit changes in method. Rather, it insists that there be a good reason for any change and that the change be disclosed in the financial statements. Otherwise, constant changes in method would lead to manipulation of income.

LOWER-OF-COST-OR-MARKET RULE

Thus far, this chapter has discussed ways of finding the cost of inventory. Once the cost is known it should be compared to the market, or current price. *Market* refers to the price which would have to be paid to replace the inventory at the time the inventory is counted. The lower of the two figures should be shown on the balance sheet. This is called the *lower-of-cost-or-market rule.* The lower-of-cost-or-market rule follows the conservatism principle. The *principle of conservatism* means that accountants choose the more conservative alternative, or the one which leads to a lower value for assets or income.

GROSS PROFIT METHOD OF ESTIMATING INVENTORIES

There may be times when an ending inventory figure is needed, but a physical count is impossible or too expensive. For example, a firm may wish to prepare financial statements every month but does not want to incur the cost of counting the stock on hand. For interim statements of this type, the firm may estimate the cost of goods in the inventory using the gross profit method. *Interim statements* are financial statements that are prepared before the end of the regular accounting period.

A second type of situation in which a firm may desire to know the ending inventory, but may be unable to take a physical count, is in the case of a disaster such as a fire or theft. Should such a disaster occur, the firm would need to know the ending inventory to prove its loss to an insurance company. In this situation, it is necessary to use the gross profit method to estimate the inventory. The *gross profit method* is based on the assumption that the gross profit rate of a firm remains the same from one period to the next. The *gross profit rate* is found by dividing gross profit by net sales. This can be expressed in the following equation:

$$\text{Gross Profit Rate} = \frac{\text{Gross Profit}}{\text{Net Sales}}$$

Or, to find the gross profit when the gross profit rate is known, Gross Profit = Net Sales × Gross Profit Rate. [Recall that Net Sales = Sales – (Sales Returns and Allowances + Sales Discounts).]

To calculate inventory by the gross profit method, begin by preparing an income statement in the normal manner. The figures for sales, sales returns and allowances, and sales discounts are recorded and the Net Sales determined. Beginning inventory and net cost of purchases are also shown in the accounts. Thus, the income statement can be prepared through Goods Available for Sale. The next line – Ending Inventory – is not known at this point. A question mark can be placed here until it is determined.

The next step is to estimate gross profit based on the gross profit rate for previous years. The second equation given earlier is used for this purpose. Once gross profit has been estimated, it is easy to solve algebraically for the cost of goods sold and the ending inventory figures. The following equations are used:

Cost of Goods Sold = Net Sales – Gross Profit
Ending Inventory = Goods Available for Sale – Cost of Goods Sold

For example, assume that a fire destroyed the warehouse and all of the inventory of a firm. The accounting records were saved and the following accounts had these balances:

Sales	$120,000
Sales Discounts	6,000
Sales Returns and Allowances	4,000
Purchases	40,000
Purchase Returns and Allowances	3,000
Purchase Discounts	2,000
Merchandise Inventory (Beginning)	50,000

In looking at past income statements, the gross profit rate has been 30% of net sales. Using this information, an income statement can be prepared by computing the gross profit at 30% of net sales, and then working backwards to find cost of goods sold and the ending inventory. The income statement information would be determined as follows:

Sales			$120,000
Less: Sales Returns and Allowances	$ 6,000		
Sales Discounts	4,000		10,000
Net Sales			$110,000
Cost of Goods Sold:			
Beginning Merchandise Inventory		$50,000	
Add: Purchases	$40,000		
Less: Purchase Discounts	2,000		
Purchase Returns & Allowances	3,000		
Net Purchases		35,000	
Goods Available for Sale		$85,000	
Less: Ending Inventory ($85,000 - 77,000)		8,000	
Cost of Goods Sold ($110,000 - 33,000)			77,000
Gross Profit (30% X $110,000)			$ 33,000

Thus, the value of the ending inventory lost in the fire was $8,000. The steps in finding the missing information in this problem can be summarized as follows:

1. Prepare the income statement through Goods Available for Sale.
2. Calculate the estimated Gross Profit (30% X $110,000 = $33,000).
3. Calculate the Cost of Goods Sold ($110,000 - 33,000 = $77,000).
4. Calculate the Ending Inventory ($85,000 - 77,000 = $8,000).

It should be noted that the gross profit method is only an estimate. In fact, it is not accepted by the Internal Revenue Service for tax purposes. Thus, it can only be used for interim statements or when the inventory has been destroyed.

THE RETAIL INVENTORY METHOD

The *retail inventory method,* so called because it is commonly used by retail stores such as department stores and grocers, is another method of estimating inventory value. Its use requires a record of the marked retail price of inventory in addition to the record of the cost of inventory kept by all firms. The following example illustrates the use of this method.

A firm's books show a beginning inventory of $8,000. The goods were marked to sell at $10,700. Purchases for the period were $22,000 and were marked to sell at $29,300 retail. Sales were $25,000. The data is arranged in the following way:

	Cost	Retail
Beginning Inventory	$ 8,000	$10,700
Purchases	22,000	29,300
Goods Available for Sales	$30,000	$40,000

The goods that the firm had available during the period cost $30,000. The were marked to sell at $40,000. The ratio between cost and selling price for the entire period was 75%, determined as follows:

$$\frac{30,000}{40,000} = 75\%$$

The firm had $40,000 of goods available for sale (at marked retail prices). Of those goods, $25,000 worth were sold. Therefore, the ending inventory must be $15,000 ($40,000 - $25,000) at marked retail prices. However, this amount cannot be used on the financial statements – it is the cost of inventory that must appear on the statements. Thus, the cost of inventory must be estimated. Since, for the period as a whole, cost was 75% of retail price, it is assumed that this is true for the ending inventory. The cost of the ending inventory is computed as 75% of $15,000, or $11,250. The $11,250 is the amount that appears on the financial statements.

The retail inventory method is a fairly accurate estimator of inventory value. The cost percentage for the entire period is known. The only assumption is that the year-end percentage is identical to the average for the period.

Practice Problem

A firm had sales of $60,000 during the past year. The following cost information is available from the accounts. The retail data is available from supplemental records kept by the firm. Use the retail inventory method to compute the cost of the ending inventory.

Solution

	Cost	Retail
Beginning Inventory	$ 6,300	$ 9,900
Purchases	48,900	70,500
Purchase Returns	(200)	(300)
Freight-in	1,070	
Goods Available for Sale	56,070	80,100

$$\text{COST PERCENTAGE} = \frac{56,070}{80,100} = 70\%$$

Minus Sales	60,000
Ending Inventory at Retail	20,100
X Cost Percentage	X .7
Ending Inventory at Cost	$14,070

The retail inventory method can also be used to determine losses due to theft. For instance, the above example shows that the marked retail price of the ending inventory should be $20,100. The firm could take a physical inventory at retail prices to determine if $20,100 is really on hand. If the physical count totals only $19,900, it indicates that $200 worth (at marked prices) is missing. Thus, goods marked to sell for $200 have been stolen. The cost of this theft to the firm is $140 (70% of $200).

SUMMARY

Inventory is the only account which appears on both financial statements. Thus, an error in finding the value of merchandise inventory causes both statements to be inaccurate. Also, since the ending inventory becomes the beginning inventory for the next period, the following period's income statement will also be incorrect. However, the balance sheet for the second year will be correct because the net income errors offset each other. The relationship between errors in the ending inventory and beginning inventories and other amounts on the financial statements can be summarized as follows:

	If ending inventory is:	Effect on Net Income	Effect on Total Assets	Effect on Ending Capital
Year 1	**overstated**	overstated	overstated	overstated
	understated	understated	understated	understated
	If beginning inventory is:			
Year 2	**overstated**	understated	none	none
	understated	overstated	none	none

The ending merchandise inventory is shown as a current asset on the balance sheet using the lower-of-cost-or-market rule. Market is the current replacement cost of the inventory. Cost of the inventory may be found in any of these four ways: (1) specific identification; (2) weighted average; (3) first-in, first-out (FIFO); or (4) last-in, first-out (LIFO). There are several considerations involved in the selection of one of these methods. The consistency principle requires that a firm choose one method and stay with that method, unless there is a good reason for changing. The gross profit method may be used to estimate inventory for purposes of interim statements or to prove a loss after a disaster.

REVIEW

1. Which of the three inventory methods (FIFO, LIFO, or weighted average) will show the highest cost of goods sold during an inflationary period?

2. Which of the inventory methods will result in the least income-tax expense during an inflationary period?

3. Which of the three inventory methods listed in the first question would match the physical flow of goods for an inventory of gasoline at a filling station?

4. Which of the three inventory methods would match the physical flow of goods for the bread department of a grocery store?
5. Which of the three inventory methods will show the highest net income during a deflationary period (a period in which costs are decreasing)?
6. Which inventory method will result in the most income-tax expense during a deflationary period?
7. Which of the inventory methods would match the physical flow of goods for a coal dealer?
8. During an inflationary period, which method will result in the highest net income?
9. What method of inventory valuation can be used when the inventory has been destroyed?
10. When the phrase *lower-of-cost-or-market* is used, what does the word *market* mean?
11. Which inventory valuation method is not acceptable for tax purposes?
12. If a firm overstates its ending inventory, what will be the effect on net income?
13. If a firm understates its beginning inventory, what will be the effect on net income?

EXERCISES

1. If, on December 31, 1981, an error is made in valuing the ending inventory by overstating it by $700, what effect would this have on the following statements?
   a. The income statement prepared on December 31, 1981.
   b. The balance sheet prepared on December 31, 1981.
   c. The income statement prepared on December 31, 1982.
   d. The balance sheet prepared on December 31, 1982.
2. A firm's entire inventory was destroyed in a fire. The following account balances were available from the accounting records: Sales, $100,000; Merchandise Inventory, $12,000; Purchases, $71,000. The firm's gross profit rate has averaged 39% for the past few years. Use the gross profit method to estimate the amount of inventory destroyed.
3. A company had the following beginning inventory and purchases during the past year:

Beginning Inventory	200 units @ $2.00 each
January 9 Purchases	200 units @ $2.10 each
May 20 Purchases	300 units @ $2.20 each
December 3 Purchases	300 units @ $2.40 each

There are 400 units in the company's ending inventory.
   a. How many units were sold during the year?
   b. Assuming the company uses the weighted average method of inventory valuation, what is the value of the ending inventory?

c. Assuming the company uses LIFO, what is the value of the ending inventory?

d. Assuming the company uses FIFO, what is the value of the ending inventory?

e. Assuming the company uses LIFO, what is the cost of goods sold during the period?

4. During a year a company purchased merchandise costing $49,500. What was the company's cost of goods sold if there were:

a. Beginning and ending inventories of zero?

b. A beginning inventory of $1,500 and an ending inventory of zero?

c. A beginning inventory of $13,000 and an ending inventory of $9,300?

d. A beginning inventory of zero and an ending inventory of $12,000?

5. Errors in determining the merchandise inventory at the end of the first year of operations resulted in its being greatly overstated. The error was not discovered, and the inventory at the end of the following year was correctly stated. Indicate the effect of the error on the financial statements at the end of the first year and the second year.

6. A firm had sales of $12,000 during the past month. The following data is available from the accounts and other records:

	Cost	Retail
Beginning Inventory	$16,200	$24,400
Purchases	18,000	25,600
Freight-in	300	

a. Use the retail inventory method to determine the cost of the ending inventory.

b. If the firm's physical count showed an ending inventory at retail of $37,000, how much was missing due to theft (at cost)?

PROBLEMS

1. The beginning inventory and purchases of Item X for the period were as follows:

Inventory, beginning	6 units @ $40 each
First purchase	8 units @ $41 each
Second purchase	5 units @ $43 each
Third purchase	5 units @ $45 each

There were 7 units of Item X in the inventory at the end of the period. Find the cost of the 7 units in the inventory by each of the following methods: first-in, first-out; last-in, first-out; and weighted average.

2. A company had 200 widgets in its ending inventory. It began the year and had purchased widgets as follows:

January 1	Inventory	100 units @ $.40 each
March 15	Purchased	300 units @ $.50 each
June 3	Purchased	300 units @ $.60 each
October 8	Purchased	200 units @ $.80 each
December 1	Purchased	100 units @ $.70 each

Determine the total cost that should be assigned to the ending inventory and to the cost of goods sold under the following assumptions:

a. A first-in, first-out basis was used to price the ending inventory.
b. A last-in, first-out basis was used to price the ending inventory.
c. The ending inventory was priced on a weighted average cost basis.

3. A company having a 30% average gross profit rate over each of the past five years sold $102,000 of merchandise at retail during the first quarter of this year. If its accounts show an $18,000 beginning-of-the-quarter inventory, $66,000 of goods purchased, and $4,000 paid for the freight on purchases during the quarter, what is its end-of-the-quarter inventory calculated by the gross profit method?

4. Flash Corporation had the following beginning inventory and purchases during the past year. Determine the proper value of the ending inventory under (1) FIFO; (2) LIFO; (3) weighted average. Also, find the cost of goods sold for the year.

January 1, Beginning Inventory	100 units @ $6.00 each
February 8, Purchase	100 units @ $6.10 each
May 1, Purchase	400 units @ $6.20 each
July 31, Purchase	200 units @ $6.30 each
November 1, Purchase	100 units @ $6.50 each

There is a total of 350 units in the ending inventory on December 31. All sales during the year were made at a price of $10 per unit.

5. A firm had sales of $140,300 during the past year. The following data is available from the accounts and other records:

	Cost	Retail
Beginning Inventory	$ 19,200	$ 43,700
Purchases	140,300	157,300
Purchase Returns	600	1,000
Freight-in	1,100	

Use the retail inventory method to determine the cost of the ending inventory.

SECTION 3

Accounting for Assets

14
Cash Control

OBJECTIVES

After studying this chapter, the student will be able to:

- Describe the internal control procedures for cash.
- Reconcile a bank statement.
- Make journal entries from the bank reconciliation.
- Journalize entries for a petty cash fund.
- Use a Cash Over and Short account.

INTERNAL CONTROL OF CASH

In larger businesses, the owner cannot personally handle all of the firm's transactions. He or she would be unable to write all of the checks or receive all of the payments resulting from the firm's activities. Therefore, various duties are assigned to other employees. However, since the owner is no longer involved in every transaction, he or she loses the direct control that is possible in a small business. To compensate for this lack of direct control, the management of a larger business must develop a system of procedures to assure that the funds of the firm are handled properly. This system is referred to as *internal control.* The purposes of internal control procedures are to protect assets from fraud and waste, and to provide accurate accounting data. Internal control over cash is particularly important because cash is easily misused or stolen.

Separation of Duties

One of the most important principles of internal control of cash is *separation of duties.* When an operation involves a chain of tasks, these tasks should be divided among two or more persons. For example, no one individual should be allowed to receive money, take the money to the bank, and keep the records. Separation of duties makes theft unlikely unless two or more employees work together to defraud the firm. In addition, with a separation of duties, errors made by one person should be caught by the person who performs the next step in the procedure. Without separation of duties, it is possible for one individual to embezzle cash and then juggle the books to cover up the theft.

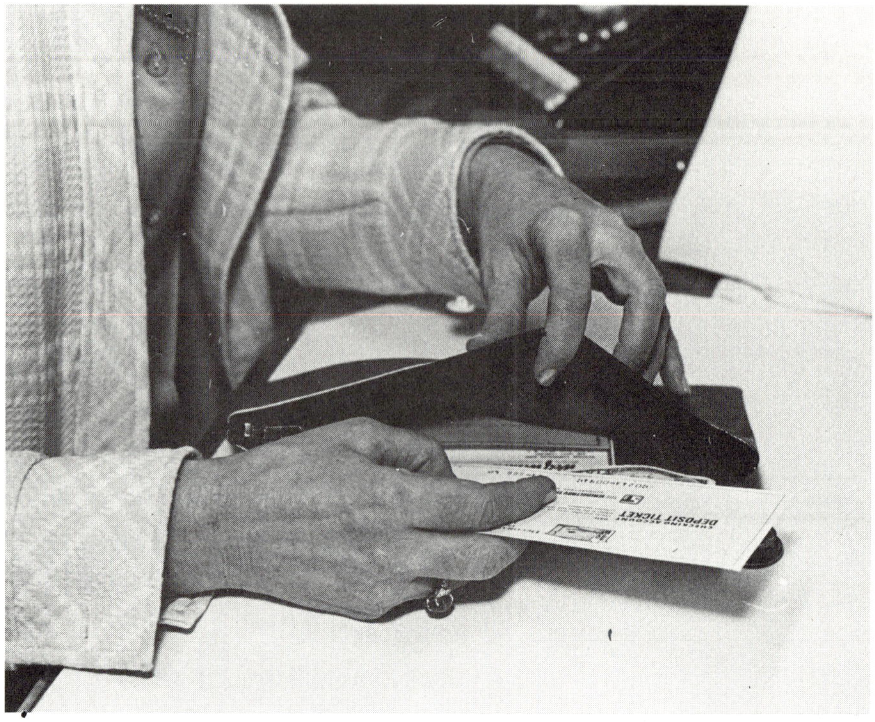

Fig. 14-1. Depositing cash receipts daily is essential for good cash flow control.

Daily Cash Deposits

A second rule of internal control for cash is that all cash receipts should be deposited in the bank, intact, daily, figure 14-1. (*Intact* means in their entirety, without any cash being removed.) Unbanked cash invites theft. The deposit slip given by the bank acts as a second record of the cash receipts in addition to the accounting records.

Payments Made by Check

The third principle of control is that all cash payments should be made by checks drawn on the firm's bank account. Thus, the check serves as a record of payment. As a further safeguard, only authorized officials should be allowed to sign checks. The bank account allows the firm to keep a double record of cash. Since all cash is deposited in the bank and all payments are made by check, the bank's records should be the same as those of the firm.

BANK RECONCILIATIONS

Once a month the bank sends its customers a bank statement which shows the account balance at the beginning and end of the month and all deductions and deposits. Canceled checks are also returned. These are the checks which were written by the firm and have been cashed or cleared by the bank. The firm's account is a liability to the bank and has a credit balance. To the firm, this same account is an asset called *Cash* or *Cash in Bank* and has a debit balance.

If all cash receipts are deposited in the bank account and all cash payments are made by checks drawn on that account, the bank account balance should be the same as the Cash account balance on the books of the firm. However, the balance shown on the bank statement probably will not agree with the Cash balance on the books due to errors or time lag. Differences in the two records are a result of:

Outstanding checks. These are checks that have been written and recorded on the firm's books but have not been received by the bank by the time it sends out the statement. The bank has not deducted these checks and they are not included among the canceled checks sent out with the bank statement.

Deposits in transit. These are deposits which were made too late to appear on the bank statement. It takes a day or two for the bank to record the data on the bank statement. Deposits which are in transit will have been added to the Cash account on the books but not to the bank statement.

Service charges. These are the charges that the bank deducts from the customer's account for its services. These charges will be shown on the bank statement. The firm will not have recorded these charges on its books.

NSF checks. *NSF* stands for *not sufficient funds.* Such checks have been accepted by the firm and added to the cash account. However, the bank has not paid the amount of the check because the writer did not have adequate funds to cover it. The bank deducts the amount of such checks from the depositor's account.

Debit and credit memoranda. The bank sends debit or credit memoranda with the bank statement to notify the firm of changes made in its account. Since the firm's account is a liability to the bank, the bank debits the account to show a decrease and credits it to show an increase. The firm does just the opposite to show the change in its asset account. An example of a credit memorandum is a collection made by the bank on behalf of the firm. The bank adds the proceeds of the collection to the account of the firm and sends the firm a credit memorandum.

Errors. Errors made by either the bank or the firm will cause a difference in the two records.

Outstanding checks and deposits in transit are not recorded by the bank and do not appear on the bank statement. Service charges, NSF checks, and debit and credit memoranda are not recorded by the firm in its Cash account. These discrepancies make it necessary to reconcile the bank balance with the book balance. In accounting, to *reconcile* means to make two items consistent with each other, or to make them agree. A *bank reconciliation* makes the bank balance agree with the balance shown on the books.

A bank reconcilation is prepared using the following form:

Balance per books		Balance per bank statement	
Add: Credit memorandum		*Add:* Deposits in transit	
Book errors		Bank errors	
Less: Service charges		*Less:* Outstanding checks	
NSF checks		Bank errors	
Debit memorandum			
Book errors			
Adjusted Book Balance	______	Adjusted Bank Balance	______

The adjusted balances should agree. This amount is the correct amount of cash and is the amount which should be shown on the balance sheet for that date.

Example of a Bank Reconciliation

For example, to prepare a bank reconciliation for the Head Company the following information is needed:

- Balance per books as of June 30 – $2,552.99
- Balance shown on bank statement as of June 30 – $3,659.20
- Deposits in transit – $816.78
- Outstanding checks: Check #513 – $1,061.39
  Check #551 – $435.00
  Check #555 – $48.60
- Credit memorandum for note collected by bank from Bob Smith – $400.00
- Service charges – $3.00
- Check #563 for $732.76 was recorded in the Cash account as 723.76. This check was for payment of an Account Payable.
- NSF check for $10.00 from Fred Bundy.

The bank reconciliation for the firm appears in figure 14-2.

Head Company
Bank Reconciliation
June 30, 19–

Balance per books		$2,552.99	Balance per bank statement		$3,659.20
Add: Credit memorandum for note collected from Bob Smith		400.00	*Add:* Deposits in transit		816.78
		$2,952.99			$4,475.98
			Less: Outstanding checks		
Less: Service charges	$ 3.00		#513	$1,061.39	
Error in recording check #563	9.00		#551	435.00	
NSF chk., F. Bundy	10.00	22.00	#555	48.60	1,544.99
Adjusted Book Balance		$2,930.99	Adjusted Bank Balance		$2,930.99

Fig. 14-2. A bank reconciliation.

GENERAL JOURNAL Page______

Date		Account Titles and Explanation	Post. Ref.	Debit	Credit
19–					
June	30	Cash		400 00	
		Notes Receivable			400 00
		To record Bob Smith note collected by bank.			
	30	Service Charge Expense		3 00	
		Accounts Payable		9 00	
		Accounts Receivable		10 00	
		Cash			22 00
		To record service charge, Fred Bundy NSF			
		check and error.			

Fig. 14-3. Adjusting entries resulting from the bank reconciliation.

Journal Entries from the Bank Reconciliation

All of the items listed on the book side of the bank reconciliation have not been recorded in the Cash account on the books of the firm. After the bank reconciliation is done, journal entries must be made for these changes so that the balance of the Cash account is equal to the adjusted book balance.

The journal entries for Head Company are shown in figure 14-3. Note that the NSF check was recorded by a debit to Accounts Receivable. Since the check bounced, the firm will have to try and collect this amount from the customer. The balance in the Cash account should now equal the adjusted book balance as follows:

	Cash (Debit)	Cash (Credit)
Beginning Balance	*2,552.99*	*22.00*
	400.00	
	2,930.99	

PETTY CASH FUND

There are times when it is impossible or impractical to write a check in payment for charges. Charges for items such as postage, delivery services, and emergency supplies can best be paid for with cash. A firm uses a petty cash fund for these items. A *petty cash fund* is a small amount of cash that is kept on hand to provide money for making small payments.

A petty cash fund is started by estimating the amount of cash needed for a given period of time. For example, a period of a month might be decided upon. A check is then written for that amount and cashed. This cash is given to the person assigned to be *petty cashier* and who is then responsible for the fund. At the time the petty cash fund is started the following journal entry is made:

Petty Cash
    Cash (or Cash in Bank)

The petty cashier is authorized to use cash from the fund and is limited only by certain restrictions as to the maximum amount and purpose of payments. Each time a payment is made from the fund, the petty cashier records the details of the payment on a *petty cash voucher,* secures the signature of the person receiving the cash, and signs the voucher. No journal entry is made at the time the payment is made from the fund. The fund will be made up of cash and petty cash vouchers. The total of the cash and the vouchers should always be equal to the total amount of the petty cash fund.

The petty cash fund should be replenished or reimbursed on two occasions: (1) when cash in the fund is low and (2) at the end of each accounting period. When the fund is nearly out of cash, the cash in the fund should be brought back up to the original amount and the vouchers should be recorded. A journal entry is made at this time, debiting the expense or asset accounts as shown on the vouchers and crediting Cash in Bank. A check is written and cashed for this amount, the money is given to the petty cashier and the cycle begins again. The same process is repeated at the end of the accounting period even if the fund is not low, since expenses and assets must be recorded in the proper accounting period.

Note that the only journal entry to the Petty Cash account is the original entry to start the fund. No other journal entries will be made to the Petty Cash account unless at some later time the amount of the petty cash fund is permanently increased or decreased. Payments from the fund are not recorded in the accounts until the fund is replenished.

CASH OVER AND SHORT

The *Cash Over and Short* account is used to show the difference between the cash on hand and the balance of the Cash account. For example, at the end of the day the amount of cash in the cash register may not agree with the sales amount shown on the cash register tape. If no mistake can be found on the record of sales, it is assumed that the difference is due to an error in making change. This difference can be recorded in the Cash Over and Short account. As an example, assume that the cash register tape shows that sales totaling $1,020 were made for the day, but the cash in the drawer is only $1,015. This journal entry would be made:

Cash	1,015	
Cash Over and Short	5	
Sales		1,020
To record cash sales for the day and a shortage.		

If there were more cash in the drawer (an overage) than the sales figure showed, the Cash Over and Short account would be credited. The Cash Over and Short account may also be used to record errors in the petty cash fund.

When there is a debit balance in the Cash Over and Short account at the end of the accounting period, the balance is shown as an expense on the income statement. If the Cash Over and Short account has a credit balance, then this amount is shown as miscellaneous or other revenue on the income statement.

Example

The Pen Company starts a petty cash fund of $50 on May 1. The entry at this time is:

May 1	Petty Cash	50.00	
	Cash		50.00
	To start a petty cash fund.		

On May 31, the fund is replenished. There is $4.64 in the fund and vouchers for these expenses:

Postage	$ 4.38
Delivery	11.85
Supplies	12.79
Office Equipment	14.13
Miscellaneous Expense	3.21

The total of the vouchers is $46.36. However, as already stated, there is $4.64 in the fund. An error must have been made in giving out the cash, since this is $1.00 more than should be in the fund. To balance the entry used to replenish the fund, a credit for $1.00 must be made to Cash Over and Short. Thus, the May 31 entry is:

May 31	Postage Expense	4.38	
	Delivery Expense	11.85	
	Supplies	12.79	
	Office Equipment	14.13	
	Miscellaneous Expense	3.21	
	Cash		45.36
	Cash Over and Short		1.00
	To replenish petty cash fund.		

SUMMARY

All firms should have a set of procedures for internal control. Internal control over cash is especially important. Three rules should be followed by all firms. There should be a separation of duties in the handling of cash. All cash receipts should be deposited in the bank, intact, daily. All cash payments should be made by checks drawn against the bank account.

Each month when the firm receives the bank statement, a bank reconciliation is prepared. A bank reconciliation makes the bank balance agree with the Cash balance on the books. A bank reconciliation is prepared using a standard form. One side of the form shows the balance as stated in the firm's books, while the other side shows the balance stated on the bank statement. After the causes of difference in the balances have been listed on both sides, the adjusted bank balance should agree with the adjusted book balance. The adjusted balance is the true amount of cash which should be shown on the balance sheet. Journal entries are made for all items shown on the book side of the bank reconciliation. These correct the Cash balance on the books.

A petty cash fund is the small amount of cash that is kept on hand to provide money for small payments. When a petty cash fund is started, a journal entry is made with a debit to Petty Cash and a credit to Cash. The petty cash fund is replenished when the fund is low or at

Fig. 14-4. The Small Business Administration (SBA) provides many helpful pamphlets on the topic of cash control. These and other publications are available free of charge from local SBA offices.

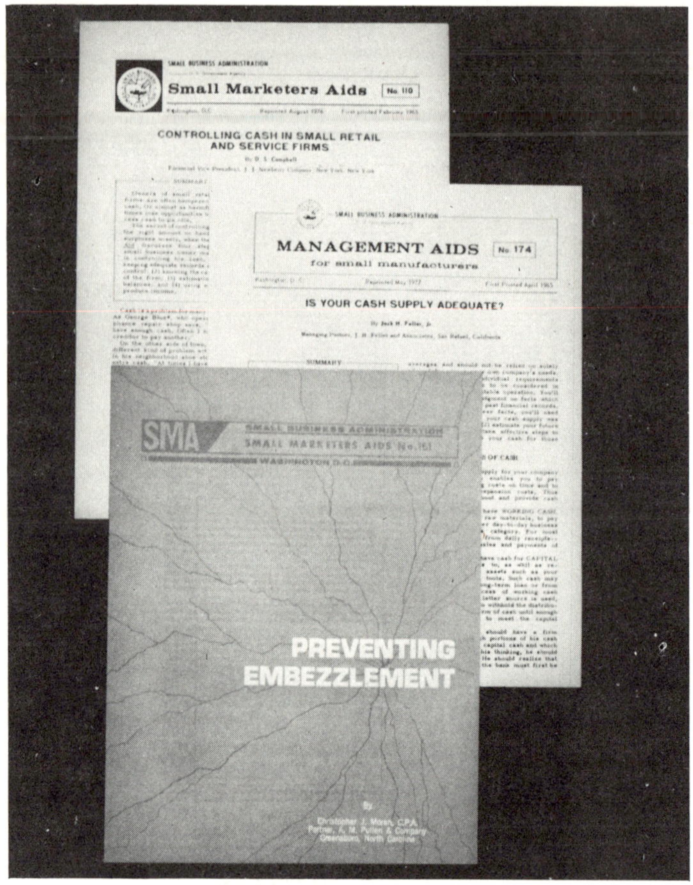

the end of the accounting period. When replenished, the expense or asset accounts shown on the petty cash vouchers are debited and Cash is credited. The only entry to Petty Cash is made when the fund is started or permanently increased or decreased.

A Cash Over and Short account is used to show the difference between the cash on hand and the balance in the Cash account. When there is a debit balance in this account, it is shown as an expense. When a credit balance is shown, it is listed as a revenue.

REVIEW

1. What are the three basic rules of cash control?
2. Why should different people be appointed to receive cash and to record the journal entry?
3. What is the meaning of the rule which states that all receipts should be deposited, intact, daily?
4. What is a petty cash voucher?
5. Under what two conditions should a petty cash fund be replenished?
6. Why must a petty cash fund be replenished at the end of each accounting period?
7. What is a bank statement?
8. What is a NSF check?

9. On which side of a bank reconciliation will an error be shown?

10. Describe the purpose and operation of the Cash Over and Short account.

11. Why must journal entries be made after a bank reconciliation is completed?

12. What types of entries will be made to the Petty Cash account?

EXERCISES

1. a. Prepare a bank reconciliation from the following information:

Balance per book	$863.00
Balance per bank statement	711.00
Service charge	4.00
Outstanding checks	100.00
NSF check	17.00
Deposit in transit	231.00

b. Record any journal entries required as a result of the reconciliation.

2. Prepare a bank reconciliation and adjusting entries for the Bandello Firm based on the following data:

Balance per Cash account			$1,631.00
Balance per bank statement			1,540.00
Outstanding checks:	#730	$ 38.00	
	#732	50.00	
	#740	107.00	
Deposit in transit			365.00
Debit memorandum for service charge			3.00
Credit memorandum for note collected			100.00
Debit memorandum for NSF check			18.00

3. Give the journal entries for the following transactions:

May 1: Started a petty cash fund with a $100 balance.

18: Replenished the fund. The following paid vouchers were in the petty cash box along with $11.00 in cash:
- Postage – $18.80
- Supplies – $32.90
- Gas and oil – $37.30

31: Replenished the fund. The following paid vouchers were in the petty cash box along with $69.00 in cash:
- Postage – $15.50
- Supplies – $16.50

PROBLEMS

1. Reconcile a bank statement for the T. S. Rivers Company using the following information:

(1) Balance per bank statement – $17,189.13

(2) Balance per books – $12,539.56

(3) Outstanding checks:

	$1,000.72
	1,600.00
	1,004.00
	$3,604.72

(4) Deposit in transit – $309.89

(5) A deposit of $738 in the middle of the month was incorrectly shown on the bank statement as $728.

(6) The bank collected a $1,000 note for the firm and deducted a $5 collection fee.

(7) A check of $100.39 was incorrectly recorded in the Cash account as $1,003.90. The check was for office equipment.

(8) There was a debit memorandum from the bank for a $5 monthly service charge.

(9) A customer's check was returned as a NSF check, $488.77.

(10) A check of $440 was incorrectly recorded as $400 in the Cash account. The check was for office supplies.

2. The following information pertains to the banking activities of Cobb Company with State National Bank during the month of September, 1981.

(1) The balance per ledger on September 1, 1981, is $16,245.18.

(2) Cash receipts for September are $45,634.92; checks during the month total $52,911.34.

(3) The statement from the bank shows a balance of $6,652.02 at the end of the month.

(4) Included in the returned checks is a memo stating that the check of M. Price has been returned marked NSF; the amount is $876.47.

(5) An examination of the checks reveals that the following are outstanding: No. 1593, $30.50; No 1812, $110.38; No. 1962, $69.12; No. 2008, $117.39; No. 2009, $4.82; and No. 2010, $29.11.

(6) The bank has deducted from the account, in error, a check of Sprot, Inc.; the amount of the check is $546.33.

(7) There is a deposit of $2,100.30 in transit at the end of September.

(8) The bookkeeper made an error in recording a check received from R. Mason; the amount recorded was $94.76; it should have been $947.60.

(9) A debit memo shows that service charges amounted to $7.80.

a. Prepare a bank reconciliation as of September 30,1981.
b. Give any journal entries required as of September 30,1981.

3. From the following information, prepare a bank reconciliation. Also prepare all adjusting entries that are required by the completed reconciliation.

(1) December 31, 1983 balance per books – $800.

(2) December 31, 1983 balance per bank statement ____?____ (This figure must be calculated.)

(3) Monthly service charge – $6.

(4) Note collected by bank and not yet recorded on books – $217 ($200 note, $17 interest).

(5) Deposit in transit – $452.

(6) Outstanding checks – $871.

(7) Check No. 214 for $304 was incorrectly recorded in the journal as $340. The check was correctly written and properly cashed by the bank as $304.

(8) A customer's NSF check in the amount of $88 was returned.

15 Statement of Changes in Financial Position

OBJECTIVES

After studying this chapter, the student will be able to:

- Explain the need for a statement of changes in financial position.
- Prepare the work sheet for a statement of changes in financial position.
- Prepare a statement of changes in financial position using either a cash or working capital basis.

THE NEED FOR A THIRD FINANCIAL STATEMENT

In some instances, the income statement and the balance sheet present an inadequate picture of a firm. For example, at the end of one year, the Great Products Firm had no cash assets. Thus, the owner believed that the firm had suffered a loss for the year. However, when completed, the income statement showed a large net income for the year. The question is, "Where did all of the cash go if the firm had such a large net income?"

The Simple Gadgets Company, on the other hand, finished the year with a great deal of cash. The owner said he had never been so rich. However, when the income statement was prepared, it showed a huge net loss for the year. The question is, "Where did all of the cash come from if the firm had such a net loss?"

These two questions can be answered with the help of a third financial statement which is designed to show the sources and uses of a firm's cash during an accounting period. The proper title of this statement is *statement of changes in financial position.* It is also known as a *statement of sources and uses of cash,* a *funds statement,* a *statement of sources and application of funds,* or a *cash flow statement.*

The rules of financial reporting require that this third statement be prepared whenever a balance sheet and an income statement are prepared. A second situation in which the statement of changes in financial position takes on added importance is when a firm is applying for a bank loan. The bank usually requests a copy of this statement to determine how the firm has used its cash and whether or not it should receive a loan.

The statement of changes in financial position has two sections. These are: (1) Sources of Cash, and (2) Uses of Cash. The following items are included under Sources of Cash:

- net income from operations
- sale of a fixed asset or investment
- investment by the owner in the firm
- borrowing money

A firm's uses of cash might include the following:

- net loss from operations
- purchase of a fixed asset or investment
- withdrawals by the owner
- paying off loans

Example of a Work Sheet for a Statement of Changes in Financial Position

A special work sheet is used as a guide when completing a statement of changes in financial position. The work sheet itself is prepared from two balance sheets – the one at the beginning of the period and the one at the end of the period. Figure 15-1 is a combined balance sheet showing the end-of-year information on the left and the beginning of the year information on the right.

Hard Rock Company
Balance Sheets
December 31, 1980 and 1981

	1981	1980
ASSETS:		
Cash	$ 1,000	$ 4,000
Accounts Receivable	3,000	3,500
Merchandise Inventory	5,000	3,000
Land	6,000	4,000
Building	16,000	10,000
Accumulated Depreciation	(3,000)	(2,000)
	$28,000	$22,500
LIABILITIES & OWNER'S EQUITY:		
Accounts Payable	4,000	3,000
Notes Payable	14,000	15,000
Jim Rock, Capital	10,000	4,500
	$28,000	$22,500

Additional Information:

a. Net income for 1981 was $9,000.
b. The owner withdrew $3,500 during the year.
c. The firm bought land, $2,000, and building, $6,000.

Fig. 15-1. Balance sheets for the Hard Rock Company.

The first step in preparing a statement of changes in financial position is to calculate a *check figure* against which to match the final amount on the statement. The check figure is determined by looking at the Cash account as shown on the balance sheet. Since the whole objective of the statement of changes in financial position is to explain the change in the Cash account, the bottom line of the statement should match the amount of the change in Cash shown on the balance sheet. In the case of the Hard Rock Company, the change in Cash was a decrease of $3,000. The firm started the year with $4,000 in cash. At year end there was only $1,000 left. Thus, Cash decreased by $3,000. The $3,000 amount is the check figure which should appear on the formal statement.

The next step is to fill in the work sheet by listing all accounts other than cash. Any time the Cash account is changed, some other account is also affected. The easiest way to figure out the change in the Cash is to look at the changes in the other accounts. For this reason, only the non-cash accounts are placed on the work sheet. Figure 15-2 shows the work sheet with the account balances.

Note that there are a pair of debit and credit columns on the work sheet. These are known as *reconstruction entry columns* and are

Hard Rock Company
Work Sheet for a Statement of Changes in Financial Position
For Year Ended December 31, 1981

	1981	*1980*	DEBIT	CREDIT
Accounts Receivable	*3,000*	*3,500*		
Merchandise Inventory	*5,000*	*3,000*		
Land	*6,000*	*4,000*		
Building	*16,000*	*10,000*		
Accumulated Depreciation	*(3,000)*	*(2,000)*		
Accounts Payable	*4,000*	*3,000*		
Notes Payable	*14,000*	*15,000*		
Jim Rock, Capital	*10,000*	*4,500*		
			SOURCES	USES
	NORMAL OPERATIONS:			
	OTHER SOURCES AND USES:			

Fig. 15-2. A work sheet for a statement of changes in financial position.

used to reconstruct the journal entries that were made during the year. The idea is to determine what entries were made during the year and reconstruct them (to the extent possible) on the work sheet. A reconstruction entry can be thought of as an inclusive entry that summarizes all entries that were made to an account during the year.

The work sheet is completed as follows. Accounts Receivable decreased from $3,500 to $3,000. Thus, that account must have been credited for $500. The debit would have been to Cash, but this account is not on the work sheet. Since the debit cannot be made to any of the accounts shown at the top of the sheet, it is recorded in the Sources and Uses section at the bottom. This procedure is used whenever only one part of the entry can be shown on the top half of the work sheet. It is the Sources and Uses section that is actually used to prepare the formal statement of changes in financial position. Entry *a* on the work sheet in figure 15-3 shows how the reconstruction is recorded for Accounts Receivable.

As seen from the balance sheet, Merchandise Inventory has increased during the year. Thus, the entry is a debit to Merchandise

Hard Rock Company
Work Sheet for a Statement of Changes in Financial Position
For Year Ended December 31, 1981

	1981	*1980*	DEBIT	CREDIT
Accounts Receivable	*3,000*	*3,500*		(a) **500**
Merchandise Inventory	*5,000*	*3,000*		
Land	*6,000*	*4,000*		
Building	*16,000*	*10,000*		
Accumulated Depreciation	*(3,000)*	*(2,000)*		
Accounts Payable	*4,000*	*3,000*		
Notes Payable	*14,000*	*15,000*		
Jim Rock, Capital	*10,000*	*4,500*		

	SOURCES	USES
NORMAL OPERATIONS:	(a) **500**	
OTHER SOURCES AND USES:		

Fig. 15-3. Work sheet entry for accounts receivable.

Hard Rock Company
Work Sheet for a Statement of Changes in Financial Position
For Year Ended December 31, 1981

	1981	1980	DEBIT	CREDIT
Accounts Receivable	*3,000*	*3,500*		*(a)* *500*
Merchandise Inventory	*5,000*	*3,000*	**(b) 2,000**	
Land	*6,000*	*4,000*		
Building	*16,000*	*10,000*		
Accumulated Depreciation	*(3,000)*	*(2,000)*		
Accounts Payable	*4,000*	*3,000*		
Notes Payable	*14,000*	*15,000*		
Jim Rock, Capital	*10,000*	*4,500*		
			SOURCES	USES
NORMAL OPERATIONS:				
Decrease in Receivables			*(a)* *500*	
Increase in Inventory				**(b) 2,000**
OTHER SOURCES AND USES:				

Fig. 15-4. Work sheet entries for merchandise inventory.

Inventory of $2,000. (See entry *b* on figure 15-4.) Since the only time the Merchandise Inventory account is used during the year is in the closing entries, the credit must have been to Income Summary. Since the Income Summary account is not on the work sheet, the credit has to be placed at the bottom of the work sheet as shown in figure 15-4.

The reconstruction entry that will explain the change in the Land account is a $2,000 debit to Land and a credit to Cash (entry *c*). Again, since Cash is not on the work sheet, that half of the entry is placed down below the line in the Uses section. Since the purchase of Land does use cash, this is a reasonable procedure. However, notice the difference between this entry and the previous ones as shown in figure 15-5. The accounts receivable and inventory changes were the result of normal operations and were entered on this section of the work sheet. Accounts Receivable and Merchandise Inventory are expected to change. Accounts such as Land and Building, however, do not change as a result of normal operations. Most firms do not buy and sell land every year.

Hard Rock Company
Work Sheet for a Statement of Changes in Financial Position
For Year Ended December 31, 1981

	1981	*1980*	DEBIT	CREDIT
Accounts Receivable	*3,000*	*3,500*		*(a) 500*
Merchandise Inventory	*5,000*	*3,000*	*(b) 2,000*	
Land	*6,000*	*4,000*	**(c) 2,000**	
Building	*16,000*	*10,000*	**(d) 6,000**	
Accumulated Depreciation	*(3,000)*	*(2,000)*		
Accounts Payable	*4,000*	*3,000*		
Notes Payable	*14,000*	*15,000*		
Jim Rock, Capital	*10,000*	*4,500*		
			SOURCES	USES
NORMAL OPERATIONS:				
Decrease in Receivables			*(a) 500*	
Increase in Inventory				*(b) 2,000*
OTHER SOURCES AND USES:				
Purchased Land				**(c) 2,000**
Purchased Building				**(d) 6,000**

Fig. 15-5. Work sheet entries for land and building.

Thus, entries for these accounts are placed at the far bottom of the work sheet in the Other Sources and Uses section.

The entry to explain the change in the Building account is also shown in figure 15-5 (entry *d*). It is a debit to Building and a credit to Cash. The credit is put at the bottom of the work sheet. Note that since the purchase of a building is not part of the normal day-to-day operations of the firm, it is recorded with the land purchase under Other Sources and Uses.

The reconstruction entry to explain the change in Accumulated Depreciation is a debit to Depreciation Expense and a credit to Accumulated Depreciation, figure 15-6. This is simply a reconstruction of the only entry that was made to Accumulated Depreciation during the year. Since the Depreciation Expense is not on the work sheet, the debit part of the entry has to be put on the bottom of the sheet. Depreciation is the result of normal operations. Thus, the debit is placed in the Normal Operations section of the work sheet as entry *e*.

Accounts Payable increased $1,000 during the year. This is shown by entry *f* in figure 15-6, debiting Purchases and crediting Accounts

Hard Rock Company
Work Sheet for a Statement of Changes in Financial Position
For Year Ended December 31, 1981

	1981	1980	DEBIT	CREDIT
Accounts Receivable	3,000	3,500		(a) 500
Merchandise Inventory	5,000	3,000	(b) 2,000	
Land	6,000	4,000	(c) 2,000	
Building	16,000	10,000	(d) 6,000	
Accumulated Depreciation	(3,000)	(2,000)		(e) 1,000
Accounts Payable	4,000	3,000		(f) 1,000
Notes Payable	14,000	15,000	(g) 1,000	
Jim Rock, Capital	10,000	4,500	(i) 3,500	(h) 9,000
			SOURCES	USES
NORMAL OPERATIONS:				
Decrease in Receivables			(a) 500	
Increase in Inventory				(b) 2,000
Depreciation Expense			(e) 1,000	
Increase in Accounts Payable			(f) 1,000	
Net Income			(h) 9,000	
OTHER SOURCES AND USES:				
Purchased Land				(c) 2,000
Purchased Building				(d) 6,000
Paid off Notes Payable				(g) 1,000
Withdrawals by the owner				(i) 3,500

Fig. 15-6. Work sheet entries for accumulated depreciation, accounts payable, notes payable, and capital.

Payable. Since Purchases is not on the work sheet, the debit is placed below the line in the Source section.

From the balance sheet, it can be seen that Notes Payable decreased during the year. The firm must have paid off part of its debt, resulting in a debit to Notes Payable and a credit to Cash. The financing of a firm with a note is not considered a part of normal operations. Thus, when reconstructing the entries, the credit is placed in the Other Sources and Uses section of the work sheet. This is shown as entry *g* in figure 15-6.

The owner's capital account was changed by two entries during the year. (See the balance sheet in figure 15-1.) One was the net income. The other was the withdrawal. The entry for the net income is a $9,000 debit to Income Summary and a credit to Jim Rock, Capital. This is shown as entry *h* in figure 15-6. The withdrawal during the year resulted in a decrease of $3,500 in the Capital account. Even though the original entry would have been to Jim Rock, Drawing, it still resulted in a decrease in Capital. Thus, it is assumed that the original entry was a debit to Jim Rock, Capital, and a credit to Cash. Since a withdrawal is not the result of normal operations, the credit is entered in the Other Sources and Uses section as entry *i* in figure 15-6.

THE FORMAL STATEMENT

Once all of the changes in the non-cash accounts have been explained with reconstruction entries, the bottom half of the work sheet can be used to prepare the formal statement of changes in financial position. An example of a formal statement of changes in financial position is given in figure 15-7. Note that the formal statement has the same date heading as an income statement and two sections: Sources of Cash and Uses of Cash.

The American Institute of CPAs (AICPA) requires that sources from normal operations appear first in the Sources of Cash section. Cash from other sources is listed following sources from operations. Note that the sources and uses from normal operations are netted against each other in the Sources section. Next, the Uses of Cash section shows the uses not resulting from operations. The next figure on the statement is a Uses of Cash total. This amount is subtracted from the Sources of Cash total. In figure 15-7 this results in a $3,000 cash decrease. Note that this amount exactly matches the check figure determined from the balance sheets.

Hard Rock Company
Statement of Changes in Financial Position
For Year Ended December 31, 1981

SOURCES OF CASH:		
Income from Operations:	$9,000	
Add: Depreciation Expense	1,000	
Decrease in Receivables	500	
Increase in Accounts Payable	1,000	
Less: Increase in Inventory	(2,000)	
Total Sources from Operations		$ 9,500
Other Sources:		
(None)		
TOTAL SOURCES OF CASH		9,500
USES OF CASH:		
Purchased Land		2,000
Purchased Building		6,000
Paid off Notes Payable		1,000
Withdrawals by the Owner		3,500
TOTAL USES OF CASH		12,500
DECREASE IN CASH		$ 3,000

Fig. 15-7. Statement of changes in financial position for the Hard Rock Company.

EXTRAORDINARY GAINS AND LOSSES

A type of entry that was not shown in the Hard Rock Company example is one for the disposal of a fixed asset in an unusual manner. The result of such a transaction is called an *extraordinary gain or loss*, since the cash obtained or lost is not directly related to the normal operations of the firm.

For example, suppose that the XY Firm owns a truck which is shown at $4,000 less $1,000 accumulated depreciation. Thus, it has a book value of $3,000. The truck is lost in a fire, and the firm collects $2,900 from the insurance company. The journal entry to record the loss of the truck is:

Cash	2,900	
Accumulated Depreciation	1,000	
Loss of Truck	100	
Truck		4,000
To record disposal of lost truck.		

The reconstruction entry for this item is shown in figure 15-8. Note that the $2,900 received for the truck is debited in the Other Sources and Uses section in the lower part of the entry since it was not from normal operations. The $100 loss, however, is debited in the Normal Operations section. The reason for this procedure is that the $100 loss will mean an adjustment to net income. Net income for the XY Firm was $5,000. The entry for net income is shown as entry *b* on figure 15-8. This was for income after extraordinary items. Income from Normal Operations is $5,100. The last three lines of the income statement would be as follows:

Income from Operations	$5,100
Less: Loss on Sale of Truck	100
NET INCOME	$5,000

It is only the Net Income ($5,000) that is closed to the owner's capital account. The statement of changes in financial position however, begins with Income from Operations. Thus, the net income figure has to be adjusted to show any gains or losses to arrive at the correct figure for Income from Operations. This is why gains and losses are placed in the Normal Operations section of the work sheet.

	1981	1980		
Truck	0	4,000		(a) 4,000
Accumulated Depreciation	0	1,000	(a) 1,000	
Charles Byrd, Capital	5,000	0		(b) 5,000
NORMAL OPERATIONS:				
Net Income			(b) 5,000	
Loss on Sale of Truck			(a) 100	
OTHER SOURCES AND USES:				
Sale of Truck			(a) 2,900	

Fig. 15-8. Reconstruction entry for an extraordinary loss.

NON-CASH TRANSACTIONS

There are some types of transactions that do not affect Cash. For example, if a firm buys a new truck on credit (Notes Payable), the entry would be a debit to Truck and a credit to Notes Payable. Therefore, one might assume that the reconstruction entry on the work sheet would be the same as that for the original entry. However, this is not the case. The AICPA feels that a statement of changes in financial position should show all changes in financial resources. Since a firm's ability to borrow is one of its financial resources, changes in the liability accounts must also be shown on the formal statement. This is done even though Cash is not actually affected by the original transaction.

A different type of entry is needed to reconstruct these non-cash transactions on the work sheet. The correct procedure is to record two reconstruction entries. Although the original entry was a debit to Truck and a credit to Notes Payable, it is shown by the following reconstruction entries:

Cash
    Notes Payable
  Borrowed money on a note.
Truck
    Cash
  Bought a truck.

In other words, it is assumed that the cash was borrowed and was then used to buy the truck. When the reconstruction entries are made, the one original transaction will show up as both a source and a use. The formal statement of changes in financial position will also show the transaction as both a source and use of cash.

Hope Book Company
Balance Sheets
December 31, 1980 and 1981

	1981	1980
ASSETS:		
Cash	$ 6,750	$ 5,300
Accounts Receivable	4,970	4,800
Merchandise Inventory	5,000	5,210
Prepaid Rent	1,300	1,200
Investment in X Company	0	4,100
Land	3,000	3,000
Building	15,000	15,000
Accumulated Depreciation	(4,000)	(3,000)
	32,020	35,610
LIABILITIES AND OWNER'S EQUITY:		
Accounts Payable	1,000	4,100
Notes Payable	15,000	10,000
James Hope, Capital	16,020	21,510
	$32,020	$35,610

Additional Data:

a. The owner withdrew $12,000 during the year.
b. Net income was $6,510.
c. The investment in X Company was sold for $6,000.

Fig. 15-9. Balance sheets for the Hope Book Company.

Hope Book Company
Work Sheet for a Statement of Changes in Financial Position
For Year Ended December 31, 1981

	1981	1980	DEBIT	CREDIT
Accounts Receivable	4,970	4,800	(a) 170	
Merchandise Inventory	5,000	5,210		(b) 210
Prepaid Rent	1,300	1,200	(c) 100	
Investment in X Company	0	4,100		(d) 4,100
Land	3,000	3,000		
Building	15,000	15,000		
Accumulated Depreciation	4,000	3,000		(e) 1,000
Accounts Payable	1,000	4,100	(f) 3,100	
Notes Payable	15,000	10,000		(g) 5,000
James Hope, Capital	16,020	21,510	(i) 12,000	(h) 6,510
			SOURCES	USES
NORMAL OPERATIONS:				
Increase in Receivables				(a) 170
Decrease in Inventory			(b) 210	
Increase in Prepaid Rent				(c) 100
Gain on Sale of Investment				(d) 1,900
Depreciation Expense			(e) 1,000	
Decrease in Accounts Payable				(f) 3,100
Net Income			(h) 6,510	
OTHER SOURCES AND USES:				
Sold Investments			(d) 6,000	
Borrowed Money on Note			(g) 5,000	
Withdrawals				(i) 12,000

Fig. 15-10. Work sheet for the Hope Book Company.

An Example

The balance sheets for the Hope Book Company are shown in figure 15-9. The completed work sheet for a statement of changes in financial position appears in figure 15-10. Study the work sheet carefully. The formal statement of changes in financial position is shown in figure 15-11. Note that the bottom line of the statement is the same as the change in the Cash account (found by subtracting the 1980 cash amount from the 1981 cash amount on the balance sheets, figure 15-9).

The statement of changes in financial position can be interpreted as follows. Note that the Income from Operations is the difference between the Net Income ($6,510) and the portion of the income that was an extraordinary gain, $1,900. Thus, the Income from Operations was $4,610. A non-cash expense (Depreciation) was added to Income from Operations. The firm also gained some cash by decreasing part of

Hope Book Company
Statement of Changes in Financial Position
For Year Ended December 31, 1981

SOURCES OF CASH:		
Income from Operations:	$4,610	
Add: Decrease in Inventory	210	
Depreciation Expense	1,000	
Less: Increase in Receivables	(170)	
Increase in Prepaid Rent	(100)	
Decrease in Accounts Payable	(3,100)	
Total Sources from Operations		$ 2,450
Other Sources:		
Sales of Investments		6,000
Borrowed Money on Note		5,000
TOTAL SOURCES OF CASH		13,450
USES OF CASH:		
Withdrawals by the Owner		12,000
INCREASE IN CASH		$ 1,450

Fig. 15-11. Formal statement of changes in financial position for the Hope Book Company.

its inventory ($210). Some of the cash generated by operations was reinvested in the operation of the firm. Some of it went into receivables ($170), prepaid rent ($100), and the largest portion went to pay off the accounts payable ($3,100). Thus despite the net income, the firm was ahead only $2,450 in its Cash account. Since the owner withdrew $12,000, the firm would have experienced financial difficulties had it not sold its investments ($6,000) and borrowed money from the bank ($5,000).

CHANGES IN WORKING CAPITAL

This chapter has emphasized the preparation of the statement of changes in financial position as prepared on a cash basis. Some firms prepare the statement of changes in financial position on a *working capital basis.* In other words, the statement shows the sources and uses of working capital. *Working capital* is defined as current assets minus current liabilities.

The procedures for preparing a statement on the working capital basis are similar to those for preparing a statement on the cash basis. When cash is emphasized, the work sheet analyzes the changes in the non-cash accounts. When working capital is emphasized, the work sheet analyzes the changes in the non-working capital accounts. Thus, the work sheet only shows those accounts that are not current assets or current liabilities.

Refer to the data in figure 15-9. If a work sheet is prepared from that data on a working capital basis, only the non-current accounts are used. Figure 15-12 shows the work sheet. Note that none of the current assets or the current liabilities appears on the work sheet. The

Hope Book Company
Work Sheet for a Statement of Changes in Financial Position
For Year Ended December 31, 1981

	1981	*1980*	DEBIT	CREDIT
Investment in X Company	*0*	*4,100*		*(d) 4,100*
Land	*3,000*	*3,000*		
Building	*15,000*	*15,000*		
Accumulated Depreciation	*4,000*	*3,000*		*(e) 1,000*
James Hope, Capital	*16,020*	*21,510*	*(i) 12,000*	*(h) 6,510*
			SOURCES	USES
NORMAL OPERATIONS:				
Gain on Sale of Investment				*(d) 1,900*
Depreciation Expense			*(e) 1,000*	
Net Income			*(h) 6,510*	
OTHER SOURCES AND USES:				
Sold Investments			*(d) 6,000*	
Withdrawals				*(i) 12,000*

Fig. 15-12. Work sheet for a statement of changes in financial position using the working capital basis.

explanations for the reconstruction entries are the same as given earlier for the cash basis. Note that there are fewer reconstruction entries since a smaller number of accounts are being analyzed. The firm that uses this method is not interested in all effects on cash. Instead, only the net effect on working capital is being analyzed.

A statement of changes in financial position can be prepared on either a cash basis or a working capital basis. Figure 15-13 shows the formal financial statement under the working capital method. Compare figure 15-13 with figure 15-11. Note that the cash basis statement (figure 15-11) is simply an expanded form of the working capital basis statement (figure 15-13).

Hope Book Company
Statement of Changes in Financial Position
For Year Ended December 31, 1981

SOURCES OF WORKING CAPITAL:		
Income from Operations:	$4,610	
Add: Depreciation Expense	1,000	
Total Sources from Operations		$ 5,610
Other Sources:		
Sales of Investments		6,000
TOTAL SOURCES OF WORKING CAPITAL		11,610
USES OF WORKING CAPITAL:		
Withdrawals by the Owner		12,000
DECREASE IN WORKING CAPITAL		$ 390

Fig. 15-13. Formal statement of changes in financial position on a working capital basis.

The formal statement shows that working capital decreased during the year by $390. The accuracy of this figure can be checked by computing the amount of working capital at the beginning of the year and at the end of the year as follows:

	1981	1980
CURRENT ASSETS:		
Cash	$ 6,750	$ 5,300
Accounts Receivable	4,970	4,800
Merchandise Inventory	5,000	5,210
Prepaid Rent	1,300	1,200
Total Current Assets	18,020	16,510
CURRENT LIABILITIES:		
Accounts Payable	1,000	4,100
Notes Payable	15,000	10,000
Total Current Liabilities	16,000	14,100
WORKING CAPITAL	$ 2,020	$ 2,410

The firm began the year with $2,410 of working capital. It ended the year with only $2,020 of working capital. Thus, working capital decreased by $390. The statement of changes in financial position explains why this decrease occurred.

SUMMARY

The statement of changes in financial position is known by many different names including a funds statement, or a statement of sources and uses of cash. The last name is probably the most descriptive since the statement is used to explain where cash came from and where it went. This statement will often answer questions that cannot be explained by either the income statement or the balance sheet.

The preparation of this third financial statement requires the following steps:

1. First, assemble two balance sheets for the firm – one for the beginning of the period and one for the end of the period. From the balance sheets, determine the check figure for the change in cash
2. Next, copy all of the amounts for the non-cash accounts onto a work sheet.
3. Explain the changes in all of the accounts on the work sheet by reconstructing the actual entries that were made to those accounts. If the account for half of the entry is not on the work sheet, place that half of the entry at the bottom of the work sheet in the Sources and Uses section. This section is divided into two parts, one for normal operations and one for other sources and uses.
4. Once all of the non-cash account changes have been explained, the bottom section of the work sheet is used to prepare the formal financial statement.

The only exception to the above guidelines occurs when a firm has some non-cash transactions. The AICPA requires that these non-cash transactions be treated as if they were two separate transactions for purposes of preparing the statement.

REVIEW

1. What is the proper name for the third financial statement?
2. Name three sources of cash other than those from normal operations.
3. Name three uses of cash other than for normal operations.
4. Why is Depreciation Expense added to Income from Operations on the formal statement?
5. Why are only the non-cash accounts examined when it is the Cash account that is being explained?
6. a. Why does a firm need a statement of changes in financial position?
   b. Give examples of situations where a statement of changes in financial position can be a useful tool.
7. Why do bankers like to see the statement of changes in financial position for a firm?

EXERCISES

1. The following information appears on two simple balance sheets of a firm. Prepare a work sheet for a statement of changes in financial position and the formal statement.

	1981	1980
Cash	$400	$100
Merchandise Inventory	190	280
Furniture	500	400
Accumulated Depreciation	(350)	(300)
	740	480
Accounts Payable	340	300
Capital	$400	$180

There were no withdrawals or additional investments during the year.

2. Given the following balance sheets of Trike Company, prepare a work sheet and a formal statement of changes in the financial position for the firm.

	1981	1980
ASSETS:		
Cash	$ 3,200	$ 5,100
Accounts Receivable	5,000	4,000
Equipment	14,000	16,000
Accumulated Depreciation	(6,000)	(5,000)
	16,200	20,100
LIABILITIES AND OWNER'S EQUITY		
Accounts Payable	2,200	14,100
Capital	14,000	6,000
	$16,200	$20,100

Additional Data:

(1) The owner invested an additional $1,000 during the year. There were no withdrawals.

(2) A piece of equipment was sold during the year for $1,700. The equipment had cost $2,000 and had accumulated depreciation of $500.

3. The following are two balance sheets for the Rapid Repair Shop. The net income for the year was $7,800. Prepare the work sheet for a statement of changes in financial position and the formal statement.

	1981	1980
ASSETS:		
Cash	$ 105	$1,270
Accounts Receivable	2,240	1,230
Shop Supplies	1,450	800
Equipment	8,300	4,200
Accumulated Depreciation	(2,200)	(1,050)
Land	5,000	0
	14,895	6,450
LIABILITIES AND OWNER'S EQUITY		
Accounts Payable	2,200	300
Notes Payable	5,000	0
Art Alexander, Capital	7,695	6,150
	$14,895	$6,450

PROBLEMS

1. Given the following balance sheets for Meta Company, prepare a formal statement of changes in financial position for 1982.

	1982	1981
ASSETS:		
Cash	$ 2,000	$ 1,000
Accounts Receivable	1,000	500
Inventory	8,000	6,000
Investments	0	1,000
Equipment	10,000	8,000
Accumulated Depreciation	(3,000)	(2,500)
	18,000	14,000
LIABILITIES AND OWNER'S EQUITY		
Accounts Payable	1,000	500
Wages Payable	1,000	500
Bonds Payable	8,000	10,000
Capital	8,000	3,000
	$18,000	$14,000

Additional Data:

(1) Net Income for the year 1982 was $7,000.

(2) Withdrawals during the year were $2,000.

(3) The only equipment sold during the year was a fully depreciated piece that had cost $1,000. It was sold for $100 and the gain is included in the net income figure above.

(4) The long term investments were sold for $1,300. The gain is included in the above net income figure.

2. The following information appears on the two balance sheets for the Fort Night Company. Prepare a work sheet and a formal statement of changes in financial position.

	1981	1980
ASSETS:		
Cash	$16,459	$ 3,740
Accounts Receivable	7,380	13,520
Merchandise Inventory	7,937	18,293
Land	6,000	12,000
Building	35,000	35,000
Accumulated Depreciation	(6,000)	(4,000)
	66,776	78,553
LIABILITIES AND OWNER'S EQUITY:		
Accounts Payable	12,880	9,750
Mortgage Payable	23,500	25,000
Denise Knight, Capital	30,396	43,803
	$66,776	$78,553

Additional Data:

(1) The owner withdrew $12,000 during the year.

(2) A piece of land was sold for $7,500.

3. The net changes in the balance sheet accounts of X Company for the year 1980 are shown below:

	DEBIT	CREDIT
Cash	$37,400	
Investments		$25,000
Land	3,200	
Buildings	35,000	
Machinery	6,000	
Office Equipment		1,500
Accumulated Depreciation:		
Buildings		2,000
Machinery		900
Office Equipment	600	
Capital		52,800

Additional Data:

(1) The investments were sold for $27,500.

(2) A building which cost $45,000 and had a depreciated basis of $40,500 was sold for $50,000.

(3) The following entry was made to record an exchange of an old machine for a new one:

Machinery	13,000	
Accumulated Depreciation: Machinery	5,000	
Machinery		7,000
Cash		11,000
To record an exchange.		

(4) A fully depreciated office machine which cost $1,500 was thrown away. The account balance was written off the books.

(5) There were no withdrawals or investments by the owner during the year.

Using this information, prepare a formal statement of changes in financial position for the year.

4. Use the data in problem 2 to prepare a work sheet and a formal statement of changes in financial position on a working capital basis.

16 Receivables Management

OBJECTIVES After studying this chapter, the student will be able to:

- Discuss the practice of matching current bad debt losses against current sales.
- Account for bad debts using both the allowance and direct write-off methods.
- Estimate bad debts by aging accounts receivable or by using a percentage of accounts receivable.
- Find the amount of the adjusting entry for bad debts by taking a percentage of credit sales or net sales.
- Make the journal entry for recovery of an account previously written off.

When goods or services are sold on credit, there may be customers who never pay the balances of their accounts. A firm usually tries to collect the money owed by its debtors. However, in some cases this is impossible. These uncollectible accounts are called *bad debts*. Most firms expect some losses from bad debts. However, because they feel that their sales are increased by offering credit, they continue to do so. As long as bad debt losses are not too high, a firm earns a greater net income by selling on credit. Thus, bad debts are considered to be one of the expenses of doing business. When an account receivable is determined to be bad (uncollectible), an entry must be made in the firm's accounting records. There are two ways of recording bad debts. One is known as the direct write-off method. The other is the allowance method. The direct write-off method is the easier method to use for recording bad debts.

METHODS OF BAD-DEBT ACCOUNTING

The Direct Write-off Method

Using the direct write-off method, an entry is made debiting Bad Debt Expense and crediting Accounts Receivable. Before making this entry, referred to as *writing off an account,* every effort should be made to collect. After the firm has unsuccessfully written and called the customer, a collection agent should be hired to try to collect the account. If this final step fails, the account should be written off since it is no longer an asset.

If a firm decides that the $100 account of Tom Rose is bad, it would make the following entry:

Bad Debt Expense	100	
Accounts Receivable		100
To write off bad debt of Tom Rose.		

The above entry takes the $100 out of the asset account and puts it into an expense account. The account Bad Debt Expense is shown on the income statement with all of the other selling expenses.

Violation of the Matching Principle. Although the direct write-off method is easy to use, most accountants do not approve of it because it violates the matching principle. Recall that the matching principle says that revenues and expenses should be matched to the period to which they apply.

In this case, Bad Debt Expense should be matched to the year in which the bad debt occurred. However, when can it be said that a bad debt occurs? Is it when the sale is made, or is it at a later time when the firm gives up trying to collect the money? The answer is that the loss occurs when the sale is made. The bad debt is incurred when the customer carries the goods out of the store without paying for them. The expense occurs at this time, although the firm does not know it until a later time. Since the expense occurs in the period in which the sale is made, it should be matched to that same period. Because of the interval spent trying to collect the debt, the direct write-off method usually fails to accomplish this matching. Collection may take a year or more, and by the time the entry is made, the firm has entered a new accounting period. Thus, the expense on the income statement is not matched to the period when the expense really occurred. For this reason, the direct write-off method is not commonly used.

However, the direct write-off method may be used in certain cases, such as when the bad debts are small in comparison with total sales. Here, the materiality principle of accounting offsets the matching principle. The *materiality principle* says that other principles may be violated if the violation does not materially affect the financial statements. (See page 425.)

THE ALLOWANCE METHOD

Another method of recording bad debts is the allowance method. Most firms use this method when accounting for bad debts. The allowance method follows the matching principle. Hence, the bad debt expense is recorded in the same period in which the sale is made. This is done by estimating the bad debt expense for the period.

For example, assume that at year-end a firm has accounts receivable of $10,000. Based on past experience, the firm estimates that about $500 of this amount will become bad debts. Using this estimate, the firm makes an adjusting entry in which Bad Debt Expense is debited for $500. Even though the firm does not know which debts will turn out to be bad, it is reasonably sure that the bad accounts will total about $500. Thus, Bad Debt Expense is debited for the expected loss of $500. The credit, however, is not made to Accounts Receivable even though it is the Accounts Receivable that is decreased. The credit is made to a new account because the decrease in value is simply an estimate. Hence, a contra account (or valuation account) is credited. The contra account is called *Allowance for Bad Debts.* Thus the entry to record the bad debts for the year is:

December 31	Bad Debt Expense	500	
	Allowance for Bad Debts		500
	To record expected bad debt loss.		

The Current Asset section of the balance sheet on December 31 is shown as follows:

Accounts Receivable	$10,000	
Less: Allowance for Bad Debts	500	
Net Realizable Value		$9,500

All three amounts should be shown on the balance sheet. The $10,000 is the total receivables that the firm is trying to collect. The $500 is the amount that the firm does not expect to collect. The $9,500, called *net realizable value,* is the true value of the firm's receivables. This $9,500 (not the $10,000) is added to the firm's other assets.

In effect, the Allowance for Bad Debts is an amount set aside to absorb any future losses. When the firm writes off an account, the allowance account is used to absorb the write-off. For example, assume that a firm using the allowance method finds out that a customer who owes $88 has filed for bankruptcy. This means that the firm will no longer be able to collect from the customer. To write off the account, the following entry is made:

January 2	Allowance for Bad Debts	88	
	Accounts Receivable		88
	To write off the account of Ted Miles.		

The receivable account is credited since that asset is no longer worth anything. The debit, however, is not to an expense because the expense was recorded last year. Instead, the allowance account, which was set up to absorb last year's bad debts, is debited.

If no other entries have been recorded other than the above write-off, the new balance sheet will look like this:

Accounts Receivable	$9,912	
Less: Allowance for Bad Debts	412	
Net Realizable Value		$9,500

Note that the write-off of the bad debt had no effect on the total assets of the firm. The bad debt had been expected. Thus, it had already been deducted from the assets.

For the most part, the allowance method of bad-debt accounting is not difficult. Only two entries are made. The first entry is a debit to

Bad Debt Expense, and a credit to Allowance for Bad Debts. This entry is made at the end of the period as an adjusting entry. The second entry is made when a particular bad debt is discovered. It debits the Allowance for Bad Debts and credits Accounts Receivable.

ESTIMATING BAD DEBTS

The most difficult part of accounting for bad debts is making an accurate estimate for the adjusting entry. Bad debt expense may be estimated in four ways. Two ways are based on an income statement account, and two are based on a balance sheet account.

An estimate based on the income statement is made by taking

- a percentage of credit sales, or
- a percentage of total (net) sales.

An estimate based on the balance sheet is determined by

- taking a percentage of accounts receivable, or
- aging of accounts rcccivable.

Estimates Based on the Income Statement

Percentage of credit sales. Theoretically, the best method of estimating bad debt expense is to take a percentage of credit sales. This method matches the expense to the cause of the expense. To use this method, a firm must have past experience upon which to base its estimate.

Suppose a firm has determined that about 1% of its credit sales have gone bad (been uncollectible) in the past. The account balances for the firm are shown in figure 16-1. Note that a balance from last year is still left in the Allowance account. Two-thirds of the firm's sales ($200,000) were made on credit. Thus, based on past experience, this year's bad debt expense will be $2,000 (1% of $200,000.) The expense will be recorded as follows:

Bad Debt Expense	2,000	
Allowance for Bad Debts		2,000
To record expected bad debt loss.		

The balance sheet will appear as follows:

Accounts Receivable	$30,000	
Less: Allowance for Bad Debts	2,100	
Net Realizable Value		$27,900

Note that the $2,000 added to the Allowance account this year is combined with the balance that was already in the account ($100).

Accounts Rcccivablc		*Allowance for Bad Debts*		*Sales*	
$30,000			*$100*		*$300,000*

Fig. 16-1. Account balances before recording adjusting entry.

Percentage of total sales. The second estimation method is done by taking a percentage of total sales. In other words, the total of credit sales plus cash sales is used. This method is easier than taking a percent of credit sales because total sales are given as the Sales account balance. Credit sales, on the other hand, must be computed separately. Thus, many firms base their estimates on total sales because of the availability of the figure. The second method is usually as accurate as the first, as long as the relationship between credit sales and cash sales stays the same from year to year.

Assume that the firm in figure 16-1 uses total sales as its base. Past experience has shown that bad debts normally make up about three-quarters of 1% (or .75%) of total sales. Thus, bad debt expense will be $2,250 (.0075 X $300,000). The entry will be:

Bad Debt Expense	2,250	
Allowance for Bad Debts		2,250
To record expected bad debt loss.		

The current asset section of the balance sheet based on figure 16-1 and this method is shown in the following way:

Accounts Receivable	$30,000	
Less: Allowance for Bad Debts	2,350	
Net Realizable Value		$27,650

Note that when either of the methods based on the income statement is used, the journal entry is for the amount calculated. The calculations for both methods are based on an income statement account (Sales), and thus, result in the balance of an income statement account (Bad Debt Expense). This means that a previous balance in the Allowance account has no effect on the journal entry.

Estimates Based on the Balance Sheet

Percentage of Accounts Receivable. Some firms base their bad debt estimates on the balance of Accounts Receivable. This is done by determining what percentage of accounts receivable have been bad debts in the past. Continuing with the example in figure 16-1, assume that 5% of $30,000 (accounts receivable) fall into this category. Thus an Allowance account is needed equal to 5% of the $30,000 (accounts receivable) or $1,500. Since there is already a $100 balance in the Allowance account, the entry is made for only $1,400. The journal entry is:

Bad Debt Expense	1,400	
Allowance for Bad Debts		1,400
To record expected bad debt loss.		

Note the difference between this method and the two income statement-based methods. In the first two methods the bad debt expense is estimated and the entry is for the exact amount calculated. In this third method, however, the proper balance for the Allowance account is computed. Thus, the entry is for the amount calculated less what was already in the account. The balance sheet after the entry appears as follows:

Accounts Receivable	$30,000	
Less: Allowance for Bad Debts	1,500	
Net Realizable Value		$28,500

Aging Accounts Receivable. The last method of estimating bad debts is known as *aging accounts receivable.* This method is similar to the method which uses a percentage of accounts receivable, except that it is more exact. The aging method uses different percentages for accounts receivable of different ages. The *age* of an account indicates how long it is overdue. This method assumes that the older an account, the more apt it is to be bad. Thus, the firm first determines the age of each receivable.

For example, the firm whose accounts are shown in figure 16-1 might determine the following ages of its $30,000 of receivables:

Less than 30 days old	$25,000
31–60 days old	3,000
61–90 days old	1,800
Over 90 days old	200
	$30,000

Those customers whose accounts are long past due are probably in financial trouble. Thus, there is a much greater danger of incurring a bad debt from an old account. Therefore, instead of using one percentage for all receivables, different percentages are used for each class of receivables.

For instance, the firm may determine that there is only a 1% bad-debt risk in receivables that are less than thirty days old. The risk on receivables that are from thirty-one to sixty days old is about 10%. Receivables that are sixty-one to ninety days old have a 25% risk. Of those receivables that are over ninety days old, 50% may be uncollectible. The firm performs the following calculation to get the balance needed in the Allowance account:

1% of $25,000 =	$250
10% of $3,000 =	300
25% of $1,800 =	450
50% of $200 =	100
Total Balance Needed	$1,100

Since there is already $100 in the Allowance account, a $1,000 entry is made to bring the balance up to the needed amount as follows:

Bad Debt Expense	1,000	
Allowance for Bad Debts		1,000
To record expected bad debt loss.		

The Current Asset section of the balance sheet is shown in the following way:

Accounts Receivable	$30,000	
Less: Allowance for Bad Debts	1,100	
Net Realizable Value		$28,900

Note that when either of the balance sheet-based methods is used, the entry will *not* be for the amount calculated; it will be for the amount calculated less what was already in the account. The two methods are based on a balance sheet account (Accounts Receivable). The result then, is the balance of a balance sheet account (Allowance for Bad Debts). This means that any previous balance in the Allowance account has to be considered before the entry is made.

RECOVERY OF AN ACCOUNT PREVIOUSLY WRITTEN OFF

There are times when an account that has been written off is finally paid. When this happens, two entries are required. The first entry reinstates the receivable on the books. For instance, assume that Ted Miles paid the $88 that was written off as a bad debt earlier in this chapter. The first entry would be:

Accounts Receivable	88	
Allowance for Bad Debts		88
To reinstate account previously written off.		

Note that this is just the reverse of the entry that was made to write off the account. In effect, it says that the write-off entry was wrong – this was not a bad debt. Since a mistake was made, the reinstatement corrects the mistake. Once the account is back on the books, the regular entry is made for the collection of an account. In this case it is:

Cash	88	
Accounts Receivable		88
Ted Miles paid his bill.		

If only part of a previously written off account is collected, the reinstatement entry is made for only the amount collected. For example, if the bankruptcy trustee for Ted Miles sends the firm $20 on the account, the two journal entries would be made for only $20.

Practice Problem

The Bilge Pump Company began operating in 1979. They estimate their bad debts at 4% of year-end accounts receivable. Record the following information as journal entries for the firm:

December 31, 1979:	The year's sales were $200,000 and accounts receivable at year end are $20,000. (Give the adjusting entry.)
May 7, 1980:	Wrote off the account of Joe Jackson, $247.
June 9, 1980:	Wrote off the account of Bob Walker, $500.
December 31, 1980:	The year's sales were $300,000 and accounts receivable at year end are $22,000. (Give the adjusting entry.)

March 3, 1981:	Joe Jackson paid the $247 written off last year.
June 29, 1981:	Wrote off the account of Dale Rowe, $1,200.
December 31, 1981:	The year's sales were $400,000 and accounts receivable at year end are $25,000. (Give the adjusting entry.)

Solution

The completed journal should appear as shown in figure 16-2.

GENERAL JOURNAL Page ____

Date		Account Titles and Explanation	Post. Ref.	Debit	Credit
1979					
Dec.	31	Bad Debts Expense		800 00	
		Allowance for Bad Debts			800 00
		Adjusting entry.			
1980					
May	7	Allowance for Bad Debts		247 00	
		Accounts Receivable			247 00
		Wrote off account of Joe Jackson.			
June	9	Allowance for Bad Debts		500 00	
		Accounts Receivable			500 00
		Wrote off account of Bob Walker.			
Dec.	31	Bad Debt Expense		827 00	
		Allowance for Bad Debts			827 00
		Adjusting entry.			
1981					
Mar.	3	Accounts Receivable		247 00	
		Allowance for Bad Debts			247 00
		Reinstated Joe Jackson's account.			
	3	Cash		247 00	
		Accounts Receivable			247 00
		Joe Jackson paid his account.			
June	29	Allowance for Bad Debts		1200 00	
		Accounts Receivable			1200 00
		Wrote off account of Dale Rowe.			
Dec.	31	Bad Debt Expense		1073 00	
		Allowance for Bad Debts			1073 00
		Adjusting entry.			

Fig. 16-2. Journal entries for the Bilge Pump Company.

SUMMARY

Bad debts result from the inability of a firm to collect payment on a portion of the goods or services sold on credit. The two ways to account for bad debts are: (1) the direct write-off method and (2) the allowance method. The direct write-off method is easier to use. However, it is not usually acceptable under the rules of financial accounting since it violates the matching principle.

When the allowance method is used, an adjustment is made to the Bad Debt Expense account only once each period. Under the allowance method the bad debt expense is estimated for the period. The four ways of estimating bad debts are:

- Take a percentage of credit sales.
- Take a percentage of total (net) sales.
- Take a percentage of year-end receivables.
- Age the receivables.

The first two ways are income-statement oriented. An income statement account is used to calculate another income statement account. The last two ways are balance-sheet oriented. A balance sheet account is used to calculate another balance sheet account balance.

If an account that has been written off is paid, two entries are needed. The first entry puts the account back on the books. The second entry records the routine collection of that account.

REVIEW

1. When does a bad debt loss actually occur?
2. How does the direct write-off method violate the matching principle?
3. Under what circumstances is the direct write-off method acceptable?
4. What is the principle of materiality?
5. Why are estimated bad debts credited to a contra account instead of to Accounts Receivable?
6. What account will be debited when an account is written off using the direct write-off method?
7. What account will be debited when an account is written off using the allowance method?
8. If a firm using the allowance method writes off ten bad accounts during a year, how many entries will be made to the Bad Debts Expense account?
9. Theoretically, what is the best method of estimating bad debts?
10. Which is the better method of estimating bad debts – taking a percentage of receivables or aging the receivables?

EXERCISES

1. A firm intends to write off a $37 account of Judy Renaldo. Give the entry under each of the following assumptions:
   a. The firm uses the direct write-off method.
   b. The firm uses the allowance method.

2. A firm bases its bad debt estimate on an aging of accounts receivable. The year-end receivables fall into the following age classes:

1 to 30 days old	$17,000	(2%)
31 to 60 days old	5,200	(10%)
61 to 90 days old	2,000	(30%)
Over 90 days old	1,000	(60%)

The bad debt risk of each age class is shown in parentheses in the right-hand column. Give the year-end adjusting entry under each of the following assumptions:

a. The allowance account has a credit balance of $200.
b. The allowance account has a debit balance of $200.

3. On December 31, 1980, a firm estimated that it would have bad debts equal to 1% of its $865,000 of credit sales. On May 17, 1981, the $400 account of Bob East was written off. On June 20, 1981, Bob East paid the $400 he owed. Give the entries required in this situation.

4. The Round Company uses the allowance method in accounting for bad debts. During 1980 it sold $432,900 of merchandise on credit, including a $232 sale to Tom Prince. On December 31, 1980, it provided an allowance for bad debts equal to one-fourth of 1% (.25%) of its 1980 charge sales. On February 17, 1981, it wrote off as a bad debt the $232 Tom Prince account. Give the adjusting entry and the entry to write off the bad debt.

PROBLEMS

1. The following amounts are taken from the trial balance of Indy Company on December 31, 1981:

	Debit	Credit
Accounts Receivable	$130,000	
Allowance for Bad Debts		$ 400
Sales		250,000
Sales Returns and Allowances	2,500	
Sales Discounts	4,800	

Give the journal entries for the following situations:

a. Assuming that the firm estimates bad debts to be 1% of net sales, give the adjusting entry required as of December 31, 1981.
b. Assuming that the firm ages the accounts receivable and estimates that $2,000 of the total will ultimately prove to be uncollectible, give the adjusting entry required as of December 31, 1981.
c. The $500 account of Claudia Smitt proved to be uncollectible on January 15, 1982.
d. On March 8, 1982, Claudia Smitt paid the $500 that she owed.

2. The A-to-Z Company has the following account balances at the end of the year. Prepare a trial balance from the accounts, and complete a work sheet from the additional data given. Prepare an income statement and a balance sheet. Finally, record the closing entries.

Cash	$ 2,000
Accounts Receivable	10,000
Allowance for Bad Debts	150
Merchandise Inventory	10,000
Equipment	20,000
Richard Bettle, Capital	26,000
Sales	50,000
Purchases	30,000
Purchase Returns	1,000
Wage Expense	3,000
Rent Expense	1,400
Insurance Expense	750

Information necessary for adjusting entries:

(1) The physical inventory shows $12,000 worth of merchandise on hand.

(2) Management estimates that about 2% of the accounts receivable are uncollectible.

(3) The equipment was purchased on April 1 of this year and is expected to have a ten-year life and a salvage value of $1,000.

(4) Rent is $100 per month and the last rent payment, on December 1, was for $300 to cover the months of December, January, and February.

(5) Accrued wages are $220.

(6) The balance of the Insurance Expense account represents a three-year fire insurance policy bought on July 1.

3. A new firm began business in 1979. It uses the allowance method of accounting for bad debts. Bad Debt Expense is estimated to be 1% of net sales. Give the journal entries for the following situations.

December 31, 1979:	Net sales for the year were $250,000. Give the adjusting entry.
May 1, 1980:	Wrote off the account of Tom Houk, $470.
June 30, 1980:	Wrote off the account of Ann Shakespear, $2,100.
December 31, 1980:	Net sales for the year were $300,000. Give the adjusting entry.
March 19, 1981:	Wrote off the account of Fred Wagner, $182.
December 1, 1981:	Tom Houk paid $470 that was written off last year.
December 31, 1981:	Net sales for the year were $400,000. Give the adjusting entry.
June 27, 1982:	Wrote off the account of Stephanie Fox, $1,585.

August 18, 1982: Received a check for $18 for an account written off last year from Fred Wagner's bankruptcy trustee. A note with the check stated that Fred's assets had been liquidated and this was the last payment the firm would receive.

December 31, 1982: Net sales for the year were $400,000. Give the adjusting entry.

4. Make the entries for Problem 3, but this time, assume that the firm uses the aging method of estimating bad debts. The following are the amounts estimated to be uncollectible by the aging schedule as of each December 31.

December 31, 1979 = $2,450
December 31, 1980 = $2,000
December 31, 1981 = $2,000
December 31, 1982 = $1,900

17 Acquisition of Fixed Assets

OBJECTIVES

After studying this chapter, the student will be able to:

- Compute the original cost of an asset.
- Allocate costs to Land, Land Improvements, and Building accounts.
- Record the acquisition of fixed assets.
- Define capital and revenue expenditures.
- Distinguish between ordinary and extraordinary repairs.

Fixed assets are tangible assets that will be used for more than one year in the operation of a firm. Fixed assets may also be called *plant assets* or *property, plant,* and *equipment.* Examples of fixed assets are buildings, land, furniture, vehicles, and machinery. The *useful life* of a plant asset is the period of time that the firm expects to use it.

ORIGINAL COST OF AN ASSET

The *original cost* of an asset includes all reasonable and necessary expenses of acquiring the asset and putting it into service. Thus, original cost includes such expenses as sales tax, transportation, and installation. Interest expense, expenses resulting from carelessness or errors, and other costs which do not increase the usefulness of the asset are not included in the original cost but are charged to expense accounts.

Cash discounts are deducted from the original cost. If the asset is built by the firm, the cost equals all costs of construction. Once the total original cost of an asset is determined, a debit is made to an asset account for that amount.

ALLOCATING COST TO LAND, LAND IMPROVEMENT, AND BUILDING ACCOUNTS

Some fixed assets are depreciated. In other words, the cost is allocated throughout the years in which the asset is used. Land is one asset that is not depreciated. Therefore, the account for land is handled differently than those for land improvements or buildings. If a firm buys land and a building for one price, a separate cost must be allocated to each.

Allocations for this purpose are based on an appraisal value or tax-assessed value. An *appraisal value* is the value assigned by an expert. For example, land and a building are bought for $120,000. The land has an appraised value of $25,000 and the building a value of $75,000. Thus, the cost is allocated as follows:

	Appraised Value	Cost
Land	$ 25,000	$25,000/$100,000 X $120,000 = $ 30,000
Building	75,000	$75,000/$100,000 X $120,000 = 90,000
Totals	$100,000	$120,000

Since the land makes up 25% of the total appraisal value (25,000/100,000), it is assumed that the land is 25% of the total purchase price. The entry to record this purchase at $120,000 is:

Land	30,000	
Building	90,000	
Cash		120,000
To record the purchase of land and building.		

Included in the cost of the land are the title search fees, surveying costs, back taxes, clearing or grading costs, real estate agent's fees, and legal fees. If the land is to be used for a new plant and an old building must be torn down, the cost of tearing down the old structure, less any salvage proceeds, is also added to the cost of the land.

The account Land Improvements is used for items that are not as permanent as the land, but that are not associated with the building. Such items are parking lots, driveways, fences, outdoor lights, and trees and shrubs. Land improvements should be placed in a separate account and depreciated over their estimated useful lives.

CAPITAL AND REVENUE EXPENDITURES

Any amount spent on a fixed asset must be classified as a revenue or a capital expenditure. A *revenue expenditure* does not increase the value of a fixed asset; it merely maintains the asset or keeps it in shape. The benefits of a revenue expenditure are used up during the current accounting period. Thus, revenue expenditures are shown as expenses on the income statement. Routine repairs such as painting, lubrication, and changing oil and spark plugs in a car are examples of revenue expenditures. These normal repairs recur and their benefits are used up in a short time.

On the other hand, amounts spent to increase the efficiency of assets are capital expenditures. A *capital expenditure* is an amount spent for the purchase of fixed assets and for improvements that will increase the value of fixed assets. A capital expenditure will benefit the firm for several years.

Examples include adding a room to a building, putting in air conditioning, and adding an escalator. Costs that add to the life of an asset or increase its utility are recorded as assets.

Revenue expenditures maintain the asset as it was; capital expenditures improve the asset. Revenue expenditures are shown on the income statement, while capital expenditures affect the balance sheet.

When to Capitalize or Expense

Most firms will set a limit for the minimum amount which will be capitalized. To *capitalize* an item means to record it as a capital expenditure. If the amount spent is below this minimum, it will be expensed even if the benefits will last more than a year. This rule follows the materiality principle. The materiality principle as explained in chapter 16, states that if an item is too small to have an effect on the financial statements, the rules may be ignored. In other words, the materiality principle allows the rules to be broken if the costs of following them exceed the benefits.

For example, a stapler is assumed to have a life of more than one year and thus meets the definition of a fixed asset. It should be capitalized and depreciated over its useful life. If the stapler cost $2.00 and has a life of ten years, this means a depreciation of $.20 per year ($2.00/10) should be recorded. It would cost more than $.20 a year to make the entry to show the depreciation. Thus, it is not worth the cost. So, following the materiality principle, the stapler is written off as a $2.00 expense.

Extraordinary Repairs

An *extraordinary repair* is a capital expenditure that extends the life of the asset. A major repair or overhaul is an extraordinary repair and is recorded as a debit to Accumulated Depreciation. This entry increases the book value of the asset. Book value is cost of the asset minus accumulated depreciation. Since the life is lengthened, the book value is increased by canceling part of the past depreciation.

As an example, a firm bought a car for $4,000. The useful life was set at four years. The firm depreciated the car for three years at $1,000 per year ($4,000/4). Thus, the book value at the end of three years was $1,000:

Cost	$4,000
Less: Accumulated Depreciation	3,000
Book value	$1,000

At the start of the fourth year, the engine was overhauled and other major repairs were made which were expected to add two more years to the life of the car. The cost of these extraordinary repairs was $800, and this entry was made:

	Debit	Credit
Accumulated Depreciation	800	
Cash		800
To record extraordinary repairs on the car.		

Now the Accumulated Depreciation account looks like this:

Accumulated Depreciation

Debit		Credit	
Extraordinary repair	*800*	*1,000*	First year depreciation
		1,000	Second year depreciation
		1,000	Third year depreciation
		2,200	***Balance***

The book value is now $1,800, calculated as follows:

Cost	$4,000
Less: Accumulated Depreciation	2,200
Book value	$1,800

This book value will be depreciated over the remaining useful life of three years. So the depreciation for each of those years will be $1,800/3 or $600.

SUMMARY

Fixed assets are tangible assets that will be used for more than one year in the operation of the firm. When a fixed asset is acquired, an entry is made debiting an asset account for the original cost. The original cost includes all reasonable and necessary expenses of acquiring the asset and putting it into service. Since land may not be depreciated, the cost for an asset consisting of both land and buildings should be allocated to separate accounts for Land, Land Improvement, and Building.

Any amount spent on a fixed asset must be classified as a revenue or a capital expenditure. A capital expenditure benefits several accounting periods. A revenue expenditure does not increase the value of an asset. Its benefits are used up during the current accounting period. An extraordinary repair is a capital expenditure that extends the useful life of an asset. An extraordinary repair should be recorded as a debit to Accumulated Depreciation to increase the book value of the asset.

REVIEW

1. What is a fixed asset?
2. What other names may be used for fixed assets?
3. Why does cost have to be allocated to the land and building accounts?
4. What is a land improvement? Give examples.
5. Define the terms capital expenditure and revenue expenditure. Give examples of each.
6. What is the materiality principle? How does it apply to capital expenditures?
7. What is an extraordinary repair?
8. Describe the entry that would be made to record an extraordinary repair, and explain the reason for this entry.
9. What is book value?
10. Which of the following would be classified as fixed assets?
    a. Truck
    b. Plant
    c. Inventory
    d. Office supplies
    e. Patents
    f. Typewriter used by the secretary
    g. Typewriter for sale in an office equipment store

EXERCISES

1. A firm bought a machine with a price of $1,000 and terms 2/10, n/30. The firm paid within the discount period. Sales tax was $40. The machine required a special electrical outlet and the electrician charged $30 for the installation. What is the cost of the machine?

2. A firm bought land and building for $180,000 cash. An appraiser said that the land was worth $60,000 and the building was worth $140,000. Allocate the costs and give the entry which should be made.

3. Dart Company bought land for $100,000. The land was subject to delinquent property taxes of $6,900. Dart Company immediately paid these taxes, in addition to the interest charges and penalties totaling $625 applicable to the delinquent taxes. The land was immediately placed in use as a parking lot. During the first year of use, the property taxes amounted to $1,800. Give the entry for the purchase of the land.

4. Scott Ward owns a grocery store. During the year he spent the following amounts:
   a. $125 – For a set of snow tires for his delivery truck.
   b. $3,000 – For construction of a parking lot for the convenience of his customers.
   c. $75 – For a new tailpipe and muffler on his delivery truck.
   d. $500 – For painting the interior and exterior of his store.
   e. $650 – For new electric wiring throughout the store.
   f. $25 – For new glass to replace the broken pane in the meat case.

   Which of these are revenue expenditures which should be expensed?

5. A firm has owned a machine for five years. The original cost was $8,000. The estimated life was eight years and the machine has been depreciated $1,000 per year for the last five years. At the beginning of the sixth year, major repairs costing $1,000 are made which should extend the life of the machine two years. Make the journal entry to record the major repairs. What will the depreciation expense be for the sixth year?

PROBLEMS

1. Top Company bought a machine with a price of $10,000 on May 1. The terms were 1/10, n/30. Sales tax came to $300. Freight charges were $100. A special cabinet had to be built to hold the machine at a cost of $40. While lifting the machine onto the cabinet, an employee dropped the machine and damaged it. It cost $35 to repair the damage. The employees had to be trained to use the new machine, necessitating a training program that cost $95. Three months after acquisition, $20 was spent to lubricate the machine.

   Determine the cost and make all journal entries to record the above information.

2. Write the following headings across the top of a piece of paper:

Land	Land Improvements	Building	Other Accounts

Classify the following amounts in one of these four categories. Identify each amount by letter and list in the proper column.

a. Cost of property – land and building which is to be torn down	$150,000
Tax assessments: Land – $90,000; Building – $30,000	
b. Title search fees	1,000
c. Back taxes charged to purchaser	450
d. Grading the land	960
e. Tearing down old building	2,000
f. Sale of salvaged materials from old building	500
g. Architect's fee for designing new building	900
h. Surveying costs	200
i. Cost of new building	250,000
j. Landscaping	1,200
k. Cost of paved parking lot	3,000
l. Outdoor lights for parking lot	1,500
m. Window broken by the landscaper while planting new trees	50
n. Fine assessed for polluting the air during construction of building	100
o. Property taxes for first year	300

3. Record the following transactions for the Space Firm in journal entry form.

June 1: Purchased a used truck for $2,000 cash.
1: Truck was badly rusted and needed repainting. Cost of painting, $500, was put on account.
1: Replaced the battery in truck for $50 cash.
3: Bought gas for truck and paid $10 cash.
4: Bought a pencil sharpener for the office for $5 cash.
5: Paid for the paint job on the truck.
6: Driver backed the truck into the garage causing $200 damage to the truck and $100 damage to the garage. Both repair bills were paid in cash.
7: Installed a $300 CB radio in the truck. This amount was put on account.
9: Bought spark plugs for $30 cash and installed them in the truck.
9: Purchased an answering service for the office at a cost of $150.

18 Depreciation Practices

OBJECTIVES After studying this chapter, the student will be able to:

- Identify the four common depreciation methods.
- Describe the recording and reporting processes used in depreciation accounting.
- Calculate depreciation using each of the four depreciation methods.
- Explain the advantages of accelerated depreciation methods.
- Define the following terms: depreciation, scrap value, book value.

The major topic of this chapter is the allocation of the cost of fixed assets. Although a fixed asset does not change in form through use, it cannot be used forever. It is useful to a firm for a specific length of time, called its *service life*. The cost of a fixed asset must be allocated over the service life of the asset.

Each time period in the asset's life is charged with its proportionate share of the asset's cost. A charge made to record a portion of the asset's cost is called depreciation expense. If this charge (debit to expense) were not made, all of the cost of the asset would have to be charged as an expense in the time period in which the asset is taken out of service. This would cause the income of the final period to be understated and that of preceding periods to be overstated. In addition, the value of the asset on the balance sheet would not reflect its actual value during the time in which it was in use.

Depreciation is an allocation process which is based on an estimate. It is not an asset valuation technique. The object is not to show the proper value on the balance sheet. Depreciation expense does not show physical depreciation or decline in market value. Its purpose is to allocate the cost of an asset over the useful life of the asset. The matching principle, which states that revenue should be matched with the expenses incurred in earning the revenue of the period, creates the need to estimate depreciation.

Depreciation is a means of allocating the cost of assets which have a life of more than a year. An asset that does not have a limited useful life, such as land, may not be depreciated. Thus, a separate account must be kept for land. If a combination of depreciable and nondepreciable property is purchased for a lump sum, as for example, buildings and land, the total cost must be apportioned according to the value of each at the time of purchase (See chapter 17.)

RECORDING DEPRECIATION

At the end of each period, a firm will need to make an adjusting entry to record depreciation expense. This process was discussed in detail in chapter 7. A standard entry is made as follows:

Depreciation Expense	XXXX	
Accumulated Depreciation		XXXX
To record depreciation for period.		

Note that the fixed asset account is not credited. Instead, a contra-asset account, Accumulated Depreciation, is used to store or *accumulate* the depreciation taken on a fixed asset.

There are several reasons for using this method of recording depreciation. First, it is useful to know the original cost of a fixed asset. This value could not be easily determined if the asset had been credited for depreciation. Second, it is desirable to show on the balance sheet both cost and accumulated depreciation. The reader may then evaluate the provision which has been made for depreciation. Remember, the amount recorded as depreciation is an estimate. It may be incorrect and require a revision. Thus, it is better to credit a separate account. Those examining the statements can then judge for themselves the adequacy of the provision for depreciation.

In preserving the cost value, two accounts must be kept for each asset that is subject to depreciation. The first of these will show the cost of the asset. The second will show the accumulated depreciation on the asset. A third account (Depreciation Expense) will be used to record the expense charged for depreciation for each time period.

Since the depreciation expense account is an expense, it is closed to the Income Summary at the end of the fiscal period in the same manner as other expense accounts. The accumulated depreciation account is a contra-asset account, and thus is a real account. It will stay on the firm's books for as long as the asset is owned by the firm. The balance of the accumulated depreciation account increases each year.

On the balance sheet, the original cost of the asset should be shown. The accumulated depreciation that goes along with the asset should be shown separately. Original cost minus accumulated depreciation equals the book value of the asset. Study the example of the balance sheet treatment of accumulated depreciation shown in figure 18-1.

ABC Company
Balance Sheet
December 31, 19–

ASSETS:			
Current Assets:			
Cash		$5,000	
Accounts Receivable		4,000	
Merchandise Inventory		3,000	
Total Current Assets			$12,000
Fixed Assets:			
Equipment	$8,000		
Less: **Accumulated Depreciation**	**6,500**	**1,500**	
Land		8,000	
Total Fixed Assets			9,500
Total Assets			$21,500

Fig. 18-1. Partial balance sheet showing accumulated depreciation.

DEPRECIATION METHODS

Establishing a correct rate of depreciation requires estimating the probable useful life of the asset and the possible scrap or salvage value at the end of its life. *Scrap value* is the value of the asset at the time it is no longer useful to the firm and must be disposed of.

Numerous depreciation methods are acceptable for tax purposes. The four most common are the:

- Straight-line method.
- Units-of-production method.
- Double-declining-balance method.
- Sum-of-the-years'-digits method.

The first steps in computing depreciation include estimating the useful life and scrap value, and selecting the method to be used. No

Fig. 18-2. Useful life varies with each asset and the policy of the particular firm.

asset may be depreciated below its scrap value under any method. Any reasonable method of depreciation is acceptable provided that the total depreciation plus the salvage value equals the cost of the asset. The useful life is the estimated period over which the asset may be expected to be used in the particular firm, figure 18-2. For example, one firm may replace its trucks every four years, while another uses them for six years. The trucks in each firm have a different useful life.

Fixed assets may be accounted for by treating each individual item as an account, or many items may be grouped in a general account in a variety of ways. For example, depreciable assets may be grouped according to use and recorded in accounts such as Furniture and Fixtures.

Straight-Line Method

The straight-line method is the easiest way to compute depreciation. It is also the most commonly used method. Under this method, the cost of the asset less its scrap value is depreciated in equal amounts. The depreciation for each year is determined by dividing the cost, less scrap value, by the useful life. Expressed as an equation, depreciation is calculated as follows:

$$\frac{\text{Cost} - \text{Scrap Value}}{\text{Useful Life}} = \text{Annual Depreciation}$$

Note that the straight-line method provides for an equal amount of depreciation for each period.

Example. A new machine with an estimated life of five years is purchased for \$11,000. It has an estimated scrap value of \$1,000. The total depreciation for the useful life of the machine is computed by subtracting the \$1,000 scrap value from \$11,000 (\$11,000 - 1,000 = \$10,000). This amount, divided by the useful life of five years, results in a depreciation expense of \$2,000 per year. Expressed as a percentage, the annual depreciation rate would be 20%. Total depreciation rate for this asset can be summarized as follows:

	Cost-Salvage	Rate	Depreciation Expense	Accumulated Depreciation
Year 1	$10,000	20%	$ 2,000	$ 2,000
Year 2	10,000	20%	2,000	4,000
Year 3	10,000	20%	2,000	6,000
Year 4	10,000	20%	2,000	8,000
Year 5	10,000	20%	2,000	10,000
Total			$10,000	

Figure 18-3 shows the entry that would be made to record the depreciation expense at the end of the second year. The presentation on the balance sheet is also shown for the end of Year 2. Notice that all three figures, cost (\$11,000), accumulated depreciation (\$4,000), and book value (\$7,000) are shown on the balance sheet.

Depreciation Journal Entry:

Depreciation Expense	$2,000	
Accumulated Depreciation		$2,000
To record annual depreciation.		

Balance Sheet Presentation:

Equipment	$11,000	
Less: Accumulated Depreciation	4,000	
		$7,000

Fig. 18-3. Journal entry and balance sheet presentation of the second year's accumulated depreciation on ABC Company's machine.

Units-of-Production Method

Under this method, depreciation is computed using a uniform cost per unit of output. An example of a unit of output would be the miles driven by a truck. A proportion of the cost of the fixed asset is assigned directly to each unit of output (cost per mile if the asset is a truck). Thus, depreciation expense fluctuates directly with changes in the production of the fixed asset.

To compute annual depreciation expense, the cost per unit is multiplied by the number of units produced during the period. The unit rate is determined by dividing the number of units of production in the life of the asset into the cost minus salvage value. This method can be used only where output can be easily measured in units, miles, or hours.

Example. Using the same cost figures as in the previous example, assume that the machine purchased by ABC has an estimated service life of 100,000 units. Production in units for each of the five years of its life is: 20,000, 40,000, 20,000, 10,000, and 10,000 respectively. In this case, the rate of annual depreciation equals cost minus salvage value divided by life in units, or

$$\frac{\$11{,}000 - \$1{,}000}{100{,}000 \text{ units}} = \$.10 \text{ per unit of output.}$$

This rate is applied to each year's production to determine depreciation expense. Thus, for the first year, depreciation expense will be $.10 multiplied by 20,000 units, or $2,000. The second year's expense is $4,000 ($.10 X 40,000). Depreciation for the remaining years is determined in the same manner. The depreciation of the machine using the units-of-production method is shown in the following chart.

	Units of Production	Rate	Depreciation Expense	Accumulated Depreciation
Year 1	20,000	$.10	$ 2,000	$ 2,000
Year 2	40,000	.10	4,000	6,000
Year 3	20,000	.10	2,000	8,000
Year 4	10,000	.10	1,000	9,000
Year 5	10,000	.10	1,000	10,000
Total			$10,000	

The units-of-production method is especially appropriate when an asset is used more in some periods than in others. For example, an asset might be used three shifts a day during some years and only one shift per day during other years. The units-of-production method shows a higher depreciation expense when assets are used more.

Double-Declining-Balance Method

Under the double-declining-balance method, the accumulated depreciation for each year is subtracted from the cost of the asset before computing the next year's depreciation. Thus, the same depreciation rate is applied to a smaller or *declining* balance each year. Using this method, depreciation expense is greater for the first year and grows smaller in later years. The rate used is twice as great (double) that used under the straight-line method.

For example, in the straight-line example discussed earlier, the rate for the double-declining-balance method would be twice 20%, or 40%. Scrap value is not deducted from the cost in determining the annual depreciation under this method. However, the asset may not be depreciated below its reasonable scrap value.

A change may be made from the double-declining-balance method to straight-line at any time. The change to straight-line is necessary to fully depreciate any asset. The reason for this is that if a declining amount is multiplied by a constant rate, the process will go on forever and never reach zero. Thus, depreciation under the double-declining-balance method, without converting to straight-line, would go on indefinitely. Therefore, the asset would never be fully depreciated.

For this reason, at some time after the midpoint in the life of the asset, the change should be made from the double-declining-balance to straight-line. This change should be made at any time that depreciation computed under the straight-line method is greater than that under the double-declining balance method. When the change is made, the undepreciated cost (book value) less the salvage value is spread over the remaining life.

Example. Assume the facts as given in the illustration for the straight-line method. Depreciation under the double-declining-balance method is computed using twice (double) the straight-line rate: two times 20%, or 40%. This rate is applied to the undepreciated cost (book value). For the first year, depreciation equals 40% of $11,000.00, or $4,400.00. The second year, the undepreciated cost of $6,600.00 ($11,000.00 – $4,400.00) is multiplied by 40% to arrive at a depreciation for that year of $2,640.00. The third year's depreciation is found by multiplying the undepreciated cost of $3,960.00 ($6,600.00 – $2,640.00) by the rate of 40%, which equals $1,584.00.

In the fourth year, the undepreciated cost of $2,376.00 ($3,960.00 – $1,584.00) multiplied by the rate equals $950.40. However, since the life of the fixed asset is more than half expired, the idea of changing to the straight-line method should be explored. Depreciation for the fourth year under the straight-line method is found by subtracting the scrap value of $1,000.00 from the undepreciated cost of $2,376.00. This amount, $1,376.00, is divided by the remaining life of two years, which equals $688.00 per year. Because depreciation as computed under the double-declining method ($950.40) is greater than that for the straight-line method, the change to straight line should not be made until the fifth year.

In Year 5, depreciation under the straight-line method is found by subtracting the $1,000.00 scrap value from the book value of $1,425.60, giving a depreciation of $425.60 for that year. The depreciation of the asset using the double-declining balance and then the straight-line method is summarized as follows:

	Undepreciated Cost	Rate	Depreciation Expense	Accumulated Depreciation
Year 1	$11,000.00	40%	$ 4,400.00	$ 4,400.00
Year 2	6,600.00	40%	2,640.00	7,040.00
Year 3	3,960.00	40%	1,584.00	8,624.00
Year 4	2,376.00	40%	950.40	9,574.40
Year 5	1,425.60	SL	425.60	10,000.00
			10,000.00	

Note that the change to the straight-line method is indicated in the rate column.

Sum-of-the-Years'-Digits Method

Under this method, a fraction representing the rate is applied each year to the cost minus scrap value. The denominator (bottom number) of the fraction does not change. That number is the total of the digits representing the years of estimated useful life of the asset. For example, if the life is five years, the denominator is the sum of 5 + 4 + 3 + 2 + 1, or 15. A shortcut for determining the sum of the digits is to square the life, add the life, and divide by 2. In the following equation, N represents the life.

$$\frac{N^2 + N}{2} \text{ or } \frac{(5 \times 5) + 5}{2} = 15$$

The numerator (top number) of the fraction changes each year to represent the years of useful life remaining. Thus, for an asset with a five-year life, the fraction for the first year is 5/15. For the second year, the fraction is 4/15.

Example. Assume the same cost and salvage value as in the three previous illustrations. The denominator will be fifteen for all years. The numerator changes each year to represent the years of useful life remaining. The depreciation for the first year is $3,333 [$11,000 (cost) minus $1,000 (salvage value) times 5/15]. The second year depreciation expense will be $2,667 (4/15 of $10,000). For the third year, depreciation expense will be 3/15 of $10,000, or $2,000. The fraction decreases accordingly for the final two years as shown in the following chart.

	Cost-Salvage	Fraction	Depreciation Expense	Accumulated Depreciation
Year 1	$10,000	5/15	$ 3,333	$ 3,333
Year 2	10,000	4/15	2,667	6,000
Year 3	10,000	3/15	2,000	8,000
Year 4	10,000	2/15	1,333	9,333
Year 5	10,000	1/15	667	10,000
			$10,000	

COMPARISON OF METHODS

The double-declining-balance and sum-of-the-years'-digits methods are known as *accelerated* methods of depreciation. They have the effect of accelerating the depreciation process so that the expense is greater in the early years of the asset's life. This is in contrast with the equal annual installments of depreciation computed under the straight-line method.

The primary advantage of speeding up the depreciation by use of the accelerated methods lies in the income-tax savings gained in the early years. The deduction for depreciation on the tax return is greater in the first year of the life of the asset and decreases in later years. This means that less taxes are paid in the early years. It must be remembered that the sum of the depreciation expenses for all years of the life of the asset is the same for all methods. The four methods differ only in the distribution of the total depreciation over the life of the asset. Thus, the use of an accelerated method does not result in a tax savings when viewed over the entire life of the asset since the total deduction for depreciation would be the same as under straight line. However, the accelerated method permits a firm to postpone its tax payments until later years. For tax purposes, a firm may elect to use an accelerated method. This will allow a speedy recovery of its investment in the asset by taking advantage of the tax savings in the beginning years.

The patterns of the different depreciation methods can be viewed in the following comparison table showing yearly depreciation under each method.

	Straight Line	Units of Production	Double Declining Balance	Sum of the Years' Digits
Year 1	$ 2,000	$ 2,000	$ 4,400.00	$ 3,333.33
Year 2	2,000	4,000	2,640.00	2,666.67
Year 3	2,000	2,000	1,584.00	2,000.00
Year 4	2,000	1,000	950.40	1,333.33
Year 5	2,000	1,000	425.60	666.67
	$10,000	$10,000	$10,000.00	$10,000.00

RECORDING DEPRECIATION FOR A PARTIAL PERIOD

Depreciation expense is only recorded for the period of time for which an asset is owned. The previous illustrations all assumed that the fixed asset was purchased on the first day of Year 1. Normally, this is not true. Thus, when an asset is bought midway through a period, the firm should only record a part of a year's depreciation during the first year.

For example, assume that the previously discussed fixed asset was bought on April 1 of Year 1. Since the firm only had the use of the asset during the last nine months of the year, only nine months of depreciation is recorded by the end of the year. The partial year's depreciation is easy to calculate. Since nine months is equal to three-quarters of a year, the depreciation expense recorded on December 31, Year 1, would be three-quarters of the yearly figures previously calculated under the four methods. The following list shows the depreciation on the fixed asset under each method for the first nine-month period:

Straight-line	\$2,000 X 3/4 = \$1,500
Units-of-production	(based on actual production)
Double-declining-balance	\$4,400 X 3/4 = \$3,300
Sum-of-the-years'-digits	\$3,333.33 X .75 = \$2,500.00

SUMMARY

Depreciation is a means of allocating the cost of a tangible fixed asset over the periods that benefit from use of that asset. This process involves estimates and is not a valuation method. It requires an adjusting entry to record the expense in the proper period. A contra-asset account is used to preserve the original cost of the asset. Both cost and accumulated depreciation are shown on the balance sheet to present the reader with a complete picture.

A number of methods of computing depreciation are available. The four most common methods are:

- Straight-line.
- Units-of-production.
- Double-declining-balance.
- Sum-of-the-years'-digits.

The double-declining-balance and sum-of-the-years'-digits methods are known as accelerated methods of depreciation. The use of these methods places a larger portion of the depreciation in the early years of the asset's life.

The total amount of depreciation will be the same under all methods. This total will equal cost reduced by scrap value. Only the distribution over the life of the fixed asset varies with the method chosen.

REVIEW

1. What is depreciation?
2. Define the matching principle and explain how it relates to depreciation.
3. List the four most common methods of computing depreciation and state which ones are the accelerated methods.
4. Suppose that property is purchased for \$100,000 and consists of land and buildings. The land is valued at \$20,000. What problems arise from this situation? How should the problems be handled?

5. Which of the four methods of computing depreciation discussed in this chapter will result in the greatest depreciation in the first year of an asset's life?

EXERCISES

1. Select the method of depreciation which is described in each of the following statements.

   A. straight-line method
   B. units-of-production method
   C. double-declining-balance method
   D. sum-of-the-years'-digits method

   a. Provides for equal amounts of depreciation each period.
   b. Uses a fixed rate applied to a decreasing amount to compute depreciation.
   c. Depreciation under this method varies directly with production.
   d. A decreasing rate is applied to a fixed value to compute annual depreciation.
   e. Results in the highest depreciation expense in the first year of an asset's life.
   f. Salvage value is ignored in calculating the first year's depreciation.
   g. Is the easiest method to use.

2. A machine cost \$10,000, has an estimated life of ten years, and no expected scrap value. Depreciation expense is \$1,000 per year. What is the rate of depreciation?

3. A company purchases a car with an estimated four-year life and elects to use the sum-of-the-years'-digits method for depreciation. What fraction should be used to compute the depreciation for the third year?

4. Equipment is purchased for \$16,000. The estimated scrap value is \$3,000. Expected service life is eight years. What is the depreciation for the second year, using the double-declining-balance method?

5. An automobile used for business has an expected useful life of 100,000 miles and it cost \$5,000. Assume that there is no expected scrap value. In the first year, the car is driven 20,000 miles. What is the depreciation expense for the year?

PROBLEMS

1. A machine is purchased and is estimated to produce 100,000 units of product during its five-year life. The machine cost \$18,500 and is estimated to have a \$2,000 scrap value. Production for the first year was 21,000 units. Calculate depreciation for the first year using:

   a. the straight-line method
   b. the units-of-production method
   c. the double-declining-balance method
   d. the sum-of-the-years'-digits method

2. Equipment purchased at the beginning of the year for $4,800 is expected to have a useful life of five years or 10,000 operating hours. It is expected to have a scrap value of $300. Compute the depreciation for the first and second years of use by each of the following methods. (Actual operating hours were 2,200 for the first year and 1,800 for the second year.)
   a. straight-line
   b. units-of-production
   c. double-declining-balance
   d. sum-of-the-years'-digits

3. A company bought a new machine at a cost of $62,000. It was estimated that the machine would have an $11,000 scrap value at the end of its five-year life. It was also estimated that the machine would produce 90,000 widgets during its life. It actually produced 15,000, 25,000, 10,000, 22,000, and 18,000 during its five-year life. Compute the depreciation under each of the four commonly used methods for each of the five years.

4. A company bought a new truck at a price of $5,000. It was estimated that the truck could be driven for 100,000 miles. The truck was expected to have a salvage value of $800. What adjusting entry would be required at the end of Year 1 if the truck is driven 35,000 miles during the year, and the firm uses the units-of-production method of computing depreciation?

19
Disposal of Fixed Assets

OBJECTIVES After studying this chapter, the student will be able to:

- Journalize entries for discards and sales of assets.
- Record exchanges of assets.
- Make adjusting entries to bring the accounts up to date prior to disposal.

The cost of an asset and its related accumulated depreciation account remain on a firm's records as long as it owns the asset. When the firm disposes (gets rid) of the asset, it needs to remove the cost of the asset and the accumulated depreciation account from its records. Depending upon the way in which the asset is disposed of, various accounting procedures are used to accomplish this.

DISCARDING AN ASSET

When a firm no longer has a use for an asset, the firm may discard it. If the asset's accumulated depreciation equals its cost, then it is considered to be fully depreciated. When a fully depreciated asset is discarded, the entry is a debit to Accumulated Depreciation and a credit to the asset account. For example, a desk was purchased for $200 and is now fully depreciated. No one will buy the desk, so the firm takes it to a junk yard. The accounts appear as follows:

Desk			*Accumulated Depreciation*	
200				*200*

Book value is zero. When the firm throws the desk away, this entry is made:

Accumulated Depreciation	200	
Desk		200
To record discard of desk.		

A firm may discard an asset which is not fully depreciated. In this case, there is a loss. For example, a firm had a drill press which cost $2,000 and had been depreciated $1,800. The drill press can no longer be used because it is out of date. Thus, it is thrown away at the start of the year. The entry to show this is:

Accumulated Depreciation	1,800	
Loss on Disposal	200	
Drill Press		2,000
To record discard of old drill press.		

The book value of the drill press was \$200 (\$2,000 - \$1,800). Since the firm got nothing for the drill press, its loss was the undepreciated amount, or book value. The Loss on Disposal account will be shown in the income statement as an other expense.

SALE OF AN ASSET

An asset may be sold at book value or at a gain or a loss. The gain or loss is the difference between the selling price and the book value of the asset. If the asset is sold for more than book value, there will be a gain. If sold for less than book value, there will be a loss. For example, a firm owns a truck that cost \$3,000 and has been depreciated \$1,600. The book value of the truck is now \$1,400 (\$3,000 - \$1,600). If the truck is sold for \$1,400, this entry is made:

Cash	1,400	
Accumulated Depreciation	1,600	
Truck		3,000
To record the sale of truck at book value.		

There is no gain or loss if an asset is sold at book value.

If the truck is sold for \$1,700, a \$300 gain will be made. The entry is shown as follows:

Cash	1,700	
Accumulated Depreciation	1,600	
Truck		3,000
Gain on Sale of Asset		300
To record sale of truck for more than book value.		

Note that a new account is set up to record the gain. The Gain on Sale of Asset account is shown as other income on the income statement.

If the truck is sold for \$1,000, there is a loss of \$400 and this entry is made:

Cash	1,000	
Accumulated Depreciation	1,600	
Loss on Sale of Asset	400	
Truck		3,000
To record sale of truck for less than book value.		

EXCHANGE OF ASSETS

A firm may trade in an old asset to obtain a new one. The old asset counts as part of the payment for the new asset because the firm is given a trade-in allowance for the old item. The rest of the payment is in cash or a note. In a trade-in transaction, the additional amount paid with a note or cash is called *boot*. If the old and new asset are similar, this is called an *exchange*.

When the trade-in allowance is more than the book value of the asset, the firm has a gain. If the trade-in allowance is less than book value, this is a loss.

The federal income tax laws state that a gain or loss on an exchange may *not* be recognized (shown) on a tax return. In accounting, to *recognize* an amount means to enter it in the accounting records. A loss or gain that cannot be listed on an income tax return is considered an *unrecognized* loss or gain. To abide by the federal law, such a gain or loss must be reflected in the cost basis of the new asset. Thus, the cost basis of a new asset becomes the list price plus the loss or minus the gain. Another way to obtain the cost of a new asset for tax purposes is to add the boot paid to the book value of the asset.

Exchanges with an Unrecognized Loss

The following is an example of the accounting required for an unrecognized loss. Burns and Bruno Company trades in its old car for a new car at the start of the year. The old car cost $5,000 and has been depreciated $4,000. Thus, the book value is $1,000. The car dealer gives the firm a $600 trade-in allowance on a new car which lists for $6,000. This means that the firm will have to pay boot of $5,400. In making the entry for a situation such as this, take these steps:

1. Remove the old asset from the books with a debit to Accumulated Depreciation and a credit to the asset.
2. Credit Cash for the boot paid.
3. Put the new asset on the books by debiting an asset account for the difference between the debits and the credits recorded thus far. Check this amount, which is the cost of the new asset, to see that it equals book value of the old asset plus boot.

The entry for Burns and Bruno is as follows. The steps are numbered according to the procedure just described.

Step	Account	Debit	Credit
(1)	Accumulated Depreciation	4,000	
(3)	Car	6,400	
(1)	Car		5,000
(2)	Cash		5,400
	To record trade-in of old car for a new car.		

The entry can be checked by using the procedure explained earlier. The cost (for accounting purposes) of the new car is $6,400 which equals book value plus boot, or $1,000 + $5,400. This is also the list price of the new asset plus the loss, or $6,000 + $400. The loss is called an unrecognized loss because it is not shown in the accounting records. The unrecognized loss of $400 results from the fact that the firm only received a trade-in allowance of $600 for an asset that had a book value of $1,000. The loss may not be taken on the tax return. However, the depreciation which may be taken in the future is increased by this amount. Thus, the firm recognizes the loss through extra depreciation. For example, total depreciation over the life of the new car (assuming zero scrap value) will be $6,400.

Exchanges with an Unrecognized Gain

The following situation illustrates the accounting needed when a firm makes an exchange with an unrecognized gain. Tony's Tree Service buys a new chain saw by trading in its old chain saw. The new chain saw has a list price of $1,200. The firm receives a trade-in allowance of $500 and pays the boot of $700 in cash. The old chain saw cost $1,000 and has been depreciated $600. The entries for these facts, numbered according to the order in which they are recorded, are:

(1)	Accumulated Depreciation	600	
(3)	Chain Saw	1,100	
(1)	Chain Saw		1,000
(2)	Cash		700
	To record trade-in of old chain saw for a new one.		

This entry is correct, since the cost of the new chain saw is equal to the book value of the old plus the boot ($400 plus boot of $700 equals $1,100). The $100 gain on the trade-in is subtracted from the list price of $1,200 to get the new cost basis for tax purposes. The gain is not shown on the tax return so no taxes are paid on that amount. However, the depreciation which may be taken on future tax returns is reduced by the amount of that gain. In other words, $1,100 is the maximum value that can be depreciated.

FINANCIAL REPORTING OF GAINS AND LOSSES ON EXCHANGES

The rules for showing a loss from an exchange on the financial statement are different from those for income taxes. A material (relatively large) loss on an exchange should be recognized in the accounts immediately. Gains are not recognized. If the loss of $400 in the Burns and Bruno example is considered material, the following entry would be made for financial reporting purposes:

Accumulated Depreciation	4,000	
Car	6,000	
Loss on Exchange of Assets	400	
Car		5,000
Cash		5,400
To record trade-in of old car for a new car.		

Note that since there is a different basis, depreciation on the income statement will not be the same as on the tax return. This will mean keeping two sets of books, one for tax and one for financial purposes. Following the materiality principle, the benefits of recognizing the loss should be greater than the costs of keeping two sets of records.

ADJUSTING ENTRIES TO BRING THE ACCOUNTS UP TO DATE PRIOR TO DISPOSAL

If an asset is not fully depreciated, depreciation should be taken up to the time of disposal. Thus, the accountant makes an adjusting entry to bring the accounts up to date at the time of disposal.

On January 1, 1980, a firm buys a vault for $890. The firm uses straight-line depreciation over a ten-year life and $50 salvage value for the vault. On December 31, 1980, the first year's depreciation is shown. The entries for the year 1980 are:

1980			
Jan. 1	Vault	890	
	Cash		890
	Bought vault.		
Dec. 31	Depreciation Expense	84	
	Accumulated Depreciation		84
	To record first year's depreciation on vault.		

On December 31, 1981, another year's depreciation is taken:

1981			
Dec. 31	Depreciation Expense	84	
	Accumulated Depreciation		84
	To record second year's depreciation on vault.		

On May 1, 1982, the firm sells the vault for $650. First, an adjusting entry should be made to bring the accounts up to date by recording depreciation for the first four months of 1982.

1982			
May 1	Depreciation Expense	28	
	Accumulated Depreciation		28
	To record four month's of depreciation on vault (4/12 X $84).		

Now the Accumulated Depreciation account looks like this:

Accumulated Depreciation

	84 December 31, 1980
	84 December 31, 1981
	28 May 1, 1982
	196 Balance

The entry to record the sale is:

May 1	Accumulated Depreciation	196	
	Cash	650	
	Loss on Sale of Asset	44	
	Vault		890
	To record sale of vault at a loss.		

SUMMARY

A firm may dispose of an asset by a discard, sale, or exchange. At the time of disposal, the accounts are brought up to date by recording depreciation up to the time of disposal. Next, an entry should be made to remove the cost of the asset and its related accumulated depreciation from the accounting records. There may be a gain or a loss on the transactions. Under income tax laws, a gain or loss on an exchange of like assets may not be recognized. The gain or loss is absorbed into the cost basis of the new asset.

REVIEW

1. How is it determined that an asset is fully depreciated, and what does this mean?
2. How long should a firm keep the cost of an asset on its books?
3. How is the discard of a fully depreciated asset recorded?
4. Where will a loss on a disposal or sale of an asset be shown on the financial statements?
5. Where will a gain on sale of an asset be shown on the financial statements?
6. What is book value of an asset?
7. Define an exchange.
8. Is the trade-in of a car for a truck an exchange?
9. What is boot? What is a trade-in allowance?
10. Explain the income tax laws concerning gains and losses from exchanges.
11. Explain the financial reporting rules for showing gains or losses on exchanges.
12. How can you determine the cost basis of a new asset obtained in an exchange for tax purposes?
13. When would two sets of records be kept for an exchange?
14. Why is an adjusting entry necessary at the time of disposal of an asset?

EXERCISES

1. A firm buys a machine for $800. Three years later, the firm discards the asset after $700 depreciation has been taken. Make the proper journal entry to show the discard of the asset.
2. A firm sold its car on July 1, 1981, for $2,000 cash. The car had been bought on January 1, 1979 for $4,400. The estimated useful life was four years and salvage value was set at $400. Straight-line depreciation was used. Make all the journal entries necessary at the time of the sale.
3. A farmer traded one bull plus $50 for another bull. The farmer had paid $500 for his bull exactly three years ago. He had depreciated the bull using straight-line depreciation, no salvage value, and a five-year life. Record the exchange following the income tax laws.

PROBLEMS

1. Make the journal entries to show the following transactions for the year. Assume that the firm's fiscal year ends on December 31.

January 3: Discarded a calculator which had cost $250 and was fully depreciated.

January 4: Sold a desk for $200. The orignal cost was $650 and the balance in Accumulated Depreciation was $390.

May 5: Traded in an old typewriter for a new one priced at $600. Received a trade-in allowance of $100 and paid the rest in cash. The old typewriter had cost $500. The balance in the Accumulated Depreciation account at the start of the year was $350. Annual depreciation on the old typewriter was $120. Follow the income tax laws.

June 28: Discarded a printing press which had cost $840. The balance in the Accumulated Depreciation account at the start of the year was $756. Annual depreciation was $84.

August 1: Sold a chair for $200. The chair had cost $360 and had been depreciated $252 at the start of the year. Annual depreciation was $36.

2. Make the journal entries to show these transactions:

Year 1

January 3: Bought a machine for $6,000. It was estimated to have a six-year life and no salvage value.

December 31: Recorded straight-line depreciation on the machine.

Year 2

May 4: The machine was cleaned and oiled at a cost of $117.

December 31: Recorded straight-line depreciation on the machine.

Year 3

December 31: Recorded straight-line depreciation on the machine.

Year 4

January 4: A major overhaul was made on the machine that cost $1,000 and extended the life of the asset by two years.

December 31: Recorded straight-line depreciation on the machine.

Year 5

December 31: Recorded straight-line depreciation on the machine.

Year 6

June 29: A fire destroyed the machine and there was no insurance. The machine was discarded.

3. The Cook Company completed the following transactions related to its car.

1980

January 2: Bought a used car for $4,600 cash.

June 12: Paid a mechanic to do $80 worth of repairs on the car.

December 31: Made the adjusting entry for depreciation for the year. The estimated life of the car was four years with a trade-in value of $600. Used the straight-line method of depreciation.

December 31: Closed the proper accounts to Income Summary.

1981

May 15: Paid for an oil change, $24.

December 31: Made the adjusting entry for depreciation for the year.

31: Closed the proper accounts to Income Summary.

1982

March 5: Changed the spark plugs in the car and other repairs. Paid cash of $49.

May 1: Traded in old car on a new car, which had a list price of $6,600. Received a trade-in allowance of $2,400 and paid the rest in cash. Recorded depreciation up to date. Made the entry for the exchange using the income tax method.

December 31: Made the adjusting entry for depreciation for the year on the new car. The estimated life was four years, with a trade-in value of $700. Used the straight-line method of depreciation.

31: Closed the proper accounts to Income Summary.

Record the above transactions in journal entry form. Post the journal entries to the following ledger accounts: Car; Accumulated Depreciation, Car; Car Repair Expense; Depreciation Expense.

SECTION 4

Specialized Systems

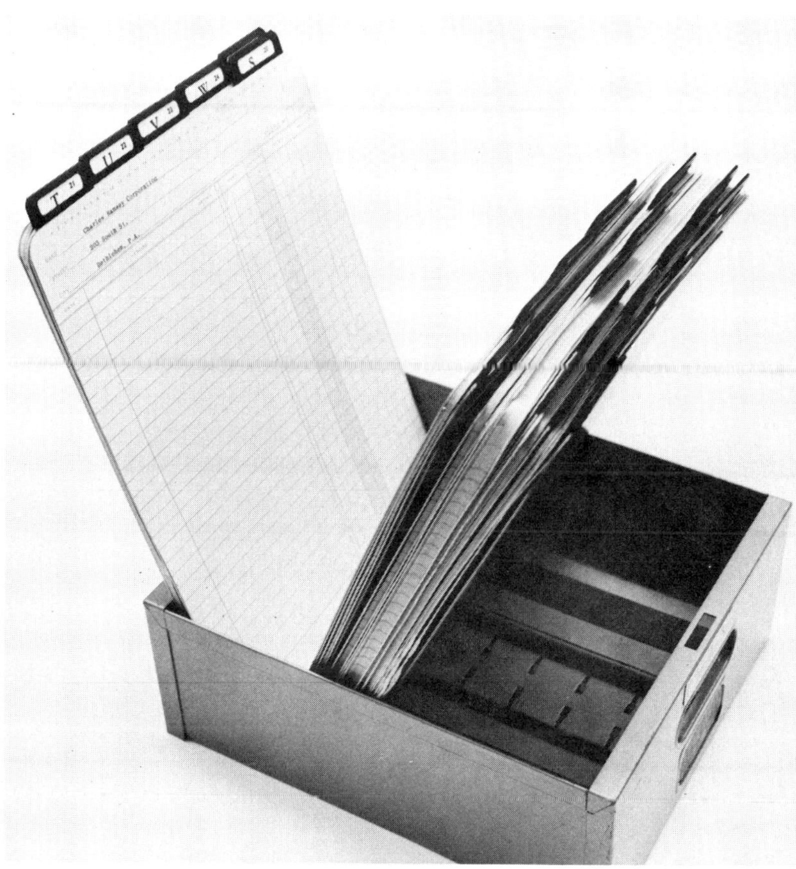

20 Subsidiary Ledgers

OBJECTIVES

After studying this chapter, the student will be able to:

- Explain the need for subsidiary ledgers.
- Identify the most common types of subsidiary ledgers.
- Define control accounts.
- Explain the importance of subsidiary ledger schedules. Record journal entries for a firm that uses subsidiary ledgers.
- Post to the accounts of a firm that uses subsidiary ledgers.

SUBDIVIDING THE LEDGER

In most firms, the number of accounts used is so great that it is difficult to keep all of them in the same ledger. For example, in this text, only one account has been used for accounts receivable. However, since a firm needs to know how much each customer owes, most firms keep a separate account for each customer. Thus, firms that have thousands of customers must use thousands of accounts receivable accounts. This subdivision of accounts is true of accounts payable as well. A separate account is used for each supplier that the firm owes. Even a small firm will have twelve or more accounts for its payables. Large firms may have thousands of liability accounts. Various asset accounts are also subdivided. For example, for each piece of equipment owned by a firm, an account must be used, rather than using one account for all equipment. This means that in addition there must be a separate accumulated depreciation account for each piece of equipment.

These extra accounts present a problem in physical handling. If they were all included in the general ledger, a thick, bulky book would result, making entries difficult. Think of the work sheet – how long would it take to complete a work sheet if there were three thousand trial balance accounts?

Since these extra accounts would be hard to work with, they usually do not appear in the trial balance. Instead, each type of account that has many accounts within it is taken out of the general ledger and put into a separate ledger. This separate ledger is known as a subsidiary ledger. A *subsidiary ledger* is defined as a special ledger that supports the general ledger.

Most firms have at least three ledgers: a general ledger, an accounts receivable subsidiary ledger, and an accounts payable subsidiary ledger. In addition, a firm with a great deal of equipment will have a fourth ledger – an equipment subsidiary ledger.

CONTROL ACCOUNTS

The debits and credits of the general ledger accounts, as expressed by the trial balance, must always be equal. If several accounts are removed from the general ledger to become a subsidiary ledger, something must be done to keep the ledger in balance. To accomplish this, a control account is substituted for the accounts that are removed. A *control account* (sometimes called a *controlling account*) is defined as an account that contains the totals of many other accounts. A control account appears in the general ledger and on the trial balance. Its balance equals the sum of many subsidiary ledger accounts.

For example, assume that a firm has the trial balance shown on the left side of figure 20-1. The firm feels that the general ledger is growing too large because of the many accounts receivable. The trial balance and work sheet would be easier to prepare if there were less accounts. Thus, the firm has decided to start using a subsidiary ledger for accounts receivable.

All six of the accounts receivable accounts are taken out of the general ledger. These six accounts are placed into a subsidiary ledger.

Book Print Shop
Trial Balance
December 31, 19–

Cash	$ 500	
Accounts Receivable – Al Barnes	250	
Accounts Receivable – Roy Jones	175	
Accounts Receivable – Charles Nelson	420	
Accounts Receivable – Ann Polk	100	
Accounts Receivable – Sam Smith	190	
Accounts Receivable – Tom Stone	330	
Prepaid Insurance	120	
Land	3,000	
Building	12,000	
Equipment	500	
Mortgage Payable		$ 8,000
Amy Jensen, Capital		9,585
	$17,585	$17,585

Book Print Shop
Trial Balance
December 31, 19–

Cash	$ 500	
Accounts Receivable	1,465	
Prepaid Insurance	120	
Land	3,000	
Building	12,000	
Equipment	500	
Mortgage Payable		$ 8,000
Amy Jensen, Capital		9,585
	$17,585	$17,585

Fig. 20-1. Trial balances before and after the use of a subsidiary ledger.

A control account (called Accounts Receivable) is put into the general ledger to replace the six accounts taken out. This control account keeps the general ledger in balance. The control account has a balance that is the same as the sum of the balances of all the accounts removed.

The new, shorter trial balance resulting from use of the control account is shown on the right side of figure 20-1. Note that both of the trial balances have the same totals. The size of the general ledger and trial balance was cut from thirteen accounts down to eight accounts. To appreciate the value of this procedure, think how much greater the savings would be if there were thousands of receivables instead of just six.

SCHEDULES OF SUBSIDIARY LEDGERS

When a group of accounts is removed from the general ledger, the trial balance will still balance because a control account replaces the accounts removed. The trial balance proves the equality of the general ledger debits and credits. There is also a need to prove the accuracy of the subsidiary ledgers. This is done by preparing a schedule for each subsidiary ledger.

A *schedule* of a subsidiary ledger is merely a list of account balances. These account balances are added up to obtain the total of all of the accounts in the subsidiary ledger. The sum of each schedule should be the same as the control account balance. A schedule of accounts receivable for the previous example is shown in figure 20-2.

Book Print Shop
Schedule of Accounts Receivable
December 31, 19—

Al Barnes	$ 250
Roy Jones	175
Charles Nelson	420
Ann Polk	100
Sam Smith	190
Tom Stone	330
TOTAL ACCOUNTS RECEIVABLE	$1,465

Fig. 20-2. Schedule of accounts receivable.

Note that the total of the schedule of accounts receivable ($1,465) is the same as the balance of the accounts receivable control account on the trial balance on the right side of figure 20-1.

RECORDING JOURNAL ENTRIES

If a firm has accounts in subsidiary ledgers, journal entries must show both the control account and the subsidiary ledger account. For example, if a firm sells $300 worth of merchandise to Ben Franks on credit, the entry is:

Accounts Receivable/Ben Franks	300	
Sales		300
To record sale on credit.		

Note that the credit is the same as shown in earlier chapters of this text. However, in the past, only Accounts Receivable was debited. Now, since the firm has a subsidiary ledger, it is necessary to also record the entry in Ben Franks' subsidiary account. There are three postings to be made for the above entry:

(1) Debit Accounts Receivable in the general ledger.
(2) Credit Sales in the general ledger.
(3) Debit Ben Franks in the subsidiary ledger.

Even though there are two debits and only one credit, the trial balance will still be in balance because one of the debits (to Ben Franks' account) will not appear on the trial balance.

When the proper account numbers have been placed in the posting reference column, the journal appears as shown in figure 20-3.

GENERAL JOURNAL Page________

Date	Account Titles and Explanation	Post. Ref.	Debit	Credit
	Accounts Receivable/Ben Franks	*112/* ✓	*300 00*	
	Sales	*411*		*300 00*
	To record sale on account.			

Fig. 20-3. Journal entry to record sale on account to Ben Franks.

Notice that the account numbers are used as reference numbers for accounts receivable and sales. However, a check mark is used instead of a number for Ben Franks' account. The reason for using a check mark is because there are no account numbers in the subsidiary ledgers. New accounts may have to be added almost every day in subsidiary ledgers. Each time a firm has a new customer, a new account will be needed. It is best to keep these accounts in alphabetical order. If the subsidiary ledger accounts were numbered, it would be impossible to add new accounts after the numbers were once assigned. Therefore, no numbers are used for the subsidiary ledger accounts.

It should be noted that some firms keep their subsidiary ledger pages on cards in a file bin instead of in a bound book. This method of handling the ledger is shown in the picture at the front of this section.

Sample Problem

The Oakra Company had a zero balance in all of its accounts before recording the following five transactions.

September 1: John Koat invested cash in new business, $1,000.
1: Bought merchandise on account from Arts Company, $350.

September 5: Bought merchandise on account from Myth and Company, $130.

11: Paid $100 to Arts Company as partial payment on September 1 purchase.

15: Bought merchandise on account from Spa Company, $400.

Required:

a. Record the above transactions in a general journal. Assume that the firm has a subsidiary ledger for accounts payable.
b. Post to the general ledger and subsidiary ledger accounts.
c. Prepare a trial balance.
d. Prepare a schedule of accounts payable.

Solutions. Figure 20-4 shows the journal after the transactions have been recorded and posted. Figure 20-5 shows the general ledger, and figure 20-6 the subsidiary ledger. Figure 20-7 illustrates the trial balance. The schedule of accounts payable is shown in figure 20-8. Notice that the total in figure 20-8 is the same as the control account balance in figure 20-7.

GENERAL JOURNAL — Page 67

Date		Account Titles and Explanation	Post. Ref.	Debit	Credit
Sept.	1	Cash	111	1 000 00	
		John Koat, Capital	311		1 000 00
		To record investment in new business.			
	1	Purchases	511	350 00	
		Accounts Payable/Arts Company	211/√		350 00
		Bought merchandise on credit.			
	5	Purchases	511	130 00	
		Accounts Payable/Myth and Company	211/√		130 00
		Bought merchandise on credit.			
	11	Accounts Payable/Arts Company	211/√	100 00	
		Cash	111		100 00
		Made partial payment on account.			
	15	Purchases	511	400 00	
		Accounts Payable/Spa Co.	211/√		400 00
		Bought merchandise on credit.			

Fig. 20-4. Journal entries for sample problem.

ACCOUNT *Cash* — Acct. No. *111*

Date		Explanation	Post. Ref.	Debit	Credit	Balance
Sept.	*1*		*67*	*1000 00*		*1000 00*
	11		*67*		*100 00*	*900 00*

ACCOUNT *Accounts Payable* — Acct. No. *211*

Date		Explanation	Post. Ref.	Debit	Credit	Balance
Sept.	*1*		*67*		*350 00*	*350 00*
	5		*67*		*130 00*	*480 00*
	11		*67*	*100 00*		*380 00*
	15		*67*		*400 00*	*780 00*

ACCOUNT *John Koat, Capital* — Acct. No. *311*

Date		Explanation	Post. Ref.	Debit	Credit	Balance
Sept.	*1*		*67*		*1000 00*	*1000 00*

ACCOUNT *Purchases* — Acct. No. *511*

Date		Explanation	Post. Ref.	Debit	Credit	Balance
Sept.	*1*		*67*	*350 00*		*350 00*
	5		*67*	*130 00*		*480 00*
	15		*67*	*400 00*		*880 00*

Fig. 20-5. General ledger accounts for sample problem.

NAME *Arts Company*
ADDRESS

Date		Explanation	Post. Ref.	Debit	Credit	Balance
Sept.	*1*		*67*		*350 00*	*350 00*
	11		*67*	*100 00*		*250 00*

NAME *Myth and Company*
ADDRESS

Date		Explanation	Post. Ref.	Debit	Credit	Balance
Sept.	*5*		*67*		*130 00*	*130 00*

NAME *Spa Company*
ADDRESS

Date		Explanation	Post. Ref.	Debit	Credit	Balance
Sept.	*15*		*67*		*400 00*	*400 00*

Fig. 20-6. Subsidiary ledger accounts for sample problem.

Oakra Company
Trial Balance
September 15, 19–

Cash	$ 900.00	
Accounts Payable		$ 780.00
John Koat, Capital		1,000.00
Purchases	880.00	
	$1,780.00	$1,780.00

Fig. 20-7. Trial balance for sample problem.

Oakra Company
Schedule of Accounts Payable
September 15, 19–

Arts Company	$250.00
Myth and Company	130.00
Spa Company	400.00
Total Accounts Payable	$780.00

Fig. 20-8. Schedule of accounts payable for sample problem.

SUMMARY

As a firm grows, the number of general ledger accounts grows as well. The problem is eased by the use of subsidiary ledgers that decrease the size of the general ledger. When there are many accounts of one type, it is possible to take all the accounts of one type out of the general ledger. These accounts are then placed in a separate ledger. One new account, called a control account, is put in the general ledger to keep the general ledger in balance. The control account has a balance that is equal to the sum of all of the accounts placed in the subsidiary ledger. The most common types of subsidiary ledgers are for accounts receivable, accounts payable, and equipment.

At the end of each period a list is made of all of the account balances in each subsidiary ledger. This list is called a schedule. The sum of each subsidiary ledger schedule should be the same as the control account in the general ledger. The purpose of preparing the schedule is to be sure that the postings to the subsidiary ledger accounts have been correct. If the schedule total is not equal to the appropriate control account, an error has been made.

Journal entries must include not only the general ledger accounts, but also the subsidiary ledger accounts. The Posting Reference column in the journal should show that postings were made to both general and subsidiary ledger accounts.

REVIEW

1. Why are subsidiary ledgers used?
2. What are the most common types of subsidiary ledgers?
3. What is a control account?
4. How many control accounts will a firm have?
5. Why are subsidiary ledger schedules prepared?
6. If the trial balance is in balance, but the Accounts Receivable Control account does not equal the total of the Schedule of Accounts Receivable, where would it be best to begin looking for the error?
7. If a purchase of merchandise on credit is recorded, how many postings are made to the accounts?
8. Why are subsidiary ledger accounts unnumbered?
9. What is a subsidiary ledger called that only contains accounts with creditors?
10. If all posting is correct, to what will the balance of a control account be equal?

EXERCISES

1. A firm does not use any subsidiary ledgers. It has the following numbers of accounts in its general ledger:

Assets (other than accounts receivables)	6
Accounts Receivable	900
Liabilities (other than accounts payable)	2
Accounts Payable	100
Owner's Equity	2
Revenues and Expenses	30
	1,040

a. How many accounts appear on the firm's trial balance?
b. How many accounts appear on the firm's work sheet?
c. If the firm decided to use one subsidiary ledger, for accounts receivable only, how many accounts would then appear on its trial balance?
d. If the firm decided to use two subsidiary ledgers, one for accounts receivable and one for accounts payable, how many accounts would appear on its trial balance?
e. How many subsidiary ledgers should the firm use?

2. Record the following entries in a general journal. Show how the posting reference column would appear after posting has been made to all general and subsidiary ledger accounts. Use the following account numbers:

110 Cash	210 Accounts Payable
112 Accounts Receivable	411 Sales
117 Merchandise Inventory	511 Purchases

January 17: Sold merchandise on credit to BR Company, $620.
18: Bought merchandise on credit from AE Company, $960.
27: Received $300 cash in partial payment from BR Company.
28: Paid AE Company $960 for balance owed.

PROBLEMS

1. The Ray Company began business on June 2. It had the following transactions during June:

June 2: Phil Ray began a new business with a $2,000 investment.
3: Bought merchandise on account from Aerco, $480.
4: Bought merchandise for cash from Tiger Company, $300.
5: Sold merchandise on credit to Roger Neal, $207.
9: Sold merchandise on credit to Al Sparks, $180.
12: Bought merchandise on account from First Company, $370.
16: Paid $480 to Aerco for June 3 purchase.
17: Sold merchandise for cash to Roger Neal, $40.
23: Bought merchandise on credit from First Company, $150.
24: Bought merchandise for cash from Tiger Company, $390.
25: Bought merchandise on credit from Second Company, $600.
30: Sold merchandise on credit to Theresa Smith, $440.

---

a. Record the transactions for the month of June in a general journal.
b. Post to the accounts.
c. Prepare a trial balance.
d. Prepare a schedule of accounts receivable.
e. Prepare a schedule of accounts payable.

2. The Pup Pet Store is operated by Ann Johnson. The firm uses a general ledger and subsidiary ledgers for accounts receivable and accounts payable. At the start of the year the firm had the following account balances:

GENERAL LEDGER	ACCOUNTS RECEIVABLE LEDGER
Cash, $500	
Accounts Receivable, $750	John Reed, $500
Merchandise Inventory, $3,400	Tom Painter, $250
Equipment, $650	
Accumulated Depreciation, $65	**ACCOUNTS PAYABLE LEDGER**
Accounts Payable, $705	Avant Supply Company, $105
Ann Johnson, Capital, $4,530	York Supply Company, $600

The firm completed the following transactions during the month of January:

January	3:	Bought merchandise on account from Avant Supply Company, $240.
	4:	Bought merchandise on account from York Supply Company, $190.
	5:	Bought merchandise on account from Lark Supply Company, $300.
	6:	Sold merchandise for cash to Nancy Miller, $80.
	7:	Sold merchandise on account to the Boy Scouts, $30.
	10:	Sold merchandise on credit to Tom Painter, $60.
	11:	Received $100 cash from John Reed in partial payment of amount owed.
	13:	Paid $105 to Avant Supply Company.
	14:	Paid $200 to York Supply Company.
	17:	Bought merchandise on credit from Lark Supply Company, $225.
	18:	Bought merchandise for cash from Avant Supply Company, $12.
	19:	Received $30 owed by the Boy Scouts.
	25:	Sold merchandise to Larry Hines on credit, $210.
	26:	Sold merchandise to Tim Booher for cash, $170.
	30:	Bought merchandise on credit from York Supply Company, $60.

---

a. Record the transactions for January in a general journal.
b. Record the beginning balances in the accounts.
c. Post the January transactions to the ledger accounts.
d. Prepare a trial balance.
e. Prepare a schedule of accounts receivable.
f. Prepare a schedule of accounts payable.

21
Special Journals

OBJECTIVES After studying this chapter, the student will be able to:

- Explain the advantages of special journals.
- List the five most common types of journals.
- Determine in which journal a transaction should be recorded.
- Post from special journals to the ledger accounts.
- Use the proper posting reference numbers for all journals.

THE NEED FOR SPECIAL JOURNALS

As a firm grows larger, the recording and posting of transactions requires more and more time. One way to save time and expense is to use special journals. Throughout this text, only a general journal has been used. All firms use a general journal. However, in addition, most firms also use several other journals. These additional journals are known as *special journals* and are used only to record a specific type of entry, such as sales of merchandise on credit.

Special journals make it possible for more than one employee to work on the recording and posting at one time. In large firms, several employees are needed to handle all of the firm's accounting. Special journals allow the firm to divide the work among several people as well as simplify some of the recording procedures.

The advantages of special journals are shown by the following example. Assume that a firm makes five sales on account (credit) to five different customers. If only a general journal is used, the entries are recorded as shown in figure 21-1.

Note that a total of twenty lines is used in the journal (counting the explanation and the blank space between entries). This results in a total of fifteen postings to the ledger accounts. These are: five debits to the Accounts Receivable Control account, five credits to Sales, and five debits to the customer accounts in the subsidiary accounts receivable ledger. Notice that some parts of the entry are the same for each of the transactions. Each entry has a debit to accounts receivable and a credit to sales. In addition, the explanation is the same for each entry.

GENERAL JOURNAL Page 2

Date		Account Titles and Explanations	Post. Ref.	Debit	Credit
May	*1*	*Accounts Receivable/LT Company*	*112/✓*	*100 00*	
		Sales	*411*		*100 00*
		To record sale on account.			
	2	*Accounts Receivable/Beck Company*	*112/✓*	*250 00*	
		Sales	*411*		*250 00*
		To record sale on account.			
	3	*Accounts Receivable/Kross Company*	*112/✓*	*80 00*	
		Sales	*411*		*80 00*
		To record sale on account.			
	4	*Accounts Receivable/Dot Company*	*112/✓*	*125 00*	
		Sales	*411*		*125 00*
		To record sale on account.			
	31	*Accounts Receivable/Rite Company*	*112/✓*	*32 00*	
		Sales	*411*		*32 00*
		To record sale on account.			

Fig. 21-1. General journal entries for five credit sales.

Since all entries for sales of merchandise on account are similar, a firm can save time and paper by using a special journal just for these sales. The special journal used for this purpose is called a *sales journal.* A sales journal is used only to record this one type of entry (sales of merchandise on credit). The same five entries can be recorded in a sales journal as shown in figure 21-2.

SALES JOURNAL Page *21*

Date		Account Debited	Invoice No.	Post. Ref.	Amount
May	*1*	*LT Company*		✓	*100 00*
	2	*Beck Company*		✓	*250 00*
	3	*Kross Company*		✓	*80 00*
	4	*Dot Company*		✓	*125 00*
	31	*Rite Company*		✓	*32 00*
				✓	*587 00*
					(112)(411)

Fig. 21-2. Use of the sales journal to record the five entries shown in figure 21-1.

Note that when a sales journal is used, it is not necessary to write the debit to the accounts receivable control account or the credit to sales. Since every entry in the journal must be a debit to Accounts Receivable and a credit to Sales, there is no need to write down these account names. It is assumed that these accounts are involved in every transaction recorded in the sales journal.

There is also no need to give an explanation for each entry. Since only one type of entry is found in the sales journal, an explanation is unnecessary. However, the customer's name, which is the subsidiary ledger account title, must still be written for every entry since this differs for every sale.

By using the special sales journal, the firm can cut its recording space for the five transactions from twenty lines to six lines (counting the total). Over a year's time this can save a firm a great deal of paperwork.

Special journals can also save unnecessary posting. Since every entry in the example has a debit to Accounts Receivable, the firm does not have to post every entry to Accounts Receivable. Instead, it can wait until the end of the month and post the total of all debits in one posting. The same is true of the credit to Sales; one posting is made at the end of the month for the total of all sales made during the month.

Posting to the subsidiary ledger accounts must be made daily, regardless of the journal system used. If the general journal is used, fifteen postings must be made. Figure 21-3 shows the posting necessary

Accounts Receivable 112

Debit	Credit
May 1 100	
2 250	
3 80	
4 125	
31 32	

Sales 411

Debit	Credit
	May 1 100
	2 250
	3 80
	4 125
	31 32

LT Company

Debit	Credit
May 1 100	

Beck Company

Debit	Credit
May 2 250	

Kross Company

Debit	Credit
May 3 80	

Dot Company

Debit	Credit
May 4 125	

Rite Company

Debit	Credit
May 31 32	

Fig. 21-3. Postings to the accounts if a general journal is used.

Accounts Receivable 112	
May 31 587	

Sales 411	
	May 31 587

LT Company	
May 1 100	

Beck Company	
May 2 250	

Kross Company	
May 3 80	

Dot Company	
May 4 125	

Rite Company	
May 31 32	

Fig. 21-4. Postings to the accounts if a sales journal is used.

if a general journal is used for the five credit sales shown in figure 21-1. On the other hand, if a sales journal is used, only seven postings are required. They are five debits to the customer subsidiary ledger accounts, one debit to the Accounts Receivable Control account (for $587), and one credit to Sales (for $587). Figure 21-4 shows the posting necessary with the use of the sales journal. The savings in time comes from posting only the totals of like kind transactions.

Types of Special Journals

The sales journal is only one type of special journal. A firm can save time by using a special journal for any type of transaction that occurs quite often. The most common types of transactions for most firms are:

- sales of merchandise
- purchases of merchandise
- receipts of cash, and
- payments of cash.

Thus, most firms have these four special journals in addition to the general journal. The five most common journals and their functions are shown in the following chart.

JOURNAL	USED TO RECORD
Sales	Sales of merchandise on credit
Purchases	Purchases of merchandise on credit
Cash Receipts	All cash receipts from all sources
Cash Payments	All cash payments for any reason
General	Any entry that does not fit in one of the special journals

THE PURCHASES JOURNAL

The purchases journal is the book of original entry for purchases of merchandise on account. It is much like the sales journal. All entries for purchases of merchandise involve a debit to purchases and credits to accounts payable and a subsidiary ledger account. Only the posting to the subsidiary ledger account has to be made daily. The debit to Purchases and the credit to the Accounts Payable control account can be made at the end of the month by posting totals only. Figure 21-5 shows a purchases journal.

Note that a check mark is placed in the posting reference column to show that the individual amounts have been posted to the subsidiary ledger accounts. Since the column total is posted at the end of each month, the reference numbers are placed in parentheses under the total. The $807 was posted as a debit to Purchases (account number 511) and as a credit to Accounts Payable (account number 211). Figure 21-6 shows the accounts after the posting has been completed.

PURCHASES JOURNAL — Page *18*

Date		Account Credited	Invoice Date	√	Amount
Jan.	*9*	*First Company*	*1-7-77*	√	*77 00*
	10	*Third Company*	*1-8-77*	√	*190 00*
	12	*Fourth Company*	*1-9-77*	√	*240 00*
	31	*Fifth Company*	*1-30-77*	√	*300 00*
					807 00
					(511)(211)

Fig. 21-5. A page from a purchases journal.

Accounts Payable 211

	Jan. 31 807

Purchases 511

Jan. 31 807	

First Company

	Jan. 9 77

Third Company

	Jan. 10 190

Fourth Company

	Jan. 12 240

Fifth Company

	Jan. 31 300

Fig. 21-6. Account balances after posting of the purchases journal.

CASH RECEIPTS JOURNAL

Page 21

Date		Account Credited	Post. Ref.	Other Accounts Cr.	Sales Cr.	Accounts Receivable Cr.	Sales Discount Dr.	Cash Dr.
May	1	Dick Stone	✓			100 00	2 00	98 00
	2	Notes Payable	212	1000 00				1000 00
	15		✓		840 00			840 00
	17	Nick Marsh	✓			300 00	6 00	294 00
	18	Purchase Returns & Allowances	512	20 00				20 00
	25	James West	✓			50 00	1 00	49 00
	31		✓		910 00			910 00
				1020 00	1750 00	450 00	9 00	3211 00
				(✓)	(411)	(120)	(412)	(110)

Fig. 21-7. The cash receipts journal.

CASH RECEIPTS JOURNAL

The same procedure of posting totals only can be used for cash receipts transactions. Since every receipt of cash means a debit to Cash, it is easy to just post one debit to the cash account each month. However, when dealing with cash receipts, the credit is not always to the same account. There are many ways for a firm to obtain cash. A cash sale means a credit to the Sales account, while a bank loan requires a credit to Notes Payable. A collection of an accounts receivable requires credits to the Accounts Receivable Control account and a subsidiary ledger account. Thus, a cash receipts journal is not as simple as the one-column journals shown for sales and purchases. At least five columns are usually used in a cash receipts journal. Figure 21-7 shows a page from a cash receipts journal.

The entries in the figure 21-7 cash receipts journal, and the posting required for each, is explained as follows:

May 1: Dick Stone paid his bill. He owed \$100, but he was given a 2% cash discount for paying promptly. The \$100 was recorded in the Accounts Receivable credit column. Cash of \$98 was received. Thus, \$98 was placed in the Cash debit column. The difference of \$2 was recorded in the Sales Discount debit column.

No daily posting is required for any item for which there is a special column. Therefore, no entries are made in the Cash, Accounts Receivable, and Sales Discounts accounts until the end of the month. At month-end, the totals of the special columns are posted to the respective accounts. In the May 1 entry the only account for which there is not a special column is Dick Stone's account. Thus, it was posted when the journal entry was made. The fact that the \$100 has been posted to Dick Stone's account is shown by a check mark in the posting reference column. The only item posted daily is the entry to the subsidiary ledger account. The general ledger accounts are taken care of at the end of the month by posting column totals.

May 2: The firm received a \$1,000 loan from the bank. This entry involves a debit to Cash and a credit to Notes Payable. Thus, \$1,000 was entered in the cash debit column. There is no special column for the notes payable credit, so the *Other Accounts Credit* column must be used. This column is for those amounts that do not properly fit in any of the special columns.

The debit to Cash was not posted to the account at the time of the journal entry. Instead, it will be posted when the monthly total is posted to the cash account. The credit to notes payable was posted immediately. Since the Other Accounts column is not a special column, its total is not posted at the end of the month. Any amount that appears in the Other Accounts column must be posted individually. Thus, there was only one immediate posting for the May 2 entry – a credit to the Notes Payable account. The account number, 212, was put in the reference column to show that the posting has been done.

May 15: Cash sales of $840 were recorded. The entry for this item is a debit to Cash and a credit to Sales. Since there is a special column for both the debit and the credit, neither was posted immediately. Note that a check mark was placed in the posting reference column even though nothing was posted. This is one method of showing that the line was examined and correctly indicates that there is no posting entry. Some accountants leave the reference column blank to indicate that no posting was done. Either method is correct.

May 17: Nick Marsh paid his bill less the 2% cash discount. This was recorded in the same way as the May 1 entry. The only posting was the $300 credit to Nick Marsh's account in the subsidiary ledger.

May 18: The firm returned some merchandise and received a $20 cash refund. This transaction required a debit to Cash, so the Cash debit column was used. The credit was to Purchase Returns and Allowances. It was necessary to use the Other Accounts column for this entry. The only posting done at the time of the entry was that of the amount in the Other Accounts column to the Purchases Returns and Allowances account. The account number, 512, was put in the reference column.

May 25: James West paid his account, less 2% cash discount. This entry was handled in the same way as the May 1 and May 17 entries. The only thing posted was the $50 credit to James West's account in the subsidiary ledger.

May 31: Cash sales of $910 were recorded. This item was handled in the same way as the May 15 entry. No posting was necessary.

At the end of the month, the cash receipts columns are handled as follows. Each column is totaled. Everything in the Other Accounts column was posted daily. Thus, nothing is done with the total. However, a check mark is placed under the $1,020 column total to show that the amount has been examined by the bookkeeper and handled properly.

The amounts in the Sales column were not posted daily. Therefore, the $1,750 total is posted as a credit to the Sales account. The

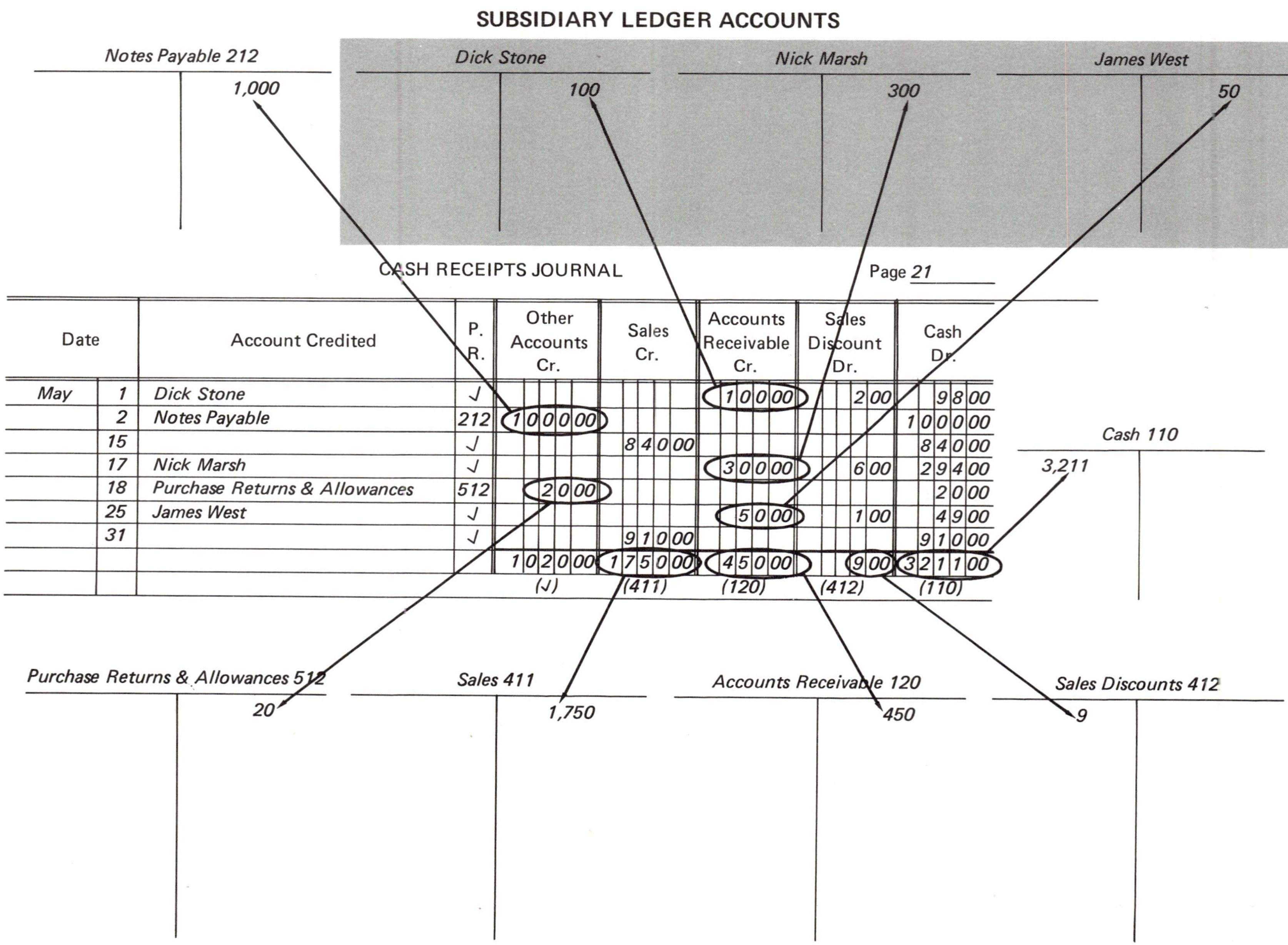

CASH RECEIPTS JOURNAL Page 21

Date		Account Credited	P.R.	Other Accounts Cr.	Sales Cr.	Accounts Receivable Cr.	Sales Discount Dr.	Cash Dr.
May	1	Dick Stone	✓			100 00	2 00	98 00
	2	Notes Payable	212	1000 00				1000 00
	15		✓		840 00			840 00
	17	Nick Marsh	✓			300 00	6 00	294 00
	18	Purchase Returns & Allowances	512	20 00				20 00
	25	James West	✓			50 00	1 00	49 00
	31		✓		910 00			910 00
				1020 00	1750 00	450 00	9 00	3211 00
				(✓)	(411)	(120)	(412)	(110)

Fig. 21-8. Posting from the cash receipts journal.

account number, 411, is placed in parentheses under the column total to show that the total was posted.

The $450 total of the Accounts Receivable column is posted as a credit to the general ledger control account. Even though each individual amount in the column was posted daily to the customers' accounts in the subsidiary ledger, there was no daily posting of any of the amounts to a general ledger account. Thus, to keep the control account in balance with the subsidiary ledger, the column total must be posted to Accounts Receivable (account number 120).

The amounts in the Sales Discount column were not posted daily. Therefore, the total for the month must be debited to the Sales Discounts account (number 412).

None of the amounts was posted to the Cash account during the month. Thus, the total debits of $3,211 is debited to Cash (account number 110). Figure 21-8 shows the entire posting process for the month.

CROSSFOOTING A MULTI-COLUMN JOURNAL

A multi-column journal such as the cash receipts journal should be crossfooted at the end of each month. To *crossfoot* means to add the column totals across to be sure that the debits and credits are equal. In figure 21-7, the crossfooting is done as follows:

Debit Column Totals		Credit Column Totals	
Sales Discounts	9.00	Other	1,020
Cash	3,211.00	Sales	1,750
		Accounts Receivable	450
TOTAL DEBITS	3,220.00	TOTAL CREDITS	3,220

The sole purpose of crossfooting a journal is to be sure the debits and credits are equal.

CASH PAYMENTS JOURNAL

The cash payments journal is used to record all credits to Cash. It is a multi-column journal. The principles of recording transactions in a cash payments journal are the same as for a cash receipts journal. Every entry is a credit to Cash, thus the Cash Credit column is used. If there is a special column for the debit, then that special column is used. If there is no special column for the account debited, then the Other Accounts column must be used. Amounts in the Other Accounts column are posted daily. Amounts in the Accounts Payable column are posted daily to the subsidiary ledger accounts. The column totals of the special columns are posted at the end of the month to the general ledger accounts.

The following transactions have been recorded in the cash payments journal page shown in figure 21-9:

June 1: Wrote check number 78 to East Company in payment of accounts payable, of $650, less the cash discount.

8: Wrote check number 79 in payment of monthly rent, $200.

10: Wrote check number 80 to West Company in payment of $100 account. A 2% discount was taken.

CASH PAYMENTS JOURNAL

Page 21

Date		Chk. No.	Account Debited	Post. Ref.	Other Accounts Dr.	Accounts Payable Dr.	Purchases Discount Cr.	Cash Cr.
June	1	78	East Company	√		650 00	13 00	637 00
	8	79	Rent Expense	620	200 00			200 00
	10	80	West Company	√		100 00	2 00	98 00
	15	81	Wild Company	√		250 00	5 00	245 00
	30	82	Purchases	510	360 00			360 00
					560 00	1000 00	20 00	1540 00
					(√)	(210)	(511)	(110)

Fig. 21-9. Sample page from a cash payments journal.

Wild Company	
June 15 250	

East Company	
June 1 650	

West Company	
June 10 100	

Cash 110	
	June 30 1,540

Accounts Payable 210	
June 30 1,000	

Purchases 510	
June 30 360	

Purchases Discounts 511	
	June 30 20

Rent Expense 620	
June 8 200	

Fig. 21-10. Accounts after posting from cash payments journal shown in figure 21-9.

June 15: Wrote check number 81 to Wild Company in payment of $250 account. A 2% discount was taken.

30: Purchased merchandise for cash, $360.

Figure 21-10 shows the accounts after the entries in the cash payments journal are posted.

Additional Columns in Special Journals

All special journals do not have the same format as those shown in this chapter. Cash receipts journals and cash payments journals often have more columns than those shown here. For example, many firms have a Purchases column in their cash payments journal. This is a useful procedure if a firm makes several cash purchases each month. The basic rule is that a firm should have a special column for each account that is used regularly. With this system, it is only necessary to post the totals each month, and not each individual transaction.

USE OF THE GENERAL JOURNAL WITH SPECIAL JOURNALS

Regardless of the number of special journals used, a firm still needs a general journal. This is because some transactions cannot be recorded in a special journal. Any entry that does not fit into a special journal must be recorded in the general journal. For example, adjusting and closing entries are still recorded in the general journal, even when special journals are used.

Also, any purchase of an asset on credit (other than merchandise) is recorded in the general journal. For example, a purchase of equipment on credit cannot be recorded in the cash or purchases journal since no cash or merchandise is involved. This transaction must be entered in the general journal.

Everything recorded in the general journal is posted daily. There are no totals to post in the general journal.

POSTING REFERENCE NUMBERS FOR USE WITH SPECIAL JOURNALS

In previous examples in this text, the journal page number was used as a posting reference number in the ledger accounts. This method is fine if a firm has only one journal. However, if a firm has more than one journal, a different way of showing references must be used. The best way is to continue to use the journal page number, but to also show the initials of the name of the journal. For example, the following codes represent each of the five journals:

S – Sales Journal
P – Purchases Journal
CR – Cash Receipts Journal
CP – Cash Payments Journal
G – General Journal

Figure 21-11 shows the Cash account and the Accounts Receivable account after several postings have been made. Note that there are only

Cash — Acct. No. *111*

Date		Explanation	Post. Ref.	Debit	Credit	Balance
Feb.	*1*	*Balance*	✓			*640 00*
	28		**CR6**	*6210 00*		*6850 00*
	28		**CP9**		*5938 00*	*912 00*

Accounts Receivable — Acct. No. *113*

Date		Explanation	Post. Ref.	Debit	Credit	Balance
Feb.	*1*	*Balance*	✓			*810 00*
	16		**G3**		*30 00*	*780 00*
	28		**S5**	*3595 00*		*4375 00*
	28		**CR6**		*4100 00*	*275 00*

Fig. 21-11. Examples of posting reference numbers for special journals.

two entries in the Cash account since all transactions are recorded in one of the two cash journals. Notice that the journal code and the page number are used as references in the posting reference column.

SUMMARY

Using special journals saves time and money. Only the totals of like kind transactions need be posted when using special journals. A firm can have any number of journals. A firm should have a special journal for each type of transaction that occurs regularly. Most firms have at least the following five journals:

Sales Journal	Cash Receipts Journal
Purchases Journal	Cash Payments Journal
General Journal	

Each one of the four special journals is used for one type of transaction only. The general journal is used to record any transaction that does not fit in any of the special journals. In addition to saving time and paper, the use of special journals permits more than one employee to work on the journals at the same time.

Firms using more than one journal use the initials of the journal and the page number as a posting reference in the accounts.

REVIEW

1. Explain how special journals can save labor and time.
2. Would an error in adding the amounts in a sales journal cause the trial balance to be out of balance? Why?
3. If a firm uses the five journals described in this chapter, which journal would be the main source of credits to customer accounts?
4. Which journal would be the main source of debits to customer accounts?
5. Does each entry in the sales journal represent a debit to the account listed in the explanation column?
6. List four different types of transactions that would be recorded in a cash receipts journal.
7. List four different types of transactions that would be recorded in a cash payments journal.
8. In which journal would the cash sale of equipment be recorded?
9. In which journal would a sales return be recorded if the return reduced the balance of the customer's account?
10. To what account is the total of the Other Accounts column of a cash receipts journal posted?
11. What would the figures *CP62* indicate in the posting reference column of the office supplies account?
12. To what accounts are the individual amounts in the Accounts Receivable column of a cash receipts journal posted?
13. Which columns of a cash payments journal are posted daily?
14. What does it mean to crossfoot the journal?

EXERCISES

1. The following are entries in the purchases journal of a firm.

Date	Account Credited	Amount
May 2	Lynn Company	260.00
9	Hawkes Company	40.00
16	Karter Company	166.00
28	Selvey Company	150.00
		616.00

The firm's general journal had the following entries:

Date	Account	Debit	Credit
May 4	Accounts Payable/Lynn Company	40	
	Purchase Returns and Allowances		40
	Returned spoiled merchandise.		
18	Accounts Payable/Karter Company	16	
	Purchase Returns and Allowances		16
	Returned spoiled merchandise.		

Post both of the journals to the general ledger and subsidiary ledger accounts.

2. A business uses a cash receipts journal, a cash payments journal, a single-column sales journal, a single-column purchases journal, and a general journal. In which journal will it record each of the following transactions?
   a. Purchase of merchandise on credit.
   b. Sale of unneeded office equipment on credit.
   c. Payment of a creditor.
   d. Sale of merchandise on credit.
   e. Correction of an entry posted to the wrong account.
   f. Purchase of office supplies on credit.
   g. Purchase of office supplies for cash.
   h. A return of merchandise by a customer; his account was reduced.
   i. Payment received from customer on account.
   j. Return of a credit purchase.
   k. A return of a cash sale.
   l. Adjusting entries.
   m. Closing entries.
   n. Purchase of office supplies for cash.
   o. Borrowing money from the bank.
   p. Paying off a bank loan.
   q. Paying employees' wages.
   r. Withdrawal by the owner of a typewriter for personal use.

PROBLEMS

1. Record the following transactions in the appropriate journals. After the entries have been recorded in the journals, post to the appropriate ledger accounts. The company has a subsidiary accounts receivable ledger as well as a general ledger.

May 1: Sold $1,200 of merchandise to Mildred Baer on credit. Terms are 2/10, n/30.

2: Sold $2,000 of merchandise to Fleisher Foundries for cash.

May 3: Sold $3,000 of merchandise to Frank Bertoli on account. Terms are 2/10, n/30.

4: Sold $20 of office supplies to the Boy Scouts for cash.

5: Sold $1,000 of merchandise to Fleisher Foundries on credit. Terms are 2/10, n/30.

11: Received a check from Mildred Baer for the amount of her May 1 purchase less the discount.

12: Sold $50 of merchandise to the Girl Scouts on credit. Terms are 1/10, n/30.

15: Fleisher Foundries paid the amount it owed on the May 5 purchase less the discount.

25: Sold merchandise for $300 cash to Mildred Baer.

26: Sold merchandise for $4,000 to Colt Industries on credit. Terms are 2/10, n/30.

29: Collected amount owed by Frank Bertoli.

29: Colt Industries returned for credit $500 of the merchandise it purchased May 26.

30: Sold office supplies of $72 to Boy Scouts on credit with a promise to pay the full amount due next week.

31: Sold an old delivery truck to Frank Bertoli for $175 cash. The delivery truck was purchased last month for $175 but was found to be unsuitable for company use; therefore the truck is being sold for the same amount that it cost the company.

31: Colt Industries paid its invoice from May 26 less the return and discount.

2. A firm uses a sales journal, a purchases journal, a cash receipts journal, a cash payments journal, and a general journal. Record each of the following transactions in the proper journal. Then post to the ledger accounts. Remember that some items must be posted daily. Others are posted only at the end of the month.

June 1: Borrowed $2,000 from the bank.

2: Bought merchandise on credit, $1,300, from ABC Supply Co.

3: Sold merchandise on account, $600, to Nick Larson.

4: Paid rent for the month, $200.

5: Bought merchandise on credit, $195, from Midwest Company.

8: Bought merchandise for cash, $30, from Phelps Company.

9: Sold merchandise for cash to Tina Johns, $82.

10: Sold $850 of merchandise on credit to Bob Beason.

11: Paid ABC Supply Co. for June 2 purchase less 2% discount.

12: Collected $588 from Nick Larson in full payment of his June 3 purchase less the 2% discount.

15: Bob Beason returned $20 worth of goods bought on June 10.

16: Paid $195 to Midwest Company in payment of June 5 invoice.

June 17: Sold merchandise to Fred Clark for $960 cash.
18: Bought a new truck on credit from Ace Motors, $4,300.
19: Sold merchandise to Nick Larson on credit, $275.
22: Bob Beason paid for his June 10 purchase less the $20 return and a 2% cash discount on the merchandise kept.
23: Sold goods on credit to Eileen Hardy, $300.
24: Purchased goods on credit from First Company, $180.
25: Purchased goods for cash of $88 from ABC Supply Co.
29: Collected $294 from Eileen Hardy in full payment of her June 23 purchase less the discount.

3. The following transactions were completed by the Karter Company during October of the current year. The terms of all sales on account are 2/10, n/30.

Oct. 3: Purchased merchandise on account from the Peer Company, $6,000; terms, n/30.
4: Sold merchandise on account to Sellers & Company, Invoice No. 833, $6,000.
5: Purchased merchandise on account from Gould & Co., $2,400; terms, 2/10, n/30.
7: Received a credit memorandum from Peer Company for defective merchandise, $300.
7: Sold merchandise on account to Trick Company, Invoice No. 834, $4,000.
11: Issued a credit memorandum to Sellers & Company for merchandise returned. Credit Memo No. 86, $200.
14: Received cash from Sellers & Company in payment of the $5,800 due on Invoice No. 833, less discount.
16: Received cash from Trick Company in payment of Invoice No. 834, less discount.
17: Issued Check No. 21 for a cash purchase of merchandise, $150.
22: Received cash for office supplies returned to the manufacturer, $80.
24: Issued Check No. 22 to Peer Company in payment of the balance due.
31: Purchased the following on account from Jet Supply Company; store supplies, $75; office supplies, $150.
31: Cash sales for October, $53,040.

Record the above transactions in the sales journal, cash receipts journal, purchases journal, cash payments journal, or two-column general journal.

4. Enter each of the following transactions in the proper journals. Five journals are used. Second, post all entries in the journals to the proper accounts.

Nov. 1: Received a $100 check from a tenant in payment of December rent.
2: Sold merchandise to James Company on credit, $830.

Nov. 3: Received merchandise and an invoice dated Nov. 2, terms 2/10, n/60 from Monroe Mfg. Co., $1,000.

4: Purchased store equipment on account from Boone Supply Co. $7,000.

5: Sold merchandise for cash to James Company, $30.

6: Sold merchandise to Mr. Wright on account, $850.

8: Paid the sales salaries for the week, $310.

10: Issued check to Monroe Mfg. Co. for payment of the Nov. 2 invoice less the discount.

12: Mr. Lear, the proprietor, withdrew $75 for the monthly payment on his personal automobile.

15: Purchased merchandise for cash from Boone Supply Co., $80.

20: Purchased merchandise on account from Monroe Mfg. Co., $807.

22: Sold merchandise on account to Frances Booth, $2,000.

23: Received check from Mr. Wright in full payment of his Nov. 6 purchase.

25: Received check from Frances Booth in payment of her Nov. 22 purchase less a 2% discount.

30: Mr. Lear took home a piece of store equipment for his personal use. The equipment was valued at $180.

22
One-Write Systems

OBJECTIVES

After studying this chapter, the student will be able to:

- Explain the advantages of a one-write system.
- Describe how a one-write system operates.
- Explain the concept of time sharing a computer.

THE ONE-WRITE SYSTEM AS A LABOR-SAVING DEVICE

Chapter 21 explained the use of special journals to cut down on posting time. Additional time can be saved by using a one-write (or pegboard) accounting system. The one-write system is so called because only *one writing* is needed to perform all of the steps of the recording process. Actually, the one-write system is simply a more sophisticated form of special journal.

For example, Bright and Company wants to make payment on its account with the Complete Office Supply Company. Without a one-write system, the firm would have to

- write the check,
- make the entry in the cash payments journal, and
- post the entry to the proper accounts payable subsidiary ledger account.

This means writing the same data three times. On the other hand, with a one-write system, only one entry is necessary. Carbon paper is the key to the one-write system. When the check is written, carbon paper transfers the same data onto a ledger card. Another sheet of carbon paper under the ledger card transfers the data to the journal page. Figure 22-1 shows the arrangement of the parts of the one-write system.

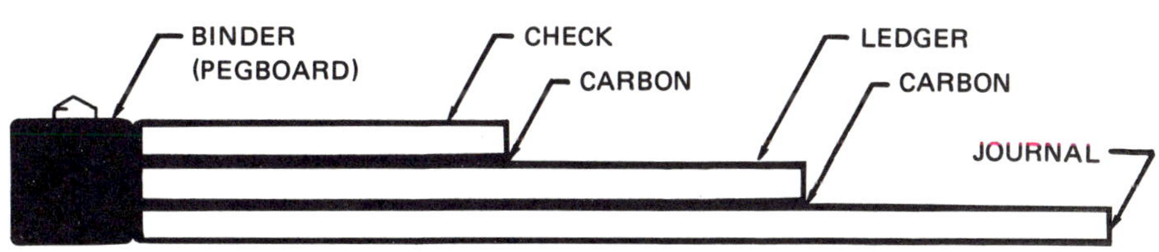

Fig. 22-1. Side view showing the basic arrangement of the one-write system.

Forms

One-write systems use specially designed checks, journal pages, and ledger cards so that all columns and spaces are the same size on all forms. In addition, the spaces are aligned so that the entries appear in the correct place on each item. Some one-write systems do not use carbon paper. Instead, the forms have a special treatment on the back side that acts in the same way as carbon paper.

Several different companies specialize in printing forms for one-write systems. Forms for one-write systems are more expensive then standard forms. If a firm is considering the use of a one-write system, an office supply store can often provide the names of sales people who sell them.

The Pegboard

A one-write system is sometimes called a pegboard system because a pegboard is used to hold the various forms in place. The name *pegboard* comes from the pegs located along one side of the board. The forms used have holes on one side. These holes fit over the pegs on the pegboard. When the forms are properly placed over the pegs, all of the lines and columns of all forms are properly aligned. Figure 22-2 shows an actual one-write system with a pegboard. The top form is a check. Under the check is the accounts payable ledger card. The bottom sheet is the cash payments (disbursements) journal page.

STANDARD USES OF THE ONE-WRITE SYSTEM

Cash Receipts Journal

Figure 22-3 shows a one-write system used for a cash receipts journal. The top form (the first writing) is a receipt to be given to the person making the payment. The next item is the subsidiary ledger card for Robert J. Smith. The bottom copy is the cash receipts journal page. Note that with a one-write system there can be no posting errors. Whatever is written on the check or receipt is also recorded in the journal and ledger by means of carbon paper. Thus, the number of errors is reduced. This is one of the major advantages of a one-write system. Of course, the other main advantage is that time is saved since recording and posting is done all in one step.

Payroll

A one-write system can also save time in the preparation of payroll. Figure 22-4 shows a one-write system for payroll. Procedures for payroll will be explained further in chapter 23.

Purchases

Figure 22-5 shows a one-write system for purchases. Although this system does not save as much time as those previously shown (since there is no check or receipt to be written), it still eliminates posting to the subsidiary ledger and reduces errors.

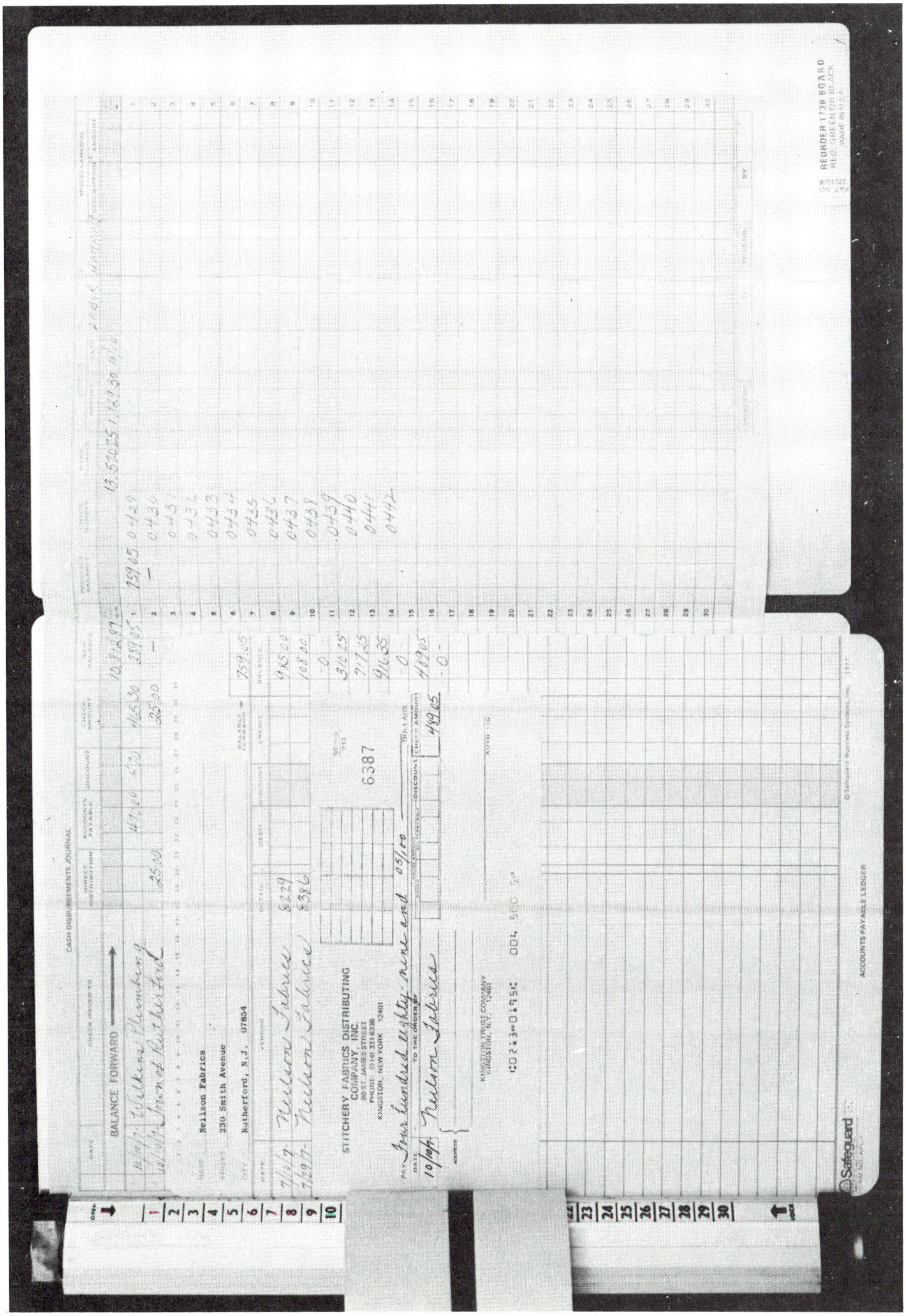

Fig. 22-2. A one-write system for accounts payable.

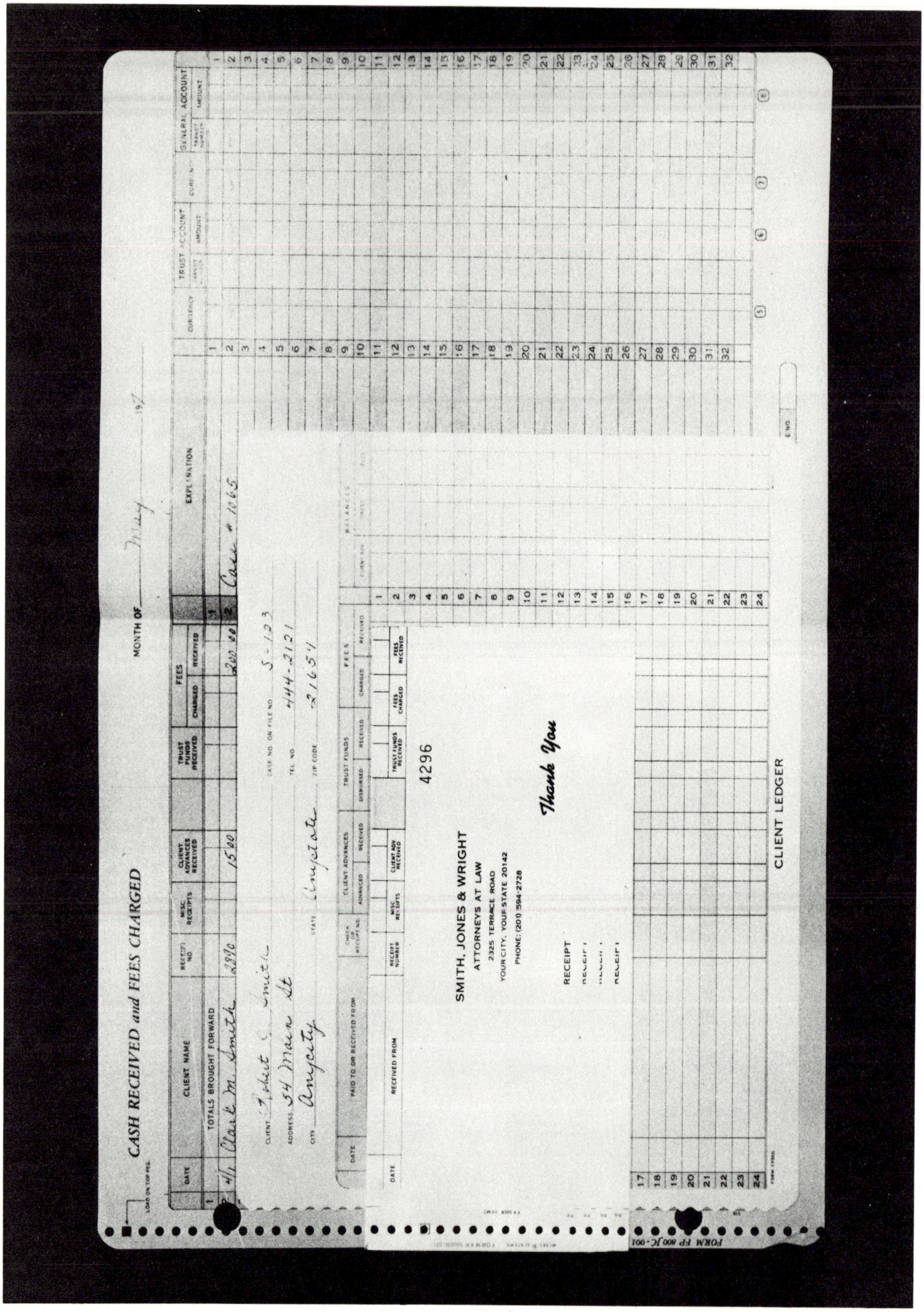

Fig. 22-3. A one-write system for cash receipts.

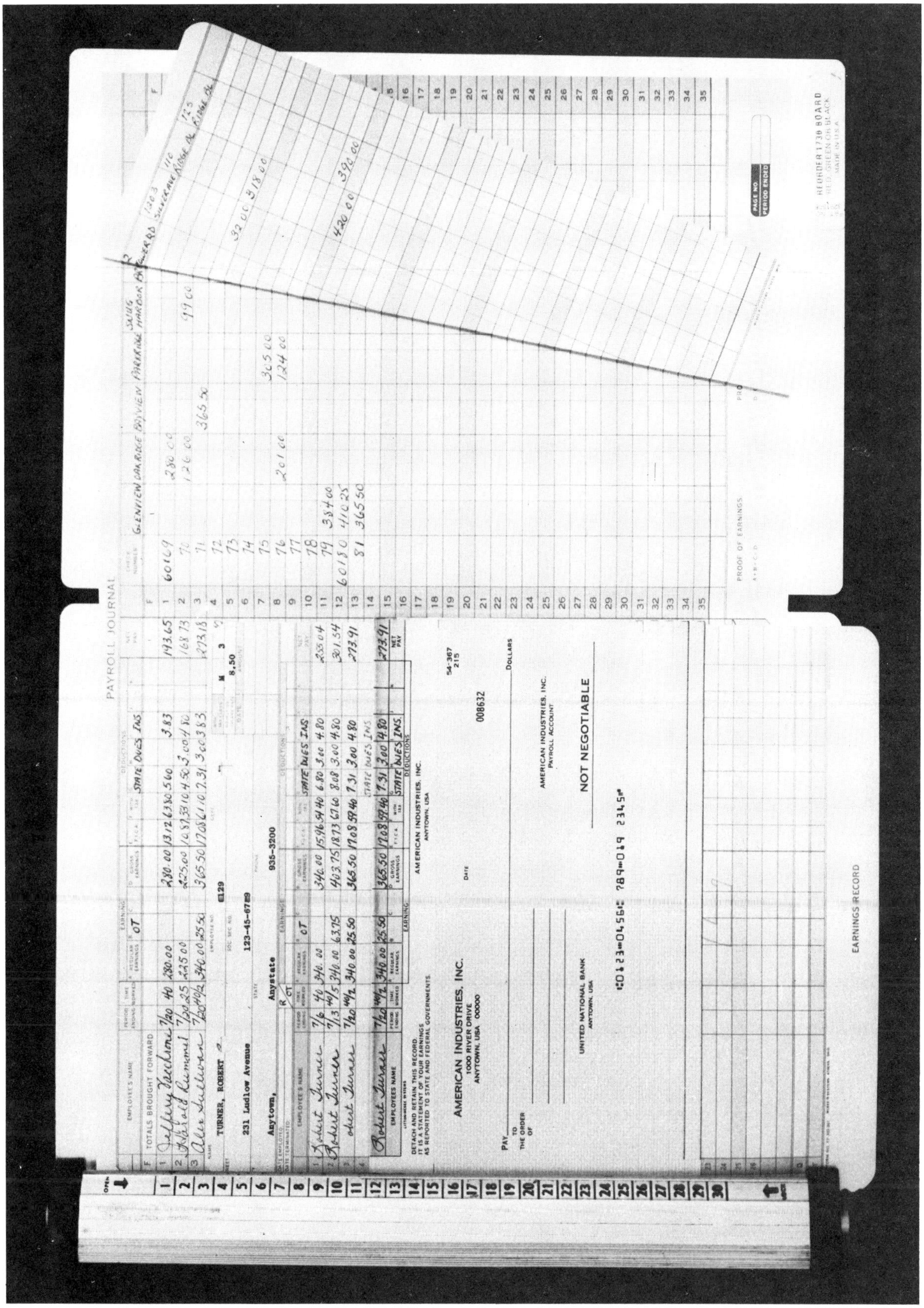

Fig. 22-4. A one-write system for payroll.

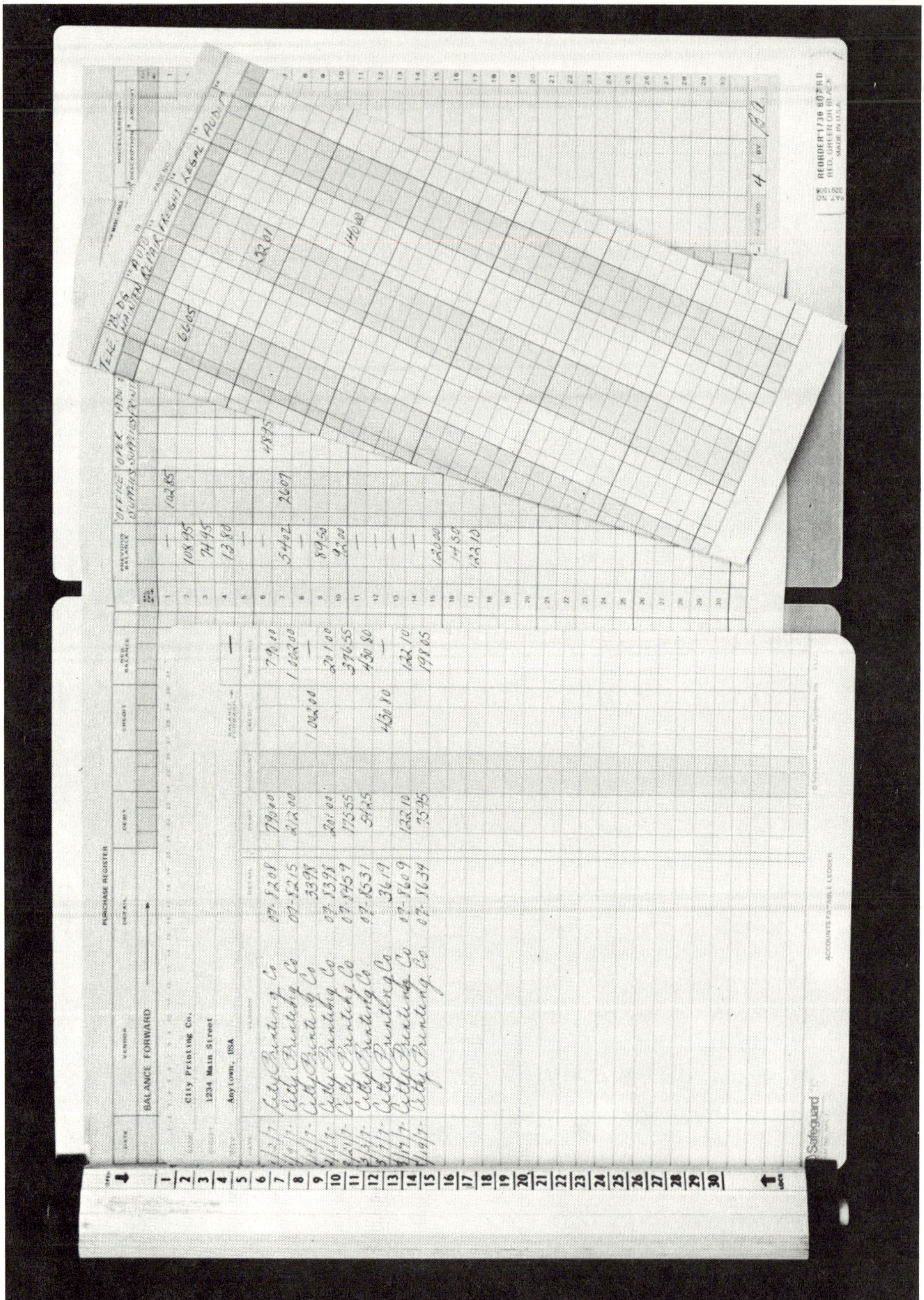

Fig. 22-5. A one-write system for purchases.

Fig. 22-6. A sophisticated pegboard system for recording payroll.

The man in figure 22-6 is using an elaborate pegboard to record transactions on a one-write system. Figure 22-7 explains its use. Most firms have simpler pegboards similar to the one in figure 22-8.

OTHER TYPES OF SYSTEMS

The procedures described in the first three sections of this text are suitable for most small firms. Their accounting can be handled with one journal and one ledger. As a firm grows larger, time and money can be saved by using subsidiary ledgers and special journals. At some point, the firm may wish to save additional labor by using one-write systems. If a company becomes so large that manual systems cannot handle the accounting required, it may take the final step in labor-saving devices – the use of a computer to record accounting data.

While large firms usually have their own computers, a firm need not buy its own computer. A small firm that cannot afford its own computer can share one with other firms. This is called *time sharing* because many firms share the computer time. Many public accountants have computers in their offices that are shared by the accountants' clients. Public accountants can supply a firm with information about time sharing.

No effort will be made in this text to detail the use of computer-kept accounting records. A complete course on computers is necessary to fully understand their operation. However, all accounting procedures described in this text also apply in a computerized system. The

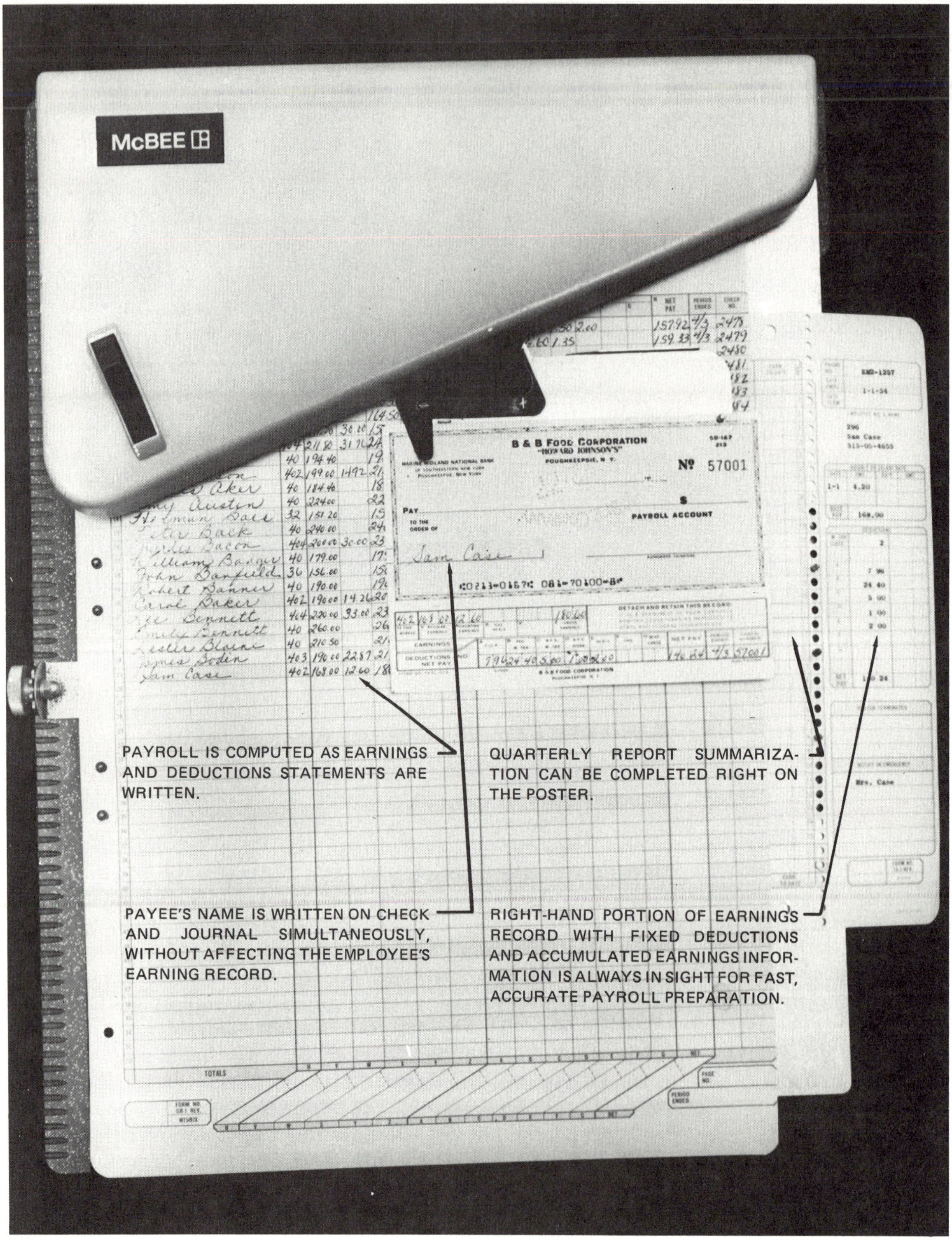

Fig. 22-7. Explanation of the payroll system shown in figure 22-6.

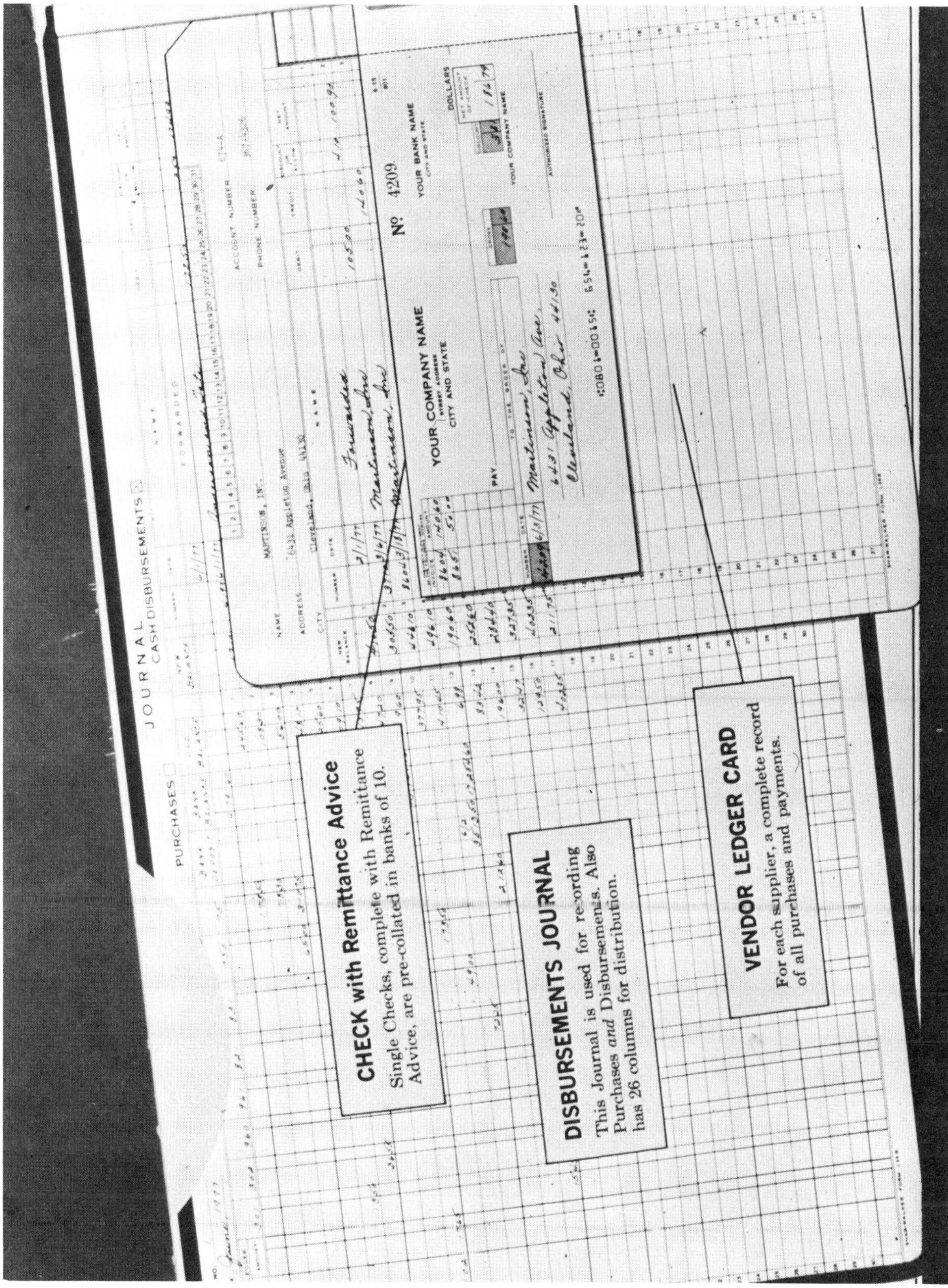

Fig. 22-8. A simple pegboard system for cash payments.

only difference is that the computer does all of the calculations and storing of records.

SUMMARY

A one-write system is a time- and labor-saving device. Carbon paper or specially treated paper is used to eliminate copying the same data in three different places. If forms are properly aligned, it is possible to make one writing do the work of three. A one-write system is also called a pegboard system since a pegboard is used to get all of the forms properly aligned.

Since the journal and subsidiary ledger are carbon copies of the check or receipt, it is impossible to make an error when transferring numbers from one sheet of paper to another. Thus, the two main advantages of a one-write system are:

- reduction of recording and posting time, and
- elimination of posting and recording errors.

The most sophisticated way to record accounting data is to use a computer. A firm may have its own computer or it may rent time on one owned by another company. Renting time on a computer used by several firms is called time sharing. Whether a firm uses a computer, or does its accounting work by hand, the basic principles of accounting are the same.

REVIEW

1. What are the two main advantages of a one-write system?
2. Describe how a one-write system for cash payments works.
3. Describe how a one-write system for cash receipts works.
4. Describe how a one-write system for purchases works.
5. What is another name for a one-write system? Why is this name appropriate?
6. If a firm using a one-write system grows larger, what would be the next step the firm would take to cut its cost of recording accounting data?
7. What is it called when a firm rents the use of another firm's computer?

23 Payroll Preparation and Recording

OBJECTIVES After studying this chapter, the student will be able to:

- Describe the types of deductions made from employees' wages.
- Explain the various federal labor laws.
- Describe the timekeeping process.
- Calculate employee earnings.
- Determine the amount of income tax to be withheld from employees' wages.
- Compute FICA (social security) taxes for individual employees.
- Keep individual employee earnings records as required by the Internal Revenue Service.
- Prepare a payroll register.
- Record the journal entry for payroll.

Up to this point, payroll has been recorded with a very simple entry – a debit to Wage Expense and a credit to Cash. However, as anyone who has ever had a job knows, the employee does not receive the full amount of wages earned. Instead, there are many deductions made from an employee's wages before the paycheck is ever written. Deductions are made for federal and state income taxes, social security taxes, pension plans, health insurance, group life insurance, savings bonds, union dues, and several other things. There may be as many as fifty different deductions from employee wages. Fortunately, not all fifty apply to each employee. Most employees have only five or six deductions made from their pay. But, as a result of these deductions, the entry to record payroll is not as simple as the one that has been described up to this point in the text.

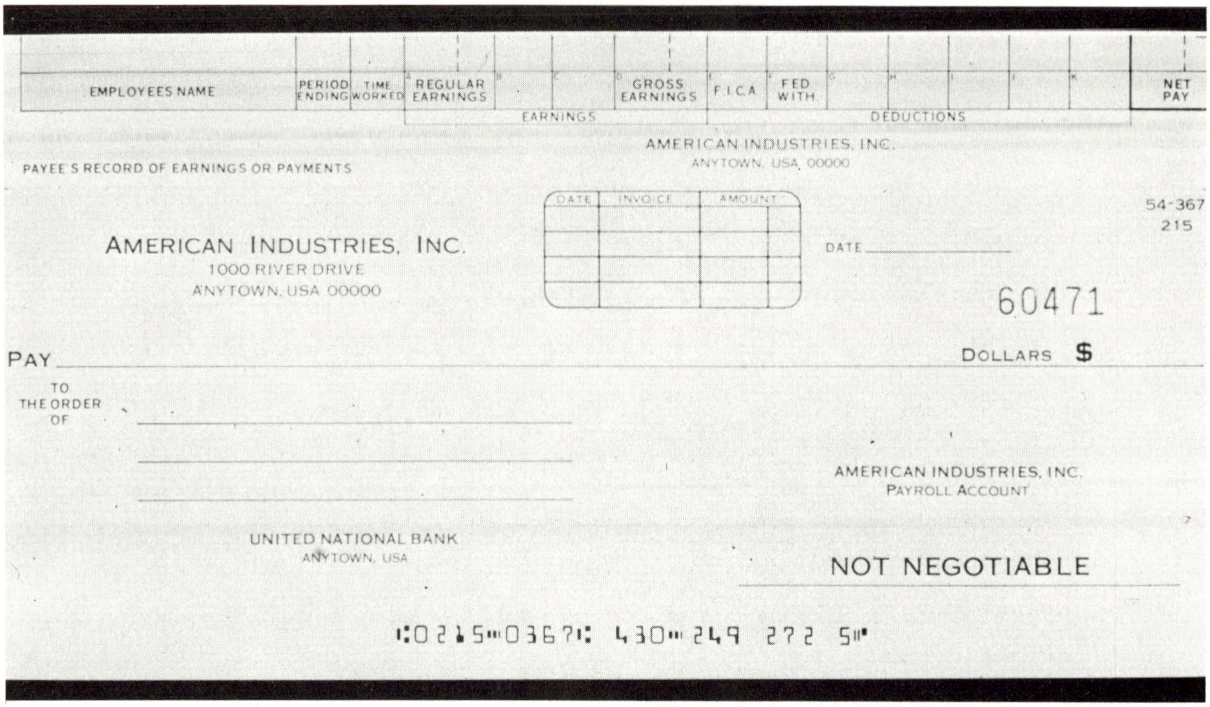

EMPLOYEES NAME | PERIOD ENDING | TIME WORKED | REGULAR EARNINGS | GROSS EARNINGS | F.I.C.A. | FED WITH | NET PAY

EARNINGS — DEDUCTIONS

AMERICAN INDUSTRIES, INC.
ANYTOWN, USA 00000

PAYEE'S RECORD OF EARNINGS OR PAYMENTS

AMERICAN INDUSTRIES, INC.
1000 RIVER DRIVE
ANYTOWN, USA 00000

DATE | INVOICE | AMOUNT

54-367
215

DATE

60471

PAY ____ DOLLARS $

TO THE ORDER OF

AMERICAN INDUSTRIES, INC.
PAYROLL ACCOUNT

UNITED NATIONAL BANK
ANYTOWN, USA

NOT NEGOTIABLE

⑆0215⑈0367⑆ 430⑈ 249 272 5⑈

Fig. 23-1. A standard payroll check.

LAWS AFFECTING PAYROLL

The following is a brief discussion of some of the laws that affect payroll.

Federal Withholding Taxes

Since 1943 the Internal Revenue Service (IRS) has required employers to withhold federal income taxes from employees' wages. The amount of wages earned by each employee and the amount of taxes withheld must be reported to the IRS four times per year. This information is reported on Form 941, which will be discussed in the next chapter. Once a year, the employer must report earnings and taxes withheld to each employee. This yearly report is made in January on Form W-2. Form W-2 will also be discussed in chapter 24.

In addition to federal withholding, most states, and many large cities, also require that income taxes be withheld from employees' wages. Each state has its own forms for the reporting of these taxes. The owner of a new business should always write to the state department of revenue to determine the requirements for wages and taxes.

In addition to keeping records of wages and taxes, employers must also keep records of their employees' names and addresses, and when wages were paid.

Social Security Taxes

All employees must pay social security taxes. These taxes are also called *FICA taxes* because they were created by the Federal Insurance Contributions Act (FICA). The FICA taxes help pay for old age security, disability benefits, and Medicare. During an employee's working years, funds are set aside from earnings. When the employee retires or is disabled, monthly cash benefits are paid to replace part of the earnings the individual or his family has lost.

Although the FICA tax rate has changed several times during the past few years, the current rate is 6.13%.* This rate applies only to the first $25,900 earned by each employee each year. Thus, if a person earns $100.00 during a week, the FICA tax that will be withheld is $6.13 (6.13% of $100.00). If a person earns $25,900 during a year, the total tax withheld for the year would be $1,587.67 (6.13% of $25,900). If a person earns more than $25,900, there is no additional tax on any excess earnings. For instance, if a worker earns $30,000 during a year, the total FICA tax withheld would still be $1,587.67.

Fair Labor Standards Act

The Federal Fair Labor Standards Act is often called the Wages and Hours Law. This law requires that employers pay a minimum wage to workers and time and one-half for overtime. *Overtime* is defined as any hours in excess of forty per week. Thus, if an employee who earns $3.00 per hour works forty-one hours during a week, he would receive $3.00 for each of the first forty hours and $4.50 (1½ times $3.00) for the hour in excess of forty, or a total of $124.50. Most states set minimum wage standards for those firms that are not covered by the federal law.

OBTAINING AN EMPLOYER IDENTIFICATION NUMBER

The first thing that a firm must do when starting in business is to obtain an *employer identification number.* This is similar to the social security number of an individual. Form SS-4, figure 23-2, is used to obtain an employer identification number from the Internal Revenue Service. The employer identification number is used on all tax forms that a firm must file.

CALCULATING THE PAYROLL

Determining the Number of Hours Worked

The first step in calculating payroll is knowing how many hours each employee works. In very small firms the employees may keep their own records of hours worked. The owner or manager might also keep track of how much each employee works. As a firm grows larger, however, it usually becomes necessary to have a time clock. A *time clock* is used to record on a card each employee's time of arrival and departure each day. As employees enter or leave the building, they place their time cards into a slot in the clock. The clock stamps the date and time on the card. At the end of the week, all of the cards are turned into the payroll department.

Payroll Register

A *payroll register* is used to summarize all payroll data at the end of each payroll period. Each line has a different employee's name,

*This rate is established by Congress and is subject to change. The rate given here and used in examples in this text is the rate at time of publication.

For clear copy on both parts, please typewrite or print with ball point pen and press firmly
(See Instructions on pages 2 and 4)

Form SS-4 (Rev. 8-76)
Department of the Treasury
Internal Revenue Service

Application for Employer Identification Number
(For use by employers and others as explained in the Instructions)

1 Name (True name as distinguished from trade name. If partnership, see Instructions on page 4)

2 Trade name, if any (Enter name under which business is operated, if different from item 1)

3 Social security number, if sole proprietor

4 Address of principal place of business (Number and street)

5 Ending month of accounting year

6 City and State

7 ZIP code

8 County of business location

9 Type of organization
☐ Governmental (See Instr. on page 4)
☐ Individual
☐ Nonprofit organization (See Instr. on page 4)
☐ Partnership
☐ Corporation
☐ Other (specify)

10 Date you acquired or started this business (Mo., day, year)

11 Reason for applying
☐ Started new business
☐ Purchased going business
☐ Other (specify)

12 First date you paid or will pay wages for this business (Mo., day, year)

13 Nature of business (See Instructions on page 4)

14 Do you operate more than one place of business? ☐ Yes ☐ No

15 Peak number of employees expected in next 12 months (If none, enter "0") ▶ Nonagricultural | Agricultural | Household

16 If nature of business is manufacturing, state principal product and raw material used

17 To whom do you sell most of your products or services?
☐ Business establishments
☐ General public
☐ Other (specify)

18 Have you ever applied for an identification number for this or any other business? ☐ Yes ☐ No

If "Yes," enter name and trade name (if any). Also enter the approximate date, city, and State where you first applied and previous number if known. ▶

Date | Signature and title | Telephone number

Fig. 23-2. Form SS-4 is used to obtain an employer identification number.

wage rate, hours worked, and deductions recorded. Figure 23-3 shows a partial page from a payroll register. Note that there is a separate column for regular pay, overtime pay, gross pay, each deduction, and net pay.

The payroll clerk first records the name of each employee in the register. Next, the hours worked are taken from the clock cards and recorded in the register. Then regular, overtime, and gross pay are calculated. The next step is to calculate the deductions for income taxes and FICA taxes. Finally, all other deductions are recorded in the register and the net pay is calculated. The *net pay* is the amount the employees will actually receive.

					Earnings			Deductions					Payment	
Employee's Name	Clock Card No.	Total Hours	O.T. Hours	Reg. Pay Rate	Reg. Pay	O.T. Pay	Gross Pay	FICA Taxes	Fed. Inc. Taxes	Un. Dues	Med. Ins.	Tot. Ded.	Net Pay	Chk. No.

Fig. 23-3. A partial page from a blank payroll register.

Calculating Income Taxes

As mentioned earlier, the employer is required to withhold income taxes from the wages of employees. The amount to be withheld depends upon two things: (1) the amount earned by the employee, and (2) the number of exemptions claimed. Each exemption reduces the amount of tax that an employee has to pay. Thus, the more exemptions an employee has, the less the tax that will be withheld. An employee is allowed an exemption for himself or herself plus one for each dependent. The employee notifies the employer of the number of exemptions to be used by giving the employer a copy of Form W-4. Form W-4, (figure 23-4), is called the Employee's Withholding Allowance Certificate. The employee must fill out a Form W-4 when first hired. A new W-4 form should be prepared whenever a change takes place in the employee's family size (such as the birth of a child or the marriage of an older child).

The employer uses a *wage bracket withholding table* to find the amount to be withheld from each employee's wages for tax purposes. The IRS supplies separate tables for weekly, biweekly, semimonthly, and monthly pay periods. A sample table is shown in figure 23-5.

The amount to be withheld is found by the following steps. First, find the employee's wage bracket in the first two columns. Then read across that line to the column for the proper number of exemption allowances. The amount in this column is the tax to be withheld.

For example, if an employee is married and has no children, he would be entitled to two exemptions. If the employee has a gross pay of $127 during a week, the amount of tax to be withheld is $8.70. This tax is determined by reading down the first two columns of figure 23-5 to the *at least $125 but less than $130* line. Moving across to the column for two exemptions, the amount shown is $8.70.

Form **W-4**
(Rev. May 1977)
Department of the Treasury
Internal Revenue Service

Employee's Withholding Allowance Certificate
(Use for Wages Paid After May 31, 1977)
This certificate is for income tax withholding purposes only. It will remain in effect until you change it. If you claim exemption from withholding, you will have to file a new certificate on or before April 30 of next year.

Type or print your full name		Your social security number
Home address (number and street or rural route)	Marital Status	☐ Single ☐ Married ☐ Married, but withhold at higher Single rate
City or town, State, and ZIP code		**Note:** *If married, but legally separated, or spouse is a nonresident alien, check the single block.*

1 Total number of allowances you are claiming . . . . ______
2 Additional amount, if any, you want deducted from each pay (if your employer agrees) . . . . $______
3 I claim exemption from withholding (see instructions). Enter "Exempt" . . . .

Under the penalties of perjury, I certify that the number of withholding exemptions and allowances claimed on this certificate does not exceed the number to which I am entitled. If claiming exemption from withholding, I certify that I incurred no liability for Federal income tax for last year and that I anticipate that I will incur no liability for Federal income tax for this year.

Signature ▶ ______________________ Date ▶ ______________, 19____

Fig. 23-4. The W-4 form is used to report exemptions.

MARRIED Persons—WEEKLY Payroll Period

And the wages are—		And the number of withholding allowances claimed is—										
At least	But less than	0	1	2	3	4	5	6	7	8	9	10 or more
		The amount of income tax to be withheld shall be—										
$0	$48	$0	$0	$0	$0	$0	$0	$0	$0	$0	$0	$0
48	49	.10	0	0	0	0	0	0	0	0	0	0
49	50	.20	0	0	0	0	0	0	0	0	0	0
50	51	.40	0	0	0	0	0	0	0	0	0	0
51	52	.60	0	0	0	0	0	0	0	0	0	0
52	53	.80	0	0	0	0	0	0	0	0	0	0
53	54	.90	0	0	0	0	0	0	0	0	0	0
54	55	1.10	0	0	0	0	0	0	0	0	0	0
55	56	1.30	0	0	0	0	0	0	0	0	0	0
56	57	1.40	0	0	0	0	0	0	0	0	0	0
57	58	1.60	0	0	0	0	0	0	0	0	0	0
58	59	1.80	0	0	0	0	0	0	0	0	0	0
59	60	1.90	0	0	0	0	0	0	0	0	0	0
60	62	2.20	0	0	0	0	0	0	0	0	0	0
62	64	2.50	.10	0	0	0	0	0	0	0	0	0
64	66	2.90	.40	0	0	0	0	0	0	0	0	0
66	68	3.20	.80	0	0	0	0	0	0	0	0	0
68	70	3.60	1.10	0	0	0	0	0	0	0	0	0
70	72	3.90	1.40	0	0	0	0	0	0	0	0	0
72	74	4.20	1.80	0	0	0	0	0	0	0	0	0
74	76	4.60	2.10	0	0	0	0	0	0	0	0	0
76	78	4.90	2.50	0	0	0	0	0	0	0	0	0
78	80	5.30	2.80	.40	0	0	0	0	0	0	0	0
80	82	5.60	3.10	.70	0	0	0	0	0	0	0	0
82	84	5.90	3.50	1.00	0	0	0	0	0	0	0	0
84	86	6.30	3.80	1.40	0	0	0	0	0	0	0	0
86	88	6.60	4.20	1.70	0	0	0	0	0	0	0	0
88	90	7.00	4.50	2.10	0	0	0	0	0	0	0	0
90	92	7.30	4.80	2.40	0	0	0	0	0	0	0	0
92	94	7.60	5.20	2.70	.30	0	0	0	0	0	0	0
94	96	8.00	5.50	3.10	.60	0	0	0	0	0	0	0
96	98	8.30	5.90	3.40	1.00	0	0	0	0	0	0	0
98	100	8.70	6.20	3.80	1.30	0	0	0	0	0	0	0
100	105	9.40	6.80	4.30	1.90	0	0	0	0	0	0	0
105	110	10.40	7.70	5.20	2.70	.30	0	0	0	0	0	0
110	115	11.40	8.60	6.00	3.60	1.10	0	0	0	0	0	0
115	120	12.40	9.60	6.90	4.40	2.00	0	0	0	0	0	0
120	125	13.40	10.60	7.70	5.30	2.80	.40	0	0	0	0	0
125	130	14.40	11.60	8.70	6.10	3.70	1.20	0	0	0	0	0
130	135	15.40	12.60	9.70	7.00	4.50	2.10	0	0	0	0	0
135	140	16.40	13.60	10.70	7.80	5.40	2.90	.50	0	0	0	0
140	145	17.40	14.60	11.70	8.80	6.20	3.80	1.30	0	0	0	0
145	150	18.40	15.60	12.70	9.80	7.10	4.60	2.20	0	0	0	0
150	160	19.90	17.10	14.20	11.30	8.40	5.90	3.50	1.00	0	0	0
160	170	21.90	19.10	16.20	13.30	10.40	7.60	5.20	2.70	.30	0	0
170	180	23.90	21.10	18.20	15.30	12.40	9.50	6.90	4.40	2.00	0	0
180	190	25.60	23.10	20.20	17.30	14.40	11.50	8.60	6.10	3.70	1.20	0
190	200	27.30	24.80	22.20	19.30	16.40	13.50	10.60	7.80	5.40	2.90	.50
200	210	29.00	26.50	24.10	21.30	18.40	15.50	12.60	9.80	7.10	4.60	2.20
210	220	30.70	28.20	25.80	23.30	20.40	17.50	14.60	11.80	8.90	6.30	3.90
220	230	32.40	29.90	27.50	25.00	22.40	19.50	16.60	13.80	10.90	8.00	5.60
230	240	34.10	31.60	29.20	26.70	24.30	21.50	18.60	15.80	12.90	10.00	7.30
240	250	35.80	33.30	30.90	28.40	26.00	23.50	20.60	17.80	14.90	12.00	9.10
250	260	37.50	35.00	32.60	30.10	27.70	25.20	22.60	19.80	16.90	14.00	11.10
260	270	39.20	36.70	34.30	31.80	29.40	26.90	24.50	21.80	18.90	16.00	13.10
270	280	41.70	38.40	36.00	33.50	31.10	28.60	26.20	23.70	20.90	18.00	15.10
280	290	44.20	40.60	37.70	35.20	32.80	30.30	27.90	25.40	22.90	20.00	17.10
290	300	46.70	43.10	39.50	36.90	34.50	32.00	29.60	27.10	24.70	22.00	19.10
300	310	49.20	45.60	42.00	38.60	36.20	33.70	31.30	28.80	26.40	23.90	21.10
310	320	51.70	48.10	44.50	40.90	37.90	35.40	33.00	30.50	28.10	25.60	23.10

22

(Continued)

Fig. 23-5. A page from the federal wage bracket withholding table.

Employee's Name	Clock Card No.	Total Hours	O.T. Hours	Reg. Pay Rate	Earnings: Reg. Pay	Earnings: O.T. Pay	Earnings: Gross Pay	Deductions: FICA Taxes	Deductions: Fed. Inc. Taxes	Deductions: Un. Dues	Deductions: Med. Ins.	Deductions: Tot. Ded.	Payment: Net Pay	Payment: Chk. No.
Rita Sparks		*40*		*3.00*	*120.00*		*120.00*	*7.36*	*7.70*	*1.00*	*5.00*	*20.96*	*98.94*	
Charles Barnes		*44*	*4*	*4.00*	*160.00*	*24.00*	*184.00*	*11.28*	*14.40*	*1.00*	___	*26.53*	*157.32*	
					280.00	*24.00*	*304.00*	*18.64*	*22.10*	*2.00*	*5.00*	*47.49*	*256.26*	

Fig. 23-6. Payroll register for Downtown Distributors.

If a state or city also requires the employer to withhold income taxes, the procedure is the same as for federal taxes. The state (or city) provides a wage bracket withholding table that is used in the same way as the federal table.

Example. Downtown Distributors has two employees, Rita Sparks and Charles Barnes. Sparks has two exemptions and Barnes has four exemptions. Sparks earns $3 per hour. Barnes earns $4 per hour. During the first week in January, Sparks worked forty hours and Barnes worked forty-four hours. Both people have union dues of $1 per week withheld from their wages. In addition, Sparks has $5 per week withheld for health insurance. The payroll register for the week is shown in Figure 23-6.

RECORDING THE PAYROLL

Once the payroll register is completed, the entry to record the payroll can be recorded. As mentioned earlier, the entry is not a simple one. The entry to record the payroll shown in figure 23-6 is:

Jan. 7	Wage Expense	304.00	
	Employees Fed. Income Taxes Payable		22.10
	FICA Taxes Payable		18.64
	Employees Union Dues Payable		2.00
	Employees Health Ins. Premiums Payable		5.00
	Accrued Payroll Payable		256.26
	To record Jan. 7 payroll		

Note that the credits of this entry are all taken from the column totals of the payroll register. All of the credits are current liability accounts. The balances in Employees Federal Income Taxes Payable and FICA Taxes Payable will be paid to the federal government. Employees Union Dues Payable is a liability that will be paid to the union. Employees Health Insurance Premiums Payable will be paid to an insurance company. The Accrued Payroll Payable is the net pay and will be paid to the employees.

The entry to pay the employees is made in the cash payments journal. A check is made out to each employee for his or her net pay. The effect of writing the checks is a debit to Accrued Payroll Payable and a credit to Cash.

INDIVIDUAL EMPLOYEE'S EARNINGS RECORD

The Internal Revenue Service requires that all employers keep a record of the amounts earned by each employee. This information is

Name Rita Sparks | Social Security No. 123-45-6789 | No. of Exemptions 2

Address 123 Circle Street, Ourtown, NC

Rate $3.00

	Date	Check Number	Total Hours	O.T. Hours	Reg. Pay	O.T. Pay	Gross Pay	Fed. Inc. Taxes	FICA Taxes	Union Dues	Insur. Prem.	Net Pay
1	1 - 7		40		120.00		120.00	7.70	7.36	1.00	5.00	98.94
2												
3												
4												

Fig. 23-7. Individual employee's earnings record.

usually kept on cards with a separate card used for each employee. An example is shown in figure 23-7.

The name, address, social security number, and number of exemptions is taken from the W-4 form filled out by the employee. The other data is taken from the payroll register. Thus, the payroll clerk must remember to post all of the information each week from the payroll register to the individual employee's earnings record. A new card must be started each year. At the end of each year the information for each employee is reported to the IRS on a W-2 form.

SUMMARY

Several federal and state laws affect the calculation of payroll. The Fair Labor Standards Act requires that a minimum wage be paid and that an overtime premium be given. The Internal Revenue Service requires that income taxes and FICA taxes be withheld from employees' wages. Labor contracts and state laws may require that additional deductions be made from wages. The Small Business Administration offers information concerning payroll problems in several of its publications, figure 23-8.

The basic payroll data is summarized in a payroll register. This data is then posted to an individual employee's earnings record. The data is also recorded with a journal entry. The basic steps of calculating and recording payroll are:

- Record names, hours worked, and pay rates in the payroll register.
- Calculate the gross payroll.
- Calculate the federal and state income taxes to be withheld.
- Calculate the FICA taxes to be withheld.
- Make any other required deductions (such as union dues, insurance premiums, savings plans, or pensions).
- Determine the net payroll.
- Add up the columns of the payroll register.
- Record the payroll register totals with a journal entry.
- Post the data from the payroll register to the individual employee earnings records.

Fig. 23-8. Publications from the Small Business Administration (SBA) help to explain the duties of employers.

All of the steps must be done each payroll period (usually weekly). Care must be taken to avoid errors. Since the payroll steps are performed so often, the slightest error can be repeated many times before it is caught. Although employees would be quick to report an underpayment, overpayments are usually not reported. Thus, an error by the payroll clerk can be very costly to the firm.

REVIEW

1. What does the Fair Labor Standards Act require of an employer?
2. What are FICA taxes?
3. Who completes the W-4 form?
4. What is the purpose of the W-4 form?
5. List at least five items that are often deducted from employees' wages.
6. What is the current FICA tax rate?

7. How is a time clock used in a business?
8. Why are individual employee earnings records required?
9. How often is the payroll register prepared?
10. What is the purpose of Form SS-4?

EXERCISES

1. Tom worked fifty hours during the first week in January. He earns $4 per hour. His firm is covered by the Federal Fair Labor Standards Act. Tom is married and has one child. Calculate his a) regular pay, b) overtime pay, c) gross pay, d) FICA taxes, and e) income taxes (use the wage bracket withholding table in this chapter). If Tom was the only employee of the firm, how would the week's payroll be recorded?

2. A firm's payroll register had the following column totals for the second week of January:

Regular Pay	3,000
Overtime Pay	1,200
Gross Pay	?
Federal Income Taxes	680
FICA Taxes	?
Health Insurance	150
Net Pay	?

   a. Calculate the totals that are not given.
   b. Record the payroll in the general journal.

3. George is married and has three children. His wife does not work. George earned $300 for the past week. So far this year, he has earned $22,000.
   a. Use the wage bracket withholding table in this unit to calculate the amount of income taxes to be withheld from George's paycheck.
   b. Calculate the amount of FICA taxes to be withheld from his check.
   c. If no other deductions are made, what is George's net pay for the week?

PROBLEMS

1. A firm has five employees. Individual data is as follows:

Employee	Wage Rate	Exemptions	Earnings to End of Previous Week	Hours Worked This Week
Fred Ami	4.00	3	8,100	40
Janet Farbes	5.00	4	12,000	44
Tom Cain	4.00	2	8,000	40
Dick Eades	10.00	5	21,000	52
Bill Jones	4.50	3	1,200	46

All employees except Bill Jones have health insurance premiums of $3 withheld from their wages. Eades has $106.90 withheld for federal income taxes.

   a. Use the above information to prepare a payroll register for the week.
   b. Record the payroll data with a general journal entry.
   c. Explain why Fred Ami's net pay is more than Tom Cain's when they both have the same gross pay.

2. A payroll register for the first week of January had the following totals:

Regular Pay	4,000
Overtime Pay	?
Gross Pay	?
Federal Income Taxes	900
State Income Taxes	120
FICA Taxes	?
Insurance Premiums	100
Union Dues	120
Total Deductions	?
Net Pay	3,000

a. Calculate the unknown figures in the list.
b. Make the journal entry to record the payroll for the week.

3. A firm has six employees. Individual data on each is:

Employee	Wage Rate	Exemptions	Earnings to End of Previous Week	Hours Worked This Week
Nancy Hanks	3.50	2	4,200	40
Ann Royce	4.00	3	2,000	40
Joan Smith	9.00	5	19,000	56
Charles Speer	10.00	2	21,000	50
Lisa Queen	5.00	4	10,000	41
Mary Todd	5.00	4	8,000	40

All employees have \$4 per week withheld for health insurance. All except Joan Smith and Charles Speer have \$1 withheld for union dues. Smith had \$103.50 withheld for federal income taxes; Speer had \$111.70 withheld.

a. Use the above information to prepare a payroll register for the week.
b. Record the payroll register with a general journal entry.

4. The following is the individual employee earnings record for David Goldman. Some information is omitted and is replaced with letters. Determine what figures should appear in place of the letters.

Name David Goldman — Social Security No. 123-54-6798 — No. of Exemptions A

Address 595 Adler Street, East City, Indiana 46000

Rate B

	Date	Check Number	Total Hours	O.T. Hours	Reg. Pay	O.T. Pay	Gross Pay	Fed. Inc. Taxes	FICA Taxes	Union Dues	Insur. Prem.	Net Pay
1	1 - 7		40		C		D	13.30	9.81			136.89
2	1 - 14		E	F	G	6.00	166.00	13.30	H			I
3	1 - 21		40	3	J	K	178.00	15.30	L			M
4	1 - 28		40	N	O	P	172.00	15.30	Q			R
5												
6												

24
Payroll Reports and Regulations

OBJECTIVES After studying this chapter, the student will be able to:

- Identify the various types of payroll reports and forms.
- Compute the amount of payroll taxes due.
- Prepare government payroll reports.
- Explain the rules and regulations pertaining to payroll record keeping.

The filing of payroll tax records is one accounting task that is done on a regular basis by all firms. Payroll tax forms must be completed periodically for

- FICA taxes (social security taxes).
- Federal unemployment taxes.
- State unemployment taxes.

Payroll taxes are an unwelcome subject with the owners of many small businesses. To many, it seems that some type of tax form is due to be filed almost every month. Tax payments may have to be made on a monthly basis, or sometimes even more often. However, payroll taxes are not as complicated as some people believe. They cease to be threatening when a person has adequate knowledge of the payroll tax laws. Well-managed firms rarely have problems in meeting tax obligations. Establishing a systematic approach to taxes lessens the possibility of forgetting to file a return or failing to make a payment.

The Small Business Administration (SBA) has prepared the following suggestion list to help small businesses manage their tax law obligations.

- Know what kind of taxes must be paid.
- Know how much taxes are due.
- Know when taxes are due.
- Set aside funds necessary to pay various tax bills.
- Pay taxes on time to avoid penalties for late payment.
- Get advice from an expert, such as an accountant or other tax counselor.

REPORTING FICA TAXES

As noted in the previous chapter, employers are required to withhold social security (FICA) taxes from each employee's wages. The FICA tax rate, as established in 1980, is 6.13%.* This rate is somewhat misleading, however, since the employer must also pay FICA taxes on each employee. The employer's rate is also 6.13%. Consequently, the FICA tax rate is really 12.26% (6.13 + 6.13%). The rules for computing the employer's share of the tax are exactly the same as for computing the employee's share of the tax. For instance, only the first $25,900 of wages earned in a year are taxed.

Example. Assume that an employee earns $1,000 in a month. The employer withholds $61.30 (6.13% of 1,000.00) from the employee's paycheck. In addition, the employer must match the $61.30 paid by the employee with another $61.30. Therefore, the total FICA tax on the $1,000 salary is $122.60, or 12.26%. The employer must pay this $122.60 to the federal government. It is important to note that both the employer and the employee must pay FICA taxes.

In addition, the employer must file a quarterly tax form reporting the amounts of tax withheld and paid. Form 941 is used for this purpose. Both FICA taxes and income taxes withheld from employees' wages are reported on this form.

Example. A firm begins business on June 1 with one employee. The employee is paid $1,000 per month, on the last day of the month. The firm withholds $196 from the employee's wages each month for federal income taxes. The journal entry to record the payment of the employee on June 30 is as follows:

June 30	Salary Expense	1,000.00	
	Employees Fed. Inc. Taxes Payable		196.00
	FICA Taxes Payable		61.30
	Cash		742.70
	To record monthly payroll.		

The entry to record the employer's share of the FICA taxes for the month is:

June 30	Payroll Tax Expense	61.30	
	FICA Taxes Payable		61.30
	To record employer's share of FICA taxes.		

Note that the total balance of the liability account, FICA Taxes Payable, is now $122.60.

The quarterly payroll tax report, form 941, must be filed within one month after the end of each calendar quarter. For example, the report for the first quarter of the year (January, February, and March) must be filed by April 30. The report for the second quarter of the year (April, May, and June) must be filed before the end of July. Thus, in the preceding example, a report must be filed for the June payroll by July 31. That report is shown in figure 24-1.

*This rate is subject to change.

Form **941**
(Rev. April 1978)
Department of the Treasury
Internal Revenue Service

Employer's Quarterly Federal Tax Return

1 **First Quarter Only.**—Number of employees (except household) employed in the pay period that includes March 12th . . . ▶	
2 Total wages and tips subject to withholding, plus other compensation . . . ⟶	1,000 00
3 Total income tax withheld from wages, tips, annuities, gambling, etc. (see instructions) . . .	196 00
4 Adjustment of withheld income tax for preceding quarters of calendar year . . .	
5 Adjusted total of income tax withheld . . . ⟶	196 00
6 Taxable FICA wages paid . . . $ 1,000.00 multiplied by =TAX . .	122 60
7 Taxable tips reported . . . $ multiplied by =TAX . .	
8 Total FICA taxes (add lines 6 and 7) . . .	
9 Adjustment of FICA taxes (see instructions) . . . ⟶	122 60
10 Adjusted total of FICA taxes . . .	
11 Total taxes (add lines 5 and 10) . . . ⟶	122 60 318 60

Record of Federal Tax Deposits (See instructions on page 4)

Deposit period ending:		I. Tax liability for period	II. Date of deposit	III. Amount deposited
Overpayment from previous quarter. . . .				
First month of quarter	1st through 7th day . . .			
	8th through 15th day . . .			
	16th through 22d day . . .			
	23d through last day . . .			
A First month total . . .	A			
Second month of quarter	1st through 7th day . . .			
	8th through 15th day . . .			
	16th through 22d day . . .			
	23d through last day . . .			
B Second month total . . .	B			
Third month of quarter	1st through 7th day . . .			
	8th through 15th day . . .			
	16th through 22d day . . .			
	23d through last day . . .	318 60		
C Third month total . . .	C	318 60		
D Total for quarter (add items A, B, and C) .		318 60		
E Final deposit made for quarter. (Enter zero if the final deposit made for the quarter is included in item D) . . .			7-1	318 60

12 Total deposits for quarter (including final deposit made for quarter) and overpayment from previous quarter. (See instructions on page 4) . . .	318 60
Note: *If undeposited taxes at the end of the quarter are $200 or more, deposit the full amount with an authorized financial institution or a Federal Reserve bank according to the instructions on the back of the Federal Tax Deposit Form 501. Enter this deposit in the Record of Federal Tax Deposits and include it in line 12.*	
13 Undeposited taxes due (subtract line 12 from line 11—this should be less than $200). Pay to Internal Revenue Service and enter here . . . ⟶	– 0 –

14 If line 12 is more than line 11, enter overpayment here ▶ $ and check if to be: ☐ Applied to next return, or ☐ Refunded.

15 If you are not liable for returns in the future, write **"FINAL"** (See instructions) ▶ Date final wages paid ▶

Under penalties of perjury, I declare that I have examined this return, including accompanying schedules and statements, and to the best of my knowledge and belief it is true, correct, and complete.

Date ▶ **Signature** ▶ **Title** ▶

T	
FF	
FD	
FP	
I	
T	

Your name, address, employer identification number, and calendar quarter of return. (If not correct, please change) ▶

Name (as distinguished from trade name) — *CORNER COMPANY*
Date quarter ended — *JUNE 30*
Trade name, if any
Employer identification number
Address and ZIP code — *MAIN STREET*
OLDTOWN, VT 05035

If address is different from prior return, check here ▶ ☐

Please file this form with your Internal Revenue Service Center.
(See instructions on "Where to file")

Form **941** (Rev. 4–78)

Fig. 24-1. Form 941, used to report withholding for income and social security tax.

The form 941 in figure 24-1 shows that a total of $318.60 of taxes are due. This figure matches the balances of the two liability accounts on the firm's books (Employees Federal Income Taxes Payable, $196 + FICA Taxes Payable, $122.60).

Several different rules and regulations govern when and how payroll tax is paid to the government. These regulations are listed in a pamphlet that accompanies the deposit forms. Normally, the payment is not mailed to the government, but is deposited at any local bank to the account of the United States Treasury Department. The taxes must be paid within a short time after the end of the payroll period. Thus, a firm pays its FICA taxes and withholding taxes at the bank whenever the total reaches $200. If the total has not reached $200 by the end of the quarter, then the total tax is payable at the time that form 941 is filed.

In figure 24-1, the total tax is $318.60. Thus, that amount had to be deposited before form 941 was filed. For this reason line 21 of the form shows that a zero balance is due. The only time an amount is shown on line 21 is when less than $200 is owed. When the taxes are paid, the entry is simply to record the payment of a liability. For example:

June 30	FICA Taxes Payable	122.60	
	Employees Federal Income Taxes Payable	196.00	
	Cash		318.60
	Deposited tax payment at local bank.		

RECEIPTS FOR EMPLOYEES

Employers are required to give each employee a copy of form W-2 during January of each year. Form W-2, figure 24-2, must show the total wages paid during the preceding calendar year, the amount of income taxes withheld, and the amount of FICA taxes withheld. In addition to giving a copy of form W-2 to employees, a copy must also be sent to the Internal Revenue Service.

1 Control number 222 | 2 Employer's State number

For Official Use Only

3 Employer's name, address, and ZIP code

4 Sub-total ☐ Cor-rection ☐ Void ☐

5 Yes ☐ Jan–Mar No ☐ | 6 Yes ☐ Apr–Jun No ☐

7 Employer's identification number

8 Yes ☐ Jul–Sep No ☐ | 9 Yes ☐ Oct–Dec No ☐

10 Employee's social security number | 11 Federal income tax withheld | 12 Wages, tips, other compensation | 13 FICA tax withheld | 14 Total FICA wages

15 Employee's name (first, middle, last) | 16 Pension plan coverage? Yes/No | 17* | 18 FICA tips

20 State income tax withheld | 21 State wages, tips, etc. | 22 Name of State

23 Local income tax withheld | 24 Local wages, tips, etc. | 25 Name of locality

19 Employee's address and ZIP code

Wage and Tax Statement

COPY A For Social Security Administration
*See Instructions for Forms W-2 and W-2P and back of Copy D

Form **W-2**

Department of the Treasury—Internal Revenue Service

Fig. 24-2. W-2 form.

Form **940**
Department of the Treasury
Internal Revenue Service

Employer's Annual Federal Unemployment Tax Return

T	
FF	
FD	
FP	
I	
T	

If incorrect, make any necessary change ▶

Name (as distinguished from trade name)

Calendar Year 1978

Trade name, if any FRESHER GROCERY

Employer identification number

Address and ZIP code RT. 1
ANYTOWN, NC

Name of State 1	State reporting number as shown on employer's State contribution returns 2	Taxable payroll (as defined in State act) 3	Experience rate period 4 From—	To—	Experience rate 5	Contributions had rate been 2.7% (col. 3 × 2.7%) 6	Contributions payable at experience rate (col. 3 × col. 5) 7	Additional credit (col. 6 minus col. 7) 8	Contributions actually paid to State 9
NC	123456	6,000.00			2.7%	162.00	162.00	– 0 –	162.00
	Totals ▶	6,000.00							162.00

10 Total tentative credit (column 8 plus column 9—see instructions on page 4)			162.00
11 Total remuneration (including exempt remuneration) paid during the calendar year for services of employees			12,000.00
Exempt Remuneration (See Instructions on Page 4)	(a) New jobs credit wages	(b) Amount paid	
12 Exempt remuneration. (Explain each exemption shown, attaching additional sheet if necessary) ▶			
13 Remuneration in excess of the first $4,200 in column (a), and the first $6,000 in column (b), paid to individual employees exclusive of exempt amounts entered on line 12. Do not use State wage limitation		6,000	
14 Total exempt remuneration (line 12 plus line 13)		6,000	
15 a New jobs credit total wages (subtract line 12, column (a) from line 11)			
b New jobs credit wages (subtract line 14, column (a) from line 11)			
c Total taxable FUTA wages (subtract line 14, column (b) from line 11)			6,000.00
16 Gross Federal tax (multiply line 15c by .034)			204.00
17 Maximum credit (multiply line 15c by .027)			
18 Line 10 or line 17 whichever is smaller			
19 Amount, if any, of wages on line 15c attributable to Rhode Island $........ × .003			
20 Credit allowable (subtract line 19 from line 18)			162.00
21 Net Federal tax (subtract line 20 from line 16)			42.00

Record of Federal Tax Deposits for Unemployment Tax (Form 508)

Quarter	Liability by period	Date of deposit	Amount of deposit
First			
Second			
Third			
Fourth			

22 Total Federal tax deposited	– 0 –
23 **Balance due** (subtract line 22 from line 21—this should not exceed $100). Pay to Internal Revenue Service ▶	42.00
24 **Overpayment** (subtract line 21 from line 22) ▶	
25 If no longer in business at end of year, write "Final" here ▶	

Under penalties of perjury, I declare that I have examined this return, including accompanying schedules and statements, and to the best of my knowledge and belief, it is true, correct and complete, and that no part of any payment made to a State unemployment fund claimed as a credit was or is to be deducted from the remuneration of employees.

Date ▶ Signature ▶ Title (Owner, etc.) ▶

Form **940** (1978)

Fig. 24-3. Completed form 940.

UNEMPLOYMENT TAXES

Employers are required to pay unemployment taxes based upon the amount of wages paid to employees. Unemployment taxes may not be withheld from employees' wages. These taxes are an expense of the employer. Both the federal government and the state governments require unemployment taxes. The federal unemployment tax rate as established in 1980 is .7% of the first $6,000 paid to each employee each year.* Although state rates may vary, most states have a rate of 2.7% of the first 6,000 paid to each employee each year. Some states provide for lower rates (merit rates) for some firms. These lower rates apply to firms who rarely lay off their employees.

Refer to the example in which $1,000 was earned by the employee during the month of June. The following journal entry is made to record the unemployment taxes for the month:

June 30	Payroll Tax Expense	34	
	Federal Unemployment Taxes Payable		7
	State Unemployment Taxes Payable		27
	To record payroll taxes for month.		

Federal unemployment taxes must be paid (deposited) within one month after any calendar quarter in which the total liability reaches $100. If the total liability does not reach $100 during a year, the full amount must be paid at the end of the year when form 940 is filed. Form 940 must be filed on or before January 31 following the close of the calendar year for which the tax is due.

Figure 24-3 is a completed copy of form 940. The example is for a company with only one employee who earned $1,000 per month for twelve months (a total of $12,000). Note that the tax is only computed on the first $6,000.

The state unemployment tax is paid at various times depending upon the state laws. Many states require that a form be filed and the tax paid on a quarterly basis. The owner of a small business should ask the local state unemployment department when forms are to be filed and the taxes paid.

Example

The S Company has two employees. Employee A earned $7,000 during January. Employee B earned $1,000. Income taxes were withheld from A's wages in the amount of $900. Income taxes of $196 were withheld from B's wages.

Solution. The following three journal entries are required to record the monthly payroll and taxes.

Jan. 31	Salary Expense	8,000.00	
	Employees Fed. Inc. Taxes Payable		1,096.00
	FICA Taxes Payable (6.13% of 8,000)		490.40
	Cash		6,413.60
	Recorded monthly payroll.		

*This rate is subject to change.

Jan. 31	Payroll Tax Expense	490.40	
	FICA Taxes Payable		490.40
	To record employer's share of FICA taxes.		
31	Payroll Tax Expense	238.00	
	Fed. Unemployment Taxes Payable (.7%)		49.00
	St. Unemployment Taxes Payable (2.7%)		189.00
	To record unemployment taxes.		

Note that the last entry is based on the full $1,000 of B's wages, but on only $6,000 of A's wages. In future months, no unemployment taxes will have to be paid on A's wages since the maximum wages subject to unemployment tax is $6,000 per year.

RECORDS TO BE KEPT

A firm must keep all payroll records available for inspection by the Internal Revenue Service. The following data are required:

- The names, addresses, and social security numbers of all employees.
- The amounts and dates of all wage payments.
- Each employee's tax withholding exemption certificate (form W-4).
- Duplicate copies of all quarterly and annual returns filed.
- Dates and amounts of tax payments made (usually deposited with a local bank).

All of the above records should be kept for at least four years.

OTHER TAXES

In addition to the payroll taxes listed previously, most firms pay several other state and local taxes. For example, most states have sales taxes. Thus, firms must file monthly sales tax reports and pay the taxes that have been collected from customers.

Most states, counties, and cities have property taxes which must be paid once or twice a year. In addition, many local governments also have income taxes. The employer must withhold these additional income taxes from employees' wages and file tax forms regularly.

Figure 24-4 illustrates a worksheet that a firm can use to help summarize its tax responsibilities. (Copies of this worksheet can be obtained free from the Small Business Administration. Ask for *Small Marketers Aid No. 142*).

SUMMARY

Small Business owners must keep in mind that taxes should be managed in the same systematic business manner as any other part of the business. Tax reports should always be filed when they are due and taxes should be paid on time. Failure to file and pay on time can result in penalties such as fines, interest, and even jail sentences. A business person should plan ahead so that the necessary cash is on hand when taxes are due. Some firms put the required funds aside each week in a separate bank account. Thus, the money is always available on the due date of the tax.

In addition to the many state tax forms that must be filed, there are two Federal forms that have to be filed regularly. These are form

WORKSHEET FOR MEETING TAX OBLIGATIONS

This worksheet is designed to help the owner-manager to manage the firm's tax obligations. You may want your accountant or bookkeeper to prepare the worksheet so you can use it as a reminder in preparing for and paying the various taxes.

Kind of Tax	Due Date	Amount Due	Pay to	Date for Writing The Check
FEDERAL TAXES				
Employee Income Tax and Social Security Tax				
Excise Tax				
Owner-Manager's and/or corporation's income tax				
Unemployment Tax				
STATE TAXES				
Unemployment Taxes				
Income Taxes				
Sales Taxes				
Franchise Tax				
Other				
LOCAL TAXES				
Sales Tax				

Fig. 24-4. Tax work sheet.

941 (federal income taxes withheld and FICA taxes) which is filed quarterly, and form 940 (federal unemployment taxes) which is filed each January.

Failure to file payroll taxes on time can result in serious trouble for a firm. Therefore, the wise owner of a small business gives careful attention to payroll taxes.

REVIEW

1. What form must be given to all employees every January?
2. What form must be filed to report FICA taxes withheld?
3. What form must be filed to report federal income taxes withheld from employees' wages?
4. What form must be filed to report federal unemployment taxes due?
5. What percentage of an employee's wages is withheld for social security taxes?
6. What percentage of an employee's wages is withheld for federal unemployment taxes?
7. Where does an employer pay the taxes that are withheld from an employee?
8. How often, and by what date, must the following federal forms be filed: form 941? form 940? form W-2?
9. How many years should payroll records be kept?
10. What is the due date of form 941 covering wages paid in August?

EXERCISES

1. Answer the following question for a firm that has only one employee who earns $10,000 per year.
   a. How much FICA tax expense will the firm incur?
   b. How much federal unemployment tax expense will the firm incur?
   c. How much state unemployment tax expense will the firm incur, assuming that the firm is not eligible for a merit rate?
2. A firm's employees earn $1,000 in the month of January and a total of $100 is withheld for income taxes.
   a. What is the total payroll tax expense for the month?
   b. What are the total liabilities on the firm's books for payroll taxes?
3. If an employee earns $100 per week and $10 is withheld for income taxes, what is his take-home pay?

PROBLEMS

1. The M&W Company opened for business on December 1, 1980. Its two employees, Micky Maloney and Lee Wright, are each paid $1,000 per month. Maloney has $120 per month withheld for federal income taxes and Wright has $95 withheld. There are also state income taxes to be withheld in the amount of $30 for Maloney and $25 for Wright. Give all journal entries to record the December 31 payroll and the payroll taxes.

2. Using the data in problem number 1, fill in the form 941 to be filed prior to January 31. Maloney's social security number is 987-65-4321. Wright's social security number is 985-99-9999.

3. Using the data in the two preceding problems, fill in form 940 for the year ending December 31, 1980.

4. The New Tech Company has three employees, all of whom are paid monthly on the last day of the month. Through the end of April the employees had earned the following wages for the current year:

Employee	Monthly Wage	Total Wages Through April
C. Terello	$4,000	$25,000
F. Wong	1,400	5,600
R. MacDonald	500	2,000

Give the entries at the end of May to record the $5,900 monthly payroll and the payroll taxes. Terello has $600 withheld for income taxes, Wong $300, and MacDonald $30.

SECTION 5

Alternate Forms of Business Organization

25 Partnership Accounting Problems

OBJECTIVES After studying this chapter, the student will be able to:

- Define and describe a partnership.
- Discuss the advantages and disadvantages of partnership.
- Make journal entries to divide the net income or net loss of a partnership.
- Record the entries to end a partnership.
- Journalize the entries for the liquidation of a partnership.

DEFINITION OF PARTNERSHIP

The three basic forms of business are

- single (or sole) proprietorship.
- partnership.
- corporation.

The firms discussed thus far in this text have been *sole proprietorships* – businesses having only one owner. This section of the text discusses accounting procedures for the two other types of businesses – partnerships and corporations. Partnerships are the subject of this chapter; corporations are described in chapter 26.

A *partnership* is a contractual agreement between two or more people for the purpose of operating a business. This agreement (or *contract*) may be oral or written. However, a written contract which spells out the details of how the partnership is to be run is preferable.

Characteristics of Partnership

There are four main characteristics of the partnership form of business.

Limited Life. A partnership ends whenever there is a change in partners. If a partner dies, goes into bankruptcy, becomes insane or otherwise becomes incapable of conducting business, then the partnership ends. The ending of a partnership due to a change in the partners is called a *dissolution.*

Unlimited Liability. Each partner in a firm is responsible *(liable)* for all the debts of the partnership. This means that if the partnership is not able to meet its obligations, creditors can make claims on the personal assets of the partners. In other words, partners can lose their own homes, cars, and other personal assets if the firm cannot pay its debts. This situation, referred to as *unlimited liability,* is often considered to be the greatest disadvantage of the partnership form of business.

Mutual Agency. Each partner may act as an *agent* for the firm. That is, any partner may sign an agreement using the name of the partnership and it will be a binding contract. This means that partners must trust each other to make sound business decisions. Every partner has an equal say in running the business.

Not Recognized as a Legal Entity. The federal tax laws do not recognize a partnership as a separate entity or being. Because a partnership does not exist under the law, it does not pay federal income taxes. Any income earned by the firm is distributed to the partners. The partners pay taxes on their share of the income as reported on their individual tax returns.

Advantages of a Partnership

The prime advantage of partnership is that by forming an association of two or more people, the partners are thus able to pool their resources and managerial talents, figure 25-1. These resources may include time, talent, ability, knowledge, and money. Also, it is simple to form a partnership. A further advantage is that partnerships do not have to pay income taxes.

Fig. 25-1. Partners discussing a new display.

Disadvantages of Partnership

One disadvantage of partnership is its limited life. For example, if two partners work hard to build up their business over their lifetime, the firm can be ended by the death of either partner.

Mutual agency and unlimited liability are also disadvantages of the partnership form of business since they increase the risk of the partners. If Partner A invested only $1,000 in a firm, and Partner B makes a poor decision, Partner A may lose not only the $1,000, but additional personal assets such as his home.

ACCOUNTING FOR PARTNERSHIPS

Accounting for a partnership is the same as that for a sole proprietorship, except in the handling of owners' equity accounts. Since there is more than one owner, a separate capital account is needed for each partner. Each partner also has a separate drawing account.

Initial Investment

Each partner's capital account is opened by making an entry to record the net assets contributed to the firm. Any additional investments by the partners are credited to their individual accounts. A withdrawal of assets by a partner for personal use is shown in the drawing account assigned to that partner.

To illustrate the above points, assume that Tom Adams and Susan Blue form a partnership. Adams invests $10,000 and Blue $8,000. The entry to record the investment is:

March 1	Cash	18,000	
	Tom Adams, Capital		10,000
	Susan Blue, Capital		8,000
	To record the original investments of the partners.		

A month later, Blue finds that she needs cash for her personal use and takes $1,000 out of the partnership cash. This is recorded as follows:

April 1	Susan Blue, Drawing	1,000	
	Cash		1,000
	To record the withdrawal of cash by Susan Blue.		

The drawing accounts are closed out to each partner's capital account at the end of the year.

Division of Earnings

At the end of the accounting period it is necessary to divide the earnings and distribute each partner's share to his or her capital account. This is accomplished by closing the Income Summary account to the capital accounts of the partners. There are several methods that may be used to divide net income or loss. The following is a discussion of some of these methods.

Fixed Ratio. The easiest way to divide profits is to use a ratio or fraction. This ratio should be specified in the partnership agreement. If there is no agreement as to division of profits, then either income or loss are divided equally. Any ratio may be used as long as the partners agree. For example, Blue and Adams may divide the profit in any of the following ways.

1 to 1 (1:1) or 1/2, 1/2
3 to 1 (3:1) or 3/4, 1/4
3 to 2 (3:2) or 3/5, 2/5

A ratio may be expressed in any one of these ways, or as a percent. For example, if the profit is to be divided using a ratio of 1 to 2 (1:2), one partner receives 1/3 or 33 1/3% while the other partner receives 2/3 or 66 2/3%. (*Note:* the denominator of a fraction formed from a ratio is the total of the figures – in this case, 3.) In determining the ratio, partners should consider the amount of time, ability and money each contributed to the firm.

Using the Adams and Blue partnership as an example, assume that they made $100,000 in net income in the first year. Their agreement calls for a division of profit using a ratio of 3:2. This means that any profits are divided in five parts with Adams getting three parts, or 3/5, and Blue taking two parts, or 2/5. In terms of the income, Adams receives $60,000 and Blue $40,000.

The entry to close out the income for the year is:

Dec. 31	Income Summary	100,000	
	Tom Adams, Capital		60,000
	Susan Blue, Capital		40,000
	Closing entry to divide the net income for the year.		

A loss would be divided in the same way and the entry would show a debit to decrease the capital accounts and a credit to the income summary to close that account. Losses are generally divided using the same ratio used for net income. For example, if the Adams and Blue partnership had lost $8,000 during the past year, the entry to split the loss would be:

Dec. 31	Tom Adams, Capital	4,800	
	Susan Blue, Capital	3,200	
	Income Summary		8,000
	Closing entry to divide the net loss for the year.		

Capital Ratio. A *capital ratio* allows profits and losses to be divided based on the partners' investments. To illustrate, consider the C & D partnership with partners Chris Robb and Doug Betts. Assume a $100,000 net income for the year. Robb had a beginning capital balance of $90,000. Betts had a beginning capital balance of $30,000. The partnership agreement says that profits and losses will be divided on the basis of the beginning capital balances. The total capital investment is $120,000. Since Robb provided 3/4 of the capital (90,000/120,000), he is entitled to 3/4 of any profits or losses. Betts receives 1/4 of any income or loss. To divide a $100,000 net income in this way, the entry is:

Dec. 31	Income Summary	100,000	
	Chris Robb, Capital		75,000
	Doug Betts, Capital		25,000
	Closing entry to divide net income for the year.		

If the firm had a loss of $8,000, the entry would be:

Dec. 31	Chris Robb, Capital	6,000	
	Doug Betts, Capital	2,000	
	Income Summary		8,000
	Closing entry to divide net loss for the year.		

Salaries, Interest and Remainder Method. This method may be used to divide income on the basis of both effort (or experience) and capital invested. To do this, an allowance is made for salary and interest on the capital investments of the partners. Note that this is merely an allowance – it is not really salary and interest. The salary allowance is not shown as salary expense on the books and it does not represent cash paid to the partners. The interest allowance is not recorded on the books or paid to the partners.

Remember, the only way that a partner can take money out of the partnership is to use the drawing account. The allowances for salary and interest are just part of the formula set up in the partnership contract to divide net income or loss fairly.

As an example of this method, consider the E & F Partnership made up of Robert Eaves and Paula Friend. Their partnership agreement calls for a salary allowance of $10,000 per year to Eaves and $15,000 to Friend. The contract also allows an interest allowance equal to 10% of their beginning capital balances. Any remainder is to be divided equally. Eaves has a capital balance of $80,000 and Friend of $40,000. Net income for the year was $100,000. The division of the $100,000 is shown in figure 25-2. The entry to record this division of income is:

Dec. 31	Income Summary	100,000	
	Robert Eaves, Capital		49,500
	Paula Friend, Capital		50,500
	Closing entry to divide net income for the year.		

The example shows how a net income would be divided using the salaries, interest and remainder method. Assume that instead of a net income there was a net loss for the year of $20,000. Using the same agreement for division as that for net income, the $20,000 loss would be divided as shown in figure 25-3.

NET INCOME				$100,000
	Eaves	Friend	Total	
Salary Allowances	$10,000	$15,000	$ 25,000	
Interest Allowances				
Eaves = 10% of $80,000	8,000			
Friend = 10% of $40,000		4,000	12,000	
Income Allocated in First Two Steps	18,000	19,000	37,000	(37,000)
REMAINDER				63,000
Remainder Divided Equally				
Eaves = ½ of $63,000	31,500			
Friend = ½ of $63,000		31,500	63,000	
TOTAL	$49,500	$50,500	$100,000	

Fig. 25-2. Allocation of $100,000 income of E & F partnership.

NET INCOME (LOSS)				($20,000)
	Eaves	Friend	Total	
Salary Allowances	$10,000	$15,000	$25,000	
Interest Allowances				
Eaves = 10% of $80,000	8,000			
Friend = 10% of $40,000		4,000	12,000	
Income Allocated in First Two Steps	18,000	19,000	37,000	(37,000)
REMAINDER				(57,000)
Remainder Divided Equally				
Eaves = ½ of ($57,000)	(28,500)			
Friend = ½ of ($57,000)		(28,500)	(57,000)	
TOTAL	($10,500)	($ 9,500)	($20,000)	

Fig. 25-3. Allocation of $20,000 loss of the E & F partnership.

Note that the method for dividing a loss is the same as for dividing a net income. The division of the net loss in figure 25-2 can be summarized as follows:

Step 1: Allocate the salary allowances to the two partners.

Step 2: Allocate the interest allowances to the two partners. After $37,000 of income is allocated for salaries and interest, the remainder is a negative $57,000, which is shared equally.

Step 3: The $28,500 negative remainder for each partner is subtracted from the positive amounts allocated in steps 1 and 2. The partner's shares are thus negative amounts, or a decrease in their capital.

This entry is made:

Dec. 31	Robert Eaves, Capital	10,500	
	Paula Friend, Capital	9,500	
	Income Summary		20,000
	Closing entry to divide net loss for the year.		

NET INCOME (LOSS)				($ 500)
	Eaves	Friend	Total	
Salary Allowances	$10,000	$15,000	$25,000	
Interest Allowances				
Eaves = 10% of $80,000	8,000			
Friend = 10% of $40,000		4,000	12,000	
Income Allocated in First Two Steps	18,000	19,000	37,000	(37,000)
REMAINDER				(37,500)
Remainder Divided Equally				
Eaves = ½ of ($37,500)	(18,750)			
Friend = ½ of ($37,500)		(18,750)	(37,500)	
TOTAL	($ 750)	$ 250	($ 500)	

Fig. 25-4. Allocation of $500 loss.

Assume for the next example that the E & F Partnership has a loss of $500 for the year and all other facts are the same. The $500 loss would be divided as shown in figure 25-4. In this case, the loss of $500 results in a decrease of $750 for Eaves and a $250 increase for Friend. This entry is made:

Dec. 31	Robert Eaves, Capital	750	
	Income Summary		500
	Paula Friend, Capital		250
	Closing entry to divide net loss for the year.		

Thus, it is possible for one partner to have a loss, while the other partner's capital account is increased as if there had been a net income. In this example the reason this occurred is that Friend received a larger salary allowance. Friend worked more for the firm during the year than Eaves. Thus, she does not have to bear as large a share of the loss.

The entire process for the salaries, interest, and remainder method is summarized in figure 25-5.

Fig. 25-5. Steps in the salaries, interest and remainder method.

- ☐ Determine net income or loss for the period.
- ☐ Allocate salary allowance to each partner.
- ☐ Allocate interest allowance to each partner.
- ☐ Determine the total amount of income allocated so far and subtract from the net income (or loss) for the period. This difference is the remainder.
- ☐ Allocate the remainder equally among the partners.
- ☐ Add up the total of all three allocations for each partner. The total for each partner is then recorded with a journal entry to close out the income summary account.

ENDING A PARTNERSHIP

Any change in the members of a partnership causes the dissolution or ending of a partnership. This change may come about for many reasons, some of which are discussed below. When a partnership dissolves, the remaining partners may choose to go on with the firm and form a new partnership. If this occurs, there will be little change except to correct the names of the partners' capital accounts and to decide how profits and losses should be divided in the new partnership. However, if the partners decide not to go on with the business, then there will be a liquidation.

Sale of a Partnership Interest

If a partner desires to leave the partnership, he or she may sell his or her interest to someone else. This sale is a business transaction between two individuals and the firm is not directly involved. The only change needed on the partnership books is a change in the name of the capital account. If the remaining partner or partners agree, a new partnership is formed.

For example, assume that C. Host has a capital balance of $7,000 and sells this interest to T. Hernandez for $10,000. The entry on the books of the partnership is:

C. Host, Capital	7,000	
T. Hernandez, Capital		7,000
To transfer Host's equity to Hernandez.		

Note that the entry is for $7,000 because it was Host who received the $10,000 – not the partnership. The owner's equity purchased by Hernandez is the same as that possessed by Host – $7,000. The entry would be the same regardless of the selling price. Even if Host had sold his share of the firm for $1, the entry would still be made for $7,000.

Withdrawal of a Partner

Another way in which a partner may leave a partnership is to quit, or *withdraw.* In the event of a withdrawal, the partnership contract usually calls for a *revaluation* of the assets of the partnership to show their current values. Thus, there are usually two steps in recording the withdrawal of a partner:

- Revaluation of assets.
- Withdrawal of the partner.

For example, Mr. Wertz is retiring from the GWL Partnership. The firm's balance sheet before the revaluation of the assets is shown in figure 25-6. Appraisers value the inventory at $18,000 rather than $12,000, and the partners decide to revalue the inventory. Gains or losses as a result of revaluation are divided among the partners as provided in their agreement. Genelli, Wertz, and Lipski have agreed

ASSETS:		OWNERS' EQUITY:	
Cash	$10,000	Genelli, Capital	$10,000
Inventory	12,000	Wertz, Capital	7,000
Total Assets	$22,000	Lipski, Capital	5,000
		Total Owners' Equity	$22,000

Fig. 25-6. Balance sheet of GWL Partnership before revaluation.

to share profits and losses using a rato of 3:2:1. The entry for revaluation is:

Inventory	6,000	
Genelli, Capital		3,000 [3/6 of 6,000]
Wertz, Capital		2,000 [2/6 of 6,000]
Lipski, Capital		1,000 [1/6 of 6,000]
To record the revaluation of the inventory.		

After revaluation, the balance sheet appears as shown in figure 25-7.

If Wertz agrees to withdraw and take $9,000 in cash (capital shown on figure 25-6 plus $2,000 from revaluation) this would be the entry:

Wertz, Capital	9,000	
Cash		9,000
To record the withdrawal of Wertz.		

There are times when the other partners are anxious for the withdrawal of the retiring partner. Thus, they may offer the retiring partner more than his or her capital balance to encourage a speedier withdrawal. For example, Genelli and Lipski might offer Wertz $11,000. If this occurs, the extra $2,000 is deducted from the capital accounts of Genelli and Lipski according to their profit and loss ratio. Genelli and Lipski share profits and losses in a ratio of 3:1. A retiring partner may withdraw assets in any form, and Wertz asks for $9,000 in cash and $2,000 in inventory. The entry to record the withdrawal of Wertz from the firm with these assets is:

Wertz, Capital	9,000	
Genelli, Capital	1,500	
Lipski, Capital	500	
Cash		9,000
Inventory		2,000
To record the withdrawal of Wertz.		

ASSETS:		OWNERS' EQUITY:	
Cash	$10,000	Genelli, Capital	$13,000
Inventory	18,000	Wertz, Capital	9,000
Total Assets	$28,000	Lipski, Capital	6,000
		Total Owners' Equity	$28,000

Fig. 25-7. Balance sheet of GWL partnership after revaluation.

Since Wertz received more than his capital account balance, it is said that he was paid a *bonus* to withdraw. The $2,000 bonus is split between the other two partners in their profit and loss ratio. Genelli has to bear $1,500 (3/4 of $2,000) of the bonus and Lipski has to bear $500 (1/4 of $2,000) of the bonus.

In some cases, the retiring partner may be the party who is anxious to leave the firm. If so, the retiring partner may agree to receive less than his or her capital balance in order to withdraw as soon as possible. For example, assume that Wertz agrees to take $5,000 in cash as full payment for his $9,000 capital balance. The extra $4,000 is divided between Genelli and Lipski using their profit and loss ratio of 3:1 as follows:

Wertz, Capital	9,000	
Cash		5,000
Genelli, Capital		3,000 [3/4 of $4,000]
Lipski, Capital		1,000 [1/4 of $4,000]
To record the withdrawal of Wertz.		

This last entry is sometimes called giving a bonus to the remaining partners.

Liquidation of a Partnership

To *liquidate* a partnership means to go out of business. In a liquidation the assets are sold, thc liabilities are paid off, and any remaining cash is given to the partners. To record a liquidation, four steps are required. Entries are made for the

- sale of assets;
- division of gain or loss on sale of assets, using the partners' profit and loss sharing ratio;
- payment of liabilities; and
- distribution of remaining cash to partners based on the credit balances in their capital accounts.

When all four steps are completed, all accounts should have a zero balance. The following examples show how these steps are carried out under various conditions. All examples refer to the balance sheet in figure 25-8.

Blackmore, Greenman, and Erikson
Balance Sheet
June 30, 19–

ASSETS:		LIABILITIES AND OWNERS' EQUITY:	
Cash	$12,000	Accounts Payable	$10,000
Inventory	68,000	Blackmore, Capital (3)	25,000
Total Assets	$80,000	Greenman, Capital (2)	35,000
		Erikson, Capital (1)	10,000
		Total Owners' Equity	$80,000

Fig. 25-8. Balance sheet for Blackmore, Greenman and Erikson partnership.

Assets Sold at a Profit. If the inventory of the Blackmore, Greenman and Erikson partnership is sold for $86,000, the first entry is:

Cash	86,000	
Inventory		68,000
Gain on Sale of Assets		18,000
To record final sale of assets.		

Second, the gain of $18,000 is divided among the partners using their profit and loss ratio of 3:2:1, thus closing the Gain on Sale of Assets account.

Gain on Sale of Assets	18,000	
Blackmore, Capital		9,000 [3/6 of $18,000]
Greenman, Capital		6,000 [2/6 of $18,000]
Erikson, Capital		3,000 [1/6 of $18,000]
To close out Gain account.		

The third step is to pay the liabilities. The following entry is used:

Accounts Payable	10,000	
Cash		10,000
To pay off liabilities.		

At this point the remaining cash is distributed to the partners based on the credit balances in their capital accounts. To determine the balance in cash and the capital account, accounts may be used to show the effects of the first three entries, see figure 25-9. Note that the balance in cash is equal to the total of all of the capital accounts. In the final step, the remaining accounts are closed out by the following entry:

Blackmore, Capital	34,000	
Greenman, Capital	41,000	
Erikson, Capital	13,000	
Cash		88,000
To distribute cash to partners and close out accounts.		

Assets Sold at a Loss: Partners' Capital Accounts Large Enough to Absorb Loss. If the firm sells its inventory for $44,000 then the four entries are as follows:

Cash	44,000	
Loss on Sale of Assets	24,000	
Inventory		68,000
To record the sale of assets at a loss.		

Blackmore, Capital	12,000	
Greenman, Capital	8,000	
Erikson, Capital	4,000	
Loss on Sale of Assets		24,000
To divide the loss among the partners.		

ACCOUNT *Cash* — Acct. No. *111*

Date		Explanation	Post. Ref.	Debit	Credit	Balance
				12,000 00		12,000 00
				86,000 00		98,000 00
					10,000 00	88,000 00

ACCOUNT *Blackmore, Capital* — Acct. No. *311*

Date		Explanation	Post. Ref.	Debit	Credit	Balance
					25,000 00	25,000 00
					9,000 00	34,000 00

ACCOUNT *Greenman, Capital* — Acct. No. *313*

Date		Explanation	Post. Ref.	Debit	Credit	Balance
					35,000 00	35,000 00
					6,000 00	41,000 00

ACCOUNT *Erikson, Capital* — Acct. No. *315*

Date		Explanation	Post. Ref.	Debit	Credit	Balance
					10,000 00	10,000 00
					3,000 00	13,000 00

Fig. 25-9. Accounts after posting final entries: gain example.

Accounts Payable	10,000	
Cash		10,000
Paid off liabilities.		

After these three entries, the account balances are as follows:

Cash	46,000	Greenman, Capital	27,000
Blackmore, Capital	13,000	Erikson, Capital	6,000

The following final entry closes these accounts:

Blackmore, Capital	13,000	
Greenman, Capital	27,000	
Erikson, Capital	6,000	
Cash		46,000
To distribute remaining cash to partners and close accounts.		

Assets Sold at a Loss: Partners' Capital Accounts Not Sufficient to Absorb Loss. If, instead, the inventory of the partnership is sold for $14,000, these entries are needed:

Cash	14,000	
Loss on Sale of Assets	54,000	
Inventory		68,000
To record sale of assets at a loss.		

Blackmore, Capital (3/6)	27,000	
Greenman, Capital (2/6)	18,000	
Erikson, Capital (1/6)	9,000	
Loss on Sale of Assets		54,000
To divide the loss among the partners.		

At this point, the account balances appear as shown in figure 25-10.

ACCOUNT *Cash* Acct. No. *111*

Date		Explanation	Post. Ref.	Debit	Credit	Balance
				12,000.00		12,000.00
				14,000.00		26,000.00
					10,000.00	16,000.00

ACCOUNT *Blackmore, Capital* Acct. No. *311*

Date		Explanation	Post. Ref.	Debit	Credit	Balance
					25,000.00	25,000.00
				27,000.00		(2,000.00)

ACCOUNT *Greenman, Capital* Acct. No. *313*

Date		Explanation	Post. Ref.	Debit	Credit	Balance
					35,000.00	35,000.00
				18,000.00		17,000.00

ACCOUNT *Erikson, Capital* Acct. No. *315*

Date		Explanation	Post. Ref.	Debit	Credit	Balance
					10,000.00	10,000.00
				9,000.00		1,000.00

Fig. 25-10. Accounts after posting final entries: loss of $54,000.

Blackmore's capital account is not large enough to cover his share of the loss. He must pay $2,000 to the firm to cover this shortage. Blackmore's payment to the partnership is recorded as follows:

Cash	2,000	
Blackmore, Capital		2,000
To record investment by Blackmore.		

After this payment is made, the four accounts appear as shown in figure 25-11.

ACCOUNT *Cash* Acct. No. *111*

Date		Explanation	Post. Ref.	Debit	Credit	Balance
				12000 00		12000 00
				14000 00		26000 00
					10000 00	16000 00
				2000 00		18000 00

ACCOUNT *Blackmore, Capital* Acct. No. *311*

Date		Explanation	Post. Ref.	Debit	Credit	Balance
					25000 00	25000 00
				27000 00		(2000 00)
					2000 00	-0-

ACCOUNT *Greenman, Capital* Acct. No. *313*

Date		Explanation	Post. Ref.	Debit	Credit	Balance
					35000 00	35000 00
				18000 00		17000 00

ACCOUNT *Erikson, Capital* Acct. No. *315*

Date		Explanation	Post. Ref.	Debit	Credit	Balance
					10000 00	10000 00
				9000 00		1000 00

Fig. 25-11. Accounts after Blackmore pays in $2,000.

ACCOUNT *Cash* Acct. No. *111*

Date		Explanation	Post. Ref.	Debit	Credit	Balance
				12000 00		12000 00
				14000 00		26000 00
					10000 00	16000 00

ACCOUNT *Blackmore, Capital* Acct. No. *311*

Date		Explanation	Post. Ref.	Debit	Credit	Balance
					25000 00	25000 00
				27000 00		(2000 00)
					2000 00	–0–

ACCOUNT *Greenman, Capital* Acct. No. *313*

Date		Explanation	Post. Ref.	Debit	Credit	Balance
					35000 00	35000 00
				18000 00		17000 00
				1333 00		15667 00

ACCOUNT *Erikson, Capital* Acct. No. *315*

Date		Explanation	Post. Ref.	Debit	Credit	Balance
					10000 00	10000 00
				9000 00		1000 00
				667 00		333 00

Fig. 25-12. Accounts after division of Blackmore's deficit.

The final entry to close the other partners' capital accounts and cash is:

Greenman, Capital	17,000	
Erikson, Capital	1,000	
Cash		18,000
To distribute the remaining cash and close the accounts.		

Sometimes, however, one partner may be unable to pay his or her share as required by a loss. For example, if Blackmore cannot pay the additional $2,000, Greenman and Erikson must cover Blackmore's shortage out of their accounts. In this case, Greenman and Erikson divide the $2,000 shortage in their profit and loss ratio of 2:1. The entry is as follows:

Greenman, Capital (2/3)	1,333	
Erikson, Capital (1/3)	667	
Blackmore, Capital		2,000
To close out debit balance in Blackmore's Capital account.		

After this entry, the accounts appear as shown in figure 25-12. The final entry the firm makes is:

Greenman, Capital	15,667	
Erikson, Capital	333	
Cash		16,000
To distribute remaining cash and to close the accounts.		

SUMMARY

A partnership is a contractual agreement between two or more people for the purpose of operating a business. The disadvantages of partnership are limited life, unlimited liability, and mutual agency. A partnership is not recognized as a separate legal entity. The major advantage of this business form is the opportunity it provides for several people to pool their resources.

The accounting process for partnerships differs from the one used for sole proprietorships only in the handling of the owner's equity accounts. Separate capital and drawing accounts are used for each partner. The earnings of a partnership can be divided among the partners using several methods, including fixed ratio; capital ratio; or salaries, interest and remainder method.

Any change in the members of a partnership ends or dissolves the partnership. A dissolution may result from a sale of a partnership interest or the withdrawal of a partner.

The liquidation of a partnership occurs when the firm goes out of business. Recording a liquidation requires four steps.

It should be noted that all of the partners may not share in the distribution of cash at liquidation. In fact, some of the partners may owe money to the partnership at the time the firm goes out of business.

REVIEW

1. What are the advantages of the partnership form of business?
2. What are the disadvantages of the partnership form of business?
3. If the partners cannot agree as to how net income should be divided, what should be done?
4. What does the phrase *mutual agency* mean?
5. What does *unlimited liability* mean to a partner?
6. What events automatically cause a partnership to end?
7. If a partnership liquidates, how is the remaining cash divided among the partners?

8. Is a partner entitled to receive interest on his or her capital investment?

9. One partner in a firm feels that he is entitled to more income than the other partners since he has contributed more time and has invested more capital than the other partners. Is he correct? Why or why not?

EXERCISES

1. The following balance sheet is for the AdGenDa partnership. The partners, Adams, Gentle, and Dante share profits and losses in the ratio of 5:3:2, respectively.

ASSETS		LIABILITIES AND OWNERS' EQUITY:	
Cash	$ 30,000	Total Liabilities	$ 70,000
Other Assets	270,000	Adams, Capital	140,000
Total Assets	$300,000	Gentle, Capital	80,000
		Dante, Capital	10,000
		Total Liabilities and Owners' Equity	$300,000

Assume that the original partners have agreed to liquidate the partnership by selling the other assets. If the other assets are sold for $200,000, which of the following divisions of the remaining capital will take place?

a. Adams, $102,500; Gentle, $57,500; Dante, $0.
b. Adams, $103,000; Gentle, $57,000; Dante, $0.
c. Adams, $105,000; Gentle, $59,000; Dante, $4,000.
d. Adams, $140,000; Gentle, $80,000; Dante, $10,000.

2. The following data is from the April 30, 19– balance sheet for the partnership of Lang, Monte, and Newton. The partners share profits and losses in the ratio of 2:2:6, respectively.

Assets, at cost	$100,000
Accounts Payable	$ 9,000
Lang, Capital	15,000
Monte, Capital	31,000
Newton, Capital	45,000
Total	$100,000

Lang is retiring from the partnership. By mutual agreement, the assets are to be adjusted to their fair value of $130,000 at April 30, 19–. Monte and Newton agree that the partnership will pay Lang $37,000 cash for her partnership interest. Give the journal entries for

a. the revaluation of the assets, and
b. the withdrawal of Lang.
c. Which of the following represents the balance of Newton's account after withdrawal of Lang?
(1) $51,000
(2) $53,000
(3) $59,000
(4) $63,000

3. The partnership agreement of Baker and Young specifies that: (1) Baker shall receive a monthly salary of $200 and Young a monthly salary of $300, (2) at the end of the year each partner shall be credited with 8% interest on his investment at the beginning of the year, and (3) the remainder shall be shared equally. At the end of the fiscal year, after all income and expense accounts have been closed, the accounts show the following balances: Baker, Capital (at the beginning of the year), $45,300; Young, Capital (at the beginning of the year), $36,900; and Income Summary (credit balance) $12,856.

   Prepare the journal entries necessary to distribute the income and close the Income Summary account.

4. X had a $32,500 equity in Partnership XYZ. He sold his share of the partnership to A for $22,750. Make the proper entry to record this transaction on the books of the partnership.

5. Rudd and Peel are partners. They are trying to decide upon the best way to divide profits and losses. State the income for each partner if profits of $20,000 were shared in each of the following ways:
   a. No decision could be reached as to how profits and losses should be divided.
   b. Profits are to be divided 60% to Rudd and 40% to Peel.
   c. Profits are to be divided on a 5 to 3 ratio.
   d. Rudd is to receive a salary allowance of $10,000 and Peel to receive a salary allowance of $5,000, with any remainder divided equally.

6. Refer to the data in exercise 5. How would a loss of $3,000 be divided under each of the provisions (a-d)?

PROBLEMS

1. Valdez and Wesson invested $8,000 and $12,000 respectively in a partnership business they began one year ago. The business earned $14,100 during the year. Give the share of each partner in the net income under each of the following conditions:
   a. The partners could not agree in advance as to the method by which they would share earnings.
   b. The partners agreed to share earnings in their beginning-of-the year capital ratio.
   c. The partnership agreement calls for a $6,000 per year salary allowance to Valdez, a $7,500 per year salary allowance to Wesson, and any remainder to be shared equally.
   d. The partnership agreement calls for interest allowance at 10% on investments, salary allowances of $6,000 per year to Valdez, and $7,500 per year to Wesson, and any remainder to be shared equally.

2. Assume that instead of earning a profit, the company of Valdez and Wesson in problem 1 incurred a loss of $3,000 for the year. How would the loss be divided between the two partners under each of the conditions listed in problem 1?

3. Terence Able had a $6,345 equity in the partnership of Able and Bell which he has just sold to Karen Collette for $7,000.
   a. Assuming that Bell is willing to accept Collette as a partner, give the entry(s) necessary to record the sale.
   b. What would the entry have been if Collette paid only $1,145 for Able's share of the partnership?

4. Bench and Cruz form a partnership with investments of $40,000 and $20,000 respectively. Determine their participation in a net income of $45,000 for the year under each of the following assumptions.
   a. There is no agreement as to division of income.
   b. Income is to be divided according to original capital investments.
   c. Interest is to be allowed at the rate of 5% on original investments. In addition there is to be a salary allowance on $5,000 and $10,000 respectively. The balance is to be divided equally.
   d. The same arrangement specified in part c is used, but the net income for the year is only $13,500.
   e. The same agreement specified in part c is used, but there is a net loss of $18,000 for the year.

   Give the general journal entry to record the distribution of net income as determined in part c above.

5. The following is the latest balance sheet of Darrell and Roemer partnership. The partnership is to be liquidated. The non-cash assets are sold for $18,000 in cash and the liabilities are paid. Prepare the journal entries to liquidate the partnership. The profit sharing ratio is 2:1.

Darrell and Roemer
Balance Sheet
June 30, 1985

ASSETS:		LIABILITIES:		
Cash	$ 4,500	Accounts Payable		$ 3,500
Other Assets	15,000	OWNERS' EQUITY:		
Total Assets	$19,500	Darrell, Capital	8,200	
		Roemer, Capital	7,800	
		Total Owners' Equity		16,000
		Total Liabilities and Owners' Equity		$19,500

6. Partnership ABC is to be liquidated. The other assets are sold for $80,000. Partner B has no personal funds to make up any deficiency on his part, and the profits are shared in the ratio 3:2:2. Using the following information, prepare the journal entries to end the ABC partnership.

Cash	Other Assets	Liabilities	A, Cap.	B, Cap.	C, Cap.
20,000	150,000	60,000	65,000	15,000	30,000

7. Telesky, Odell and Earl are partners. Their capital account balances are: Telesky, $30,000; Odell, $25,000; and Earl, $10,000. They share profits in a 4:3:2 ratio. Earl wishes to withdraw from the firm. It has been agreed that all of the assets are fairly valued on the firm's books except for land. Land is carried on the books at $20,000, but it is now worth $38,000. The partners agree to revalue the land before Earl withdraws from the firm.

a. Give the entry needed to revalue the land.
b. Give the entry for the withdrawal of Earl, assuming that she receives cash equal to her capital account balance.
c. Give the entry for the withdrawal of Earl assuming that she receives $8,000 in cash.
d. Give the entry for the withdrawal of Earl assuming that she receives $20,000 in cash.

26 Corporation Accounting

OBJECTIVES

After studying this chapter, the student will be able to:

- List the advantages and disadvantages of the corporate form of business.
- Describe the organization and management of a corporation.
- Make journal entries for the issuance of par value and no-par value stock.
- Describe the different types of capital stock.
- Journalize entries for the declaration and issuance of cash dividends and stock dividends.
- Record the journal entries for the purchase and sale of treasury stock.
- Differentiate between a stock dividend and a stock split.
- Prepare a retained earnings statement.
- Define the following terms: corporation, stock (issued, outstanding, and treasury), par value, dividend.

DEFINITION OF A CORPORATION

A *corporation* is an organization created by a charter from the government. In effect, a corporation is an artificial being created by law. It is a separate legal entity owned by stockholders. Its charter grants the corporation most of the legal rights possessed by individuals. It may own property, enter into contracts and exercise other legal rights.

Advantages of Corporations

There are five main advantages of the corporate form of business.

Ease of Raising Large Amounts of Capital. Because it can sell shares to many individuals, a corporation can obtain as much capital as it needs. Some industries, such as the auto industry, require a great deal of capital to operate. A single person in a sole proprietorship probably would not have enough money to start an auto manufacturing firm. If enough partners were obtained to raise a large sum of money, there would be too many people to run the business. Thus, a corporation is the only form of business in which great sums of money can be raised without creating management problems.

Limited Liability. A corporation must pay its own debts. The owners or stockholders are not responsible for the debts of the firm. Stockholders can lose only the amount that they have invested in the firm. This reduces the risk to the owners. Recall that a sole proprietor or partner is personally liable for business debts. In other words, partners can lose their personal homes or other personal assets if the firm goes bankrupt. In a corporation, however, the owners are not responsible if the firm goes bankrupt. This is often the most important advantage of the corporation in the eyes of an investor in a small business.

Easy Transfer of Ownership. To buy ownership in a corporation a person buys stock, and thus becomes a stockholder. The stockholder is free to do what he or she pleases with this stock. The stock may be sold or given away as a gift without permission from the corporation. Compare this freedom with that of a partner who cannot sell his or her share of the firm without the approval of all partners. The corporate form of business is much more convenient if the owner desires to sell.

Continuous Existence. A corporation may exist forever; it is not affected by a change in owners. This is a very important advantage for people who want a firm to continue after their death.

No Mutual Agency. Stockholders may not enter into binding contracts on behalf of the corporation. A stockholder need not be active in the corporation since professionals may be hired to run the firm. This is an important advantage. It means that one partner is not forced to trust the business judgment of the other owners as in the case of a partnership.

Disadvantages of Corporations

There are two main disadvantages of the corporation.

Additional Taxes. Since corporations are separate legal entities under the law, they must pay federal and state income taxes. When the income remaining after taxes is paid out to the stockholders in the form of dividends, it is considered income to the individual and is taxed again. This is known as *double taxation* since the earnings of a corporation are eventually taxed twice. The current income tax rate on corporations may be as great as 46%. This high taxation is the major disadvantage of the corporate form of business.

Government Regulation. Since corporations are created and operate under a grant from the state, the state has more control over these firms than other forms of business. Regulation by state and federal governments means more rules and record keeping for the firm.

OPERATION OF CORPORATIONS

Organizing a Corporation

To form a corporation, an application for a charter is sent to the secretary of state's office of the state in which the firm is to be incorporated. The charter includes the following information.

- the name and address of the firm
- the names of the incorporators
- the nature of the business to be conducted
- the type and amount of capital stock to be authorized and issued.

A fee must be sent in with the application.

After the charter is approved, the stockholders meet and adopt bylaws. These bylaws, together with the charter, form the rules to govern the firm. The bylaws specify such things as: the time, place, and nature of meetings of the stockholders and directors, how directors are chosen; the appointment of officers and their duties; the issue and transfer of capital stock, and the fiscal year.

Organization Costs

There are costs involved in starting a corporation. These include the fee paid to the state, the attorney's fee to draw up the charter, costs of printing stock certificates, and accounting fees. However, these costs benefit the firm during its entire life. They are entered in an account called *Organization Costs* which is a long-term intangible asset. An intangible asset is *amortized,* or written off, over its useful life. However, the income tax laws allow a firm to write off its organization costs over a period of five years or more. Thus, most coporations write off their organization costs over the first five years. Intangible assets are shown below Plant and Equipment on the balance sheet.

Management of a Corporation

The owners of a corporation are called *stockholders.* The stockholders elect a *board of directors* who have the authority to supervise the affairs of the corporation. The directors act as policy makers. Directors may or may not be stockholders. The board delegates authority to officers who are appointed to run the firm. The number of officers to be appointed is set out in the firm's bylaws. They commonly include a president, several vice-presidents, a secretary and a treasurer. The officers may then hire employees to carry out the work of the firm. A basic organizational chart of a corporation is shown in figure 26-1. Note that the stockholders are shown at the top of the chart. As the owners of the firm, they have the final authority.

Stock Certificates

Ownership in a corporation is represented by a stock certificate. A *stock certificate* is a document showing how many shares of stock

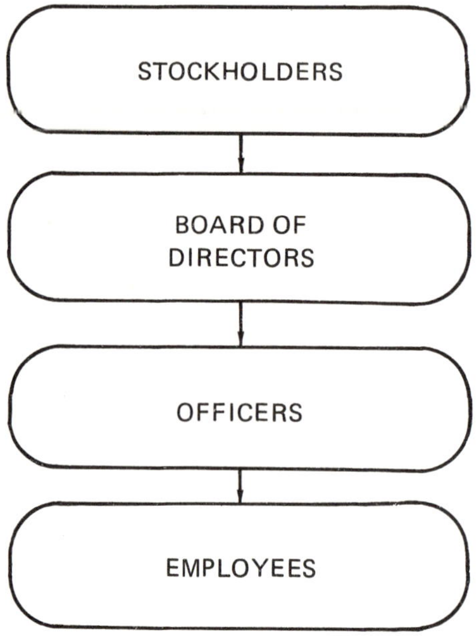

Fig. 26-1. Corporate organizational chart.

a particular stockholder owns. If a stockholder wishes to sell his or her share of the firm, then the stock certificate is signed on the back, just like a check, and turned over to the new owner. The new owner or a stockbroker must then register the sale with the corporation. When the old, signed certificate is turned in, the corporation issues a new certificate made out in the name of the new owner.

One of the first steps in forming a corporation is to print the stock certificates. Usually a firm has its blank certificates bound into a stock certificate book. As shares are issued, the blank forms are torn out of the book and given to stockholders. Figures 26-2 (A and B) show the front and back sides of a corporate stock certificate.

Fig. 26-2 (A). Front of a corporate stock certificate.

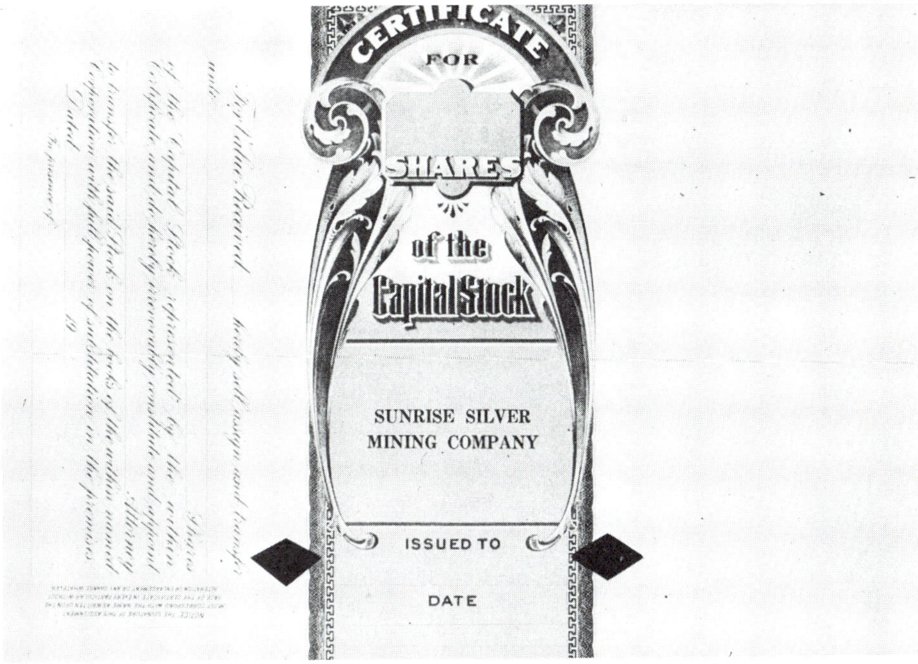

Fig. 26-2 (B). Back of a corporate stock certificate.

Rights of Stockholders

The stockholders of a firm have the following rights:

Voting. At the annual meeting, the stockholders vote on the election or removal of directors, amendments to the charter and bylaws, appointment of auditors and other major decisions. If a stockholder is unable to attend the meeting, he may vote by proxy. A *proxy* is the written authority to act for another. A proxy allows a person who is attending the meeting to vote for someone who cannot attend.

Profit Sharing. A stockholder is entitled to receive his or her share of dividends when a dividend is declared by the board of directors. *Dividends* are a distribution of assets to stockholders. There is no guarantee of dividends; there is merely the right to a share of any dividends declared.

Distribution of Assets Upon Liquidation. When a firm is in liquidation or is going out of business, the assets are sold and the debts are paid. If there are any remaining assets, they are distributed to the stockholders on a pro rata basis (according to their number of shares in the firm). Note that the stockholders are the last to receive assets if the firm ceases to operate.

Preemptive Right. This is the right to buy a pro rata share of any new capital stock the corporation is about to issue. Each stockholder's preemptive right is determined by the stock he or she already owns. For instance, if a stockholder now owns 20% of all stock outstanding, then he or she has the right to buy 20% of any new stock issued. This right enables a stockholder to maintain his or her percentage of ownership.

Transfer Rights. The stockholder has the right to sell or otherwise dispose of the stock.

CORPORATION ACCOUNTING

Corporation accounting differs from other types of accounting in its handling of the owners' equity section of the balance sheet. Since the owners are stockholders, the name of the owners' equity section of the balance sheet will be changed to *Stockholders' Equity*.

There are two sources of stockholders' equity. These are: paid-in capital and retained earnings. The law requires that separate accounts be used to record these two sources because in most states a dividend can only be paid out of retained earnings.

Paid-in capital is the total amount of cash, property, and services paid into a corporation by its stockholders or others. In a corporation, the net income or net loss is closed out to the Retained Earnings account from Income Summary. Dividends are paid out of retained earnings. Thus, the balance in the Retained Earnings account is the amount of earnings that have been retained by the corporation. A debit balance in Retained Earnings is called a *deficit*.

Capital Stock

Capital stock is the shares of ownership in a corporation. When a corporation is set up, the number of shares of stock which may be sold are stated in the charter. This is the authorized stock. *Authorized* shares are the number of shares of capital stock that may be issued by the corporation. Stock that has been sold to investors is called *issued stock*. Issued stock includes all shares that have ever been sold. All shares owned currently by stockholders are called *outstanding stock*. The difference between issued and outstanding stock is treasury stock, as shown by the following equation:

OUTSTANDING STOCK = ISSUED STOCK – TREASURY STOCK

Treasury stock is stock that has been reacquired by the corporation; that is, it has been issued but is not currently owned by stockholders because it is in the hands of the corporation. Treasury stock is discussed in greater detail later in this chapter.

The first type of capital stock issued by a corporation is *common stock*. All corporations issue common stock. Common stockholders have the controlling interest in the firm and have all rights granted to stockholders. If a second type of stock is issued it is called *preferred stock*. Preferred stockholders are given preference over common stockholders in receiving dividends and also assets upon liquidation. However, preferred stockholders usually do not have the right to vote. If a corporation has issued both perferred and common stock, separate accounts are used to record each, and they are shown separately on the balance sheet.

Par Value

Par value is the arbitrary value assigned to each share of stock for accounting and legal purposes. Par value does not indicate worth or price. Stock may be sold for an amount equal to, above, or below its par value. Par value is the amount entered in the capital stock account. One of the purposes of setting a par value is to establish legal capital. *Legal capital* is the amount of capital which must be retained by a corporation for the protection of creditors. Dividends may not be paid out of legal capital. Thus, stockholders cannot be paid dividends before the firm's creditors are satisfied.

Preferred Stock

Preferred stock has first claim on dividends and assets upon liquidation of the corporation. The corporation must pay the preferred stockholders before the common stockholders. The dividend on preferred stock is stated as a dollar amount or as a percent of par. For example, \$1.10, \$100.00 par value preferred stock would be paid a dividend of \$1.10 per share each year. A 6%, \$100.00 par value preferred stock would receive a dividend equal to 6% of \$100.00, or \$6.00 per share each year.

The following is a brief explanation of the various types of preferred stock.

Cumulative and Noncumulative Preferred Stock. Dividends are paid only when declared by the board of directors. Thus, dividends may not be paid every year. However, the dividends on cumulative preferred stock accumulate until paid. These accumulated unpaid dividends are called *dividends in arrears.* Thus, *cumulative preferred stock* can be defined as stock on which the dividends accumulate until paid. Since preferred stock has preference over common stock in dividends, common stockholders may not receive any dividends until dividends are paid in full to the preferred stockholders. This is not a guarantee of dividends – only an assurance that the preferred stockholders will be paid first if any dividends are paid. On the other hand, unpaid dividends, and also share additional dividends along with common stockholders. Since preferred stockholders have preference over common,

Participating and Nonparticipating Preferred Stock. Stockholders who own *participating preferred stock* receive its fixed share of dividends, and also share additional dividends along with common stockholders. Since preferred stockholders have preference over common, they first receive their regular dividend. Next, the common stockholders get the same percentage as a dividend. Then the remainder of the dividends are divided on a pro rata basis to both preferred and common stock. For those who own *nonparticipatinging preferred stock,* dividends are limited to the fixed rate. The majority of preferred stocks are cumulative and nonparticipating.

RECORDING TRANSACTIONS INVOLVING STOCK

Selling Stock for Cash at Par

When stock is sold for cash, the entry is a debit to cash for the amount received and a credit to capital stock for par value. There should be a separate account for each class, or type of stock. These capital stock accounts show the entire amount of stock sold. In addition, the firm must maintain a separate record of the names and addresses of stockholders and the number of shares owned by each. This is called a *stockholders' ledger.*

An example of selling stock for cash at par value is the sale of 100 shares of $100 par value preferred stock and 5,000 shares of $10 par value common stock for cash at par value. The entry is:

Cash	60,000	
Preferred Stock		10,000
Common Stock		50,000
To record the sale of stock.		

Note that a separate account is used for each type of stock. Once the stock has been paid for, the stock certificates are given to the stockholders and the stock is said to have been issued.

Stock Premiums and Discounts

Stock may be sold for more or less than its par value. If stock is sold for more than par value, it is said to have been sold *at a premium.* The premium should be recorded in a separate account. The entry for stock sold at a premium is a debit to Cash for the amount received, a credit to a capital stock account for par value, and a credit to the Premium account for the amount paid in excess of par value. The Premium account is a paid-in capital account just like Common Stock or Preferred Stock.

For example, assume that 100 shares of $100 par value common stock is sold for $110 per share. The entry is:

Cash	11,000	
Common Stock		10,000
Premium on Common Stock		1,000
To record the sale of stock.		

If stock is sold for less than par value, it is sold at a discount. This is illegal in some states. In other states, the stockholder is liable for the amount of the discount since not enough was paid in to cover the legal capital. Therefore, the sale of stock at a discount is unusual.

As an example of the entry for the sale of stock at a discount, assume that 100 shares of $10 par value preferred stock is sold for $8 per share. The entry is:

Cash	800	
Discount on Preferred Stock	200	
Preferred Stock		1,000
To record the sale of stock at a discount.		

STOCKHOLDERS' EQUITY:		
Preferred Stock, $10 par value, 100 shares issued	$ 1,000	
Less: Discount on Preferred Stock	200	$ 800
Common Stock, $100 par value, 100 shares issued	10,000	
Premium on Common Stock	1,000	11,000
Total Paid-in Capital		11,800
Retained Earnings		5,000
Total Stockholders' Equity		$16,800

Fig. 26-3. Stockholders' Equity section of a balance sheet.

The Preferred Stock account is credited for par value. The Discount account is a contra-paid-in-capital account and is deducted from the capital stock account on the balance sheet.

Using the two preceding examples and assuming a balance in the Retained Earnings account of $5,000, the Stockholders' Equity section of the balance sheet would appear as shown in figure 26-3.

SELLING STOCK FOR ASSETS OTHER THAN CASH

Corporations may take assets other than cash in exchange for stock. In such a case, the board of directors determines the fair market value of the asset or services rendered. For example, a firm acquires land and a building in exchange for 10,000 shares of $25 par value common stock. An appraiser estimates that the current value of the building is $200,000 and the current value of the land is $50,000. The entry is:

Building	200,000	
Land	50,000	
Common Stock		250,000
To record exchange of stock for land and building.		

Accountants and attorneys may accept stock from a corporation in exchange for their services in setting up the new business. If an attorney accepts 200 shares of $25 par value common stock in exchange for services in organizing the corporation for which he normally charges $6,000, this entry would be made:

Organization Costs	6,000	
Common Stock		5,000
Premium on Common Stock		1,000
To record exchange of stock for attorney's services.		

No-par Stock

No-par stock is capital stock which has no specified par value. One reason no-par stock is issued is to avoid having to issue stock at a discount. (Remember, the issuance of stock at a discount is illegal in some states.) Another reason is that par value may be deceiving. If the par value of a stock is printed on the certificate, some investors may think that it indicates the value of the stock, which it does not.

If no-par value stock is issued, the entire amount received may be credited to the capital stock account. Suppose that 1,000 shares of no-par common stock are sold at $16 per share. The entry is:

Cash	16,000	
Common Stock		16,000
To record the sale of no-par stock.		

In some cases, the no-par stock is assigned an arbitrary value which is called *stated value.* Stated value is treated in much the same way as par value. In other words, the capital stock account is credited for the stated value. The excess of the amount received for the stock over its stated value is credited to an account called *Paid-in Capital in Excess of Stated Value,* which is just like a premium account. For example, assume that 1,000 shares of no-par common stock with a stated value of $10 per share are sold for $16 per share. The entry is:

Cash	16,000	
Common Stock		10,000
Paid-in Capital in Excess of Stated Value		6,000
To record the sale of common stock.		

STOCK VALUES

There are several values used when talking about stock. *Par value* is the arbitrary amount which is given to par value stock to establish the amount of legal capital. *Stated value* is the abitrary figure assigned to no-par stock. Par values or stated values are the amounts entered in the capital stock accounts. *Market value* is the price at which the stock is selling.

Book Value

Another term that is used is book value. *Book value* is the equity of one share of stock in the assets of the corporation. In other words, book value is total stockholders' equity divided among the shares outstanding. When a corporation has only common stock outstanding, the total stockholders' equity is divided by the number of shares of common stock outstanding. For example, consider a corporation with the following stockholders' equity:

Common Stock, $5 par value, 10,000 shares outstanding,	$50,000
Retained Earnings	10,000
Total Stockholders' Equity	$60,000

The book value per share would be calculated as follows:

$$\frac{\$60{,}000}{10{,}000 \text{ shares}} = \$6 \text{ per share book value}$$

If preferred stock is outstanding, the preferred stockholders have preference over the common stockholders in dividends and assets at liquidation. These amounts are deducted from stockholders' equity to determine the amount left for the common stockholders. Thus, the liquidation value of the preferred stock (usually par value) plus any dividends in arrears are allocated to the preferred stock to compute book value per share for preferred stock. The remaining stockholders' equity is available to the common stockholders.

For example, a firm has the following accounts in its Stockholders' Equity section. The book value calculations would be as shown below.

Preferred Stock, 6% cumulative, \$100 par, 100 shares issued and outstanding (One year's dividends are in arrears)	\$10,000	
Premium on Preferred Stock	1,000	\$ 11,000
Common Stock, \$5 par, 10,000 shares issued and outstanding	50,000	
Premium on Common Stock	10,000	60,000
Total Paid-in Capital		71,000
Retained Earnings		85,000
Total Stockholders' Equity		\$156,000

$$\text{Preferred Stock Book Value} = \frac{\$10{,}000 + \$600}{100 \text{ shares}} = \$106 \text{ per share.}$$

$$\text{Common Stock Book Value} = \frac{\$156{,}000 - \$10{,}600}{10{,}000 \text{ shares}} = \$14.54 \text{ per share.}$$

DIVIDENDS

Cash Dividends

A dividend is a distribution of assets to shareholders on a per share basis. A *cash dividend* is a distribution of cash. The three requirements which must be met before a cash dividend can be paid are:

Cash. There must be enough cash available to pay the dividend.

Retained Earnings. Cash dividends reduce retained earnings. Thus, there must be a sufficient credit balance in the Retained Earnings account to cover the dividend.

Formal Action by the Board of Directors. In a formal meeting, the board of directors must pass a motion declaring that a cash dividend be paid. In this declaration they specify the amount of dividend to be paid per share, the date of record, and the date the dividend will be paid.

There are three important dates to keep in mind when discussing dividends. These are:

Date of Declaration. This is the date of formal action by the board of directors to declare the dividend. This action establishes a liability. The entry required is to reduce retained earnings and record the liability with a debit to Retained Earnings and a credit to Dividends Payable. Dividends Payable is a current liability account on the balance sheet.

Date of Record. This is the date that ownership of shares is to be determined as stated in the dividend declaration. Those owning the stock on the date of record receive the dividend. No entry is required at this time. It is just a matter of preparing a list of those who are stockholders on this date.

Date of Payment. This is the day the checks are mailed out to pay the liability. The entry includes a debit to Dividends Payable and a credit to Cash.

For example, assume that the board of directors of a firm meets on September 1 and declares a $1 per share dividend to be paid September 30 to the September 15 stockholders of record. There are 5,000 shares outstanding. The entries are as follows:

Sept. 1	Retained Earnings	5,000	
	Dividends Payable		5,000
	To record the declaration of $1 per share cash dividend.		
15	[No entry is required on this date but a list of the names and addresses of those owning stock should be prepared.]		
30	Dividends Payable	5,000	
	Cash		5,000
	To record the payment of a cash dividend.		

As a further explanation of the date of record, note that a stockholder who sells his stock on September 16 will still receive the dividend on September 30. The important fact is who owns the stock on the date of record, September 15.

Stock Dividends

A *stock dividend* is a distribution of shares of stock to stockholders on a pro rata basis. The dividend is paid in additional shares of a firm's own stock. Usually, it is a dividend of common stock to common stockholders. The effect of a stock dividend is to transfer an amount out of retained earnings into paid-in capital. There is no change in total assets or total stockholders' equity.

For example, on May 31, the board of directors declares a 10% stock dividend to be issued on June 30 to stockholders of record on June 15. At this time the market price of one share of stock is $24. A partial balance sheet follows:

Common Stock, $10 par value, 20,000 shares outstanding	$200,000
Premium on Common Stock	40,000
Retained Earnings	134,000
Total Stockholders' Equity	$374,000

Journal entries are made on the declaration date and the date of payment. On the date of declaration, retained earnings are reduced and paid-in capital accounts are increased. Retained Earnings is debited for the fair market value of the dividend. The value of the dividend is the total market value of the shares to be distributed. The number of shares is found by taking the percent of the dividend times the number of shares outstanding. In this case, the value of the dividend is 10% times 20,000 shares, or 2,000 shares times $24 per share, or $48,000. Thus, the following entry is made:

Retained Earnings	48,000	
Common Stock Dividend Distributable		20,000
Premium on Common Stock		28,000
To record the declaration of a 10% stock dividend.		

The account, *Common Stock Dividend Distributable* is a temporary paid-in capital account. It shows the par value of the stock to be distributed. The excess of the value of the stock over par is added to the premium account.

One additional note is needed on recording the payment of stock dividends. In this example, market value was used to record the value of the dividend. This procedure is followed only for a small stock dividend. A *small stock dividend* is defined as a dividend of less than 20% to 25%. If a large stock dividend is declared (more than 25%), par value (or stated value) is used in the debit to Retained Earnings.

On the payment date the following entry is made to record the fact that the new shares have been mailed out.

June 30	Common Stock Dividend Distributable	20,000	
	Common Stock		20,000
	To record issuance of a 10% stock dividend.		

To see the effect of the stock dividend, study the Stockholders' Equity section of the balance sheet before and after the dividend.

	Before	After
Common Stock	$200,000	$220,000
Premium on Common Stock	40,000	68,000
Retained Earnings	134,000	86,000
Total	$374,000	$374,000

Note that total stockholders' equity stays the same because there is a transfer of $48,000 out of Retained Earnings into Common Stock and the Premium account. No assets were paid out so that total assets remain the same.

Suppose that Stockholder G owned 1,000 shares of this stock before the dividend. His ownership percentage (portion of the company he owns) was 1,000/20,000 or 5%. The book value of one share before the dividend was $374,000/20,000 shares, or $18.70 per share. Thus, the book value of stock owned by Stockholder G was 1,000 X $18.70, or $18,700. After the dividend, Stockholder G owns 1,100 shares, and the ownership percentage is 1,100/22,000 = 5%. The book value of one share is $374,000/22,000 shares, or $17 per share. The book value of 1,100 shares is 1,100 X $17, or $18,700. Thus, there is no effect on a person's ownership percentage or the book value of his or her holdings when a stock dividend is received.

Even though a stock dividend has little or no effect on the firm's assets or the shareholders' equity, there are some good reasons for its issuance. First, stockholders expect dividends from a profitable firm.

However, the firm may not have adequate cash or may wish to use its cash for investment. So, to make the stockholders feel that their investment is profitable, the board of directors may declare a stock dividend. Thus, stockholders feel that they have received something and that they are sharing in the profits made by the firm.

If the market value of the stock remains the same, the shareholder may actually make money on a stock dividend. However, a stock dividend often reduces the market value of a share of stock. This is advantageous for the firm since it may cause more people to invest in the stock. Also, stock dividends have an advantage over cash dividends because stock dividends are not taxed.

STOCK SPLIT

To *split* stock, the firm calls in its stock, reduces the par or stated value, and issues a proportionate number of new shares. For example, a corporation may call in 10,000 shares of $20 par value common stock and have a *two-for-one* stock split. The firm cuts the par value in half (to $10) and issues twice as many shares (20,000). In a two-for-one split, the stockholders receive two shares of new stock for every share of old stock that had been held. A split has no effect on any account and thus no journal entry is required. A memoradum entry is made to show the change in par value and the number of shares outstanding.

The purpose of a stock split is to reduce the market price of the stock by increasing the number of shares on the market. The hope is that the lower price will attract more investors. Also, it has been found that if there are more shares outstanding, there will be more shareholders. These new shareholders often become customers due to the loyalty felt for their own company. Therefore, a firm may have a stock split to increase shareholders, who, in turn, become new customers. Figure 26-4 illustrates a typical release announcing a stock split.

TREASURY STOCK

Treasury stock is a firm's own stock that it has reacquired through purchase or donation. It is not a part of capital stock outstanding. Treasury stock does not receive dividends and has no rights. When bought, it is recorded at cost and is shown as a deduction in the Stockholders' Equity section of the balance sheet. The entry to record the purchase of treasury stock is to debit Treasury Stock at cost, and credit Cash. For example, the XYZ firm purchases 1,000 shares of its own $5 par common stock at $30 per share, the entry is as follows:

Treasury Stock-Common	30,000	
Cash		30,000
To record purchase of 1,000 shares of treasury stock.		

A firm may reacquire its own stock for several reasons. The market price of the stock may be low, and the firm may wish to stimulate activity. This is called *supporting the market.* The firm may need the stock to distribute to employees as a part of a pension, bonus, or stock-purchase plan. The stock may be held as treasury stock, or it may be reissued, or it may even be retired.

GAT

Press Release

FROM: The Amaron Company
Crescent Highway
Anaheim, California 90010

FOR: GAT, INC.

Immediate Release

GAT VOTES THREE-FOR-TWO STOCK SPLIT;
CASH DIVIDEND TO BE INCREASED

NEW YORK, NEW YORK, January 6, 1979 -- The board of directors of GAT, Inc. today voted a three-for-two stock split of the common stock. The directors also stated their intention to maintain a 8-1/2 cents per share quarterly dividend on the increased number of shares to be outstanding following the stock split. This would constitute a 50 percent increase in the cash dividend.

The stock distribution will be made on approximately May 15, 1979 to shareholders of record January 15, 1979.

Shareholders will receive one additional share for each two shares presently held. There are currently 3,205,000 shares of common stock outstanding.

Steven M. Scisson, president of GAT Inc., stated: "The action of the board in voting the three-for-two stock split and the board's intention to increase quarterly cash dividend payments reflects the significant improvement in operating results, a favorable outlook for our business and the company's sound financial condition. In addition, it is believed that the increase in the number of shares outstanding will assist in broadening the shareholder base of our company as well as improve the marketability of the common stock."

(more)

3206 Lincoln Avenue • New York, New York 23980

Fig. 26-4. News release announcing a stock split.

If the firm sells, or reissues, the treasury stock, an entry is made to record the sale. Assume that the XYZ Firm in the preceding example later sells 200 shares of the treasury stock for $40 per share. This entry is made:

Cash	8,000	
Treasury Stock		6,000
Paid-in Capital from Treasury Stock Sales		2,000
To record the sale of 200 shares of treasury stock at $40.		

Note that the Treasury Stock account was credited for $30 per share which was the original cost of the treasury stock.

At a still later date, the XYZ Firm sells 200 more shares of the treasury stock for $25 per share. This sale is recorded as follows:

Cash	5,000	
Paid-in Capital from Treasury Stock Sales	1,000	
Treasury Stock		6,000
To record the sale of 200 shares of treasury stock at $25.		

When treasury stock is sold below cost, as occurs here, the Paid-in Capital from Treasury Stock Sales account is debited if it has a balance. However, if there is no balance in the Paid-in Capital from Treasury Stock Sales account, then Retained Earnings is debited.

Donated Treasury Stock

If a corporation is in financial trouble and needs cash, the stockholders may decide to give a part of their stock back to the firm. This stock is then sold to the public to obtain cash. To record the donation, only a memorandum entry is used. The transaction is also shown as a notation in the Stockholders' Equity section of the balance sheet, but without any money values.

If the donated treasury stock is sold, this increases assets and stockholders' equity. The entry for the sale of donated treasury stock is a debit to Cash and a credit to an account called *Paid-in Capital From Sale of Donated Treasury Stock.*

DONATIONS OF CAPITAL BY OUTSIDERS

A city, county, or a country may offer free land or factories to a firm if the firm will locate in their area and help the local economy. This donation is recorded at the current fair market value by debiting the asset account and crediting the Paid-in Capital from Donation. For instance, if a firm receives a building and some land from a county, an appraisal must be made to learn the fair value. If the land is worth $10,000 and the building $80,000, the following entry is made:

Land	10,000	
Building	80,000	
Paid-in Capital from Donation		90,000
To record donation of capital.		

T & D Corporation Statement of Retained Earnings For Year Ended December 31, 1981		
Beginning Balance of Retained Earnings, January 1, 1981		$49,554
Net Income for the Year		6,785
		56,339
Less: Cash Dividends	$5,500	
Stock Dividends	3,600	- 9,100
Ending Balance of Retained Earnings, December 31, 1981		$47,239

Fig. 26-5. A retained earnings statement.

STATEMENT OF RETAINED EARNINGS

A corporation may use another statement to supplement the balance sheet and income statement. This additional statement is a *statement of retained earnings.* This statement shows the changes in the retained earnings account resulting from dividends and net income or loss for the period. An example of a retained earnings statement is shown in figure 26-5.

SUMMARY

A corporation is a form of business created by the law. The major advantages of corporations over other forms of business are:

- Ease of raising large amounts of capital.
- Limited liability.
- Easy transfer of ownership.
- Continuous existence.
- No mutual agency.

The main disadvantages of the corporate form of business are:

- High taxation.
- Greater government regulation.

A corporation is run by officers who are appointed by the board of directors. The directors are elected by the stockholders. If a stockholder cannot attend a meeting, he or she can still vote by means of a proxy.

Common stockholders of a corporation have the right to:

- Vote.
- Share in profits.
- Share in assets at liquidation.
- Maintain their share of ownership (preemptive right).
- Transfer their stock to others.

With the exception of owners' equity, the accounting process for corporations is the same as that for other types of firms. The owners' equity (called stockholders' equity) accounts must be kept separate according to source. The two major categories of stockholders' equity are paid-in capital and retained earnings. Stock is recorded in the

Preferred Stock
Premium on Preferred Stock
Discount on Preferred Stock
Common Stock
Premium on Common Stock
Discount on Common Stock
Paid-in Capital from Donation
Paid-in Capital from Sale of Donated Treasury Stock
Paid-in Capital from Sales of Treasury Stock
Treasury Stock
Retained Earnings
Common Stock Dividend Distributable

Fig. 26-6. Typical stockholders' equity accounts.

accounts at its par or stated value. Market value is the current selling price of the stock on the open market. Book value is the equity per share.

If a firm has a second class of stock it is called preferred stock. The word *preferred* means that its owners have preference over common stockholders in receiving dividends and assets at liquidation. However, preferred stockholders usually have no voting rights.

There are two types of dividends. Cash dividends are paid in cash and stock dividends are paid in stock. Stock dividends do not result in any change in the total stockholders' equity. The three important dividend dates are the declaration date, the record date, and the payment date. Journal entries are made on the declaration date and the payment date.

A stock split is sometimes made to reduce the market value per share of stock. No entry is made to record a stock split.

Treasury stock is a firm's own stock that it has reacquired. Treasury stock has no rights and receives no dividends. It is recorded at its cost. The Treasury Stock account has a debit balance. It is shown on the balance sheet as a contra account to stockholders' equity. Figure 26-6 shows some of the stockholders' equity accounts that might appear on a balance sheet. Most firms would not have all of these accounts. However, the student of accounting should become familiar with all of the accounts, since all do appear regularly.

Even if a person never works with accounting, a knowledge of corporation accounting is vital for personal investment purposes. Nearly one American out of every six owns stock. A thorough knowledge of this chapter provides a solid basis for profitable investment decisions.

REVIEW

1. Explain the concept of mutual agency.
2. How are the earnings of corporations taxed twice?
3. What are the five rights of stockholders?

4. List five advantages of the corporate form of business.
5. What is a proxy?
6. What are the disadvantages of the corporate form of business?
7. Explain the preemptive right of stockholders.
8. What is a deficit.
9. What is the first type of stock that a corporation issues?
10. What are the three important dates relating to dividends?
11. What is treasury stock?
12. How is book value of preferred stock calculated?
13. How is book value of common stock calculated?
14. What is par value?
15. How do the members of a corporation's board of directors obtain their positions?
16. Explain the difference between cumulative and noncumulative preferred stock.
17. Explain the difference between participating and nonparticipating preferred stock.
18. What are the two types of dividends?
19. What is the difference between a stock split and a stock dividend?
20. How are a stock split and a stock dividend alike?
21. What are dividends in arrears?

EXERCISES

1. Mountaintop Crafts, Inc., a large craft manufacturer needs to raise capital for expansion. It issues 25,000 shares of its $10 par common stock for $22 per share.
   a. Give the entry.
   b. What would the entry have been if the stock had been sold for only $9 per share?

2. After Hours, a new coffee house, is incorporating. The owners do not have much capital so they have given their lawyer 500 shares of their $10 par common stock to take care of all legal matters concerning their organization and incorporation. Normally the lawyer's fee for such work is $6,000. What entry should be made?

3. Give the entries for the following transactions.
   a. Oil, Inc., has 4,000 shares of $100 par common authorized, with 600 shares issued and outstanding. Directors of the company declare a 5% stock dividend. The current market value of Oil stock is $180 per share.
   b. The stock dividend from Oil, Inc. is distributed.
   c. Six months after the stock dividend, Oil common stock has a four-for-one split.

4. Give the entries for the following transactions.
   a. Alcan Airlines, Inc., has previously issued 10,000 shares of $20 par common at $40. They repurchased this stock off the open market for $65.
   b. Alcan Airlines reissues the above stock six months later at $73.
5. The following is the Shareholders' Equity section from a corporation's balance sheet.

   SHAREHOLDERS' EQUITY

Preferred Stock, $100 par value, 8% cumulative and nonparticipating, 1,000 shares authorized and issued	$100,000
Common Stock, $10 par value, 50,000 shares authorized, 40,000 shares issued	400,000
Retained Earnings	172,000
Total Shareholders' Equity	$672,000

   If no dividends are in arrears:
   a. What is the book value of the preferred stock per share?
   b. What is the book value of the common stock per share?

   If three years' dividends are in arrears on the preferred stock:
   c. What is the book value of the preferred stock per share?
   d. What is the book value of the common stock per share?
6. On April 1, when its stock was selling for $16 per share, the balance sheet of a corporation showed the following stockholders' equity:

Common Stock, $10 par value, 30,000 shares authorized, 20,000 shares issued	$200,000
Premium on Common Stock	142,000
Retained Earnings	102,000
Total Stockholders' Equity	$444,000

   The next day the board of directors declared a 10% stock dividend distributable on May 7 to the May 1 stockholders of record. Give entries to record the declaration and distribution of the dividend.
   a. What was the book value per share of the corporation's stock on April 1?
   b. What was the book value per share after the dividend distribution?
   c. If Stockholder B owned 100 shares of the corporation on April 1, what was the total book value of the shares?
   d. If the same stockholder neither bought nor sold any of the company's shares between April 1 and May 7, what was the book value of all of the shares after the dividend shares were received?

PROBLEMS

1. Write the letter of the word or phrase in the left-hand column which is best described by each of the definitions given in the right-hand column.

   a. Common stock
   b. Deficit
   c. Imprest
   d. Proxy
   e. Preferred stock
   f. Participating preferred stock
   g. Cumulative preferred stock
   h. Dividends in arrears
   i. Preemptive right
   j. Common stock dividend distributable
   k. Treasury stock
   l. Par value
   m. Book value
   n. Convertible stock

   1. Stock which has a limited or fixed maximum return.
   2. The name given to stock when only one class of stock is issued.
   3. A negative amount of retained earnings.
   4. The right of first opportunity to buy a certain percentage of a new issue of common stock.
   5. A preferred stock having the right to share in earning beyond a fixed basic percentage.
   6. Gives an agent the right to vote in the stockholders' meeting.
   7. Preferred stock on which undeclared dividends accumulate each year until paid.
   8. Unpaid back dividends.
   9. The equity of one share of stock in the assets of the issuing corporation.
   10. Arbitrary value established for a share of stock in the charter of the issuing corporation.

2. A corporation issues 10,000 shares of common stock to its principal incorporator in exchange for land valued at $100,000. Give the required journal entry under each of the following assumptions:

   a. The stock is $10 par.
   b. The stock is $25 par.
   c. The stock is $5 par.
   d. The stock is no-par without a stated value.
   e. The stock is no-par with a $10 stated value.

3. Section A is a list of terms. From this list select the letter of the word that best fits the numbered definitions in Section B.

Section A

a. book value	g. limited liability	m. premium
b. capital stock	h. market value	n. retained earnings
c. charter	i. officers	o. stated value
d. corporation	j. par value	p. treasury stock
e. cumulative	k. participating	q. unissued
f. directors	l. preemptive	

Section B

1. An artifical being created by law.
2. Those elected by the stockholders.
3. Price stock may be sold or bought on an open market.
4. Common name for accumulated earnings.
5. Account from which dividends are declared.
6. The exemption of a corporation's stockholders from responsibility for the debts of the company provided the stock held was originally fully paid.
7. The right of a stockholder to purchase a proportionate number of any new shares of stock the corporation might issue.
8. A type of preferred stock that entitles its owners to receive a specified rate of dividend and, if the directors do not pay this amount in any year, there can be no common stock dividends until any such "missed" or "skipped" preferred dividends have been paid.
9. A type of preferred stock that entitles its owners to receive certain amounts of dividends and, also, to share with common stockholders in any additional amount distributed as dividends.
10. Essentially the same thing as par value, but relates to shares that, technically, have no par.
11. Stock that has been authorized but not issued.
12. A document which, after approval by the appropriate state official, gives legal existence to a corporation.
13. Shares of a corporation's own stock which are held by that company.

4. From the following information prepare in good form the Stockholders' Equity section of the balance sheet for the Riverside Corporation for the year ending December 31, 1980: preferred stock, \$50 par, cumulative and nonparticipating, authorized shares, 10,000, issued shares, 6,000; common stock, \$10 par value, 10,000 shares authorized and issued; premium on preferred, \$18,000; contributed capital from treasury stock, \$1,500; treasury stock, common, 400 shares \$4,500; retained earnings, \$80,000.

5. A company has the following accounts in the Stockholders' Equity section of its balance sheet on December 31, 1981.

Preferred Stock (6%, \$100 par, cumulative, nonparticipating)	\$100,000
Common Stock (\$5 par, 100,000 shares issued and outstanding)	500,000
Premium on Common Stock	50,000
Retained Earnings	100,000
	\$750,000

State the effect of each of the following transactions which occurred during 1982 on the total stockholders' equity and the total retained earnings of the corporation.

Feb. 1: The Company buys 100 shares of common treasury stock at $20 per share.

a. What is the new total stockholders' equity?
b. What is the new total retained earnings?

Apr. 3: The firm declared a $.10 per share cash dividend on common stock and a $6.00 per share dividend on preferred stock.

c. What is the new total stockholders' equity?
d. What is the new total retained earnings?

9: Paid the previously declared cash dividends.

e. What is the new total stockholders' equity?
f. What is the new total retained earnings?

Aug. 1: The corporation received a gift of land from the city. It was worth $10,000.

g. What is the new total stockholders' equity?
h. What is the new total retained earnings?

Oct. 1: The company sold 100 shares of treasury stock at $40 per share.

i. What is the new total stockholders' equity?
j. What is the new total retained earnings?

Nov. 1: The company declared a two-for-one stock split on common stock.

k. What is the new total stockholders' equity?
l. What is the new total retained earnings?

Dec. 1: The firm declared a 2% stock dividend on common stock when the market price was $20 per share.

m. What is the new total stockholders' equity of the firm?
n. What is the new total retained earnings of the company?

6. Stockholders' Equity in a corporation appeared as follows on May 1:

Common Stock, $10 par value, 200,000 shares authorized, 150,000 issued and outstanding	$1,500,000
Premium on Common Stock	200,000
Retained Earnings	320,000
	$2,020,000

a. What is the book value per share at this time?
b. On May 2 the corporation purchased 1,000 shares of its own stock at $25 per share. Give the entry for the purchase.
c. On August 31 the corporation sold 600 of the shares they had purchased on May 2. The selling price was $30 per share. Give the entry for the sale.
d. On September 30 the corporation's board of directors declared a cash dividend of $1 per share to be paid on October 31 to the October 15 stockholders of record. Give the entry that would be made on September 30.
e. Give the entry that would be made on October 15.
f. Give the entry that would be made on October 31.
g. Give the book value per share after the entries in b-f have been posted.

7. The following transactions were completed by the Himmel Corporation during its first two years of business.

198A

Jan. 17: Received a charter from the state authorizing the firm to issue 10,000 shares of $10 par common stock and 1,000 shares of $100 par, 6% cumulative preferred stock.

20: Sold 5,000 shares of common at $11 per share.

30: Sold 1,000 shares of preferred at $99 per share.

Feb. 1: Issued 100 shares of common to lawyer in payment of a bill for $1,200. The expenses were incurred in forming the corporation.

July 8: Sold 4,000 shares of common at $15 per share.

Dec. 31: Net income for the year was $30,000.

198B

Mar. 6: Bought 200 shares of our own stock at $13 per share.

Aug. 29: Sold 100 shares of treasury stock at $16 per share.

Nov. 1: Sold 100 shares of treasury stock at $9 per share.

Dec. 22: Declared dividends on common and preferred stocks totaling $15,000. (Use two separate liability accounts, one for preferred and one for common.)

31: Recorded the $18,000 net income for the year.

---

a. Record the above transactions in general journal form.

b. Prepare the Stockholders' Equity section of a balance sheet at the end of the second year.

c. What is the book value per share at the end of the second year?

SECTION 6

Accounting for Manufacturing Concerns

27
The Elements of Manufacturing Cost

OBJECTIVES After studying this chapter, the student will be able to:

- Identify the basic elements of manufacturing cost.
- Describe the nature of the cost data which must be recorded for control of manufacturing costs.
- List and describe the accounts needed to record manufacturing costs.
- Record the journal entries for a manufacturing firm.

THE MANUFACTURING BUSINESS

Thus far, this text has discussed accounting for service and merchandising firms. Businesses that perform a service include doctors, lawyers, accountants, and plumbers. Firms that sell finished goods fall into the merchandising category. Some examples are grocery stores, department stores, and clothing stores. This section of the text deals with a third type of business, the manufacturing firm. A *manufacturing firm* buys raw materials and then makes the goods that it sells. Bakeries, construction firms, and automobile plants are all examples of manufacturing firms.

The accounting records for a manufacturing firm must show the cost of making the goods that are sold. To handle this information, manufacturing firms require six accounts in addition to those already introduced. The basic elements of cost that are involved in the manufacture of a product are accounted for separately. In this way, the management of a firm can determine the cost of making the product.

ELEMENTS OF MANUFACTURING COST

There are three basic elements involved in the manufacture of a product. These three elements are raw materials, direct labor, and factory overhead.

Raw Materials

Raw materials are the materials that become a part of the finished product. Raw materials may also be called *direct materials* because they enter directly into the finished product. For example, in making a book, paper and ink are the major raw materials used. Leather is the raw material used to make shoes.

Direct Labor

Direct labor is composed of the wages paid to employees who work directly on the raw materials to produce the finished product. These are the people directly involved in the manufacturing process. The wages paid to these factory employees should be recorded separately from the wages paid to other employees.

Factory Overhead

Factory overhead can be defined as all costs incurred in the operation of the factory other than raw materials and direct labor. One part of factory overhead consists of indirect materials. *Indirect materials* are materials which cannot be associated with specific units of product. They do not become a major part of the product, but rather, are supplies used in the factory. Examples of indirect materials include the following: sandpaper, glue, and the oil and grease used to lubricate machinery during the manufacturing process.

Another component of factory overhead is indirect labor. *Indirect labor* is made up of the wages paid to employees who work in the factory, but do not work directly on the product. These are the employees who supervise the work, repair the machinery, clean up the factory, and transport materials to and from the stockroom.

The final category of overhead consists of all other indirect manufacturing costs. These overhead costs cannot be associated directly with the units produced. They include depreciation expense for plant and equipment, utilities to run the plant, and insurance and taxes on the factory building. The following list further illustrates the nature of the costs in this group. This is only a partial list; there may be many more in some industries. Note that this list does not include selling or front office expenses. Only costs incurred in production are included.

Examples of Overhead Costs

- factory supplies
- salaries of supervisors and foremen
- wages of janitors, maintenance workers, and watchmen
- salaries of inspectors
- power and utilities
- fuel
- depreciation
- taxes
- insurance on factory and equipment
- rent for factory assets
- repairs of equipment
- payroll taxes on factory employees

ACCOUNTS NEEDED FOR MANUFACTURING COSTS

Six accounts distinguish manufacturing firms from other companies.

Fig. 27-1. All manufacturing firms must account for the three basic elements of manufacturing cost: raw materials, direct labor, and factory overhead. Identify each of these elements in this photograph.

Raw Materials Purchases

This account is to be used to record the cost of all raw materials purchased. Raw Materials Purchases should be debited every time raw materials are bought.

Direct Labor

As mentioned earlier, the wages of employees who work directly on the product must be recorded separately from the wages of other workers. The Direct Labor account is used for this purpose.

Freight-in on Raw Materials

This new account is used to record the cost of having the raw materials delivered to the firm. It is just an additional cost of getting the raw materials. The Freight-in on Raw Materials account has a normal debit balance.

Raw Materials Inventory

This account is used to record the inventory of raw materials that are on hand. When a periodic inventory method is used, the inventory on hand at the end of the year is found by a physical count. It is recorded with a closing entry. Raw Materials Inventory is a current asset account and has a normal debit balance.

Goods-in-Process Inventory

This account is used to record the inventory of partly completed products on hand. These are the products that are in the in-between stage. Some of the manufacturing work has been done, so these units cannot be called raw materials. But, since they are not finished, they cannot be included with finished goods. In some firms, this account is called Work-in-Process Inventory. Under a periodic inventory system, a physical count is taken and the cost of goods in process is recorded by a closing entry at the end of the accounting period.

Finished Goods Inventory

This account shows the inventory of completed products that are on hand and ready to be sold. If a periodic inventory system is in use, a closing entry will be made at the end of the accounting period to record the inventory as determined by a physical count. Finished Goods is not really a new account. It is merely a different name for the Merchandise Inventory account that is used by merchandising firms.

Note that in a manufacturing firm there are three types of inventories – raw materials, goods-in-process, and finished goods. All of these inventories are classified as current assets, and thus, all have debit balances. The ending inventories of raw materials, goods-in-process, and finished goods are shown on the balance sheet of a manufacturing firm.

Journal Entries for Manufacturing Firms

The Solid-Built Company buys $5,000 worth of raw materials for cash. The following journal entry is made:

Raw Material Purchases	5,000	
Cash		5,000
Bought raw materials.		

Freight costs of $40 are incurred to obtain the above shipment. The entry to pay the freight is as follows:

Freight-in on Raw Materials	40	
Cash		40
To record payment of freight charges.		

The entry to record manufacturing wages is a compound entry since both direct and indirect labor are involved. If Solid-Built has $800 of direct labor during a week, the entry would be:

Direct Labor	800	
Indirect Labor	200	
FICA Taxes Payable		61.30
Employees Federal Income Taxes Payable		100.00
Cash		838.70
To record weekly manufacturing payroll.		

Overhead costs are recorded in the same manner as any expense. The overhead accounts all have debit balances. The costs should be recorded when they are incurred.

The journal entries and other accounting procedures for a manufacturing firm are not very different from those of any other type of business. The important point is to keep manufacturing costs separated in different accounts from the selling and administrating expenses. To accomplish this separation, additional accounts are needed. Chapter 28 explains how these accounts affect the financial statements.

SUMMARY

Manufacturing businesses differ from other firms in that they both make and sell products. Accounting records for this type of firm are expanded to show the cost of manufacturing. The elements of manufacturing costs must be recorded separately.

There are three elements of manufacturing cost: raw materials, direct labor, and factory overhead. Raw materials and direct labor are considered direct costs because they can be associated directly with the units which are produced. Raw materials are resources that become a part of the finished product. Direct labor is made up of the wages paid to employees who work directly on the raw materials to produce the final product. Overhead costs are indirect manufacturing costs. Overhead consists of all manufacturing costs except raw materials and direct labor.

Six special accounts are needed to record the manufacturing costs. Three of these are inventory accounts: raw materials, goods-in-process, and finished goods. These inventories are shown as current assets on the balance sheet. The accounting records of a manufacturing firm aid its management in determining, analyzing, and controlling the costs of making the product.

REVIEW

1. How does a manufacturing firm differ from other types of businesses (i.e., service and merchandising)? How does this affect the accounting records?
2. What are the elements of manufacturing cost? Describe each of these elements.
3. How does overhead differ from raw materials and direct labor?
4. Give at least five examples of factory overhead costs.
5. What special accounts are needed in the accounting records of a manufacturing firm? Classify those accounts and state their normal balances.
6. How is the balance sheet of a manufacturing firm different from the balance sheet of a merchandising firm?

EXERCISES

1. A manufacturing firm incurs production costs of \$30,000 during a month. These include \$4,000 of raw materials and \$18,000 of overhead. How much direct labor is used during the month?
2. A manufacturing firm buys \$300 worth of raw materials for cash from Pine Sales Company. Give the journal entry (in general journal form) for the transaction.

3. The firm in Exercise 2 must pay $20 to have the raw materials delivered. What entry would be made for the payment to the trucking company that delivered the materials?

4. Which of the following accounts are overhead costs accounts?
   a. Indirect Labor
   b. Direct Labor
   c. Heat, Light and Power
   d. Freight-in on Raw Materials
   e. Work-in-Process Inventory
   f. Finished Goods Inventory
   g. Raw Materials Inventory
   h. Depreciation Expense – Machinery

5. Which of the following accounts appear on the balance sheet?
   a. Raw Materials Purchases
   b. Raw Materials Inventory
   c. Finished Goods Inventory
   d. Accumulated Depreciation – Machinery
   e. Work-in-Process Inventory

6. Make the journal entry to record the weekly payroll for the first week of January if the following wages are earned: Office workers, $200; Direct Labor, $1,000; and Indirect Labor, $500. The total of the federal income taxes withheld is $330. (Hint: Remember to include the FICA taxes.)

PROBLEMS

1. The following is a list of manufacturing costs. Classify these costs as raw materials, direct labor, or factory overhead.
   a. insurance on factory equipment
   b. utilities expense
   c. machinery repairs
   d. janitorial work
   e. wages of person who varnishes furniture
   f. supervisory salaries
   g. gathering scrap and waste
   h. depreciation of plant
   i. taxes on building
   j. sawing lumber for furniture
   k. wood used to produce a baseball bat
   l. sandpaper used to sand baseball bat
   m. tape put on handle of baseball bat

2. State for each of the following costs whether it is a manufacturing cost, general and administrative expense, or selling expense. If the cost is manufacturing, state whether it is raw material, direct labor, or factory overhead.
   a. bad debt expense
   b. salary expense – company president
   c. salary expense – factory foreman
   d. salary expense – sales manager
   e. depreciation of accountant's adding machine
   f. depreciation of factory machinery

g. advertising expense
h. raw materials
i. interest expense
j. rent expense – office building
k. rent expense – factory building
l. rent expense – retail store
m. direct labor
n. indirect labor
o. salary expense – accountant
p. repair expense – factory equipment
q. repair expense – office equipment
r. freight-in on raw materials
s. office supplies used
t. factory supplies used
u. insurance expense – factory
v. heat, light & power – factory

3. Make the journal entries in general journal form for each of the following transactions.

June 19: Bought $700 worth of raw materials on credit from Boone Supply Company.
19: Paid freight charges on the raw materials, $60.
23: Paid the utility bill for the factory, $40.
24: Paid the employees their weekly pay. Direct labor was $600 and indirect labor was $100. FICA taxes were $40.95 and federal withholding taxes were $50.
26: Bought $1,300 worth of raw materials for cash from Gap Sales Company.
26: Paid $50 to have the materials from Gap Sales delivered.
30: Recorded depreciation for the month on the factory machinery, $119.

28 The Manufacturing Statement

OBJECTIVES After studying this chapter, the student will be able to:

- Prepare a manufacturing statement.
- Explain the relationship of the manufacturing statement to the income statement.
- Identify the contents of each section of the manufacturing statement.
- Describe the income statement and balance sheet of a manufacturing firm.

Chapter 27 introduced six accounts which make it possible to calculate the cost of goods manufactured. If all of these accounts were added to the income statement, it would become quite long and confusing.

For this reason, the additional accounts and the calculation of the cost of goods manufactured is shown on a separate statement. This statement is called a *manufacturing statement* or a *statement of cost of goods manufactured.* It supplements, or serves as a supporting schedule to, the income statement. The last figure on the manufacturing statement is the cost of goods manufactured. Therefore, this statement must be prepared before the income statement can be completed.

THE MANUFACTURING STATEMENT

The manufacturing statement is divided into three sections – raw materials, direct labor, and factory overhead.

Raw Materials

In the first section, the cost of raw materials used is calculated. This calculation is made in the following way:

Beginning Inventory of Raw Materials
Add: Raw Material Purchases
Add: Freight-in
Equals: Total Raw Materials Available for Use
Less: Ending Inventory of Raw Materials
Equals: Raw Materials Used

The beginning inventory of raw materials is the balance shown in the Raw Materials Inventory account for the beginning of the accounting period. The amount of raw materials which have been purchased during the accounting period is shown by the balance in the Raw Materials Purchases account. Another separate account shows the amount of freight-in. The ending inventory of raw materials is found by taking a physical count of the raw materials on hand at the end of the period. The following example shows the raw material section of the manufacturing statement for the DE Company. The beginning inventory of the firm was $700 and the ending inventory is $380.

Beginning Inventory of Raw Materials	$ 700
Add: Raw Material Purchases	1,140
Add: Freight-in	50
Total Raw Materials Available for Use	1,890
Less: Ending Inventory of Raw Materials	380
Raw Materials Used	$1,510

Direct Labor

The second section of the manufacturing statement shows the amount of direct labor as taken from the Direct Labor account balance.

Overhead

The third part of the statement includes a listing of all overhead account balances. These overhead items are totaled and added to the Raw Materials Used and Direct Labor figures.

Total Manufacturing Costs

The three elements calculated thus far, when added together, equal the total manufacturing costs placed into production this period. Using the DE Company example, the three elements added together appear as follows:

Raw Materials Used		$1,510
Direct Labor		2,000
Factory Overhead:		
Indirect Labor	$500	
Depreciation – Factory	270	$ 770
Total Manufacturing Costs		4,280

Goods-in-Process

In addition to the manufacturing costs of production during this accounting period, some costs were brought over into this period as goods-in-process inventory. These goods were partially finished during the last accounting period. Thus, part of the raw materials, direct labor and factory overhead costs had already been incurred for these units in the previous period. The beginning goods-in-process inventory is added to the total manufacturing costs to determine the total of all goods-in-process during the period. The beginning goods-in-process inventory is the balance in the Goods-in-Process Inventory account. All of the goods that were in process during the period have probably not been completed at the end of the period. The goods which are only partly completed are counted and valued at the end of each period to find the ending goods-in-process. This figure is then subtracted from the total goods-in-process during the period to find the cost of goods manufactured. This is the last figure on a firm's manufacturing statement.

Remember, every financial statement should start with a heading that tells the name of the firm, the name of the financial statement and the time period covered by the statement. Such a heading is used in figure 28-1, a manufacturing statement for the Domestic Manufacturing Company for the year ended December 31, 1981. The date line on a manufacturing statement is always the same as the date line in the income statement heading.

DOMESTIC MANUFACTURING COMPANY
Manufacturing Statement
For Year Ended December 31, 1981

Raw Materials:		
Beginning Inventory		$ 400
Add: Purchases	$3,000	
Add: Freight-in	150	
Total Purchases		3,150
Cost of Materials Available		3,550
Less: Ending Inventory		120
Raw Materials Used		3,430
Direct Labor		1,870
Factory Overhead:		
Indirect Labor	330	
Heat – Factory	500	
Depreciation Expense	700	
Total Overhead		1,530
Total Manufacturing Costs		6,830
Add: Goods-in-Process, Beginning		300
Cost of Goods-in-Process During Year		7,130
Less: Goods-in-Process, Ending		320
Cost of Goods Manufactured		$6,810

Fig. 28-1. Manufacturing statement for Domestic Manufacturing Company.

DOMESTIC MANUFACTURING COMPANY Income Statement For Year Ended December 31, 1981		
Revenue:		
Sales		$10,000
Cost of Goods Sold:		
Finished Goods Inventory, Beginning	$ 500	
Cost of Goods Manufactured (per statement)	6,810	
Cost of Goods Available for Sale	7,310	
Less: Finished Goods Inventory, Ending	560	
Cost of Goods Sold		6,750
Gross Profit		3,250
Administrative and General Expenses:		
Heat – Office	220	
Bad Debt Expense	100	
Total Expenses		320
Net Income		$ 2,930

Fig. 28-2. Income statement for Domestic Manufacturing Company.

INCOME STATEMENT FOR A MANUFACTURING FIRM

The income statement for a manufacturing firm is the same as that for a merchandising firm, except for the Cost of Goods Sold section. Cost of goods sold is determined as follows:

Beginning Finished Goods Inventory
Add: Cost of Goods Manufactured
Equals: Cost of Goods Available for Sale
Less: Ending Finished Goods Inventory
Equals: Cost of Goods Sold

The beginning finished goods inventory is the balance in the Finished Goods Inventory account. Cost of goods manufactured is the final figure on the manufacturing statement. Usually, the reader is referred to the manufacturing statement for the details of how this cost was calculated.

Note that Cost of Goods Manufactured replaces Purchases which appears in the Cost of Goods Sold section of an income statement for merchandising firms. The ending finished goods inventory is found by taking a physical count. The income statement for the Domestic Manufacturing Company is shown in figure 28-2. Note the reference to the manufacturing statement.

BALANCE SHEET FOR A MANUFACTURING FIRM

The balance sheet for a manufacturing firm is the same as that for a merchandising firm, except for the Current Assets section. The ending raw materials, goods-in-process, and finished goods inventories are shown as current assets. These three inventory figures are determined by physical counts taken at the end of the accounting period. The balance sheet for Domestic Manufacturing Company is shown in figure 28-3.

DOMESTIC MANUFACTURING COMPANY
Balance Sheet
December 31, 1981

ASSETS:			LIABILITIES AND STOCKHOLDERS' EQUITY:			
Cash		$ 100	Liabilities:			
Accounts Receivable		200	Accounts Payable			$ 200
Raw Materials Inventory		120	Stockholders' Equity:			
Goods-in-Process Inventory		320	Common Stock	$1,000		
Finished Goods Inventory		560	Retained Earnings:			
Total Current Assets		1,300	Beginning Balance	470		
Factory Equipment	5,000		Net Income	2,930		
Less: Accumulated Depreciation	(1,700)	3,300	Ending Balance		$3,400	
			Total Stockholders' Equity			4,400
Total Assets		$4,600	Total Liabilities and Stockholders' Equity			$4,600

Fig. 28-3. Balance sheet for Domestic Manufacturing Company.

ACCOUNTING EXAMPLE FOR A MANUFACTURING FIRM

Practice Problem

The following is the adjusted trial balance for the Lake Company as of December 31, 1981.

Account	Debit	Credit
Cash	$ 1,000	
Accounts Receivable	2,000	
Allowance for Bad Debts		$ 400
Raw Materials Inventory	3,500	
Goods-in-Process Inventory	1,850	
Finished Goods Inventory	3,200	
Factory Equipment	18,000	
Accumulated Depreciation		3,600
Accounts Payable		4,000
Wages Payable		600
Common Stock		10,000
Retained Earnings		12,365
Sales		70,000
Raw Materials Purchases	32,000	
Freight-in	175	
Direct Labor	16,000	
Indirect Labor	3,100	
Depreciation – Factory Equipment	1,800	
Heat & Power – Factory	1,150	
Utility Expense – Office	690	
Salary Expense – Office	14,000	
Bad Debt Expense	300	
Rent – Factory Building	1,200	
Rent – Office	1,000	
	$100,965	$100,965

The Lake Company took its annual inventory on December 31, 1981. The following amounts of each inventory were on hand.

Raw Materials	$4,200
Goods-in-Process	2,200
Finished Goods	3,650

Using this information, prepare the following three financial statements for the Lake Company:

- manufacturing statement.
- income statement.
- balance sheet.

Solution. Figure 28-4 shows the manufacturing statement for the Lake Company. Study the information given and how it is calculated. Note that the manufacturing statement includes only those accounts that deal with producing the product. For example, Bad Debt Expense has nothing to do with production. It is a selling expense. Therefore, Bad Debt Expense does not appear on the manufacturing statement. The bottom line of the manufacturing statement is carried over to the income statement.

Lake Company
Manufacturing Statement
For Year Ended December 31, 1981

Raw Materials		
Beginning Inventory		$ 3,500
Add: Raw Materials Purchases	$32,000	
Add: Freight-in – Raw Materials	175	
Net Cost of Purchases		32,175
Raw Materials Available for Use		35,675
Less: Ending Raw Materials Inventory		4,200
Raw Materials Used		31,475
Direct Labor		16,000
Factory Overhead		
Indirect Labor	3,100	
Depreciation – Factory Equipment	1,800	
Heat and Power – Factory	1,150	
Rent – Factory Building	1,200	
Total Overhead		7,250
Total Manufacturing Costs		54,725
Add: Beginning Goods-in-Process Inventory		1,850
Total Goods-in-Process During Year		56,575
Less: Ending Goods in Process Inventory		2,200
Cost of Goods Manufactured		$54,375

Fig. 28-4. Manufacturing statement for Lake Company.

Fig. 28-5. Income statement for Lake Company.

Lake Company
Income Statement
For Year Ended December 31, 1981

Revenue:		
Sales		$70,000
Cost of Goods Sold:		
Beginning Finished Goods Inventory	$ 3,200	
Add: Cost of Goods Manufactured (Per Statement)	54,375	
Goods Available for Sale	57,575	
Less: Ending Finished Goods Inventory	3,650	
Cost of Goods Sold		53,925
Gross Profit		16,075
Operating Expenses:		
Utility Expense	690	
Salary Expense	14,000	
Bad Debt Expense	300	
Rent	1,000	
Total Expenses		15,990
Net Income		$ 85

Fig. 28-6. Balance sheet for Lake Company.

Lake Company
Balance Sheet
December 31, 1981

ASSETS:			
Current Assets:			
Cash		$ 1,000	
Accounts Receivable	$2,000		
Less: Allowance for Bad Debts	(400)	1,600	
Raw Materials Inventory		4,200	
Goods-in-Process Inventory		2,200	
Finished Goods Inventory		3,650	
Total Current Assets			$12,650
Fixed Assets:			
Factory Equipment		18,000	
Less: Accumulated Depreciation		3,600	14,400
Total Assets			$27,050
LIABILITIES:			
Current Liabilities:			
Accounts Payable		$ 4,000	
Wages Payable		600	
Total Current Liabilities			4,600
EQUITIES:			
Stockholders' Equity:			
Common Stock		10,000	
Retained Earnings		12,450	
Total Stockholders' Equity			22,450
Total Equities			$27,050

The income statement for the Lake Company is shown in figure 28-5. Notice that all of the production accounts are summarized in one line – Cost of Goods Manufactured.

The balance sheet is the last step in the preparation of statements. The balance sheet for the Lake Company appears in figure 28-6. Note that the three inventory accounts have the balances that were on hand at the end of the year, rather than the amounts that appeared on the trial balance. The figure for retained earnings ($12,450) is the sum of $12,365 that appeared on the trial balance and the $85 net income for the year.

SUMMARY

Manufacturing firms use a separate statement to supplement the income statement. Called a manufacturing statement, it shows the cost of the goods that have been made by the firm. It must be prepared before the income statement can be completed.

The manufacturing statement consists of a separate section for each of the three types of manufacturing costs. Only the costs of manufacturing are shown on this statement. Costs incurred by the sales staff or in the office do not appear.

The only change in the income statement required for manufacturing firms is in the Cost of Goods Sold section. On an income statement for a manufacturing firm the Purchases line is replaced by a Cost of Goods Manufactured line. On the balance sheet of a manufacturing firm, the three inventories are all shown as current assets. These three types of inventories are raw materials, goods-in-process, and finished goods.

REVIEW

1. What account appears on the income statement of a merchandising firm but not on the income statement of a manufacturing firm?
2. In what order are the three financial statements of a manufacturing firm prepared?
3. What information is given in the first section of a manufacturing statement?
4. Which is the shortest section of a manufacturing statement?
5. If ending raw material inventory is greater than beginning raw material inventory, which of the following is higher?
   a. the raw materials purchased
   b. the raw materials used
6. If a firm had no beginning or ending finished goods inventories, which of the following would be higher?
   a. the cost of goods manufactured
   b. the cost of goods sold

EXERCISES

1. If a firm put $12,000 worth of manufacturing costs into production, had a beginning goods-in-process inventory of $400, and an ending goods-in-process inventory of $150, what was the cost of goods manufactured for the period?

2. Given the following account balances and information:
   a. Prepare the Raw Materials section of a manufacturing statement.
   b. What amount will appear on the balance sheet for raw material inventory?

Raw Materials Inventory	$ 8,000
Raw Materials Purchases	13,000
Freight-in, Raw Materials	500

   An actual count of raw materials on hand at the end of the period totaled only $1,700.

3. Supply the missing figures in the following manufacturing statements.

Raw Materials Beginning Inventory	5,000	F	4,000	P
Raw Materials Purchases	25,000	3,000	K	5,000
Freight-in	1,000	500	1,000	1,000
Raw Materials Available	A	G	10,000	Q
Ending R.M. Inventory	B	1,000	2,000	12,000
Raw Materials Used	16,000	7,500	L	R
Direct Labor	C	18,000	M	18,000
Factory Overhead	7,000	H	6,000	18,000
Total Manufacturing Costs	38,000	30,000	N	S
Beginning Goods-in-Process Inventory	2,000	I	3,000	19,000
Total Goods in Production	D	J	24,000	73,000
Ending Goods-in-Process Inventory	E	9,000	1,000	T
Cost of Goods Manufactured	33,000	22,000	0	60,000

4. Supply the missing figures for the following income statements.

Sales	100,000	E	I	60,000
Beginning Finished Goods Inventory	A	16,000	22,000	M
Cost of Goods Manufactured	30,000	F	10,000	14,000
Goods Available for Sale	B	50,000	J	29,000
Ending Finished Goods Inventory	35,000	12,000	K	N
Cost of Goods Sold	35,000	G	3,000	O
Gross Profit	C	H	37,000	39,000
Operating Expenses	5,000	3,000	L	P
Net Income	D	6,000	5,000	2,000

5. Supply the missing information for the following statements.

	I	II
Cost of Raw Materials Used	$381,700	$100,400
Direct Labor	85,600	64,400
Manufacturing Expenses	58,500	52,300
Goods-in-Process – Beginning	4,100	33,700
Goods-in-Process – Ending	3,000	34,200
Finished Goods – Beginning	8,600	7,000
Finished Goods – Ending	8,600	5,900
Cost of Goods Manufactured	A	C
Cost of Goods Sold	B	D

PROBLEMS

1. The following manufacturing cost accounts were taken from the adjusted trial balance of Batt Manufacturing Company. The firm prepares financial statements once a year. The adjusted trial balance was dated December 31, 1981.

Depreciation Expense	700
Direct Labor	19,300
Heat, Light & Power	1,200
Indirect Labor	2,600
Raw Materials Inventory	5,000
Raw Materials Purchases	40,000
Rent Expense	1,800
Freight-in	2,250
Goods-in-Process Inventory	6,000

The following quantities of inventories were on hand at December 31, 1981, according to a physical count made on that date.

Raw Materials	3,700
Goods-in-Process	180

Using the correct form, prepare a manufacturing statement for the firm.

2. The adjusted trial balance shown below is for the Big X Manufacturing Company as of December 31, 1981. Statements are prepared once a year.

Cash	$ 3,000	
Accounts Receivable	21,000	
Allowance for Bad Debts		$ 100
Raw Materials Inventory	3,330	
Goods-in-Process Inventory	4,440	
Finished Goods Inventory	5,550	
Prepaid Insurance	180	
Factory Machinery	19,000	
Accumulated Depreciation		5,700
Accounts Payable		2,000
FICA Taxes Payable		580
Common Stock		10,000
Retained Earnings		10,210
Sales		100,000
Raw Materials Purchases	27,090	
Freight-in – Raw Materials	1,120	
Direct Labor	13,900	
Indirect Labor	5,200	
Depreciation – Machinery	1,900	
Heat, Light, & Power – Factory	3,600	
Utility Expense	4,250	
Telephone Expense	840	
Advertising Expense	500	
Salary Expense – Office	10,400	
Bad Debt Expense	50	
Insurance Expense – Factory	240	
Rent Expense – Factory	1,800	
Rent Expense – Office	1,200	
	$128,590	$128,590

The year-end inventories were as follows:

Raw Materials	5,000
Goods-in-Process	4,000
Finished Goods	3,000

Prepare the following year-end statements for the firm:
a. manufacturing statement.
b. income statement.
c. balance sheet.

3. The following adjusted trial balance is for the Wolf Manufacturing Company as of December 31, 1981. The amounts are for the entire year. (The accounts are listed alphabetically to provide practice in sorting the accounts to the proper statements.)

Accounts Payable		$ 1,200
Accounts Receivable	$ 8,100	
Accumulated Depreciation – Factory Building		2,200
Accumulated Depreciation – Factory Equipment		1,100
Advertising Expense	1,150	
Allowance for Bad Debts		200
Bad Debt Expense	300	
Cash	4,000	
Common Stock		20,000
Depreciation Expense – Factory Building	1,000	
Depreciation Expense – Factory Equipment	500	
Direct Labor	22,220	
Factory Building	20,000	
Factory Equipment	10,000	
Finished Goods Inventory	6,200	
Freight-in – Raw Materials	250	
Goods-in-Process Inventory	8,400	
Heat, Light & Power – Factory	1,300	
Indirect Labor	6,630	
Prepaid Rent	300	
Raw Materials Inventory	1,500	
Raw Materials Purchases	15,100	
Rent Expense – Office	2,400	
Retained Earnings		18,500
Salary Expense – Office	10,600	
Salaries Payable		200
Sales		80,000
Telephone Expense	1,500	
Utility Expense – Office	1,950	
	$123,400	$123,400

The year-end physical counts showed the following inventories on hand:

Raw Materials	$1,870
Goods-in-Process	8,450
Finished Goods	3,300

Prepare (a) a manufacturing statement, (b) an income statement, and (c) a balance sheet for the firm.

4. The following transactions were completed by the Peltz Manufacturing Company during its first month of operation.

1981

June 1: Charles Peltz invested $20,000 to establish the firm as a proprietorship.

2: Bought raw materials for cash, $3,000.

3: Bought factory equipment on credit from Excel Company, $5,000.

June 4: Placed advertisement in newspaper, $25.
8: Bought raw materials on credit from First Company, $7,000. Paid freight-in expense of $30.
10: Paid factory rent for the month, $100.
15: Paid office rent for the month, $150.
22: Bought raw materials on credit from First Company, $3,700.
23: Paid for the raw materials bought on June 8.
29: Received $24,000 from sale of products.
29: Paid utility bill for the office, $100, and for the factory, $330.
30: Paid the employees one month's wages. The total of $5,000 was divided up as Direct Labor, $3,000; Indirect Labor, $1,000; Office Wages, $1,000. A total of $590 was withheld for federal income taxes.
30: Recorded depreciation on the equipment for the month, $10.

The month-end inventories included $1,000 of raw materials, $700 worth of goods in process and $1,250 of finished goods.

---

a. Record the transactions in general journal form.
b. Post to T-accounts.
c. Prepare a manufacturing statement.
d. Prepare an income statement.
e. Prepare a balance sheet.

29 Work Sheet for a Manufacturing Firm

OBJECTIVES

After studying this chapter, the student will be able to:

- Prepare a work sheet for a manufacturing firm.
- Record the ending inventories on the work sheet.
- Use the work sheet to complete the financial statements.

Recall from previous chapters that a work sheet is a tool used to summarize and sort the information needed to complete the financial statements. Adjustments are easily determined from the work sheet and noted on it. It allows the accountant to sort the accounts into columns according to their relationship to the financial statements when dealing with a manufacturing firm. The cost of goods manufactured and net income are also computed on the work sheet.

PREPARATION OF THE WORK SHEET

The work sheet of a manufacturing firm has an extra set of columns to accommodate the information shown on the manufacturing statement. The procedure for preparing the manufacturing firm's work sheet is the same as for a merchandising firm. Figure 29-1 is a work sheet for the Domestic Manufacturing Company introduced in chapter 28. Study the work sheet and the following explanation of the steps necessary for its completion.

Step 1

Enter the trial balance amounts in the first set of columns. Add these columns to be sure that the debits and credits balance. Note that this step is the same as the first step for a merchandising firm's work sheet.

Step 2

Enter the adjustments in the adjustments columns. The adjustments are the same as those for a merchandising firm. In this example, there is only one adjustment needed. The adjustments columns are added to show that the debits and credits are equal.

Domestic Manufacturing Company
Work Sheet
For Year Ended December 31, 1981

	Trial Balance		Adjustments		Manufacturing Statement		Income Statement		Balance Sheet	
	Dr.	Cr.	Dr.	Cr.	Dr.	Cr.	Dr.	Cr.	Dr.	Cr.
Cash	100								100	
Accounts Receivable	200								200	
Raw Materials Inventory	400				400	120			120	
Goods-in-Process Inventory	300				300	320			320	
Finished Goods Inventory	500						500	560	560	
Factory Equipment	5,000								5,000	
Accumulated Depreciation		1,000		700						1,700
Accounts Payable		200								200
Common Stock		1,000								1,000
Retained Earnings		470								470
Sales		10,000						10,000		
Raw Materials Purchases	3,000				3,000					
Freight-in Raw Materials	150				150					
Direct Labor	1,870				1,870					
Indirect Labor	330				330					
Heat — Factory	500				500					
Heat — Office	220						220			
Bad Debt Expense	100						100			
	12,670	12,670								
Depreciation Expense			700		700					
			700	700	7,250	440				
Cost of Goods Manufactured						6,810	6,810			
					7,250	7,250	7,630	10,560		
Net Income							2,930			2,930
							10,560	10,560	6,300	6,300

Fig. 29-1. Work sheet for the Domestic Manufacturing Company.

Step 3

Add the amounts in the trial balance columns and the amounts in the adjustments columns and sort them to the proper statement column. An adjusted trial balance may or may not be used. For each account, two decisions must be made. First, does the account have a debit or credit balance? Second, which statement should each account be shown on? All accounts must be placed in the debit or credit column of either the manufacturing statement, the income statement, or the balance sheet. The following lists show the division of the accounts among the three columns.

Manufacturing Statement	Income Statement	Balance Sheet
Raw Materials	Revenues	Assets
Goods-in-Process	Finished Goods	Liabilities
Direct Labor	Cost of Goods Manufactured	Owner's Equity
Factory Overhead	Selling & Administrative Expense	

In figure 29-1, note the distribution of expenses on the manufacturing statement and income statement. For example, consider the accounts for heat expense. Heat expense has been allocated to two accounts – one for the factory and one for the office. The expense of heating the factory is a part of the cost of manufacturing. Therefore, it is shown on the manufacturing statement. However, the expense of heating the office is a general and administrative expense which is placed on the income statement. Since the depreciation expense is on factory equipment used for manufacturing, this account is sorted into the manufacturing statement columns. In summary, when sorting expenses, those related to the manufacturing process are placed on the manufacturing statement, while selling expenses and general expenses appear on the income statement.

Step 4

After sorting all accounts into one of the last six columns, enter the ending inventory figures on the work sheet. Since the ending raw materials and goods-in-process inventories appear on the manufacturing statement, these amounts are entered in the manufacturing credit columns. These ending inventory amounts are subtracted from all of the other figures on the manufacturing statement. Thus, they appear in the work sheet credit column which is the opposite column from all of the other amounts that appear on the manufacturing statement.

The ending inventory amounts are current assets on the balance sheet. Thus, these figures are placed in the balance sheet debit column. Note the treatment of the $120 and $320 inventory amounts in figure 29-1.

The ending finished goods inventory appears on the income statement and is entered in the income statement credit column of the work sheet. The ending finished goods inventory also appears on the balance sheet as a current asset. Therefore, it is shown in the balance sheet debit column of the work sheet. Note the $560 finished goods inventory in figure 29-1.

Step 5

Add up the manufacturing columns of the work sheet. Initially, the columns will not balance. The debit column will be greater than the credit column. The difference between these two columns is the cost of goods manufactured. Add this number to the credit column. Now the manufacturing statement columns should be equal.

Since a credit is added, a debit of the same amount must be placed somewhere to maintain equality. The Cost of Goods Manufactured amount is placed on the debit side of the income statement columns for this purpose. Remember, the Cost of Goods Manufactured amount appears on both the manufacturing statement and the income statement. Thus, since it appears on both statements, it must also appear in both work sheet columns. Note the handling of the Cost of Goods Manufactured amount ($6,810) in figure 29-1.

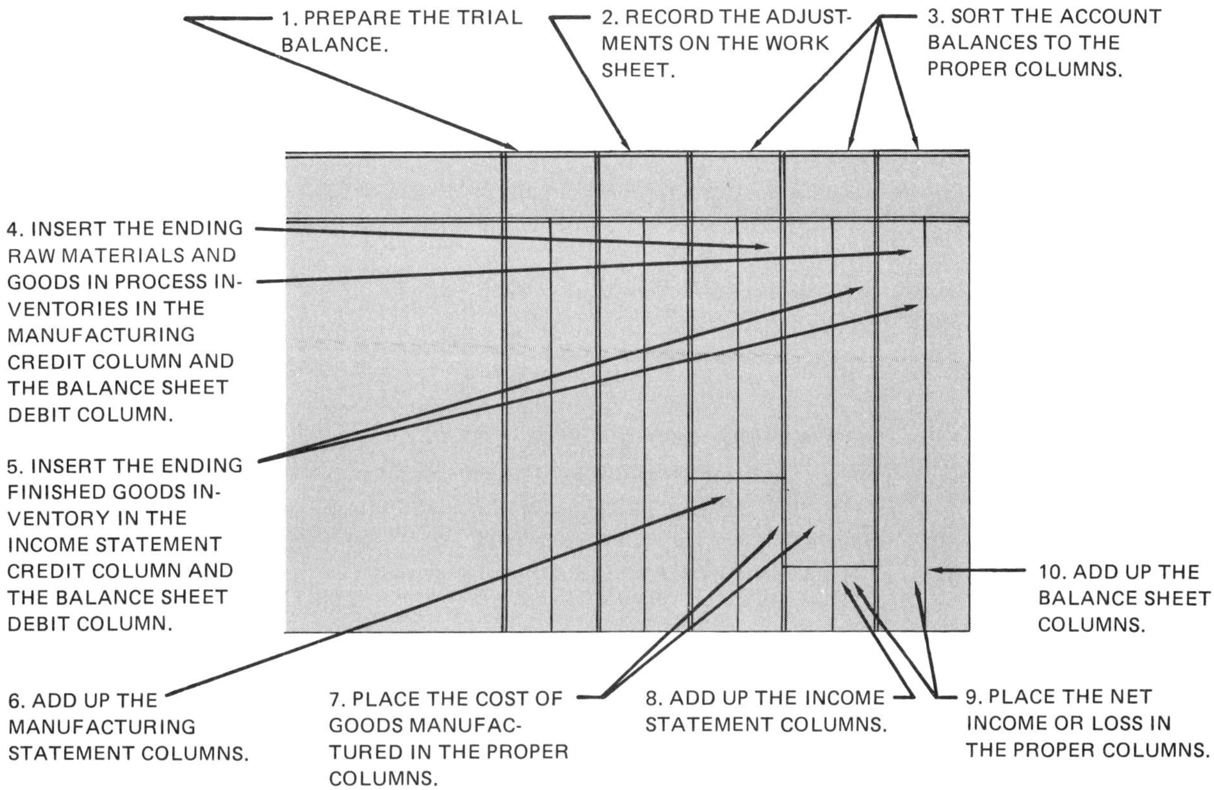

Fig. 29-2. Summary of work sheet preparation for a manufacturing firm.

Another way to remember that the Cost of Goods Manufactured amount is placed in the income statement debit column is to relate it to the work sheet of a merchandising firm. Remember, a merchandising firm will have Purchases in the income statement debit column. Since Cost of Goods Manufactured replaces Purchases on the income statement, it also replaces Purchases on the work sheet.

Step 6

Finish the work sheet in the usual way. Add the income statement columns. The difference between the two columns is the net income or loss. This figure is placed in the appropriate income statement and balance sheet columns. Note the placement of the $2,930 net income in figure 29-1. At this point, all of the sets of columns on the work sheet are in balance, and the work sheet is complete.

Figure 29-2 summarizes the entire process of preparing a work sheet for a manufacturing firm.

PREPARATION OF FINANCIAL STATEMENTS

When the work sheet is completed, the cost of goods manufactured and the net income amounts are known. All of the information needed to prepare each of the statements is on the work sheet. The amounts in the columns for each statement should be arranged in proper order. Refer to the manufacturing statement, income statement, and balance sheet in chapter 28 to see how these statements were prepared from the work sheet shown in this chapter.

ADJUSTING ENTRIES

When the work sheet and financial statements are completed, the adjustments shown in the adjustments columns of the work sheet are entered on the books. Journal entries for each of these adjustments should be made in the journal and posted to the ledger. The one adjustment necessary for Domestic Manufacturing Company is:

Depreciation Expense	700	
Accumulated Depreciation		700

SUMMARY

The work sheet helps the accountant to prepare the financial statements for a manufacturing firm. The work sheet is used to summarize and sort information. It shows the effects of adjustments before the entries are made and allows the accountant to compute the cost of goods manufactured and net income before the statements are prepared. The preparation of this work sheet is the same as that for a merchandising firm except for the addition of a set of columns for the manufacturing statement information. The ending inventories appear on two statements and thus are shown in two sets of columns on the work sheet.

When the work sheet is completed, the financial statements are prepared. Finally, the adjusting entries are made in the journal and posted to the ledger.

REVIEW

1. Which inventories, the beginning or the ending, appear on the trial balance of a manufacturing firm?
2. Which inventories, the beginning or the ending, appear on the adjusted trial balance of a manufacturing firm?
3. In which work sheet column, or columns, does the beginning raw material inventory appear?
4. In which work sheet column, or columns, does the ending raw materials inventory appear?
5. In which work sheet column, or columns, does the beginning goods-in-process inventory appear?
6. In which work sheet column, or columns, does the ending goods-in-process inventory appear?
7. In which work sheet column, or columns, does the beginning finished goods inventory appear?
8. In which work sheet column, or columns, does the ending finished goods inventory appear?
9. Which is prepared first, the balance sheet, the work sheet, or the adjusting entries?
10. Which is prepared first, the balance sheet, the work sheet, or the manufacturing statement?
11. In which work sheet column, or columns, does cost of goods manufactured appear?

EXERCISES

1. Each of the following accounts appears on the work sheet adjusted trial balance of a manufacturing firm. To which of the last six columns will each account be sorted? An example is provided.

Account	Column
Example: aa. Cash	*Balance Sheet Debit*
a. Accounts Payable	
b. Accounts Receivable	
c. Allowance for Bad Debts	
d. Factory Machinery	
e. Raw Materials Inventory (beginning)	
f. Goods-in-Process (beginning)	
g. Finished Goods (beginning)	
h. Accumulated Depreciation – Factory Machinery	
i. Direct Labor	
j. Indirect Labor	
k. Depreciation Expense – Factory Machinery	
l. Prepaid Rent-Factory Building	
m. Bad Debt Expense	
n. Heat, Light, and Power – Factory	
o. Advertising Expense	
p. Wages Payable	
q. Property Tax Expense – Factory	
r. Raw Materials Purchases	
s. Freight-in – Raw Materials	
t. Retained Earnings	
u. Preferred Stock	
v. Salary Expense – Office	
w. Sales	
x. Common Stock	
y. Insurance Expense – Office	

2. A firm has the following inventories:

	Beginning	Ending
Raw Materials	1,000	1,500
Goods-in-Process	2,000	1,700
Finished Goods	3,000	1,900

Show how all of these inventory figures would appear on a work sheet.

3. The following items appear in the manufacturing statement columns of Field Corporation's year-end work sheet. Use the information to prepare a formal manufacturing statement for the firm.

	Manufacturing Statement	
	Debit	Credit
Raw Materials Inventory	330	175
Goods-in-Process Inventory	817	780
Raw Materials Purchases	3,220	
Freight-in – Raw Materials	120	
Direct Labor	2,779	
Indirect Labor	1,230	
Repairs Expense	295	
Rent	2,400	
Heat and Power	1,750	
	12,941	955
		11,986
	$12,941	$12,941

PROBLEMS

1. The last six columns of a manufacturing firm's work sheet are assigned the following code letters:

A. Manufacturing debit
B. Manufacturing credit
C. Income Statement debit
D. Income Statement credit
E. Balance Sheet debit
F. Balance Sheet credit

Using these code letters, state in which column, or columns, each of the following items would appear. An example is provided.

Account	Column
Example: 0. Cash	*E*
1. Accounts Receivable	
2. Allowance for Bad Debts	
3. Raw Materials Inventory (beginning)	
4. Raw Materials Inventory (ending)	
5. Goods-in-Process Inventory (beginning)	
6. Goods-in-Process Inventory (ending)	
7. Direct Labor	
8. Sales	
9. Advertising Expense	
10. Indirect Labor	
11. Depreciation Expense – Factory Machines	
12. Depreciation Expense – Office Equipment	
13. Patents	

Account	Column
14. Accounts Payable	
15. Repair Expense – Factory Machines	
16. Factory Machines	
17. Office Equipment	
18. Finished Goods Inventory (beginning)	
19. Finished Goods Inventory (ending)	
20. Common Stock	
21. Prepaid Rent	
22. Interest Expense	
23. Rent Expense – Factory	
24. Rent Expense – Office	
25. Retained Earnings	

2. Refer to problem 3 in chapter 28. Use the adjusted trial balance in that problem to prepare the last six columns of a work sheet.

3. The following trial balance amounts and other information are supplied for Barnelli Manufacturing Company. The amounts are for the year ended December 31, 1981.

A.

Cash	$ 300	
Accounts Receivable	900	
Allowance for Bad Debts		$ 100
Raw Materials Inventory	1,100	
Goods-in-Process Inventory	2,200	
Finished Goods Inventory	3,300	
Factory Machines	10,000	
Accumulated Depreciation		1,250
Accounts Payable		1,000
R.J. Barnelli, Capital		22,950
Sales		20,000
Raw Materials Purchases	16,000	
Freight-in – Raw Materials	100	
Direct Labor	8,000	
Indirect Labor	1,170	
Heat, Light and Power – Factory	640	
Utility Expense – Office	990	
Rent Expense – Factory	600	
	$45,300	$45,300

B. Depreciation expense for the period was $250.

C. The allowance for bad debts should be increased by $50.

D. Ending inventories were:

Raw Materials	$4,000
Goods-in-Process	1,850
Finished Goods	3,900

a. Prepare the complete work sheet for the firm.
b. Record the adjusting entries in general journal form.
c. Prepare a manufacturing statement.
d. Prepare an income statement.
e. Prepare a balance sheet.

4. The following trial balance amounts and other information are given for Shalit Manufacturing Company. The statements are prepared once a year.

A.

Account	Debit	Credit
Cash	$ 8,320	
Accounts Receivable	1,140	
Allowance for Bad Debts		$ 60
Raw Materials Inventory	1,100	
Goods-in-Process Inventory	3,200	
Finished Goods Inventory	800	
Office Supplies	100	
Prepaid Insurance	240	
Factory Machinery	8,000	
Accumulated Depreciation – Factory Machinery		1,600
Office Equipment	2,000	
Accumulated Depreciation – Office Equipment		400
Accounts Payable		400
Common Stock		10,000
Retained Earnings		1,710
Sales		50,000
Raw Materials Purchases	20,000	
Freight-in – Raw Materials	270	
Direct Labor	10,400	
Indirect Labor	5,200	
Advertising Expense	1,000	
Rent Expense – Factory	2,400	
	$64,170	$64,170

B. Depreciation for the period was $800 on the factory machinery.
C. Depreciation was $400 on the office equipment for the period.
D. The allowance for bad debts should be increased by $25.
E. Prepaid insurance at year end totals $60.
Ending inventories at December 31, 1981, were:

Office Supplies	$ 20
Raw Materials	500
Goods-in-Process	1,300
Finished Goods	900

a. Prepare the complete work sheet for the firm.
b. Record the adjusting entries in general journal form.
c. Prepare a manufacturing statement.
d. Prepare an income statement.
e. Prepare a balance sheet.

30
Closing Entries for a Manufacturing Firm

OBJECTIVES After studying this chapter, the student will be able to:

- Prepare the closing entries for a manufacturing firm.
- Trace the end-of-period accounting process for a manufacturing firm.
- Describe how manufacturing inventories are valued.

After the financial statements are prepared and the adjusting entries are made in the journal, all temporary accounts are closed. Since the purpose of temporary accounts is to store data for one accounting period, they are closed after the data is used in completing period-end reports. Thus, the accounts are clear to begin storing amounts for the new period.

CLOSING ENTRIES

Manufacturing firms require two closing entries in addition to those used for merchandising firms. These entries are needed to close the accounts in the manufacturing statement columns of the work sheet. The accounts in these columns are closed out to a Manufacturing Summary account. The Manufacturing Summary account functions in the same way as the Income Summary account. This account does not appear on any financial statement. It is used only to close out the costs of manufacturing. The Manufacturing Summary account is closed out, in turn, to Income Summary.

With the first closing entry, close all accounts in the manufacturing statement debit column of the work sheet. Credit those accounts and debit the Manufacturing Summary account. Next, debit all accounts shown in the manufacturing statement credit column of the work sheet, and credit Manufacturing Summary. For the Domestic Manufacturing example used in the preceding chapters, the closing entries would be made as follows. (Refer to the work sheet in figure 29-1 while studying these entries.)

CLOSING ENTRIES

Dec. 31	Manufacturing Summary	7,250	
	Raw Materials Inventory		400
	Goods-in-Process Inventory		300
	Raw Materials Purchases		3,000
	Freight-in		150
	Direct Labor		1,870
	Indirect Labor		330
	Heat – Factory		500
	Depreciation Expense		700
Dec. 31	Raw Materials Inventory	120	
	Goods-in-Process Inventory	320	
	Manufacturing Summary		440

Note that in the first entry the debit to Manufacturing Summary is the same as the total of the manufacturing statement debit column on the work sheet. When each of the accounts are credited in this same entry, they are given a zero balance. In the second entry, the credit to Manufacturing Summary is the same as the total of the manufacturing statement credit column on the work sheet (before Cost of Goods Manufactured is added). Thus, an easy way to remember what the amount of each entry will be is to recall that the debit column total is debited to the summary account, and the credit column total is credited to the summary account. To see the effect of these two entries on the Manufacturing Summary, Raw Materials Inventory and Goods-in-Process Inventory accounts, study the way in which these entries are posted to the accounts in figure 30-1.

The balance in the Manufacturing Summary account is equal to the Cost of Goods Manufactured figure shown on the work sheet. The balances in the Raw Materials Inventory and Goods-in-Process Inventory accounts are the ending inventory figures. Remember, the ending inventory of one period becomes the beginning inventory of the next period.

One purpose of these closing entries is to close out to zero all of the manufacturing statement accounts, including the beginning inventory amounts for raw materials and goods-in-process. The second purpose is to enter the ending inventory of raw materials and goods-in-process in the accounts for the beginning of the next period. As a result of these entries, the balance in the Manufacturing Summary account will be equal to Cost of Goods Manufactured. The Manufacturing Summary account is a temporary account and is closed to Income Summary in the next closing entry.

The next step is to close all of the accounts that appear in the income statement columns of the work sheet. Close all accounts in the debit column by crediting these accounts and debiting Income Summary. This includes the amount shown for Cost of Goods Manufactured in the income statement debit column which is the balance of the Manufacturing Summary account. Next, close the accounts in the

ACCOUNT *Manufacturing Summary* Acct. No. *350*

Date		Explanation	Post. Ref.	Debit	Credit	Balance
Dec.	*31*		*52*	*7,250.00*		*7,250.00*
	31		*52*		*440.00*	*6,810.00*

ACCOUNT *Raw Materials Inventory* Acct. No. *115*

Date		Explanation	Post. Ref.	Debit	Credit	Balance
Jan.	*1*			*400.00*		*400.00*
Dec.	*31*		*52*		*400.00*	*-0-*
	31		*52*	*120.00*		*120.00*

ACCOUNT *Goods-in-Process Inventory* Acct. No. *116*

Date		Explanation	Post. Ref.	Debit	Credit	Balance
Jan.	*1*			*300.00*		*300.00*
Dec.	*31*		*52*		*300.00*	*-0-*
	31		*52*	*320.00*		*320.00*

Fig. 30-1. Account balances after first two closing entries.

income statement credit column by debiting those accounts and crediting Income Summary. For the Domestic Manufacturing example, these entries are:

Dec. 31	Income Summary	7,730	
	Finished Goods Inventory		500
	Heat – Office		220
	Bad Debt Expense		100
	Manufacturing Summary		6,810
	Finished Goods Inventory	560	
	Sales	10,000	
	Income Summary		10,560

After the above entries are posted to the accounts, the inventory and summary accounts appear as shown in figure 30-2, page 348.

The Manufacturing Summary account has served its purpose and has been closed. The beginning Finished Goods Inventory for the period has been closed and the ending inventory has been entered as the new balance to start off the next period. The balance in Income Summary is equal to the net income for the period.

ACCOUNT *Finished Goods Inventory* Acct. No. *117*

Date		Explanation	Post. Ref.	Debit	Credit	Balance
Jan.	*1*			*500 00*		*500 00*
Dec.	*31*		*52*		*500 00*	*-0-*
	31		*52*	*560 00*		*560 00*

ACCOUNT *Manufacturing Summary* Acct. No. *350*

Date		Explanation	Post. Ref.	Debit	Credit	Balance
Dec.	*31*		*52*	*7250 00*		*7250 00*
	31		*52*		*440 00*	*6810 00*
	31		*52*		*6810 00*	*-0-*

ACCOUNT *Income Summary* Acct. No. *351*

Date		Explanation	Post. Ref.	Debit	Credit	Balance
Dec.	*31*		*52*	*7630 00*		*7630 00*
	31		*52*		*10560 00*	*2930 00*

Fig. 30-2. Account balances after first four closing entries.

The final entry is to close the Income Summary account to owners' equity. In this example, the entry would be:

Dec. 31	Income Summary	2,930	
	Retained Earnings		2,930

At this point all temporary accounts are closed and a post-closing trial balance is prepared.

END-OF-PERIOD ACCOUNTING PROCESS FOR A MANUFACTURING FIRM

The following steps outline the end-of-the-period accounting process for a manufacturing firm. This process is also illustrated by figure 30-3.

1. **Prepare the work sheet.** Show adjustments and sort accounts into manufacturing statement, income statement, or balance sheet columns. Enter ending inventories. Determine cost of goods manufactured and net income.

2. **Prepare financial statements.** Use the work sheet to complete the manufacturing statement, income statement and balance sheet.

3. **Enter the adjusting entries in the journal and post to the ledger accounts.** Use the information in the adjustments columns of the work sheet to make the adjusting entries.

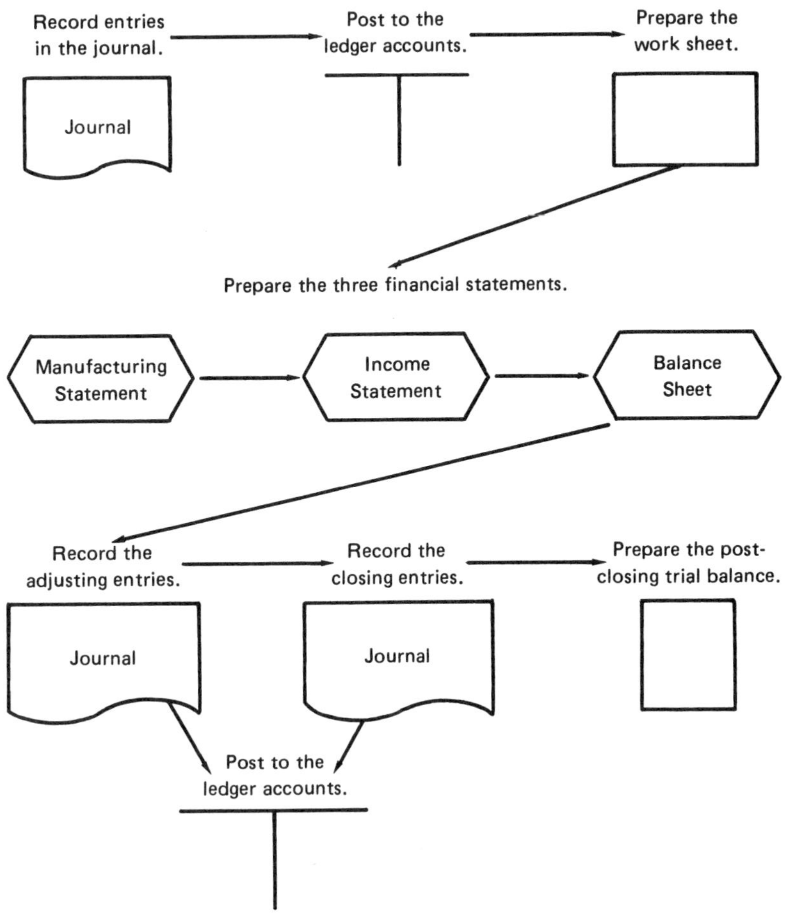

Fig. 30 3. Accounting process for a manufacturing firm.

4. **Enter the closing entries in the journal and post to the ledger.** Close all temporary accounts and transfer net income or loss to owners' equity. The work sheet column totals can be used as check figures when making the entries.

5. **Prepare a post-closing trial balance.** Test the balance of the ledger before starting the new accounting period.

HOW TO VALUE INVENTORY

Determining the value of a manufacturing firm's inventories is not always an easy task. It is not difficult to value the raw materials inventory, the quantities of raw materials on hand can be counted and valued at their cost. However, the values of the goods-in-process and finished goods inventories are not as easily determined. The firm can count the number of items of goods-in-process and finished goods that are on hand – but what is the cost of these items? Remember, each item of goods-in-process and finished goods includes raw material costs, direct labor costs, and overhead costs.

Thus, the firm must determine the cost of raw materials and direct labor for each item of inventory. Both of these costs are easy to determine. For example, LB Company knows that each item it makes requires one pound of raw material at $1 per pound. Direct laborers work one hour on each item and are paid $4 per hour. Therefore, the raw material cost is $1 and the direct labor cost is $4 for each item.

The real problem in the valuing of the inventories is the calculation of the overhead costs per unit. By definition, overhead costs are not direct costs. There is no way to directly relate an overhead cost to a single item of inventory. Thus, the firm must estimate how much overhead cost is included in each item. Firms usually base their estimates on direct labor. A standard equation is used to determine the ratio of overhead costs to direct labor.

For example, if the LB Company has $100,000 of overhead costs for the year and $200,000 of direct labor costs, the following calculation is made:

$$\frac{\text{Overhead Costs}}{\text{Direct Labor}} = \frac{\$100,000}{\$200,000} = 50\%$$

Since overhead costs represent 50% of direct labor for the whole year, it is assumed that this percent can be applied to each item of year-end inventory. In the LB Company example, direct labor is $4 per unit. Thus, overhead costs are estimated at $2 per unit (50% of $4). The total cost of each item of inventory is $7, calculated as follows:

Raw Materials	$1
Direct Labor	4
Overhead (50% of DL)	2
Total Cost per Item	$7

If the firm counts 100 items in its inventory, then the total value is $700. Since overhead is normally closely related to direct labor, this method of estimating the amount of overhead in inventory is usually quite accurate. For example, the more hours employees work, the greater are the overhead costs. Logically, more heat, light, and power will be needed if the employees work longer. Thus, higher overhead costs are caused, in part, by employees working longer hours.

Example

During the current year, Beta Corporation incurred direct labor costs of $250,000. Overhead costs were $100,000. The ending inventories of goods-in-process and finished goods have been counted. They include the following values for raw materials and direct labor:

	Goods-in-Process	Finished Goods
Raw Materials	$3,000	$2,000
Direct Labor	5,000	7,000
Overhead	?	?
Total	?	?

In order to determine the total value of each inventory, it is necessary to add overhead costs to the raw materials and direct labor costs. The *overhead percentage* for the year (sometimes called the *overhead application rate),* is 40%. This is calculated as follows:

$$\frac{\text{Total Overhead}}{\text{Total Direct Labor}} = \frac{\$100{,}000}{\$250{,}000} = 40\%$$

If 40% of direct labor is added to each inventory, the total value of goods-in-process is $10,000. The total value of the finished goods is $11,800. These are calculated as follows:

	Goods-in-Process	Finished Goods
Raw Materials	$ 3,000	$ 2,000
Direct Labor	5,000	7,000
Overhead (40% of DL)	2,000	2,800
Total	10,000	11,800

SUMMARY

After completing the financial statements and adjusting entries, the temporary accounts are closed. This clears the accounts for the start of the new period. Two new entries are needed to close the accounts of a manufacturing firm. In these two entries, the manufacturing statement accounts are closed out to a Manufacturing Summary account.

The work sheet column totals can be used to help make the closing entries. The work sheet manufacturing debit column total is debited to Manufacturing Summary. The work sheet manufacturing credit column total is credited to Manufacturing Summary. After the closing entries have been made in the journal and posted to the ledger, a post-closing trial balance is prepared to test the balance of the ledger.

When valuing goods-in-process and finished goods inventories, all three elements of cost must be considered. The overhead included in each inventory is estimated. This estimate is usually based on direct labor. Thus, the total value of goods-in-process and finished goods includes raw material, direct labor, and overhead costs.

REVIEW

1. Why are closing entries made?
2. On which financial statement does the account Manufacturing Summary appear?
3. To what account is Manufacturing Summary closed?
4. To what account is the raw material beginning inventory closed?
5. To what account is the finished goods beginning inventory closed?
6. Which are closed first, the manufacturing statement accounts or the income statement accounts? Why?
7. How is the amount of overhead to be included in inventory valuation determined? Why is it calculated in this manner?
8. Which entries are made first, the closing entries or the adjusting entries?
9. Which is prepared first, the closing entries or the post-closing trial balance?
10. Why is a post-closing trial balance prepared?

EXERCISES

1. Using the data from exercise 3 in chapter 29, prepare the first two closing entries for the firm.

2. The manufacturing statement and income statement columns of Tek Corporation's year-end work sheet are shown below. Use the data to make all closing entries.

	Manufacturing Statement		Income Statement	
	Debit	Credit	Debit	Credit
Raw Materials Inventory	*650*	*695*		
Goods-in-Process Inventory	*1,120*	*340*		
Finished Goods Inventory			*870*	*1,275*
Sales				*10,000*
Raw Materials Purchases	*4,000*			
Freight-in	*180*			
Direct Labor	*3,000*			
Indirect Labor	*690*			
Repair Expense	*135*			
Rent Expense – Factory	*1,200*			
Rent Expense – Office			*600*	
Heat and Power	*510*			
Advertising Expense			*100*	
Bad Debt Expense			*200*	
	11,485	*1,035*		
		10,450	*10,450*	
	11,485	*11,485*	*12,220*	*11,275*
				945
			12,220	*12,220*

3. Use the data from exercise 2 to prepare a manufacturing statement for the firm. Assume that it is for the year ended December 31, 1981.

4. Use the data in exercises 2 and 3 to prepare an income statement for Tek Corporation.

5. Assume that the Lox Company, a single proprietorship owned by S. Lox, had a $7,200 net income for the year.
   a. Give the final closing entry for the year.
   b. What would the entry have been if the firm had lost $3,000 during the year?

6. Refer to the data in exercise 5. What would have been the two entries if the firm had been a corporation?

7. The Mulderry Manufacturing Company had direct labor costs of $100,000 during the past year. The firm incurred overhead costs of $160,000.
   a. What is the overhead application rate?
   b. What is the total value of the goods-in-process inventory if it contains $3,000 of raw materials and $5,000 of direct labor?
   c. What is the total value of the finished goods inventory if it contains $4,000 of raw materials and $10,000 of direct labor?

8. A company has a predetermined overhead rate of 180% of direct labor. If the ending finished goods inventory has $700 of materials in it and $1,200 of direct labor, what is the total cost of the inventory?

9. The company in exercise 8 has a job with a $2,000 balance in its Goods-in-Process ledger at the end of the year. This includes $600 of direct labor. What is the raw materials cost for the job?

PROBLEMS

1. Using the data from problem 3 in chapter 29, make all of the compound closing entries for the firm.

2. The Small Company has the following balances on its adjusted trial balance as of December 31. Statements are prepared once a year.

Cash	$ 30	
Raw Materials Inventory	50	
Goods-in-Process Inventory	60	
Finished Goods Inventory	70	
Accounts Payable		$ 10
J. Small, Capital		183
Sales		100
Raw Materials Purchases	42	
Direct Labor	18	
Indirect Labor	3	
Rent Expense – Factory	10	
Rent Expense – Office	5	
Advertising Expense	5	
	$293	$293

Ending inventories are: Raw Materials, $42; Goods-in-Process, $52; Finished Goods, $62.

a. Complete the last six columns of the firm's work sheet.
b. Prepare a manufacturing statement.
c. Prepare an income statement.
d. Prepare a balance sheet.
e. Prepare all closing entries for the firm.

3. You are given the following year-end trial balance amounts and other information for Jonez Manufacturing Corporation.

A. Cash	$ 1,230	
Accounts Receivable	9,210	
Allowance for Bad Debts		$ 140
Raw Materials Inventory	1,020	
Goods-in-Process Inventory	2,230	
Finished Goods Inventory	8,200	
Office Supplies	130	
Prepaid Rent	600	
Production Equipment	6,500	
Accumulated Depreciation – Production Equipment		1,300
Office Furniture	2,500	

Accumulated Depreciation – Office Furniture		1,500
Accounts Payable		4,100
Common Stock		20,000
Retained Earnings	53,860	
Sales		100,000
Raw Materials Purchases	14,000	
Freight-in	190	
Direct Labor	18,760	
Indirect Labor	1,870	
Telephone Expense – Office	1,940	
Rent Expense – Office	3,300	
Rent Expense – Factory	1,500	
	$127,040	$127,040

B. Depreciation for the year was $650 on production equipment and $250 on Office Furniture.

C. The allowance for bad debts should be increased by $900.

D. Office rent is $300 per month. One month is prepaid at the end of the year. No factory rent is prepaid at year end.

E. Ending inventories at December 31, 1981, were:

Office Supplies	$ 45
Raw Materials	840
Goods-in-Process	2,000
Finished Goods	9,990

---

a. Prepare the complete work sheet for the firm.
b. Prepare the manufacturing statement.
c. Prepare an income statement.
d. Prepare a balance sheet.
e. Record the adjusting entries in the general journal.
f. Record the compound closing entries.

SECTION 7

Special Topics

31 Financial Statement Analysis

OBJECTIVES After studying this chapter, the student will be able to:

- Prepare comparative financial statements showing percentage changes.
- Use trend percentages.
- Prepare common-size statements.
- Compute several ratios and analyze a firm.
- Explain the treatment of extraordinary items.

Once the financial statements for a firm are completed, they may be analyzed to discover the strengths and weaknesses of the firm. Analysis is done by making comparisons to past years and to industry averages which show the success of the competition. This chapter examines some of the many ways of analyzing a firm.

COMPARATIVE FINANCIAL STATEMENTS

Comparative financial statements show data for several years side by side. In this way, the changes can be easily seen. These changes may be shown as percentages. The *percentage change* is calculated by dividing the amount of dollar change by the amount for the base year. The base year is the earliest year being considered. The percentage change is calculated as follows:

Year 1	Year 2	Change	Calculation	Percentage Change
1,000	1,500	500	500/1,000	= 50% Increase
1,000	500	500	500/1,000	= 50% Decrease
1,000	(1,000)	2,000	2,000/1,000	= 200% Decrease
(500)	1,000	1,500	1,500/(500)	= Cannot be shown as a percentage.
0	1,000	1,000	1,000/0	= Cannot be shown as a percentage.

Note that if the base year is zero or negative, the change cannot be shown as a percentage. Study the examples of comparative balance sheets and income statements shown in figures 31-1 and 31-2.

Suburban Company
Comparative Balance Sheets
at June 30, 1984 and June 30, 1985

	1985	1984	INCREASE (DECREASE)	Percentage
ASSETS:				
Current Assets:				
Cash	$ 50	$ 92	$ (42)	(45.7)
Marketable Securities	1,215	–	1,215	–
Accounts Receivable, net	2,618	1,563	1,055	67.5
Inventories	5,243	4,363	880	20.2
Prepaid Expenses	52	129	(77)	(59.7)
Total Current Assets	9,178	6,147	3,031	49.3
Noncurrent Assets:				
Goodwill	287	300	(13)	(4.3)
Other Assets	163	76	87	114.5
Plant and Equipment	5,396	4,805	591	12.3
Less: Accumulated Depreciation	(2,524)	(2,153)	371	17.3
Total Noncurrent Assets	3,322	3,028	294	9.7
Total Assets	$12,500	$9,175	3,325	36.2
LIABILITIES:				
Current Liabilities:				
Accounts Payable	$ 2,313	$3,205	(892)	(27.8)
Long Term Debt	3,050	300	2,750	916.7
Total Liabilities	5,363	3,505	1,858	53.0
STOCKHOLDERS' EQUITY:				
Common Stock, No Par	3,352	3,265	87	2.7
Retained Earnings	4,050	2,646	1,404	53.1
Less: Treasury Stock	(265)	(241)	24	10.0
Total Stockholders' Equity	7,137	5,670	1,467	25.9
Total Equities	$12,500	$9,175	3,325	36.2

Fig. 31-1. Comparative balance sheets.

Suburban Company
Comparative Income Statements
For Years Ended June 30, 1984 and June 30, 1985

	1985	1984	INCREASE (DECREASE)	Percentage
Net Sales	$20,479	$12,929	$7,550	58.4
Cost of Goods Sold	13,290	8,457	4,833	57.1
Gross Profit	7,189	4,472	2,717	60.8
Operating Expenses	3,264	2,125	1,139	53.6
Income from Operations	3,925	2,347	1,578	67.2
Interest Expense	274	72	202	280.6
Income Before Taxes	3,651	2,275	1,376	60.5
Income Taxes	1,841	1,106	735	66.5
Net Income	1,810	1,169	641	54.8
Earnings Per Share	$1.90	$1.25	.65	52.0

Fig. 31-2. Comparative income statements.

TREND PERCENTAGES

To determine trends in business in terms of percentages, the financial statements for several years are compared. The first step in finding trend percentages is to select a base year and set that base year equal to 100%. The figures for each year after the base year are then expressed as a percentage of the base year amount. Study the following example.

	1980	1981	1982	1983
Net Sales	$100,000	90,000	120,000	140,000
Gross Profit	30,000	20,000	30,000	40,000
Net Income	10,000	5,000	8,000	12,000

To show trend percentages, set the earliest year (1980 in this case), as the base year which represents 100%. Then state the other years as a percentage of the amount for 1980 as shown below:

	1980	1981	1982	1983
Net Sales	100%	90%	120%	140%
Gross Profit	100%	67%	100%	134%
Net Income	100%	50%	80%	120%

To find the net sales percentages for 1981, 1982, and 1983 the sales figures for each of the years are divided by $100,000, the amount of sales in 1980 (the base year). For the gross profit percentages, the amounts for each year after 1980 are divided by $30,000 (the gross profit figure for the base year). The divisor for the net income for years 1981, 1982, and 1983 is the base year net income $10,000.

The trend percentages for this firm show that after a drop in sales in 1981, sales steadily increased in the next two years. Gross profit also increased in the last two years. However, it did not increase as fast as sales. Net income is not keeping up the pace with either sales or gross profit. This means that the firm may be spending too much on expenses.

COMMON-SIZE STATEMENTS

Common-size statements show each line on the statement as a percentage of a key figure, or in a *common size.* On the common-size balance sheet, each line is stated as a percentage of the total assets. The key figure used as the basis of comparison on the income statement is the firm's net sales.

A common-size balance sheet for a firm is shown in figure 31-3. A common-size income statement appears in figure 31-4. Study these illustrations and the following explanation.

All figures on the balance sheet are divided by total assets to obtain the percentage. On the income statement, net sales is the common-size figure. It may be said for 1980 that for each $100 of net sales, the gross profit on the sale was $33.67 and net income was $19.08. This is better than the firm did in 1979. Common-size statements make it possible to compare companies of different sizes; that is, a big firm and a small firm in the same industry.

AB Company
Balance Sheets
May 31, 1979 and 1980

	1980	Percentage	1979	Percentage
ASSETS:				
Current Assets:				
Cash	$ 16,500	1.16	$ 26,300	1.95
Marketable Securities	28,000	1.97	58,700	4.35
Accounts Receivable	184,000	12.96	142,700	10.57
Inventory	198,000	13.95	205,800	15.24
Total Current Assets	426,500	30.04	433,500	32.11
Property and Equipment (net)	993,500	69.96	916,500	67.89
Total Assets	$1,420,000	100.00	$1,350,000	100.00
LIABILITIES:				
Current Liabilities:				
Accounts Payable	165,500	11.65	143,000	10.59
Long Term Debt	474,500	33.42	485,000	35.93
STOCKHOLDERS' EQUITY:				
Common Stock-100 par	560,000	39.44	560,000	41.48
Retained Earnings	220,000	15.49	162,000	12.00
Total Stockholders' Equity	780,000	54.93	722,000	53.48
Total Equities	$1,420,000	100.00	$1,350,000	100.00

Fig. 31-3. Common-size balance sheets.

AB Company
Income Statements
For Years Ended May 31, 1979 and May 31, 1980

	1980	Percentage	1979	Percentage
Revenues:				
Sales	$990,000	101.02	$915,000	101.67
Less: Sales Returns and Allowances	10,000	1.02	15,000	1.67
Net Sales	980,000	100.00	900,000	100.00
Cost of Goods Sold	650,000	66.33	620,000	68.89
Gross Profit	330,000	33.67	280,000	31.11
Operating Expenses	93,000	9.49	90,000	10.00
Income Before Taxes	237,000	24.18	190,000	21.11
Tax Expense	50,000	5.10	45,000	5.00
Net Income	$187,000	19.08	$145,000	16.11

Fig. 31-4. Common-size income statements.

MEANS OF COMPARISON

Various types of information can be obtained from comparison of other data on the financial statements. The basis for comparison can be the past performance of the firm or the performance of the competition. Various types of ratios are used for this purpose. By comparing current financial data with past years, certain trends and problems may be revealed. Comparisons may be made with the competition by using industry averages. The trade associations of most industries gather and publish the average figures for the firms in the industry. Some financial services and credit agencies such as Dun & Bradstreet also publish data which can be used for analysis.

WORKING CAPITAL ANALYSIS

Working capital is equal to current assets minus current liabilities. *Current* normally means a time period of one year or less. Current liabilities are those to be paid out of current assets. Thus, working capital is the amount remaining after current liabilities are paid. A firm must have working capital to operate. The amount of working capital possessed by a firm indicates its current or short term position. Firms frequently make comparisons of their own working capital from year to year.

The remaining examples in this chapter are based on the financial statements for R Company shown in figure 31-5. A comparison of the

R Company
Income Statements
For Years Ended December 31, 1980 and 1981

	1981	1980
Net Sales	$300,000	$250,000
Cost of Goods Sold	200,000	160,000
Gross Profit	100,000	90,000
Operating Expenses	62,000	50,000
Operating Income	38,000	40,000
Interest Expense	6,000	6,000
Income Before Taxes	32,000	34,000
Income Taxes	14,000	13,500
Net Income	$ 18,000	$ 20,500

All sales were on credit. The stock was selling for $20 per share on December 31, 1981.

R Company
Balance Sheets
December 31, 1980 and 1981

	1981	1980		1981	1980
ASSETS:			LIABILITIES:		
Cash	$ 20,000	$ 20,000	Accounts Payable	$ 30,000	$ 36,000
Marketable Securities	25,000	25,000	Mortgage Payable	30,000	30,000
Accounts Receivable	50,000	54,000	Bonds Payable	60,000	60,000
Inventory	65,000	63,000	Total Liabilities	120,000	126,000
Plant & Equipment (Net)	240,000	240,000	STOCKHOLDERS' EQUITY:		
			Common Stock-$100 par	200,000	200,000
			Retained Earnings	80,000	76,000
			Total Stock. Equity	280,000	276,000
Total Assets	$400,000	$402,000	Total Equities	$400,000	$402,000

Fig. 31-5. Financial statements of the R Company.

working capital of the firm in the years 1980 and 1981 is made as follows. The current assets of R Company at the end of 1981 total $160,000. These consist of cash, marketable securities, accounts receivable, and inventory. Accounts payable is the only current liability and has a balance of $30,000. Thus, working capital equals $160,000 minus $30,000, or $130,000. Working capital in 1980 was:

Current Assets	$162,000
Current Liabilities	- 36,000
Working Capital, 1980	$126,000

The comparison shows that more working capital was available in 1981 than in 1980.

It is unrealistic to compare the amount of working capital of one firm with that of other firms. For example, R Company's $130,000 of working capital might be too much for a small firm but not enough for a large firm. To make a fair comparison of two firms of different sizes, the current ratio of their working capital is used.

CURRENT RATIO

The *current ratio* equals current assets divided by current liabilities. The current ratio is the most commonly used ratio. The current ratios for the R Company in 1980 and 1981 are calculated as follows:

	1981		Ratio	1980		Ratio
Current Assets / Current Liabilities	$160,000 / $ 30,000	=	5.33	$162,000 / $ 36,000	=	4.5

The current ratio for 1981 is 5.33 to 1, which means that current assets are more than five times greater than current liabilities. It can also be seen that the current ratio for 1981 is better than the ratio for 1980. The ratio of 5.33 to 1 has more meaning when compared to the average current ratio for firms of its type. The published report of the trade association for this industry shows the average current ratio is 2 to 1. Thus, the current position of the R Company is much better than the industry average.

A current ratio that is too high or too low indicates financial problems for the firm. If the current ratio is too low, there are not enough current assets to pay off the current liabilities. The firm cannot survive long under these conditions. If the current ratio is too high, the firm has a large amount of current assets on hand, which is wasteful. Excess current assets should be invested. The desirable range for the current ratio varies from industry to industry. This also holds true for the other ratios to be studied here.

QUICK RATIO (ACID TEST RATIO)

The *quick ratio* equals quick assets divided by current liabilities. Quick assets are those assets that can quickly be turned into cash. Inventories and prepaid expenses are not easily converted to cash without taking a loss. Thus, quick assets are the current assets minus inventories and prepaid expenses. The quick ratio shows the short term liquidity of a firm, or how much of its assets can be turned into cash in a short time.

The quick ratio (sometimes called the acid test ratio) for R Company in years 1981 and 1980 is:

$$\frac{\text{Current Assets - Inventory - Prepaid Expenses}}{\text{Current Liabilities}}$$

$$1981 = \frac{\$160{,}000 - 65{,}000}{30{,}000} = 3.17 \qquad 1980 = \frac{\$162{,}000 - 63{,}000}{36{,}000} = 2.75$$

The comparison shows that the quick ratio improved in 1981. The industry average is 1 to 1. Thus, R Company has a very good quick ratio.

ACCOUNTS RECEIVABLE TURNOVER

Accounts receivable turnover is found by dividing net sales on credit by the average accounts receivable. Since the ratio measures the effectiveness of the collecting of accounts receivable, only credit sales are used. *Average accounts receivable* equals the beginning balance in accounts receivable plus the ending balance in accounts receivable, divided by two. In other words, an amount representing the average receivables for the year is used.

The accounts receivable turnover for the R Company is calculated as follows. Assume that the beginning accounts receivable for 1980 was $46,000.

$$\frac{\text{Net Sales on Credit}}{\text{Average Accounts Receivable}} \qquad \underline{1981}: \frac{\$300{,}000}{52{,}000} = 5.77 \text{ times} \qquad \underline{1980}: \frac{\$250{,}000}{50{,}000} = 5 \text{ times}$$

The average accounts receivable was computed as follows:

$$\frac{\$54{,}000 + 50{,}000}{2} = 52{,}000 \qquad \frac{\$46{,}000 + 54{,}000}{2} = 50{,}000$$

The calculations show that turnover has improved slightly in 1981. However, the industry average turnover is ten times per year. In other words, R Company is only turning over its accounts receivable about one-half as fast as the competition. This indicates a poor collection policy and/or a low rate of sales.

AVERAGE AGE OF ACCOUNTS RECEIVABLE

The average age of accounts receivable is often compared to the credit terms allowed by the firm. This shows whether or not most customers are paying on time and taking advantage of a cash discount if one is offered.

The *average age of accounts receivable,* or *days' sales uncollected* may be found by this equation:

$$\frac{\text{Accounts Receivable}}{\text{Net Sales on Credit}} \times 365 \text{ days}$$

The amount used for accounts receivable is the ending balance. The average age of accounts receivable for R Company is:

$$\underline{1981}: \frac{\$50{,}000}{\$300{,}000} \times 365 \text{ days} = 60.83 \text{ days} \qquad \underline{1980}: \frac{\$54{,}000}{\$250{,}000} \times 365 \text{ days} = 78.84 \text{ days}$$

The average age of R Company's receivables has dropped in 1981. This indicates that collections have improved somewhat, just as was shown by the improvement in accounts receivable turnover. However, if the credit terms given by the R Company are 1/10, n/60, the average age of accounts receivable shows that few customers take advantage of the cash discount. It also indicates that many customers do not pay their bills on time.

This ratio, plus the accounts receivable turnover should indicate to the management of the R Company that there is a problem in the credit policy. Accounts receivable should be collected more quickly. Perhaps the credit policy is too liberal and the firm should be more selective in granting credit to customers. Maybe a shorter credit period and a more aggressive collection process are needed. It is possible that the 1% cash discount is too low or that customers are not aware of the discount. Advertising a cash discount of 2% might speed up collections.

INVENTORY TURNOVER

Inventory turnover is the cost of goods sold divided by the average inventory. Average inventory is the beginning inventory plus the ending inventory, divided by two. This turnover shows the number of times a year that the average inventory is sold. The inventory turnovers for the R Company are shown below. Assume that the beginning inventory for 1980 was $57,000.

	1981		1980	
$\frac{\text{Cost of Goods Sold}}{\text{Average Inventory}}$	$= \frac{\$200{,}000}{\$64{,}000}$	$=$ 3.125 times	$\frac{\$160{,}000}{60{,}000}$	$=$ 2.67 times

The average inventory was computed as follows:

1981	1980
$\frac{63{,}000 + 65{,}000}{2} = \$64{,}000$	$\frac{57{,}000 + 63{,}000}{2} = \$60{,}000$

These figures show that the inventory was being sold faster in 1981 than in 1980. The industry average, however, is 9.8 times. This indicates that R Company is not selling merchandise fast enough and thus is holding too much inventory. This practice is unproductive because it ties up funds which could be better used. It also causes storage and insurance costs to be higher. In addition, the risk of loss due to drop in demand or such costs as spoilage and obsolescence increases.

DEBT RATIO

The *debt ratio* is total liabilities divided by the total assets. This ratio shows the percentage of assets financed through borrowing, or the creditors equity in the assets.

The debt ratios for R Company are:

	1981	1980
$\frac{\text{Total Liabilities}}{\text{Total Assets}} =$	$\frac{\$120{,}000}{\$400{,}000} = 30\%$	$\frac{\$126{,}000}{\$402{,}000} = 31.3\%$

These ratios show that the firm is in debt for about 30% of its assets. The industry average is 35%. Thus, R Company is less in debt than others in the industry. A low debt ratio provides greater protection for creditors. A high debt ratio means more risk to those who extend credit to the firm.

EQUITY RATIO

The *equity ratio* is total stockholders' equity divided by the total assets. This ratio shows the proportion of funding financed by stockholders.

The equity ratios for the R Company are:

		1981		1980
Total Stockholders' Equity / Total Assets =	\$280,000 / \$400,000 =	70%	\$276,000 / \$402,000 =	68.7%

The equity ratios of R Company are better than the industry average of 65%. Note that the equity ratio plus the debt ratio for each year adds up to 100%. This is always true because all assets are either financed by creditors or owners. As in the basic accounting equation: *Assets equal liabilities plus owners' equity.* All assets are either paid for, or bought on credit. A high equity ratio protects the firm's creditors.

NUMBER OF TIMES INTEREST EARNED

The *number of times interest earned* is computed by dividing the operating income by the annual interest expense. This measurement shows the extent to which earnings can fall before interest cannot be paid. Failure to pay interest can lead to legal action by creditors and possibly end in bankruptcy. *Operating income* is the income before taxes and interest are deducted. It may be found by adding net income, income taxes, and interest expense. The before-tax figure is used since interest expense may be deducted in computing income tax expense. Thus, a firm's ability to pay its interest is not affected by taxes.

The number of times interest earned for the R Company is as follows:

	1981		1980	
Operating Income / Annual Interest Expense =	\$38,000 / \$6,000 =	6.34 times	\$40,000 / \$6,000 =	6.67 times

The ability of the R Company to meet its interest obligations has decreased slightly over the two-year period. The industry average is eight times. Perhaps R Company should reduce its debts or increase its net income to cover these obligations.

RETURN ON COMMON STOCKHOLDERS' EQUITY

The *return on common stockholders' equity* is the rate of earnings made on the investment of the common stockholders. It is found as follows:

$$\frac{\text{Net Income} - \text{Preferred Dividends}}{\text{Average Common Stockholders' Equity}}$$

The return on common stockholders' equity for the R Company is calculated as follows. In this example, there is no preferred stock and the beginning stockholders' equity for 1980 was \$264,000.

1981	1980
$\frac{\$18,000}{\$278,000} = 6.5\%$	$\frac{\$20,500}{\$270,000} = 7.6\%$

The average common stockholders' equity was computed in the following way:

$$\frac{\$276,000 + \$280,000}{2} = \$278,000 \qquad \frac{\$264,000 + \$276,000}{2} = \$270,000$$

The rate of return decreased because the firm earned less on a higher investment in 1981 than it did in 1980. If the industry average is 12.8%, then R Company's return is too low. Stockholders may compare and find that they could have earned a higher return by investing somewhere else.

RETURN ON TOTAL ASSETS

This measurement shows the return or productivity of the firm's assets. Interest expense is added back to eliminate consideration of the means of financing the assets.

The return on total assets is computed in this way:

$$\frac{\text{Net Income + Interest Expense}}{\text{Average Investment in Assets}}$$

The return on total assets for the R Company is calculated as follows. Assume that total assets at the beginning of 1980 were $404,000.

1981	1980
$\frac{\$18,000 + \$6,000}{(\$402,000 + \$400,000)/2} = 5.99\%$	$\frac{\$20,500 + \$6,000}{(\$404,000 + \$402,000)/2} = 6.58\%$

The industry average is 8.5%. This analysis shows that the return on total assets is declining and is below the industry average. The cause of this problem is that net income is too low or investment in assets is too high, or both. The inventory turnover and accounts receivable turnover were both too low, two factors which contribute to the problem. The firm may also possess other unproductive assets which should be sold.

When the return on common stockholders' equity is higher than the return on total assets, it is said that the firm is using leverage. *Leverage* is the process of using other people's money to earn profits for the shareholders. Since the return on common stockholders' equity (6.5% in 1981) was higher than return on assets (5.99%), it means that the firm was able to use borrowed money to increase the return to shareholders.

BOOK VALUE PER SHARE OF COMMON STOCK

Book value per share of common stock is calculated by dividing common stockholders' equity by the number of shares of common stock outstanding. Book value was discussed in detail in chapter 26.

The book value of common stock of R Company is:

		1981			1980		
$\frac{\text{Com. Stockholders' Equity}}{\text{Shares of Com. Outstanding}}$	=	$\frac{\$280,000}{2,000}$	=	$140 per share	$\frac{\$276,000}{2,000}$	=	$138 per share

This calculation shows the value of net assets behind each share of stock and can be compared to the market price. Market price was $20 per share on December 31, 1981. It would appear to be a bargain to pay $20 for $140 worth of assets.

EARNINGS PER SHARE ON COMMON STOCK

Earnings per share on common stock shows the amount of net income allocated to each share of stock. The earnings per share figure is of particular interest to investors and is listed in the financial journals. The earnings per share must be shown on the income statement. Earnings per share may also be compared to dividends per share to find the amount of earnings retained by the firm.

Earnings per share on common stock is calculated as follows:

$$\frac{\text{Net Income} - \text{Preferred Dividends}}{\text{Shares of Common Stock Outstanding}}$$

Earnings per share for the R Company are:

1981	1980
$\frac{\$18,000}{2,000} = \$9.00$ per share	$\frac{\$20,500}{2,000} = \$10.25$ per share

From these figures, it can be seen that the earnings are declining – a point of concern for R Company's management.

PRICE-EARNINGS RATIO

The *price-earnings ratio* is the market price per share divided by earnings per share. The price-earnings ratio is quoted in financial journals (such as the *Wall Street Journal*) for the benefit of investors. The price-earnings ratio is often called the *P/E ratio.* By comparing the P/E ratio of one stock with others in the same industry, the investor can judge the reasonableness of the price of the stock.

The price-earnings ratio of the R Company stock for 1981 is:

$$\frac{\text{Market Price per Share}}{\text{Earnings per Share}} = \frac{\$20}{\$9} = 2.2 \text{ times}$$

USING FINANCIAL STATEMENT ANALYSIS

The ratios and other measurements shown in this unit may be used for decision-making purposes and financial planning. They are of value to many groups such as bankers, creditors, owners, investors, management, employees, and labor unions. Each of these groups has special interests. Thus, there are many measurements to suit these various needs.

To be valuable, ratios must be used for comparison. This comparison may be made to prior years or to industry averages. Averages vary from industry to industry, so comparisons must be made only within an industry. Such comparisons reveal the strengths and weaknesses of a firm.

The analysis of R Company shows that the current, or working capital position of the firm is strong. The debt and equity ratios are satisfactory. The weaknesses revealed are low sales, low net income, poor credit policy, excess inventory, and unproductive assets.

EXTRAORDINARY ITEMS Financial analysis is based upon the results of normal operations. Thus, anything that is extraordinary (not normal), must be shown separately on the income statement so that it will not be used when ratios are computed. *Extraordinary items* are unusual gains or losses which are material in amount and result from events significantly different from ordinary business transactions. Gains or losses that meet this definition are rare. Some examples of extraordinary items are gains or losses from a casualty such as a fire or a tornado. Extraordinary items should be shown in a separate section on the income statement, net of taxes. Earnings per share should be calculated for income before extraordinary items, and for the final net income figure. This allows investors to use either figure to determine whether the firm has been successful.

SUMMARY Many methods are used to analyze financial statements. These methods allow the firm to make comparisons with prior years as well

RATIO OR MEASUREMENT	COMPUTATION
Working Capital	Current Assets – Current Liabilities
Current Ratio	$\frac{\text{Current Assets}}{\text{Current Liabilities}}$
Quick Ratio (Acid Test Ratio)	$\frac{\text{Current Assets} - \text{Inventory} - \text{Prepaid Expenses}}{\text{Current Liabilities}}$
Accounts Receivable Turnover	$\frac{\text{Net Sales on Credit}}{\text{Average Accounts Receivable}}$
Average Age of Accounts Receivable	$\frac{\text{Accounts Receivable}}{\text{Net Sales on Credit}} \times 365 \text{ days}$
Inventory Turnover	$\frac{\text{Cost of Goods Sold}}{\text{Average Inventory}}$
Debt Ratio	$\frac{\text{Total Liabilities}}{\text{Total Assets}}$
Equity Ratio	$\frac{\text{Total Stockholders' Equity}}{\text{Total Assets}}$
Number of Times Interest Earned	$\frac{\text{Operating Income}}{\text{Annual Interest Expense}}$
Return on Common Stockholders' Equity	$\frac{\text{Net Income} - \text{Preferred Dividends}}{\text{Average Common Stockholders' Equity}}$
Return on Total Assets	$\frac{\text{Net Income} + \text{Interest Expense}}{\text{Average Investment in Assets}}$
Book Value per Share of Common Stock	$\frac{\text{Common Stockholders' Equity}}{\text{Shares of Common Stock Outstanding}}$
Earnings per Share on Common Stock	$\frac{\text{Net Income} - \text{Preferred Dividends}}{\text{Shares of Common Stock Outstanding}}$
Price-Earnings Ratio	$\frac{\text{Market Price per Share}}{\text{Earnings per Share}}$

Fig. 31-6. Methods used for financial analysis.

as with other competing firms. Changes from year to year may be seen with comparative financial statements showing the percentage of change. The direction of changes may be seen through trend percentages. Common-size statements are helpful in comparing firms of different sizes. The common-size figure used on the balance sheet is total assets, while net sales is the key figure to use on the common-size income statement. The ratios and other measurements used are summarized in figure 31-6. They are helpful for decision making and financial planning.

REVIEW

1. What amount represents 100% on a common-size income statement?
2. What amount represents 100% on a common-size balance sheet?
3. What amount represents 100% when trend percentages are calculated?
4. What is the advantage of common-size financial statements?
5. List three ratios or calculations that measure a firm's ability to pay its current debts.
6. Which is better, a high inventory turnover or a low inventory turnover?
7. Which is better, a high accounts receivable turnover or a low turnover?
8. If a firm has a debt ratio of 82%, what is its equity ratio?
9. Would a lender rather finance a firm that has a debt ratio of 10% or 90%?
10. What are quick assets?
11. What does it mean when a firm's return on common stockholders' equity is higher than its return on total assets?
12. What is another name for the quick ratio?
13. What is leverage?

EXERCISES

1. The following figures are from a firm's income statements for the past three years.

	YEAR 1	YEAR 2	YEAR 3
Sales	$200,000	$250,000	$320,000
Cost of Goods Sold	130,000	170,000	230,000
Gross Profit	70,000	80,000	90,000

   a. Restate the above figures in terms of trend percentages.
   b. What is indicated by the trend percentages?

2. The following income statement information is for two firms in the same industry.

	Small Company	Large Company
Sales	$150,000	$9,000,000
Cost of Goods Sold	80,000	5,500,000
Gross Profit	70,000	3,500,000
Selling Expenses	10,000	900,000
General Expenses	10,000	500,000
Net Income	$ 50,000	$2,100,000

a. Prepare common-size income statements for the two firms.
b. How is the small firm doing compared to its large competitor?

3. Following are the balance sheets of Nance Company for the past two years.

	YEAR 1	YEAR 2
ASSETS:		
Current Assets:		
Cash	$ 2,000	$ 1,000
Accounts Receivable	12,000	18,000
Inventory	12,000	36,000
Total Current Assets	26,000	55,000
Fixed Assets:		
Equipment	80,000	100,000
Accumulated Depreciation	36,000	45,000
Total Fixed Assets	44,000	55,000
Total Assets	$70,000	$110,000
LIABILITIES	10,000	40,000
STOCKHOLDERS' EQUITY	60,000	70,000
Total Equities	$70,000	$110,000

a. Prepare common-size balance sheets for the two years.
b. What can be said about Nance Company if the average common-size balance sheet for the industry has accounts receivable of 17, inventories of 18, and net fixed assets of 60?

4. The year-end statements of General Sales Corporation were as follows:

Income Statement

Revenue:		
Sales		$465,000
Cost of Goods Sold:		
Merchandise, January 1	$ 29,400	
Purchases	241,200	
Goods Available for Sale	270,600	
Merchandise, December 31	40,600	
Cost of Goods Sold		230,000
Gross Profit on Sales		235,000
Operating Expense		200,000
Net Income Before Taxes		35,000
Income Taxes		6,600
Net Income		$ 28,400

Balance Sheet

ASSETS:		LIABILITIES:	
Cash	$ 53,000	Accounts Payable	$ 30,000
Accounts Receivable	10,000	Mortgage Payable, secured by a lien on the fixed assets	40,000
Merchandise Inventory	40,600		
Prepaid Expense	100		
Fixed Assets, Net	140,000	STOCKHOLDERS' EQUITY:	
Total Assets	$243,700	Common Stock, $10 par	100,000
		Retained Earnings	73,700
		Total Liabilities and Stockholders' Equity	$243,700

Calculate the following:

a. current ratio
b. acid test ratio
c. days' sales uncollected
d. merchandise turnover
e. equity ratio
f. debt ratio
g. working capital

5. Use the income statement and balance sheet from exercise 4 to prepare common-size statements.

6. State whether each of the following transactions increases working capital, decreases working capital, or has no effect on working capital.
   a. Collected accounts receivable.
   b. Declared a cash dividend.
   c. Paid previously declared cash dividend.
   d. Declared stock dividend.
   e. Sold fixed assets at book value.
   f. Sold fixed assets at a loss.
   g. Sold fixed assets at a profit.
   h. Sold common stock.
   i. Borrowed money on ninety-day note.
   j. Paid accounts payable.
   k. Purchased fixed assets.
   l. Bought a long-term investment.
   m. Declared a stock split.
   n. Bought merchandise.

PROBLEMS

1. The financial statements of Whim Company appear below. (The January 1 beginning inventory was $15,000; beginning receivables were $15,000.)

Whim Company
Balance Sheet
1983

ASSETS:		LIABILITIES AND CAPITAL:	
Cash	$10,000	Accounts Payable	$12,000
Receivables	15,000	Notes Payable	7,000
Inventories	25,000	Other Current Liabilities	2,000
Total Current Assets	$30,000	Total Current Liabilities	$21,000
Net Property	26,000	Long-term Debt	15,000
Other Assets	2,000	Owner's Equity	42,000
Total Assets	$78,000	Total Claims on Assets	$78,000

Whim Company
Income Statement
for 1983

Sales		$130,000
Cost of Goods Sold		100,500
Gross Profit		29,500
Selling Expenses	$10,000	
General Expenses	8,750	18,750
Operating Profit		10,750
Less: Interest Expenses		1,250
Net Profit before Taxes		9,500
Federal Income Taxes		4,750
Net Income		$ 4,750

Using this information, complete the following chart.

Ratio	Computation	Industry Average	Better Ratio Whim or IA*
a. Current		2.7 times	
b. Quick		1.0	
c. Equity		67%	
d. Debt		33%	
e. Accts. Rec. Turnover		7.5 times	
f. Inv. Turnover		5 times	
g. Times Interest Earned		8 times	
h. Avg. Age of Accts. Rec.		22 days	

* IA = Industry Average

2. The following is the summarized balance sheet and income statement of Reshler Corporation for the year.

Balance Sheet
December 31, 19–

Assets	$200,000	Accounts Payable	$ 5,000
		Bonds Payable – 8%	50,000
		Preferred Stock – 6%	10,000
		Common Stock	60,000
		Premium on Common	35,000
		Retained Earnings	40,000
			$200,000

Income Statement
Year Ended December 31, 19–

Net Sales	$400,000
Costs & Expenses	300,000
Income Taxes	40,000
Net Income	$ 60,000

The common stock consists of 60,000 shares with a $1 par value. The 6% preferred stock outstanding consists of 10 shares with a $1,000 par value. No dividends are in arrears on the preferred stock. The common stock is currently being traded on the stock exchange at a price of $12 per share.

a. What are the earnings per share on common stock?
b. What is the price-earnings ratio of the common stock?
c. What is the rate of return on sales?
d. What is the book value of the common stock per share?
e. What is the market value of the common stock per share?
f. Without regard to the answer computed above, assume that the price-earnings ratio of Reshler Corporation is 29. A competing firm called Similar Corporation has a price earnings ratio of 46. Which corporation (Reshler or Similar) appears to be the better investment?

3. The following are the statements for the Baum Company. There are 100 shares of common stock outstanding and the current market price is $5 per share. The beginning inventory was $94. The beginning receivables were $56. The total assets at the beginning of the year were $300. Beginning stockholders' equity was $210.

Baum Company
Balance Sheet
December 31, 19–

ASSETS:			LIABILITIES:		
Cash		$ 30	Accounts payable	$ 30	
Marketable securities		22	Notes payable (6%)	30	
Net receivables		44	Other current liabilities	14	
Inventories		106	Total current liabilities		$ 74
Total current assets		$202	Long-term debt		16
Gross fixed assets	$150		Total liabilities		$ 90
Less: Depreciation	52		STOCKHOLDERS' EQUITY:		
Net fixed assets		98	Common stock	$ 76	
			Retained earnings	134	
			Total stockholder equity		210
Total assets		$300	Total claims on assets		$300

Baum Company
Income Statement
For year ended December 31, 19–

Net sales	$530	
Cost of goods sold	440	
Gross profit		$ 90
Operating expenses	49	
Depreciation expense	8	
Interest expense	3	
Total expenses		60
Net income before tax		$ 30
Taxes 50%		15
Net income		$ 15

Answer the following questions concerning the firm.

a. How much is working capital?
b. What is the current ratio?
c. What is the quick ratio?
d. What is the average age of accounts receivable?
e. What is the debt ratio?
f. What is the equity ratio?
g. What is the number of times interest earned?
h. What is the accounts receivable turnover?
i. What is the inventory turnover?
j. What is the book value per share of common stock?
k. What is the return on total assets?
l. What is the return on common stockholders' equity?
m. What is the earnings per share?
n. What is the price-earnings ratio?

4. The following information is from the financial statements of the Max Corporation for the calendar year 1980. The norms given are industry averages for the firm's industry. The beginning inventories and receivables were the same as the ending amounts.

Max Corporation
Balance Sheet
December 31, 1980

Cash	$ 40,000	Accounts payable	$ 33,000
Receivables	59,000	Notes payable (5%)	44,000
Inventory	165,000	Other current liabilities	22,000
Total current assets	$264,000	Total current liabilities	$ 99,000
Net fixed assets	121,000	Long-term debt (6%)	44,000
		Owners' equity	242,000
Total assets	$385,000	Total claims on assets	$385,000

Max Corporation
Income Statement
For year ended December 31, 1980

Sales		$550,000
Cost of goods sold:		
Materials	$209,000	
Labor	132,000	
Heat, light, and power	19,800	
Indirect labor	33,000	
Depreciation	12,100	405,900
Gross profit		$144,100
Selling expenses	$ 55,000	
General and administrative expenses	63,360	118,360
Operating profit		$ 25,740
Less: Interest expense		2,640
Income before taxes		$ 23,100
Less: Federal income taxes		11,550
Net income		$ 11,550

Using this information, complete the following chart.

Ratio	Max	Industry	Which is better?
Current		2.5 times	
Inv. turnover		9.9 times	
Average collection period		33 days	
Debt ratio		60%	
Equity ratio		40%	
Quick ratio		1.1	

5. Selected information from the financial statements of Dreski Company is as follows:

Sales (all on credit)	$800,000	Long-term debt, 9%	$100,000
Cost of goods sold	560,000	Capital stock, $10 par	120,000
Operating expenses	120,000	Total stockholders' equity	480,000
Bond interest expense	9,000	Average inventory	60,000
Net income (after income taxes)	63,000	Ending inventory	90,000
Current assets	270,000	Average receivables	48,000
Current liabilities	110,000	Ending receivables	42,000
Total assets	690,000	Income taxes expense	48,000
		Prepaid expenses	0

Compute the following:

a. gross profit rate
b. debt ratio
c. current ratio
d. quick ratio
e. inventory turnover
f. average accounts receivable turnover
g. number of times bond interest was earned (before interest and income taxes)
h. book value per share of common stock
i. earnings per share of common stock

6. Use the balance sheet and income statement for the Max Corporation in problem 4 to prepare common-size statements.

32
Implications of Income Taxes

OBJECTIVES After studying this chapter, the student will be able to:

- Outline the basic income tax formula for federal income tax.
- Identify taxable and nontaxable income.
- Explain the rules for exemptions and deductions.
- Compute personal income taxes.
- Describe the impact of taxes on decision making.

Accounting and taxes, particularly income taxes, are closely related. Income tax is based on the firm's income, as determined by the accounting process. The federal government, most states, and some cities place a tax on a firm's income. This chapter deals only with the federal income tax since it is common to all states and has the highest rates.

The federal income tax system is based on voluntary compliance, self-assessment, and a progressive rate structure. *Voluntary compliance* means that taxpayers must file their own tax returns and meet the requirements of the tax laws. A tax return is the form that a taxpayer sends to the government. *Self-assessment* is required. In other words, taxpayers determine their own tax payments: they report their income and compute the tax themselves. The federal tax system is also based on ability to pay. This means that the tax rates are *progressive* – the rates increase as the income increases. Tax rates range from 14% to 70% of taxable income for individuals. The corporate tax rate ranges from 17% to 46%.

The federal income tax system was set up by the Sixteenth Amendment to the Constitution and the Revenue Act of 1913. Today the Internal Revenue Service, a branch of the Treasury Department, is responsible for enforcing the tax laws as contained in the Internal Revenue Code.

CLASSES OF TAXPAYERS

The tax laws group taxpayers into four classes: individuals, corporations, estates, and trusts. Each taxpayer must file a tax return and

Form **1040** Department of the Treasury—Internal Revenue Service
U.S. Individual Income Tax Return

For Privacy Act Notice, see page 3 of Instructions | For the year January 1–December 31, 1978, or other tax year beginning ______, 1978, ending ______, 19__.

Use IRS label. Otherwise, please print or type.	Your first name and initial (if joint return, also give spouse's name and initial)	Last name	Your social security number
	Present home address (Number and street, including apartment number, or rural route)		Spouse's social security no.
	City, town or post office, State and ZIP code		Your occupation

▶ Do you want $1 to go to the Presidential Election Campaign Fund? ☐ Yes ☐ No
If joint return, does your spouse want $1 to go to this fund? . . ☐ Yes ☐ No
Note: *Checking Yes will not increase your tax or reduce your refund.*
Spouse's occupation

Filing Status

Check only one box.

1 ☐ Single
2 ☐ Married filing joint return (even if only one had income)
3 ☐ Married filing separate return. If spouse is also filing, give spouse's social security number in the space above and enter full name here ▶
4 ☐ Unmarried head of household. Enter qualifying name ▶ ______. See page 6 of Instructions.
5 ☐ Qualifying widow(er) with dependent child (Year spouse died ▶ 19). See page 6 of Instructions.

Exemptions

Always check the box labeled Yourself. Check other boxes if they apply.

6a ☐ Yourself ☐ 65 or over ☐ Blind
b ☐ Spouse ☐ 65 or over ☐ Blind
Enter number of boxes checked on 6a and b ▶ ☐

c First names of your dependent children who lived with you ▶
Enter number of children listed ▶ ☐

d Other dependents: (1) Name	(2) Relationship	(3) Number of months lived in your home	(4) Did dependent have income of $750 or more?	(5) Did you provide more than one-half of dependent's support?

Enter number of other dependents ▶ ☐

7 Total number of exemptions claimed . . . . . . Add numbers entered in boxes above ▶ ☐

Income

Please attach Copy B of your Forms W-2 here.

If you do not have a W-2, see page 5 of Instructions.

Please attach check or money order here.

8	Wages, salaries, tips, and other employee compensation	8
9	Interest income *(If over $400, attach Schedule B)*	9
10a	Dividends *(If over $400, attach Schedule B)* ______, 10b Exclusion ______	
10c	Subtract line 10b from line 10a	10c
11	State and local income tax refunds *(does not apply unless refund is for year you itemized deductions)*	11
12	Alimony received	12
13	Business income or (loss) *(attach Schedule C)*	13
14	Capital gain or (loss) *(attach Schedule D)*	14
15	Taxable part of capital gain distributions not reported on Schedule D (see page 9 of Instructions) . .	15
16	Net gain or (loss) from Supplemental Schedule of Gains and Losses *(attach Form 4797)*	16
17	Fully taxable pensions and annuities not reported on Schedule E	17
18	Pensions, annuities, rents, royalties, partnerships, estates or trusts, etc. *(attach Schedule E)*	18
19	Farm income or (loss) *(attach Schedule F)*	19
20	Other income (state nature and source—see page 10 of Instructions) ▶	20
21	**Total income.** Add lines 8, 9, and 10c through 20 . . . . . ▶	21

Adjustments to Income

22	Moving expense *(attach Form 3903)*	22
23	Employee business expenses *(attach Form 2106)* . .	23
24	Payments to an IRA (see page 10 of Instructions)	24
25	Payments to a Keogh *(H.R. 10)* retirement plan . . .	25
26	Interest penalty due to early withdrawal of savings	26
27	Alimony paid (see page 10 of Instructions)	27
28	**Total adjustments.** Add lines 22 through 27 . . . . . ▶	28

Adjusted Gross Income

29	Subtract line 28 from line 21	29
30	Disability income exclusion *(attach Form 2440)*	30
31	**Adjusted gross income.** Subtract line 30 from line 29. *If this line is less than $8,000, see page 2 of Instructions. If you want IRS to figure your tax, see page 4 of Instructions* . . . . . ▶	31

☆ U.S. GOVERNMENT PRINTING OFFICE: 1978—O-263-303 13-2687299 Form 1040 (1978)

Fig. 32-1 (A). Sample form 1040 (front).

Form 1040 (1978) Page 2

Tax Computation

32 Amount from line 31 32

33 If you do not itemize deductions, enter zero . . . .
If you itemize, complete Schedule A (Form 1040) and enter the amount from Schedule A, line 41 33

Caution: If you have unearned income and can be claimed as a dependent on your parent's return, check here ▶ ☐ and see page 11 of the Instructions. Also see page 11 of the Instructions if:

- *You are married filing a separate return and your spouse itemizes deductions, OR*
- *You file Form 4563, OR*
- *You are a dual-status alien.*

34 Subtract line 33 from line 32. Use the amount on line 34 to find your tax from the Tax Tables, or to figure your tax on Schedule TC, Part I 34

Use Schedule TC, Part I, and the Tax Rate Schedules ONLY if:

- *The amount on line 34 is more than $20,000 ($40,000 if you checked Filing Status Box 2 or 5), OR*
- *You have more exemptions than those covered in the Tax Table for your filing status, OR*
- *You use any of these forms to figure your tax: Schedule D, Schedule G, or Form 4726.*

Otherwise, you MUST use the Tax Tables to find your tax.

35 Tax. Enter tax here and check if from ☐ Tax Tables or ☐ Schedule TC 35

36 Additional taxes. (See page 11 of Instructions.) Enter total and check if from ☐ Form 4970, ☐ Form 4972, ☐ Form 5544, ☐ Form 5405, or ☐ Section 72(m)(5) penalty tax . . . 36

37 **Total.** Add lines 35 and 36 . . . . ▶ 37

Credits

38 Credit for contributions to candidates for public office . . 38

39 Credit for the elderly *(attach Schedules R&RP)* 39

40 Credit for child and dependent care expenses (attach Form 2441) . 40

41 Investment credit *(attach Form 3468)* 41

42 Foreign tax credit *(attach Form 1116)* 42

43 Work Incentive (WIN) Credit *(attach Form 4874)* 43

44 New jobs credit *(attach Form 5884)* 44

45 Residential energy credits (see page 12 of Instructions, attach Form 5695) . . . 45

46 **Total credits.** Add lines 38 through 45 46

47 **Balance.** Subtract line 46 from line 37 and enter difference (but not less than zero) . ▶ 47

Other Taxes

48 Self-employment tax *(attach Schedule SE)* 48

49 Minimum tax. Check here ▶ ☐ and attach Form 4625 49

50 Tax from recomputing prior-year investment credit *(attach Form 4255)* 50

51 Social security (FICA) tax on tip income not reported to employer *(attach Form 4137)* . . 51

52 Uncollected employee FICA and RRTA tax on tips *(from Form W–2)* 52

53 Tax on an IRA *(attach Form 5329)* 53

54 **Total tax.** Add lines 47 through 53 . . . . ▶ 54

Payments

Attach Forms W-2, W-2G, and W-2P to front.

55 Total Federal income tax withheld 55

56 1978 estimated tax payments and credit from 1977 return . 56

57 Earned income credit. If line 31 is under $8,000, see page 2 of Instructions. If eligible, enter child's name ▶.............. 57

58 Amount paid with Form 4868 58

59 Excess FICA and RRTA tax withheld (two or more employers) 59

60 Credit for Federal tax on special fuels and oils (attach Form 4136) . 60

61 Regulated Investment Company credit *(attach Form 2439)* 61

62 **Total.** Add lines 55 through 61 . . . . ▶ 62

Refund or Due

63 If line 62 is larger than line 54, enter amount **OVERPAID** . . . . ▶ 63

64 Amount of line 63 to be **REFUNDED TO YOU** . . . . ▶ 64

65 Amount of line 63 to be credited on 1979 estimated tax. ▶ 65

66 If line 54 is larger than line 62, enter **BALANCE DUE.** Attach check or money order for full amount payable to "Internal Revenue Service." Write your social security number on check or money order . . ▶ 66
(Check ▶ ☐ if Form 2210 (2210F) is attached. See page 14 of instructions.) ▶ $

Please Sign Here

Under penalties of perjury, I declare that I have examined this return, including accompanying schedules and statements, and to the best of my knowledge and belief, it is true, correct, and complete. Declaration of preparer (other than taxpayer) is based on all information of which preparer has any knowledge.

▶ Your signature   Date   ▶ Spouse's signature (if filing jointly, BOTH must sign even if only one had income)

Paid Preparer's Information

Preparer's signature ▶   Preparer's social security no.   Check if self-employed ▶ ☐

Firm's name (or yours, if self-employed), address and ZIP code ▶   E.I. No. ▶   Date ▶

Fig. 32-1 (B). Sample form 1040 (back).

Form **1040A** Department of the Treasury—Internal Revenue Service
U.S. Individual Income Tax Return

Use IRS label. Otherwise, please print or type.	Your first name and initial (if joint return, also give spouse's name and initial)	Last name	Your social security number
	Present home address (Number and street, including apartment number, or rural route)		Spouse's social security no.
	City, town or post office, State and ZIP code		Your occupation

Do you want $1 to go to the Presidential Election Campaign Fund? ☐ Yes ☐ No
If joint return, does your spouse want $1 to go to this fund? ☐ Yes ☐ No
Note: *Checking Yes will not increase your tax or reduce your refund.*
Spouse's occupation

For Privacy Act Notice, see page 5 of Instructions

Filing Status — Check Only One Box

1 ☐ Single
2 ☐ Married filing joint return (even if only one had income)
3 ☐ Married filing separate return. If spouse is also filing, give spouse's social security number in the space above and enter full name here ▶ ....
4 ☐ Unmarried head of household. Enter qualifying name ▶ .... See page 11 of Instructions.

Exemptions

Always check the box labeled Yourself. Check other boxes if they apply.

5a ☐ Yourself ☐ 65 or over ☐ Blind
b ☐ Spouse ☐ 65 or over ☐ Blind
Enter number of boxes checked on 5a and b ▶ ☐
c First names of your dependent children who lived with you ▶ ....
Enter number of children listed ▶ ☐

d Other dependents: (1) Name	(2) Relationship	(3) Number of months lived in your home.	(4) Did dependent have income of $750 or more?	(5) Did you provide more than one-half of dependent's support?

Enter number of other dependents ▶ ☐

6 Total number of exemptions claimed . . . . Add numbers entered in boxes above ▶ ☐

Please Attach Copy B of Forms W-2 Here

7 Wages, salaries, tips, and other employee compensation. *(Attach Forms W–2. If you do not have a W–2, see page 7 of Instructions)* 7
8 Interest income *(see page 4 of Instructions)* 8
9a Dividends .... 9b Exclusion .... Subtract line 9b from 9a ▶ 9c
(See pages 4 and 8 of Instructions)
10 Adjusted gross income *(add lines 7, 8, and 9c). If under $8,000, see page 2 of Instructions on "Earned Income Credit."* **If eligible, enter child's name ▶** 10
11a Credit for contributions to candidates for public office. *Enter one-half of amount paid but do not enter more than $25 ($50 if joint return). (See page 8 of Instructions)* . . . 11a
IF YOU WANT IRS TO FIGURE YOUR TAX, PLEASE STOP HERE AND SIGN BELOW.
b Total Federal income tax withheld *(if line 7 is larger than $17,700, see page 8 of Instructions)* 11b
c Earned income credit *(from page 2 of Instructions)* 11c

Please Attach Check or Money Order Here

12 Total *(add lines 11a, b, and c)* 12
13 Tax on the amount on line 10. *(See Instructions for line 13 on page 9, then find your tax in the Tax Tables on pages 14–25.)* 13
14 If line 12 is larger than line 13, enter amount to be **REFUNDED TO YOU** . . . . ▶ 14
15 If line 13 is larger than line 12, enter **BALANCE DUE.** Attach check or money order for full amount payable to "Internal Revenue Service." Write social security number on check or money order . . ▶ 15

Please Sign Here

Under penalties of perjury, I declare that I have examined this return, including accompanying schedules and statements, and to the best of my knowledge and belief, it is true, correct, and complete. Declaration of preparer (other than taxpayer) is based on all information of which preparer has any knowledge.

▶ Your signature Date ▶ Spouse's signature (if filing jointly, BOTH must sign even if only one had income)

Paid Preparer's Information	Preparer's signature ▶	Preparer's social security no.	Check if self-employed ▶ ☐
	Firm's name (or yours, if self-employed), address and ZIP code ▶	E.I. No. ▶	
		Date ▶	

☆ U.S. GOVERNMENT PRINTING OFFICE: 1978—O-263-332 13-2687299 Form **1040A** (1978)

Fig. 32-2. Form 1040A.

pay taxes on taxable income. Note that partnerships or sole proprietorships are not treated as separate taxable entities under the tax law. The income from these forms of business is recorded as income of the individual owners of the firm. A corporation is treated as a taxable entity and must file a return and pay taxes. Any dividends paid by a corporation to its stockholders are treated as income to the individual and are taxed again on the individual's tax return. This is called double taxation. (The taxation of estates and trusts is not covered in this text.)

BASIC INDIVIDUAL TAX OUTLINE

Individuals report their tax on form 1040 (long form), figure 32-1, or form 1040A (short form), figure 32-2. Tax returns are due on April 15 after the end of the tax year. Several other forms, called schedules, are required if form 1040 is used.

The tax laws provide a basic outline, or formula, for the individual taxpayer to follow in computing his or her tax. This basic outline is shown in figure 32-3. Each of the parts of this formula are discussed in the following explanation.

Gross Income
- Deductions from Gross Income
= Adjusted Gross Income
- Deductions from Adjusted Gross Income
  1. The larger of
     a) Standard deduction
     b) Itemized deductions
  2. Personal Exemptions
= Taxable Income
X Applicable Tax Rate
= Gross Tax
- Tax Credits and Payments
= Net Tax Payable or Refundable

Fig. 32-3. An outline for computation of individual income tax.

Gross Income

Gross income equals total income minus exclusions. The tax law defines gross income as all income from whatever source, unless expressly excluded by law. Thus, only those exclusions written into the law are recognized as nontaxable sources of income. Figure 32-4 lists some items that are included in gross income and some that are excluded. Note that the first $100 of dividend income may be excluded by each taxpayer owning stock. This means there may be a $200 exclusion on the joint return of a husband and wife.

Filing Requirements. As of 1978, a single individual under sixty-five years of age must file a return if gross income is $2,950 or more. Married persons must file if their combined gross income is $4,700 or more, provided they are filing a joint return. Married persons may combine their income and file a single tax return which is called a joint return. Any time a refund of tax is due, a return should be filed.

INCLUSIONS: TAXABLE ITEMS

Alimony
Amounts recovered after being deducted in prior years
Annuities
Awards
Back pay
Bargain purchase from employer
Bonuses
Breach of contract damages
Business income
Christmas bonus from employer
Clergy fees and contributions
Commissions
Compensation for services
Contributions to members of the clergy
Death benefit in excess of $5,000
Debts forgiven
Director's fees
Dividends in excess of $100 on stock
Embezzled funds
Employee awards
Employee bonuses
Employee benefits
Employee stock options
Estate and trust income
Farm income
Fees
Free tour
Gains from illegal activities
Gains from sale of property
Gambling winnings
Group term life insurance coverage over $50,000
Hobby income
Incentive awards
Interest
Jury duty fees
Living quarters, meals (unless furnished for employer's convenience)
Mileage allowance
Military pay (unless combat pay)
Notary fees
Partnership income
Pensions
Prizes
Professional fees
Punitive damages
Reimbursement for moving expenses
Rents
Retirement pay
Rewards
Royalties
Salaries
Severance pay
Strike and lockout benefits
Supplemental unemployment benefits
Tips and gratuities
Travel allowance
Wages

EXCLUSIONS – NONTAXABLE ITEMS

Accident insurance proceeds
Annuities (to a limited extent)
Bequests
Casualty insurance proceeds
Child support payments
Compensatory damages
Cost-of-living allowance (for military)
Damages for personal injury or sickness
Death benefits up to $5,000
Disability benefits
Disability pensions (to a limited extent)
Dividends on stock of $100 or less
Federal Employees' Compensation Act payments
Fellowship grants (to a limited extent)
Gifts
Group term life insurance paid by employer (coverage under $50,000)
Health insurance proceeds not deducted as medical expense
Inheritances
Interest on obligations of a state or political subdivision
Life insurance paid on death
Meals and lodging (furnished for employer's convenience)
Military allowances
Minister's dwelling rental value allowance
Railroad retirement benefits
Relocation payments
Scholarship grants (to a limited extent)
Sickness and injury benefits
Social Security benefits
Unemployment compensation
Veterans' benefits
Welfare payments
Workmen's compensation

Fig. 32-4.

SCHEDULE C
(Form 1040)
Department of the Treasury
Internal Revenue Service

Profit or (Loss) From Business or Profession
(Sole Proprietorship)

Partnerships, Joint Ventures, etc., Must File Form 1065.

▶ Attach to Form 1040. ▶ See Instructions for Schedule C (Form 1040).

Name of proprietor	Social security number of proprietor

C

A Main business activity (see Instructions) ▶ ______; product ▶ ______

B Business name ▶ ______

C Employer identification number ▶ ______

D Business address (number and street) ▶ ______

City, State and ZIP code ▶ ______

E Accounting method: (1) ☐ Cash (2) ☐ Accrual (3) ☐ Other (specify) ▶ ______

F Method(s) used to value closing inventory:
(1) ☐ Cost (2) ☐ Lower of cost or market (3) ☐ Other (if other, attach explanation)

	Yes	No
G Was there any major change in determining quantities, costs, or valuations between opening and closing inventory? If "Yes," attach explanation.		
H Does this business activity involve oil or gas, movies or video tapes, or leasing personal (section 1245) property to others? (See page 25 of the Instructions.)		
I Did you deduct expenses for an office in your home?		

Part I Income

1 a Gross receipts or sales	1a		
b Returns and allowances	1b		
c Balance (subtract line 1b from line 1a)		1c	
2 Cost of goods sold and/or operations (Schedule C–1, line 8)		2	
3 Gross profit (subtract line 2 from line 1c)		3	
4 Other income (attach schedule)		4	
5 **Total income** (add lines 3 and 4) ▶		5	

Part II Deductions

6 Advertising		28 Telephone	
7 Amortization		29 Travel and entertainment	
8 Bad debts from sales or services		30 Utilities	
9 Bank charges		31 a Wages	
10 Car and truck expenses		b New Jobs Credit	
11 Commissions		c Subtract line 31b from 31a	
12 Depletion		32 Other expenses (specify):	
13 Depreciation (explain in Schedule C–2)		a	
		b	
14 Dues and publications		c	
15 Employee benefit programs		d	
16 Freight (not included on Schedule C–1)		e	
		f	
17 Insurance		g	
18 Interest on business indebtedness		h	
19 Laundry and cleaning		i	
20 Legal and professional services		j	
21 Office supplies		k	
22 Pension and profit-sharing plans		l	
23 Postage		m	
24 Rent on business property		n	
25 Repairs		o	
26 Supplies (not included on Schedule C–1)		p	
		q	
27 Taxes		r	

33 **Total deductions** (add amounts in columns for lines 6 through 32r) ▶	33	
34 **Net profit or (loss)** (subtract line 33 from line 5). Enter here and on Form 1040, line 13. **ALSO** enter on Schedule SE (Form 1040), line 5a. (For "at risk" provisions, see page 25 of Instructions.) ▶	34	

Fig. 32-5 (A). Sample schedule C (front).

SCHEDULE C-1.—Cost of Goods Sold and/or Operations (See Schedule C Instructions for Part I, Line 2)

1 Inventory at beginning of year (if different from last year's closing inventory, attach explanation)	1		
2 a Purchases — 2a			
b Cost of items withdrawn for personal use — 2b			
c Balance (subtract line 2b from line 2a)	2c		
3 Cost of labor (do not include salary paid to yourself)	3		
4 Materials and supplies	4		
5 Other costs (attach schedule)	5		
6 Add lines 1, 2c, and 3 through 5	6		
7 Inventory at end of year	7		
8 Cost of goods sold and/or operations (subtract line 7 from line 6). Enter here and on Part I, line 2 ▶	8		

SCHEDULE C-2.—Depreciation (See Schedule C Instructions for line 13)

If you need more space, please use Form 4562.

Description of property (a)	Date acquired (b)	Cost or other basis (c)	Depreciation allowed or allowable in prior years (d)	Method of computing depreciation (e)	Life or rate (f)	Depreciation for this year (g)
1 Total additional first-year depreciation (do not include in items below) →						
2 Other depreciation:						
Buildings						
Furniture and fixtures						
Transportation equipment						
Machinery and other equipment						
Other (Specify)						
3 Totals					3	
4 Depreciation claimed in Schedule C-1					4	
5 Balance (subtract line 4 from line 3). Enter here and on Part II, line 13 ▶					5	

SCHEDULE C-3.—Expense Account Information (See Schedule C Instructions for Schedule C-3)

Enter information for yourself and your five highest paid employees. In determining the five highest paid employees, add expense account allowances to the salaries and wages. However, you don't have to provide the information for any employee for whom the combined amount is less than $25,000, or for yourself if your expense account allowance plus line 34, page 1, is less than $25,000.

Name (a)	Expense account (b)	Salaries and Wages (c)
Owner		
1		
2		
3		
4		
5		

Did you claim a deduction for expenses connected with:	Yes	No
A Entertainment facility (boat, resort, ranch, etc.)?		
B Living accommodations (except employees on business)?		
C Employees' families at conventions or meetings?		
If "Yes," were any of these conventions or meetings outside the U.S. or its possessions? (See page 26 of Instructions.)		
D Vacations for employees or their families not reported on Form W-2?		

☆ U.S. GOVERNMENT PRINTING OFFICE: 1978—O—263-312—E.I. # 52-0237640

Fig. 32-5 (B). Sample schedule C (back).

Deductions from Gross Income

Various expenses related to a taxpayer's business or other sources of income may be deducted from gross income. Some of these deductions are discussed in the following paragraphs.

Trade or Business Expenses. Any ordinary and necessary expenses incurred in conducting a trade or business are deducted from gross income. Schedule C shown in figure 32-5 (A) & (B) is used to compute the net income of a sole proprietorship.

Business Expenses of an Employee. An employee may deduct certain business expenses, such as transportation and travel costs, outside salesperson's expenses, and moving expenses. *Transportation costs* are the expenses of moving from one place of employment to another during the day. The cost of commuting from home to the first place of employment or from the last place of employment to home is usually not deductible. *Travel costs* are the expenses incurred for such things as transportation, meals, and lodging while away from home on business. *Expenses of outside salespersons* are the costs involved in selling away from the place of business. An employee incurs *moving expenses* in changing his place of residence to begin work at a new location. Certain requirements and limitations apply to these deductions. Only the part of the expenses not reimbursed by the employer may be deducted.

Expenses for Production of Rents and Royalties. All expenses incurred to earn rent and royalty income are deducted on Schedule E in determining adjusted gross income. Examples of such expenses are depreciation, repairs and maintenance, interest, and insurance.

Capital Gains and Losses Deduction. Generally, a taxpayer who sells or otherwise disposes of property, has either a gain or a loss. For gains or losses on sales of certain kinds of property called *capital assets,* Congress has allowed a special tax treatment to encourage investment in those assets. The most common capital assets are stocks and bonds. Capital assets are distinguished from business assets because of the difference in tax treatment.

The sale or exchange of a capital asset is reported on Schedule D. Gains and losses are classified as either short term or long term. The *holding period* or the length of time the asset was owned is the determining factor. For tax years beginning after 1977 the taxpayer must hold the property more than one year to qualify for the long-term treatment. When a taxpayer has a long-term capital gain, 60% of the gain may be deducted so that only 40% of the gain is taxed. Short-term gains are fully taxable. Short-term losses are fully deductible and long-term losses are 50% deductible (but may not exceed $3,000 per year for individuals).

Alimony. A person who pays alimony may deduct the payments from gross income. The person receiving alimony payments must include the payments as income.

Adjusted Gross Income

Adjusted gross income equals gross income minus deductions from gross income. Adjusted gross income is often abbreviated as *AGI.* It is important in finding the tax on the tables and the limit for contributions and medical expenses.

Deductions from Adjusted Gross Income

The law allows certain deductions from adjusted gross income in computing taxable income. There are two ways of taking these deductions:

- Claim the standard deduction.
- Itemize deductions on Schedule A.

The taxpayer should determine the deduction under both methods and use the one that results in the greater deduction.

Standard Deduction. A standard deduction is an allowance used to reduce adjusted gross income if the taxpayer does not itemize deductions. To *itemize* means to list deductions in detail rather than as one amount. As of 1978, the standard deduction may not exceed:

- $2,200 for a single person;
- $3,200 for married persons filing a joint return and for certain widows or widowers; or
- $1,600 for a married person filing a separate return.*

Since the tax tables assume these amounts will be deducted, they are sometimes called the *zero bracket amounts.*

Itemized Deductions. Charitable contributions, interest and certain taxes of a nonbusiness nature, medical and dental expenses, and certain losses and other expenses may be itemized as deductions on Schedule A. Records must be kept to prove these deductions. Charitable contributions are contributions to qualified organizations for religious, charitable, scientific, literary, or educational purposes, or for the prevention of cruelty to children or animals. Example of such qualified nonprofit orgainizations include churches, community chests or funds, and educational groups. Interest expenses paid on a debt which is of a personal nature, such as a home mortgage, a car loan, or bank credit card plan are deducted as itemized deductions. A sample of the form used to itemize deductions is shown in figure 32-6. The back of this form, or Schedule B, is used to record dividend and interest income. A sample Schedule B is shown in figure 32-7.

*These amounts are subject to change.

Schedules A&B—Itemized Deductions AND Interest and Dividend Income
(Form 1040)

Department of the Treasury
Internal Revenue Service

▶ Attach to Form 1040. ▶ See Instructions for Schedules A and B (Form 1040).

Name(s) as shown on Form 1040 | Your social security number

Schedule A—Itemized Deductions (Schedule B is on back)

Medical and Dental Expenses (not paid by insurance or otherwise) (See page 15 of Instructions.)

1 One-half (but not more than $150) of insurance premiums you paid for medical care. (Be sure to include in line 10 below.) . ▶

2 Medicine and drugs . . . .

3 Enter 1% of Form 1040, line 31 . . .

4 Subtract line 3 from line 2. If line 3 is more than line 2, enter zero . . . .

5 Balance of insurance premiums for medical care not entered on line 1 . . . .

6 Other medical and dental expenses:

a Doctors, dentists, nurses, etc. . . .

b Hospitals . . . .

c Other (itemize—include hearing aids, dentures, eyeglasses, transportation, etc.) ▶

7 Total (add lines 4 through 6c) . . . .

8 Enter 3% of Form 1040, line 31 . . .

9 Subtract line 8 from line 7. If line 8 is more than line 7, enter zero . . . .

10 **Total medical and dental expenses (add lines 1 and 9).** Enter here and on line 33 . ▶

Taxes (See page 15 of Instructions.)

11 State and local income . . . . . .

12 Real estate . . . .

13 State and local gasoline (see gas tax tables) .

14 General sales (see sales tax tables) . .

15 Personal property . . . .

16 Other (itemize) ▶

17 **Total taxes (add lines 11 through 16).** Enter here and on line 34 . . . . ▶

Interest Expense (See page 16 of Instructions.)

18 a Home mortgage . . . .

b Credit and charge cards . . . . .

19 Other (itemize) ▶

20 **Total interest expense (add lines 18a through 19).** Enter here and on line 35 ▶

Contributions (See page 17 of Instructions.)

21 a Cash contributions for which you have receipts, cancelled checks or other written evidence . . . .

b Other cash contributions (show who you gave to and how much you gave) ▶

22 Other than cash (see page 17 of instructions for required statement) . . . .

23 Carryover from prior years . . . . .

24 **Total contributions (add lines 21a through 23).** Enter here and on line 36 . . ▶

Casualty or Theft Loss(es) (See page 17 of Instructions.)

25 Loss before insurance reimbursement .

26 Insurance reimbursement . . . . .

27 Subtract line 26 from line 25. If line 26 is more than line 25, enter zero . . .

28 Enter $100 or amount on line 27, whichever is smaller . . . .

29 **Total casualty or theft loss(es) (subtract line 28 from line 27).** Enter here and on line 37 . ▶

Miscellaneous Deductions (See page 17 of Instructions.)

30 Union dues . . . .

31 Other (itemize) ▶

32 **Total miscellaneous deductions (add lines 30 and 31).** Enter here and on line 38 ▶

Summary of Itemized Deductions (See page 18 of Instructions.) **A**

33 Total medical and dental—from line 10 .

34 Total taxes—from line 17 . . . . .

35 Total interest—from line 20 . . . .

36 Total contributions—from line 24 . . .

37 Total casualty or theft loss(es)—from line 29 .

38 Total miscellaneous—from line 32 . .

39 **Total deductions (add lines 33 through 38)** ▶

40 If you checked Form 1040, Filing Status box:
2 or 5, enter $3,200
1 or 4, enter $2,200
3, enter $1,600 . . . .

41 Subtract line 40 from line 39. Enter here and on Form 1040, line 33. (If line 40 is more than line 39, enter zero and see "You Must Itemize Deductions" on page 11 of the Instructions.) . . . . . ▶

Fig. 32-6. Sample schedule A used to record itemized deductions.

Schedules A&B (Form 1040) 1978 **Schedule B—Interest and Dividend Income** Page **2**

Name(s) as shown on Form 1040 (Do not enter name and social security number if shown on other side) | **Your social security number**

Part I Interest Income

1 If you received more than $400 in interest, Complete Part I. Please see page 8 of the instructions to find out what interest to report. Then answer the questions in Part III, below. If you received interest as a nominee for another, or you received or paid accrued interest on securities transferred between interest payment dates, please see page 18 of the instructions.

Name of payer	Amount

2 Total interest income. Enter here and on Form 1040, line 9 . . . .

Part II Dividend Income

3 If you received more than $400 in gross dividends (including capital gain distributions) and other distributions on stock, complete Part II. Please see page 9 of the instructions. Write (H), (W), (J), for stock held by husband, wife, or jointly. Then answer the questions in Part III, below. If you received dividends as a nominee for another, please see page 18 of the instructions.

Name of payer	Amount

4 Total of line 3 . . . .

5 Capital gain distributions. Enter here and on Schedule D, line 7. See Note below . . .

6 Nontaxable distributions . . . . . .

7 Total (add lines 5 and 6) . . . .

8 Dividends before exclusion (subtract line 7 from line 4). Enter here and on Form 1040, line 10a . . . .

Note: *If you received capital gain distributions and do not need Schedule D to report any other gains or losses or to compute the alternative tax, do not file that schedule. Instead, enter the taxable part of capital gain distributions on Form 1040, line 15.*

B

Part III Foreign Accounts and Foreign Trusts

If you are required to list interest in Part I or dividends in Part II, OR if you had a foreign account or were a grantor of, or a transferor to a foreign trust, you must answer both questions in Part III. Please see page 18 of the instructions.

	Yes	No
A Did you, at any time during the taxable year, have an interest in or signature or other authority over a bank, securities, or other financial account in a foreign country (see page 18 of instructions)? . . .		
B Were you the grantor of, or transferor to, a foreign trust during any taxable year, which foreign trust was in being during the current taxable year, whether or not you have any beneficial interest in such trust? . If "Yes," you may be required to file Forms 3520, 3520–A, or 926.		

☆ U.S. Government Printing Office: 1978—O—263-309—E.I. # 52-0237640

Fig. 32-7. Sample schedule B used to show dividend and interest income.

Deductible Taxes

Real estate tax (State, local, or foreign)
General sales tax (State or local)
Income tax (State, local, or foreign)
Personal property tax (State and local)

Nondeductible Taxes

1) Federal
Federal income tax
Social security tax
Railroad retirement tax
Federal excise tax
Federal estate and gift taxes

2) State and local (other than income taxes)
Motor vehicle tax (but see personal property taxes)
Inheritance, legacy tax
Gift, succession tax
Cigarette, tobacco taxes

3) Fees and charges, such as:
Alcoholic beverage license, etc.
Driver's license
Dog tags
Hunting license
Auto inspection fees
Marriage license
Tolls for bridges, roads, etc.

Fig. 32-8.

The following taxes imposed on and paid by the taxpayer may be deducted: income tax (other than federal); real property tax; personal property tax; and sales tax. Figure 32-8 lists the taxes that are deductible and nondeductible.

The taxpayer may deduct medical and dental expenses not compensated for by insurance, but paid during the taxable year for medical care for self, spouse, or dependents, subject to certain limitations. The term *medical care* is broadly defined to include amounts paid to diagnose, cure, treat, or prevent disease, or to affect any structure or function of the body. As a general rule, medical expenses may be deducted only when their total exceeds 3% of the taxpayer's adjusted gross income. Expenses for medicines and drugs are further limited. The taxpayer must first deduct 1% of adjusted gross income, then include the remainder with the other medical expenses. Half of the taxpayer's medical insurance premiums up to $150 may be deducted without regard to the 3% limitation; the remainder should then be included with other medical costs.

For example, Taxpayer X's doctor and hospital bills are $684 for the year, and medicines and drugs cost an additional $116. Taxpayer X paid $200 during the year for medical insurance. Insurance reimbursed the taxpayer $285 for doctor and hospital bills and $25 for medicines and drugs. Taxpayer X's adjusted gross income was $8,400. The medical deduction is calculated as follows:

One-half of medical insurance premium		$100
Total cost of medicines and drugs ($116 - $25 reimbursement)	$ 91	
Less: 1% of $8,400	84	
Balance considered as medical expenses	$ 7	
Other medical expenses (including balance of insurance premiums: $684 - $285 reimbursement + $100)	499	
Total medical expenses	$506	
Less: 3% of $8,400	252	254
Total medical expense deduction		$354

Figure 32-9 lists several medical-related expenses that are not deductible.

A casualty loss as a result of theft, hurricane, fire, storm, flood and other disasters may be deductible to the extent that it exceeds $100 and is not reimbursed by insurance.

The following examples are deductible as miscellaneous deductions: union dues, political contributions, employee expenses such as uniforms and small tools, and tax counsel and assistance fees. Figure 32-10 lists several miscellaneous costs that are not deductible.

Exemptions. Every taxpayer is allowed to claim his or her own personal exemption. Married taxpayers may be entitled to claim an exemption for their spouses. Additional exemptions are allowed if the

Nondeductible Medical Expenses include:

1) Cost of a trip taken to change environment, improve morale, or health in general — even though made on the advice of a physician;

2) Social activities recommended by a doctor to improve general health or amounts paid to preserve general health, such as membership in a health club,

3) Funeral and burial expenses, including the cost of a gravestone;

4) Expenses for domestic help;

5) Cost of maternity clothes;

6) Items such as toothpaste, toiletries, and cosmetics (they do not qualify as medicine and drugs, nor do vitamins taken to maintain general health);

7) Veterinarian's fees;

8) Illegal operations or drugs;

9) Diaper service;

10) Life insurance;

Fig. 32-9.

Nondeductible expenses

Improvements and other capital expenditures
Lost or misplaced cash or property
Bar examination fees, etc.
Repayment of a debt
Corporate expenses paid by officer-stockholder
Bribes and illegal payments, including improper payments to foreign officials
Fines, tax penalties, and collateral
Hobby expenses in excess of income from the hobby
Gambling losses in excess of gains
Child adoption expenses
Support payments
Marriage license fees
Fishing and hunting licenses
Dog tags
Repairs to home
Rent on home
Driver's licenses and auto inspection fees
Insurance on home
Expenses incurred in the production of tax-exempt income.

Fig. 32-10.

taxpayer is over sixty-five years of age or blind at the end of the tax year. The taxpayer may also claim an exemption for each person who qualifies as a dependent. In general, a *dependent* is a person who (1) received over half of his or her support from the taxpayer during the year; (2) had less than $1,000 of gross income for the year or was a full-time student; (3) was a member of the taxpayer's household or was closely related to the taxpayer; (4) was a US citizen or resident; and (5) did not file a joint return. The deduction is $1,000 for each exemption.

Tax Table Income. Most taxpayers can use the tax tables to complete their taxes. In order to use the tax tables, *Tax Table Income* must be computed. If a person does not itemize, tax table income is equal to adjusted gross income. If a person itemizes, the excess of itemized deductions over the allowable zero bracket amount must be deducted from AGI. Once the tax table income is known, the tax is located on the tax table.

Computing the Tax

The tax is computed on either the taxable income or the tax table income. Depending upon the taxpayer's income (and other factors), the instruction booklet tells whether a tax table or a tax rate schedule should be used to find the tax. A sample tax table is shown in figure 32-11. A tax rate schedule appears in figure 32-12.

The status of the taxpayer determines which tax rate schedule or tax table should be used. Single status is used by all unmarried taxpayers who do not qualify for another status. Married taxpayers may file joint returns or separate returns. The tax rates for an unmarried head of household generally fall between the rates for the single and joint status. To qualify to use the head of household rates, the taxpayer must have been unmarried or legally separated on the last day of the tax year. Also, the taxpayer must have furnished more than half the cost of maintaining a household for the entire year for at least one unmarried child or grandchild, or one dependent relative.

Tax Credits and Payments

A *credit* is a direct dollar-for-dollar reduction of the tax. There are many types of tax credits. The following is a description of some of the credits common to individual tax returns.

If a taxpayer pays expenses for household services, child care, disabled dependent care, or disabled spouse care in order to be gainfully employed, he or she may be entitled to a credit. The credit is titled *Child Care and Disabled Dependent Care* and consists of 20% of the payments for such services. There is also a tax credit available for the elderly.

Political contributions may be deducted as an itemized deduction or as a tax credit. The credit may not exceed $25 on a separate return or $50 on a joint return. Foreign income taxes paid to a foreign country or United States possession may be claimed as a credit or as an

Tax Table B—MARRIED FILING JOINTLY (Box 2) and QUALIFYING WIDOW(ER)S (Box 5)

(For married persons filing joint returns or qualifying widow(er)s with tax table income of $40,000 or less who claim fewer than 10 exemptions)

To find your tax: Read down the left income column until you find your income as shown on line 34 of Form 1040. Read across to the column headed by the total number of exemptions claimed on line 7 of Form 1040. The amount shown at the point where the two lines meet is your tax. Enter on Form 1040, line 35.

The $3,200 zero bracket amount, your deduction for exemptions and the general tax credit have been taken into account in figuring the tax shown in this table. **Do not take a separate deduction for them.**

If line 34, Form 1040 is—		And the total number of exemptions claimed on line 7 is—							
Over	But not over	2	3	4	5	6	7	8	9
		Your tax is—							
If $5,200 or less your tax is 0									
5,200	5,250	4	0	0	0	0	0	0	0
5,250	5,300	11	0	0	0	0	0	0	0
5,300	5,350	18	0	0	0	0	0	0	0
5,350	5,400	25	0	0	0	0	0	0	0
5,400	5,450	32	0	0	0	0	0	0	0
5,450	5,500	39	0	0	0	0	0	0	0
5,500	5,550	46	0	0	0	0	0	0	0
5,550	5,600	53	0	0	0	0	0	0	0
5,600	5,650	60	0	0	0	0	0	0	0
5,650	5,700	67	0	0	0	0	0	0	0
5,700	5,750	74	0	0	0	0	0	0	0
5,750	5,800	81	0	0	0	0	0	0	0
5,800	5,850	89	0	0	0	0	0	0	0
5,850	5,900	96	0	0	0	0	0	0	0
5,900	5,950	104	0	0	0	0	0	0	0
5,950	6,000	111	0	0	0	0	0	0	0
6,000	6,050	119	0	0	0	0	0	0	0
6,050	6,100	126	0	0	0	0	0	0	0
6,100	6,150	134	0	0	0	0	0	0	0
6,150	6,200	141	0	0	0	0	0	0	0
6,200	6,250	149	4	0	0	0	0	0	0
6,250	6,300	156	11	0	0	0	0	0	0
6,300	6,350	164	18	0	0	0	0	0	0
6,350	6,400	171	25	0	0	0	0	0	0
6,400	6,450	179	32	0	0	0	0	0	0
6,450	6,500	186	39	0	0	0	0	0	0
6,500	6,550	194	46	0	0	0	0	0	0
6,550	6,600	201	54	0	0	0	0	0	0
6,600	6,650	209	61	0	0	0	0	0	0
6,650	6,700	216	69	0	0	0	0	0	0
6,700	6,750	224	76	0	0	0	0	0	0
6,750	6,800	232	84	0	0	0	0	0	0
6,800	6,850	240	91	0	0	0	0	0	0
6,850	6,900	248	99	0	0	0	0	0	0
6,900	6,950	256	106	0	0	0	0	0	0
6,950	7,000	264	114	0	0	0	0	0	0
7,000	7,050	272	121	0	0	0	0	0	0
7,050	7,100	280	129	0	0	0	0	0	0
7,100	7,150	288	136	0	0	0	0	0	0
7,150	7,200	296	144	0	0	0	0	0	0
7,200	7,250	304	151	4	0	0	0	0	0
7,250	7,300	312	159	11	0	0	0	0	0
7,300	7,350	320	166	19	0	0	0	0	0
7,350	7,400	328	174	26	0	0	0	0	0
7,400	7,450	336	181	34	0	0	0	0	0
7,450	7,500	344	189	41	0	0	0	0	0
7,500	7,550	352	197	49	0	0	0	0	0
7,550	7,600	360	205	56	0	0	0	0	0
7,600	7,650	368	213	64	0	0	0	0	0
7,650	7,700	376	221	71	0	0	0	0	0
7,700	7,750	384	229	79	0	0	0	0	0
7,750	7,800	393	237	86	0	0	0	0	0
7,800	7,850	401	245	94	0	0	0	0	0
7,850	7,900	410	253	101	0	0	0	0	0
7,900	7,950	418	261	109	0	0	0	0	0
7,950	8,000	427	269	116	0	0	0	0	0
8,000	8,050	435	277	124	0	0	0	0	0
8,050	8,100	444	285	131	0	0	0	0	0
8,100	8,150	452	293	139	0	0	0	0	0
8,150	8,200	461	301	146	0	0	0	0	0
8,200	8,250	469	309	154	6	0	0	0	0
8,250	8,300	476	317	162	14	0	0	0	0
8,300	8,350	484	325	170	21	0	0	0	0
8,350	8,400	491	333	178	29	0	0	0	0

Continued next column

If line 34, Form 1040 is—		And the total number of exemptions claimed on line 7 is—							
Over	But not over	2	3	4	5	6	7	8	9
		Your tax is—							
8,400	8,450	499	341	186	36	0	0	0	0
8,450	8,500	506	349	194	44	0	0	0	0
8,500	8,550	514	358	202	51	0	0	0	0
8,550	8,600	521	366	210	59	0	0	0	0
8,600	8,650	529	375	218	66	0	0	0	0
8,650	8,700	536	383	226	74	0	0	0	0
8,700	8,750	544	392	234	81	0	0	0	0
8,750	8,800	553	400	242	89	0	0	0	0
8,800	8,850	561	409	250	96	0	0	0	0
8,850	8,900	570	417	258	104	0	0	0	0
8,900	8,950	578	426	266	111	0	0	0	0
8,950	9,000	587	434	274	119	0	0	0	0
9,000	9,050	595	443	282	127	0	0	0	0
9,050	9,100	604	451	290	135	0	0	0	0
9,100	9,150	612	460	298	143	0	0	0	0
9,150	9,200	621	468	306	151	1	0	0	0
9,200	9,250	629	477	314	159	9	0	0	0
9,250	9,300	638	485	323	167	16	0	0	0
9,300	9,350	646	494	331	175	24	0	0	0
9,350	9,400	655	502	340	183	31	0	0	0
9,400	9,450	663	511	348	191	39	0	0	0
9,450	9,500	672	520	357	199	46	0	0	0
9,500	9,550	680	529	365	207	54	0	0	0
9,550	9,600	689	539	374	215	61	0	0	0
9,600	9,650	697	548	382	223	69	0	0	0
9,650	9,700	706	558	391	231	76	0	0	0
9,700	9,750	714	567	399	239	84	0	0	0
9,750	9,800	723	577	408	247	92	0	0	0
9,800	9,850	731	586	416	255	100	0	0	0
9,850	9,900	740	596	425	263	108	0	0	0
9,900	9,950	748	605	433	271	116	0	0	0
9,950	10,000	757	615	442	279	124	0	0	0
10,000	10,050	765	624	450	288	132	0	0	0
10,050	10,100	774	634	459	296	140	0	0	0
10,100	10,150	782	643	467	305	148	0	0	0
10,150	10,200	791	653	476	313	156	4	0	0
10,200	10,250	799	662	485	322	164	11	0	0
10,250	10,300	808	672	494	330	172	19	0	0
10,300	10,350	816	681	504	339	180	26	0	0
10,350	10,400	825	691	513	347	188	34	0	0
10,400	10,450	833	700	523	356	196	41	0	0
10,450	10,500	842	710	532	364	204	49	0	0
10,500	10,550	850	719	542	373	212	57	0	0
10,550	10,600	859	729	551	381	220	65	0	0
10,600	10,650	867	738	561	390	228	73	0	0
10,650	10,700	876	748	570	398	236	81	0	0
10,700	10,750	884	757	580	407	244	89	0	0
10,750	10,800	893	765	589	415	253	97	0	0
10,800	10,850	901	774	599	424	261	105	0	0
10,850	10,900	910	782	608	432	270	113	0	0
10,900	10,950	918	791	618	441	278	121	0	0
10,950	11,000	927	799	627	450	287	129	0	0
11,000	11,050	935	808	637	459	295	137	0	0
11,050	11,100	944	816	646	469	304	145	0	0
11,100	11,150	952	825	656	478	312	153	0	0
11,150	11,200	961	833	665	488	321	161	6	0
11,200	11,250	969	842	675	497	329	169	14	0
11,250	11,300	978	850	684	507	338	177	22	0
11,300	11,350	986	859	694	516	346	185	30	0
11,350	11,400	995	867	703	526	355	193	38	0
11,400	11,450	1,003	876	713	535	363	201	46	0
11,450	11,500	1,012	884	722	545	372	209	54	0
11,500	11,550	1,020	893	732	554	380	218	62	0
11,550	11,600	1,029	901	741	564	389	226	70	0

Continued on next page

Fig. 32-11. A sample tax table.

Tax Rate Schedules

If you cannot use one of the Tax Tables, figure your tax on the amount on Schedule TC, Part I, line 3, by using the appropriate Tax Rate Schedule on this page. Enter tax on Schedule TC, Part I, line 4.
Note: *Your zero bracket amount has been built into these Tax Rate Schedules.*

SCHEDULE X—Single Taxpayers Not Qualifying for Rates in Schedule Y or Z

Use this schedule if you checked **Box 1** on Form 1040—

If the amount on Schedule TC, Part I, line 3, is: / Enter on Schedule TC, Part I, line 4:

Not over $2,200............ —0—

Over—	But not over—		of the amount over—
$2,200	$2,700	14%	$2,200
$2,700	$3,200	$70+15%	$2,700
$3,200	$3,700	$145+16%	$3,200
$3,700	$4,200	$225+17%	$3,700
$4,200	$6,200	$310+19%	$4,200
$6,200	$8,200	$690+21%	$6,200
$8,200	$10,200	$1,110+24%	$8,200
$10,200	$12,200	$1,590+25%	$10,200
$12,200	$14,200	$2,090+27%	$12,200
$14,200	$16,200	$2,630+29%	$14,200
$16,200	$18,200	$3,210+31%	$16,200
$18,200	$20,200	$3,830+34%	$18,200
$20,200	$22,200	$4,510+36%	$20,200
$22,200	$24,200	$5,230+38%	$22,200
$24,200	$28,200	$5,990+40%	$24,200
$28,200	$34,200	$7,590+45%	$28,200
$34,200	$40,200	$10,290+50%	$34,200
$40,200	$46,200	$13,290+55%	$40,200
$46,200	$52,200	$16,590+60%	$46,200
$52,200	$62,200	$20,190+62%	$52,200
$62,200	$72,200	$26,390+64%	$62,200
$72,200	$82,200	$32,790+66%	$72,200
$82,200	$92,200	$39,390+68%	$82,200
$92,200	$102,200	$46,190+69%	$92,200
$102,200	....	$53,090+70%	$102,200

SCHEDULE Y—Married Taxpayers and Qualifying Widows and Widowers

If you are a married person living apart from your spouse, see page 7 of the instructions to see if you can be considered to be "unmarried" for purposes of using Schedule X or Z.

Married Filing Joint Returns and Qualifying Widows and Widowers

Use this schedule if you checked **Box 2 or Box 5** on Form 1040—

If the amount on Schedule TC, Part I, line 3, is: / Enter on Schedule TC, Part I, line 4:

Not over $3,200............ —0—

Over—	But not over—		of the amount over—
$3,200	$4,200	14%	$3,200
$4,200	$5,200	$140+15%	$4,200
$5,200	$6,200	$290+16%	$5,200
$6,200	$7,200	$450+17%	$6,200
$7,200	$11,200	$620+19%	$7,200
$11,200	$15,200	$1,380+22%	$11,200
$15,200	$19,200	$2,260+25%	$15,200
$19,200	$23,200	$3,260+28%	$19,200
$23,200	$27,200	$4,380+32%	$23,200
$27,200	$31,200	$5,660+36%	$27,200
$31,200	$35,200	$7,100+39%	$31,200
$35,200	$39,200	$8,660+42%	$35,200
$39,200	$43,200	$10,340+45%	$39,200
$43,200	$47,200	$12,140+48%	$43,200
$47,200	$55,200	$14,060+50%	$47,200
$55,200	$67,200	$18,060+53%	$55,200
$67,200	$79,200	$24,420+55%	$67,200
$79,200	$91,200	$31,020+58%	$79,200
$91,200	$103,200	$37,980+60%	$91,200
$103,200	$123,200	$45,180+62%	$103,200
$123,200	$143,200	$57,580+64%	$123,200
$143,200	$163,200	$70,380+66%	$143,200
$163,200	$183,200	$83,580+68%	$163,200
$183,200	$203,200	$97,180+69%	$183,200
$203,200	....	$110,980+70%	$203,200

Married Filing Separate Returns

Use this schedule if you checked **Box 3** on Form 1040—

If the amount on Schedule TC, Part I, line 3, is: / Enter on Schedule TC, Part I, line 4:

Not over $1,600............ —0—

Over—	But not over—		of the amount over—
$1,600	$2,100	14%	$1,600
$2,100	$2,600	$70+15%	$2,100
$2,600	$3,100	$145+16%	$2,600
$3,100	$3,600	$225+17%	$3,100
$3,600	$5,600	$310+19%	$3,600
$5,600	$7,600	$690+22%	$5,600
$7,600	$9,600	$1,130+25%	$7,600
$9,600	$11,600	$1,630+28%	$9,600
$11,600	$13,600	$2,190+32%	$11,600
$13,600	$15,600	$2,830+36%	$13,600
$15,600	$17,600	$3,550+39%	$15,600
$17,600	$19,600	$4,330+42%	$17,600
$19,600	$21,600	$5,170+45%	$19,600
$21,600	$23,600	$6,070+48%	$21,600
$23,600	$27,600	$7,030+50%	$23,600
$27,600	$33,600	$9,030+53%	$27,600
$33,600	$39,600	$12,210+55%	$33,600
$39,600	$45,600	$15,510+58%	$39,600
$45,600	$51,600	$18,990+60%	$45,600
$51,600	$61,600	$22,590+62%	$51,600
$61,600	$71,600	$28,790+64%	$61,600
$71,600	$81,600	$35,190+66%	$71,600
$81,600	$91,600	$41,790+68%	$81,600
$91,600	$101,600	$48,590+69%	$91,600
$101,600	....	$55,490+70%	$101,600

SCHEDULE Z—Unmarried or legally separated taxpayers Who Qualify as Heads of Household

Use this schedule if you checked **Box 4** on Form 1040—

If the amount on Schedule TC, Part I, line 3, is: / Enter on Schedule TC, Part I, line 4:

Not over $2,200............ —0—

Over—	But not over—		of the amount over—
$2,200	$3,200	14%	$2,200
$3,200	$4,200	$140+16%	$3,200
$4,200	$6,200	$300+18%	$4,200
$6,200	$8,200	$660+19%	$6,200
$8,200	$10,200	$1,040+22%	$8,200
$10,200	$12,200	$1,480+23%	$10,200
$12,200	$14,200	$1,940+25%	$12,200
$14,200	$16,200	$2,440+27%	$14,200
$16,200	$18,200	$2,980+28%	$16,200
$18,200	$20,200	$3,540+31%	$18,200
$20,200	$22,200	$4,160+32%	$20,200
$22,200	$24,200	$4,800+35%	$22,200
$24,200	$26,200	$5,500+36%	$24,200
$26,200	$28,200	$6,220+38%	$26,200
$28,200	$30,200	$6,980+41%	$28,200
$30,200	$34,200	$7,800+42%	$30,200
$34,200	$38,200	$9,480+45%	$34,200
$38,200	$40,200	$11,280+48%	$38,200
$40,200	$42,200	$12,240+51%	$40,200
$42,200	$46,200	$13,260+52%	$42,200
$46,200	$52,200	$15,340+55%	$46,200
$52,200	$54,200	$18,640+56%	$52,200
$54,200	$66,200	$19,760+58%	$54,200
$66,200	$72,200	$26,720+59%	$66,200
$72,200	$78,200	$30,260+61%	$72,200
$78,200	$82,200	$33,920+62%	$78,200
$82,200	$90,200	$36,400+63%	$82,200
$90,200	$102,200	$41,440+64%	$90,200
$102,200	$122,200	$49,120+66%	$102,200
$122,200	$142,200	$62,320+67%	$122,200
$142,200	$162,200	$75,720+68%	$142,200
$162,200	$182,200	$89,320+69%	$162,200
$182,200	....	$103,120+70%	$182,200

Fig. 32-12. A sample tax rate schedule.

itemized deduction. If certain new or used tangible personal property with a useful life of at least three years is acquired for use in a trade or business, an investment credit of 10% of the investment may be taken.

Tax payments are taxes that have already been paid such as federal income taxes withheld by employers. The same pay-as-you-go principle applies to individuals who have income that is not subject to withholding. These individuals make estimated tax payments quarterly and may deduct these payments from their tax liability. Other tax payments exist, but will not be discussed here.

Once the tax credits and payments have been deducted from the gross tax liability, tax refundable or payable is known. If the credits and payments are greater than the tax, then the government will refund the difference to the taxpayer. However, if the credits and payments are less than the tax liability, then the taxpayer must pay the difference to the government.

INCOME AVERAGING

Income averaging is a method that may permit part of an unusually large amount of taxable income (compared to the taxpayer's ordinary income) to be taxed in lower brackets. This reduces the amount of tax that must be paid. A great increase in income might be caused by a large raise in salary, a big prize, or a capital gain on the sale of stock.

Income averaging uses five tax years: the year the taxpayer elects the benefits of income averaging and the four years immediately before the tax year. To be eligible, the taxpayer must have been a citizen or resident of the US for all five years and must have furnished more than half of his or her own support for all of those years. The taxpayer's goal in using income averaging is to pay less tax.

FINANCIAL DECISIONS AND TAXES

Tax Planning

The income tax effect should be considered when making any financial decision. The overall goal, achieved by wise tax planning, is to keep taxes low. *Tax planning* is choosing ways of transacting business which result in the least amount of taxes. All firms try to plan their operations to keep taxes at a minimum.

Tax Avoidance v. Tax Evasion

Two activities are associated with efforts to reduce taxes: tax avoidance and tax evasion. A distinction must be made between these two terms. *Tax avoidance* is the use of legal means to reduce taxes. It is accomplished through careful planning and timing. In tax avoidance, the tax laws are used to the advantage of the taxpayer.

For example, a person may plan to marry on December 31 so that the new spouse can be claimed as an exemption for an entire year and the rates for married individuals may be used. A business could buy equipment in late December in order to take advantage of the 10% investment credit. Although the firm might prefer to wait until January to buy the equipment, there could be an earlier tax saving if it was purchased in December.

Tax evasion involves the use of illegal methods to reduce tax payments. Examples of tax evasion are failure to report all income, claiming nonexistent dependents, and inventing additional deductions. Keep in mind that tax avoidance is a legal activity, while tax evasion is not.

Situations in which Taxes are an Important Factor

Although the tax effect is not the only factor to consider in making business decisions, it is a major consideration in the following situations.

Choosing the Form of Business. A firm may be a sole proprietorship, partnership, or corporation. The form of business chosen directly affects the way in which income tax is paid. The income from a sole proprietorship or partnership is reported on the individual owner's tax return to be taxed at the personal tax rate. A corporation, on the other hand, is a taxable entity and must file a separate tax return. The net income of corporations is taxed at rates as high as 46%. When the remaining earnings of the corporation are distributed as dividends to the owners, they are taxed again on the stockholders' individual tax returns. Thus, the corporation's income is subject to higher tax rates and double taxation.

However, there are certain tax advantages to incorporation. On a corporate tax return, a reasonable salary paid to owners who work for the firm may be deducted to arrive at taxable income. This cannot be done in a sole proprietorship or a partnership. To determine the best form of business for tax purposes, estimate the tax liability under each form. Then choose the form that results in the least taxation.

Accounting Methods and Timing of Transactions. Often, there is more than one way to properly account for a business transaction. Taxes should be a factor when choosing the accounting method. Some areas in which the accounting method affects taxation are in the recording of depreciation and inventory. Proper timing of transactions can also lessen the tax burden. For example, careful planning may allow the taxpayer to take advantage of the capital gains and losses provisions of the tax law.

Financing Agreements. When a corporation needs funds, the firm may borrow money or sell more stock. However, these two options result in different tax situations. Interest paid on borrowed funds may be deducted in computing taxable income, but dividends are not deductible. Thus, the tax liability is decreased by borrowing money rather than by selling stock.

Example

Assume that a taxpayer, Walter Reiley, has income from wages of $7,769.36. This is reported to him at the end of the year by his

1 Control number	222	2 Employer's State number

3 Employer's name, address, and ZIP code	4 Sub-total / Cor-rection / Void ☐ ☐ ☐	5 Yes Jan–Mar No ☐ ☐	6 Yes Apr–Jun No ☐ ☐
ABC COMPANY RIDGEWOOD AVENUE RIDGEWOOD, NJ 07451	7 Employer's identification number	8 Yes Jul–Sep No ☐ ☐	9 Yes Oct–Dec No ☐ ☐
10 Employee's social security number 999-22-9999 / 11 Federal income tax withheld	12 Wages, tips, other compensation 7,769.36	13 FICA tax withheld 404.00	14 Total FICA wages 7,769.36
15 Employee's name (first, middle, last) WALTER REILEY	16 Pension plan coverage? Yes/No NO	17	18 FICA tips
2220 STRATFORD ROAD RIDGEWOOD, NJ 07459	20 State income tax withheld 203.86	21 State wages, tips, etc. 7,769.36	22 Name of State N.J.
19 Employee's address and ZIP code	23 Local income tax withheld 74.34	24 Local wages, tips, etc. 7,769.36	25 Name of locality N.J.
Wage and Tax Statement		**Copy B To be filed with employee's FEDERAL tax return**	

Form **W–2** **This information is being furnished to the Internal Revenue Service.** Department of the Treasury—Internal Revenue Service

Fig. 32-13. Form W-2 shows the employee's income for the year.

employer on form W-2, figure 32-13. A total of $912.24 was withheld from his wages for taxes. This is also shown on form W-2. His only other income is $730 of interest on a savings account and dividends of $520.

Walter Reiley is married and has one child. He files a joint return with his wife. The Reileys had the following deductible costs during the past year:

MEDICAL		
Health Insurance Premiums	180.00	
Doctor Bills	210.00	
Medicines	45.00	
New Glasses for Mrs. Reiley	70.00	
Total Medical		505.00
TAXES		
State Income Tax	203.86	
City Income Tax	74.34	
Property Tax	800.00	
Total Taxes		1,078.20
INTEREST		
Interest on Home		1,400.00
CONTRIBUTIONS		210.00
CASUALTY LOSS		
Car Accident – no insurance		630.00

The Reiley's adjusted gross income is calculated as follows:

Wages	$7,769.36
Interest	730.00
Dividends ($520 – $200)	320.00
Adjusted Gross Income	$8,819.36

The Reiley's itemized deductions are computed as follows:

MEDICAL			
½ of insurance premiums			90.00
Medicines	45.00		
Less: 1% of AGI	88.19		
Deductible Medicines	– 0 –		
Remaining ½ of insurance		90.00	
Doctor Bills		210.00	
Glasses		70.00	
		370.00	
Less: 3% of AGI		264.58	105.42
Total Medical Deduction			195.42
TAXES			
(Fully Deductible)			1,078.20
INTEREST			
(Fully Deductible)			1,400.00
CONTRIBUTIONS			
(Fully Deductible)			210.00
CASUALTY LOSS			
(630.00 - 100.00)			530.00
Total Itemized Deductions			3,413.62

The Reiley's tax is computed as follows:

Adjusted Gross Income		8,819.36
Itemized Deductions	3,413.62	
Less: Zero Bracket Amount	3,200.00	
Excess Itemized Deductions		213.62
Tax Table Income		8,605.74

The next step is to use the tax tables shown in figure 32-9 to determine the tax. By finding the Reiley's taxable income and reading down the column for a joint return, it is found that the tax is $375. Since this is less than they have paid in, they will receive a refund.

CORPORATE TAXATION

Corporations must pay taxes on their income. There are no such things as adjusted gross income, itemized deductions or standard deductions for a corporation. Although there are exceptions, a corporation's taxable income is often the income as computed on the income statement. This means that it is often advantageous for tax purposes to use accelerated depreciation methods and LIFO inventory valuation. There are other important areas of corporate tax planning, but they will not be dealt with in this text. A copy of the corporate tax return (form 1120, figure 32-14) is shown.

Form **1120**
Department of the Treasury
Internal Revenue Service

U.S. Corporation Income Tax Return

For calendar year 1977 or other taxable year beginning ...., 1977, ending ...., 19......
(PLEASE TYPE OR PRINT)

Check if a—	Use IRS label. Otherwise print or type.		
A Consolidated return ☐		Name	D Employer identification number
B Personal Holding Co. ☐		Number and street	E Date incorporated
C Business Code No. (See Page 8 of instructions)		City or town, State, and ZIP code	F Enter total assets from line 14, column (D), Schedule L (See specific Instructions)

IMPORTANT—Fill in all applicable lines and schedules. If the lines on the schedules are not sufficient, see instruction N. $

GROSS INCOME

	Line	
1 Gross receipts or gross sales .... **Less:** Returns and allowances	1	
2 **Less:** Cost of goods sold (Schedule A) and/or operations (attach schedule)	2	
3 Gross profit	3	
4 Dividends (Schedule C)	4	
5 Interest on obligations of the United States and U.S. instrumentalities	5	
6 Other interest	6	
7 Gross rents	7	
8 Gross royalties	8	
9 (a) Capital gain net income (attach separate Schedule D)	9(a)	
(b) Net gain or (loss) from line 9, Part II, Form 4797 (attach Form 4797)	9(b)	
10 Other income (see instructions—attach schedule)	10	
11 TOTAL income—Add lines 3 through 10	11	

DEDUCTIONS

	Line	
12 Compensation of officers (Schedule E)	12	
13 Salaries and wages (not deducted elsewhere)	13	
14 Repairs (see instructions)	14	
15 Bad debts (Schedule F if reserve method is used)	15	
16 Rents	16	
17 Taxes (attach schedule)	17	
18 Interest	18	
19 Contributions (**not over 5% of line 30 adjusted per instructions—attach schedule**)	19	
20 Amortization (attach schedule)	20	
21 Depreciation from Form 4562 (attach Form 4562) ...., less depreciation claimed in Schedule A and elsewhere on return ...., Balance ▶	21	
22 Depletion	22	
23 Advertising	23	
24 Pension, profit-sharing, etc. plans (see instructions) (enter number of plans ▶ ....)	24	
25 Employee benefit programs (see instructions)	25	
26 Other deductions (attach schedule)	26	
27 TOTAL deductions—Add lines 12 through 26	27	
28 Taxable income before net operating loss deduction and special deductions (line 11 less line 27)	28	
29 **Less:** (a) Net operating loss deduction (see instructions—attach schedule) . . 29(a)		
(b) Special deductions (Schedule I) . . 29(b)		
30 Taxable income (line 28 less line 29)	30	

TAX

	Line	
31 TOTAL TAX (Schedule J)	31	
32 **Credits:** (a) Overpayment from 1976 allowed as a credit		
(b) 1977 estimated tax payments		
(c) Less refund of 1977 estimated tax applied for on Form 4466 . ( )		
(d) Tax deposited with Form 7004 (attach copy)		
(e) Tax deposited with Form 7005 (attach copy)		
(f) Credit from regulated investment companies (attach Form 2439)		
(g) U.S. tax on special fuels, nonhighway gas and lubricating oil (attach Form 4136)		
33 TAX DUE (line 31 less line 32). See instruction G for depositary method of payment	33	
34 OVERPAYMENT (line 32 less line 31)	34	
35 Enter amount of line 34 you want: Credited to 1978 estimated tax ▶ Refunded ▶	35	

Under penalties of perjury, I declare that I have examined this return, including accompanying schedules and statements, and to the best of my knowledge and belief it is true, correct, and complete. Declaration of preparer (other than taxpayer) is based on all information of which the preparer has any knowledge.

▶ Signature of officer   Date

▶ Title

▶ Paid preparer's signature and identifying number (see instructions)

▶ Paid preparer's address (or employer's name, address and identifying number)

Fig. 32-14. The front page of form 1120, used to report corporate income tax.

SUMMARY

Taxes have a great effect on all financial situations. Thus, it is important to have a solid knowledge of tax laws. Tax planning involves making choices which minimize tax liability. A firm is justified in avoiding, but not evading, tax liability.

The owners of sole proprietorships and partnerships are taxed as individuals for their business incomes. Corporations are treated as separate entities and are taxed at higher rates. Individual income is reported on federal form 1040 and schedules A, B, C, D, and E as necessary. Tax tables and tax rate schedules help the taxpayer to compute the correct tax.

REVIEW

1. List five examples of nontaxable income.
2. What is the amount of the exemption deduction?
3. If a person were in a 20% tax bracket, what would be the tax on a $1,000 long-term capital gain?
4. How long would an investment have to be held before its sale would count as a long-term capital gain?
5. What are the four types of taxable entities?
6. A widow receives all of her income from selling candy, which she makes in her home. Her gross sales for the current taxable year were $1,250. The ingredients for the candy cost $900. Would she be required to file a tax return?
7. Answer the taxpayer who explains: "I am single, over sixty-five, and retired. I received social security checks of $1,450, and $2,000 from a pension on which there was no withholding. Do I have to file a tax return?"
8. Define gross income.
9. What is the zero bracket amount? What is the alternative to the zero bracket amount?
10. What is the difference between tax avoidance and tax evasion?
11. What is the procedure when a person is eligible for income averaging?
12. What is the limitation on medical deductions?
13. Why would a person use the standard deduction instead of itemizing deductions?

EXERCISES

1. Determine the filing status and number of exemptions in each of the following cases.
   a. John and Mary are married. Only John has an income. John is forty-five, Mary forty-four. Their fifteen-year-old son, Jim, lives with them. They provide more than half the support for John's nephew, Jack, who also lives with them and earned $450 in the last year.

b. Juan's wife died in 1974 when he was forty-two. He maintains a household for his twenty-one-year-old daughter, Bonita, who is a full-time student and lives at home. She had a gross income of $800 from a summer job. He contributes more than half her support.

c. In 1974, after obtaining a divorce, Marge's sixty-five-year-old husband died. She remarried on December 31, 1975, her sixty-first birthday. Her new husband, age sixty-two, had 1975 income of $10,000. Her only 1975 income was $20,000 from a life insurance policy. She has a blind twenty-three-year-old son, Mike, not a student, who lives at home and earned $7,200 in 1975.

2. Manny and Anna Goldstein paid the following medical expenses:

Medicine and drugs	$125.00
Hospital bills	750.00
Doctor bills	
Dr. North	250.00
Dr. Green	50.00
Hospitalization insurance	103.20
Supplementary hospitalization insurance under medicare	34.80
Doctor bills for Anna's dependent mother (Dr. May)	290.00
Medicine and drugs for dependent mother	125.00
Reimbursement from insurance	770.65

Manny and Anna's adjusted gross income for the year is $16,000. Determine the allowable medical expense deduction.

3. Frank and Nan Denelli are married and have two children under eighteen years of age. Their adjusted gross income is $10,875. They are filing a joint return and had the following medical expenses:

Doctors for husband	$1,000
Doctors for wife	500
Doctors for children	500
Medicine and drugs for husband	200
Medicine and drugs for wife	200
Medicine and drugs for children	100
Nurses for wife	500
Medical insurance	350
Taxi fare to and from doctors	60

Assume that Mr. Denelli was reimbursed from the insurance company for his doctor bill.
Determine the allowable medical expense deduction.

4. Martha Benson, age sixty-eight, has adjusted gross income of $19,000 for the year and had the following medical expenses:

Medical and hospital insurance	$ 90
Accident insurance	55
Medicare insurance (supplementary)	48
Medicine and drugs	290
Insulin	65
Dr. Tom, M.D.	800
St. John's Hospital	2,000
Dr. Sigel (Chiropractor)	30
Special shoes prescribed by Dr. Sigel	90

She further stated that her insurance company reimbursed her $1,900 on the hospital bill and $700 on the doctor bills. Determine the allowable medical expense deduction.

5. Alan Waxer has a personal residence and paid mortgage interest of $460 for the year. He also paid $65 interest on a loan he obtained from National City Bank. He requested and received notice that finance charges paid for the year on his charge account were $18.
Determine the allowable interest expense deduction for the year.

6. Give the number of personal exemptions that can be claimed in the following situations:
   a. Husband and wife are filing a joint return. Both are under age sixty-five and have good eyesight. How many personal exemptions may they claim on their joint return?
   b. Husband and wife are filing separate returns. Both had gross income, are under age sixty-five, and have good eyesight. How many personal exemptions may the husband claim on his return?
   c. Husband and wife are filing a joint return. The husband is sixty-eight and blind. The wife is sixty-four and has good eyesight. How many personal exemptions may they claim?
   d. Husband and wife are not filing a joint return. The husband is 67 and has good eyesight. The wife is 62, has good eyesight, had no gross income, and is not the dependent of another taxpayer. How many personal exemptions may the husband claim on his separate return?

7. A taxpayer states: "I don't know much about taxes. I've written down all the money I received in 1975. Could you tell me if I have to file a return?" The taxpayer's list contains the following information:

   $2,200 – Alimony received February through December
   $475 – Five weeks' salary for a job beginning in late November
   a. What is taxpayer's gross income?
   b. Does the taxpayer have to file an income tax return?

PROBLEMS

1. Tom Bradley, who is single, age thirty-two, earned $9,769.36 from the ABC Company. Tom had interest income from his savings account of $10.86 and received dividends of $27.00 from GN, Ltd. He supplied his accountant with the following information:

   Medical insurance premiums totaled $195.
   Total paid drug bills were $286.

   Mr. Bradley incurred the following medical expenses:

Dr. William – Surgeon	$390.00
Dr. James – Surgeon	$450.00
Dr. George – G.P.	$90.00
St. John's Hospital	$1,285.00
Mountainview Hospital	$720.00

   Tom Bradley also had the following expenses:

Property taxes	$108.00
Contributions	$200.00
Union Dues	$48.00
Casualty Loss	$110.00

   a. Calculate Tom Bradley's adjusted gross income.
   b. Calculate his medical deduction.
   c. Calculate Tom's itemized deductions.

2. Sherry Ho, a widow, age sixty-three, has no earned income from wages. She lives alone and has no dependents. She furnished the accountant with the following information.

   She received the following income:

Social Security	$1,780
Dividends from the following:	
ABC Company	$ 380
United, Inc.	400
City Gas Company	400
XYZ Ltd.	600
Interest from the following:	
First National Bank	$1,200
County Bank	1,300
Federal Savings & Loan	1,500

   There were no adjustments to income.

   She paid $25 for medical insurance.
   She paid the following medical bills:

Drugs	$483
Dr. George	345
Dr. Stevens	580
Dr. Joseph	690
Lab fees	85
X-rays	125
Mt. Hope Hospital	330

Ms. Ho received $1,380 medical insurance reimbursement for her doctor bills. She made payments for her estimated state tax of $284. She donated money to the following:

YMCA $75
Girl Scouts $100
National College of Arts $280
Miscellaneous charities $115

She also donated clothes to the Salvation Army which cost her $800, but were worth $125 when she made the gift. She had one passbook loan during the year, which was repaid with $12 in interest. Her car was damaged in June. She paid $780 for repairs and her insurance reimbursed her $690. A diamond ring was stolen in August. Its value was $1,500. Her insurance reimbursed her $1,415. She had no other deductions.

a. Calculate Ms. Ho's adjusted gross income.
b. Calculate her total itemized deductions.
c. Should she itemize her deductions for this year?

3. Use the following data to calculate the total itemized deductions for James and Phyllis Farr. Their AGI was $19,000.

MEDICAL AND DENTAL EXPENSES:	
Medical insurance premiums	$ 312
Prescription drugs	88
Other drugs	36
Dr. Jones – James' broken wrist	187
Dentist	150
Dr. Brown – pediatrician	225
Orthopedic shoes and braces for dependent son	315
Medical insurance reimbursement for doctor bills	418
Veterinarian fees	30
TAXES:	
State income tax withheld	$ 714
Real estate tax	526
County personal property tax	12
Sales tax	116
INTEREST:	
Home mortgage	$1,857
Car loan	121
Charge accounts	47
CONTRIBUTIONS:	
Religious Organization – $5 a week	
United Givers' Fund	$ 25
March of Dimes	10
Salvation Army	2
(All of the preceding items substantiated by checks, receipts, etc.)	
Value of three boxes of used clothing, household goods, etc., given to neighbors whose house burned	45
Value of used refrigerator given to synagogue	20

MISCELLANEOUS DEDUCTIONS:

Union dues	$ 52
Fees for Phyllis' adult education course in Chinese cooking	35
Babysitter	45
Safety workshoes	35
Dog license	5
Transportation to and from work	250
Life insurance premiums	225

4. Paul and Mary Kobi are married filing a joint return. They are both forty-six years of age.

   Gross wages – $16,000
   Federal income tax withheld – $1,450.42
   FICA withheld – $772.20
   State income tax withheld – $464.00

   They have three children, Hank, Helen, and Heidi. They present the following records for the past year.

   $480 – Premiums for hospital insurance
   220 – Medicine and drugs
   80 – Eyeglasses for daughter (Helen)
   240 – Hospital bill for son's broken arm
   60 – Reimbursement from hospital insurance
   99 – Doctor bill
   59 – Reimbursement from insurance on doctor bill
   211 – Real estate taxes on personal residence
   61 – Personal property taxes
   22 – Cost of auto tags
   1,200 – First Church of Wisconsin
   25 – American Red Cross
   300 – United Fund Campaign
   120 – Men's Golf Club dues
   120 – YMCA Family Health Club dues
   820 – Interest on home mortgage
   120 – Interest on personal loan at First National Bank
   106 – Finance charge on credit card
   160 – School lunches for children
   16 – Safe deposit box rental to keep birth certificates and old family photographs
   12 – Fee to veterinarian for rabies shot for puppy

---

a. Calculate the Kobi's adjusted gross income.
b. Calculate the total itemized deductions.

5. George Black, a widower, has adjusted gross income of $13,200. Determine his total itemized deductions.

MEDICAL AND DENTAL EXPENSES:	
Medical insurance premiums	$ 270
Medicine and drugs	86
Dr. Green – pediatrician	212
Dr. Alphonse – physical check-up	106
Dentist	616
Insurance reimbursement	182
TAXES:	
Real estate tax	$ 367
State sales tax	110
State income tax	324
INTEREST:	
Home mortgage	$1,247
Car loan	62
CONTRIBUTIONS:	
Church (paid by check)	$ 30
Miscellaneous charities (Red Cross, $2; Girl Scouts, $3; Campfire Girls, $4; and American Cancer Society, $16.)	25
CASUALTY LOSS:	
George had a fire in his store room. The damage to the room was repaired for $1,200. Three suitcases worth $140 were destroyed along with $400 worth of clothing that was stored in the room. His insurance reimbursement was $1,300.	
MISCELLANEOUS DEDUCTIONS:	
Union Dues	$ 72

33
Budgeting

OBJECTIVES

After studying this chapter, the student will be able to:

- State the main reason for preparing a budget and list the four ways in which it can be used.
- Identify and explain the two major types of budgets.
- Define a master budget.
- Prepare a master budget and its components.
- List the order in which individual sections of a budget are prepared.
- Prepare a flexible budget.

SETTING FINANCIAL GOALS

Control of costs is a major part of the manager's job in a large firm. The best way to control costs is to know how much the firm should be spending. Thus, most large firms determine ahead of time how much will be spent in a specific period. This means setting goals for the firm's operation in the future. When goals are put in monetary terms, they are called *budgets.*

All large firms use budgets, and all small firms should use them. Large firms have a budgeting staff that works all year on budgets. In small firms, the chief accountant works out the budgets. Without a budget, a firm cannot determine its financial success. The main reason for preparing a budget is to maximize the net income of the firm. This can be done by keeping costs low. A budget is actually four tools in one. It can be used as an aid in planning, controlling, motivating, and communicating.

The Budget as a Planning Tool

A budget is a written plan for the future. The managers of firms which use budgets are forced to plan ahead. Thus, these firms tend to do well because they anticipate problems before they occur. A firm without financial goals may find it difficult to make wise decisions. A firm with specific goals in the form of a budget makes many decisions ahead of time. Hence, there is no need to make quick decisions which may not be in the best interest of the firm.

The Budget as a Control Tool

A budget helps a firm to control its costs by setting guidelines for spending. Managers and foremen are discouraged from spending money for unneeded items because they know that all costs will be compared to the budget. If costs exceed the budgeted costs, an explanation will be required. Frequently exceeding the budget may even be grounds for dismissal.

The Budget as a Motivation Tool

A budget helps to motivate employees to do a good job. This is particularly true when employees help in setting up the budget. For example, if a foreman is asked to prepare a budget for his or her department for next year, that foreman will work hard to keep costs as low as possible. Many firms reward employees who are able to keep department costs below the budgeted amounts.

The Budget as a Communications Tool

In many firms, the employees are unaware of the firm's goals. A firm can use the budget to tell employees about its goals. When all employees know the firm's goals, they can work together to accomplish them.

Without a budget, employees in various departments may see different goals for the firm. For example, the sales department may want to keep as much inventory on hand as possible so that no sales will be lost. The accounting manager, on the other hand, may desire to keep the inventory as low as possible. His goal is to avoid spending cash sooner than necessary. If the firm has a budget that specifies how much inventory should be kept, this conflict is avoided, and everyone works toward the same goal.

The communications aspect of a budget is very important. For a successful operation, all of the departments in a firm must work well together. In fact, some departments cannot begin to set up their budgets until other departments have completed theirs. For example, the purchasing agent cannot do a purchases budget until after the sales department has finished the sales budget.

PREPARING A BUDGET FOR A MERCHANDISING FIRM

The complete budget for a firm is often called the *master budget.* The master budget consists of many smaller budgets. These small budgets include a sales budget, a purchases budget, expense budgets, equipment purchases budget and a cash budget. Once all of these budgets are completed, the master budget for the entire firm is prepared.

The master budget includes an income statement and a balance sheet. A firm uses the budgeted income statement to decide whether the budget results in a high enough income. If the budgeted income statement shows a very low income or a loss, the entire budgeting process begins again. The budget is reworked until a desired net income

Lark Company
Sales Budget
For Quarter Ended March 31, 19–

Sales:	Jan.		Feb.		Mar.		Total for Quarter	
	Units	$	Units	$	Units	$	Units	$
Product A	100	1,000	150	1,500	200	2,000	450	4,500
Product B	200	4,000	230	4,600	260	5,200	690	13,800
		5,000		6,100		7,200		18,300

Fig. 33-1. Sales budget.

is shown on the budgeted income statement. The firm then strives to meet the budget and earn the income shown.

Sales Budget

The sales budget is the first budget to be prepared. It is an estimate of the goods that will be sold. Once a firm has some idea of what its sales will be, it can then decide how much to purchase. Sales are usually budgeted by product or by department. Thus, all sales personnel know what products must be sold in large quantities. Sales are usually budgeted on a monthly basis as well as a yearly basis. A sales budget for the Lark Company is shown in figure 33-1.

Purchases Budget

Once a firm has estimated its sales, a purchases budget can be prepared. A purchases budget is prepared on a monthly basis. Some firms even prepare it on a weekly basis. The function of the purchases budget is to plan purchases so that the firm will never run out of inventory. At the same time, however, the firm wants to keep its inventory as low as possible because inventory costs money. Not only does the firm have to pay for the additional inventory, but there are also storage costs, higher insurance costs, and greater risks of spoilage. Thus, the goal of the purchases budget is to keep inventory as low as possible without losing sales.

When planning for inventory, a firm must also consider the quantity discounts given by suppliers. These discounts may make it profitable for a firm to buy in larger quantities. Most firms also like to keep a safety stock on hand. A *safety stock* is inventory that is kept on hand in excess of planned sales. It is used if the planned sales are greater than budgeted. Safety stock is also a safeguard in case of delays in receiving shipments. For example, a firm expects to receive delivery of merchandise on a certain day. However, there is a truck strike on that day, and the goods are not delivered. Without safety stock, the firm might run out of inventory in this situation.

Lark Company
Purchases Budget
For Quarter Ended March 31, 19—

	Jan.				Feb.				Mar.				Total for Quarter			
	A		B		A		B		A		B		A		B	
	Units	$	Units	$	Units	$	Units	$	Units	$	Units	$	Units	$	Units	$
Expected Sales — A	100	750			150	1,125			200	1,500			450	3,375		
Expected Sales — B			200	2,400			230	2,760			260	3,120			690	8,280
Desired Ending Inventory — A	160	1,200			210	1,575			220	1,650			220	1,650		
Desired Ending Inventory — B			240	2,880			270	3,240			280	3,360			280	3,360
Total Goods Needed by Month End — A	260	1,950			360	2,700			420	3,150			670	5,025		
Total Goods Needed by Month End — B			440	5,280			500	6,000			540	6,480			970	11,640
Beginning Inventory — A	110	825			160	1,200			210	1,575			110	825		
Beginning Inventory — B			210	2,520			240	2,880			270	3,240			210	2,520
Required Purchases — A	150	1,125			200	1,500			210	1,575			560	4,200		
Required Purchases — B			230	2,760			260	3,120			270	3,240			760	9,120

Fig. 33-2. Purchases budget.

Lark Company
Expense Budget
For Quarter Ended March 31, 19–

	Jan.	Feb.	Mar.	Total
Depreciation Expense (fixed)	100	100	100	300
Sales Salaries Expense (10% of Sales)	500	610	720	1,830
Supplies Expense (5% of Sales)	250	305	360	915
Administrative Salaries	800	800	800	2,400
Advertising Expense	25	25	25	75
TOTAL EXPENSES	1,675	1,840	2,005	5,520

Fig. 33-3. Expense budget.

A purchases budget for the Lark Company is shown in figure 33-2. The budget assumes that the Lark Company wants to begin each month with enough inventory to cover that month's sales, plus have a safety stock of ten units of each item (products A and B).

Expense Budgets

Once the sales budget is finished, it is given to all department heads. The department heads use the sales budget as a basis for preparing departmental expense budgets. The expense budgets are based on prior years' costs and adjusted by price changes, wage changes, and changes in sales estimates. The Lark Company has only one expense budget and it is shown in figure 33-3.

Equipment Purchases Budget

Since fixed assets are often quite costly, firms like to plan their equipment purchases in advance. The firm must know well ahead of time when cash will be needed for large purchases. The equipment purchases budget cannot be prepared until after the sales, purchases, and expense budgets are completed. This is because the firm will not know how much equipment is needed until after the activity levels are known. An equipment purchases budget for the Lark Company is shown in figure 33-4. This budget is sometimes called a capital expenditures budget. Some firms try to prepare it much more than a year ahead of time. This is necessary because some specialized types of equipment and buildings must be ordered more than a year in advance.

Lark Company
Equipment Purchases Budget
For Quarter Ended March 31, 19–

	Jan.	Feb.	Mar.	Total
New Typewriter for Office		120		120
TOTAL	0	120	0	120

Fig. 33-4. Equipment purchases budget.

Cash Budget

The cash budget is prepared after all of the other budgets have been completed. The cash budget is probably the most important part of a firm's budget program. Without proper planning, a company could find itself with inadequate cash resources. If a firm knows of a cash need far enough in advance, it can arrange for a bank loan if necessary. A bank is much more likely to lend money to a firm which does not need the money until a later time. This advance notice gives the bank time to have the necessary cash available for the firm.

All firms must prepare cash budgets at some time. Small firms may not prepare budgets on a regular basis. However, a cash budget is usually required to obtain a bank loan. The bank usually asks the firm to submit a cash budget that shows how the firm plans to pay back the loan. The cash budget for the Lark Company is shown in figure 33-5. Notice how the figures in this budget relate to the other budgets. Study the notes at the bottom of figure 33-5 that explain how the amounts are computed.

Lark Company
Cash Budget
For Quarter Ended March 31, 19—

	January	February	March
Beginning Cash Balance	50	225	30
Receipts:			
Collection from Sales*	4,900	5,550	6,650
TOTAL CASH AVAILABLE	4,950	5,775	6,680
Payments:			
Purchases**	3,150	3,885	4,620
Sales Salaries	500	610	720
Supplies	250	305	360
Administrative Salaries	800	800	800
Advertising	25	25	25
Equipment Purchases		120	
TOTAL PAYMENTS	4,725	5,745	6,525
ENDING BALANCE	225	30	155

*NOTE: Sales are ½ cash sales and ½ on credit (net 30 days). Thus, ½ of each month's sales are collected in the month of the sale and ½ are collected the following month. For example, the February collections ($5,550) were calculated as follows:

½ of January Sales	$2,500
½ of February Sales	3,050
	$5,550

**NOTE: Purchases are on terms of net 30 days. Thus, purchases are paid for in the month following the purchase. The amount paid in February ($3,885) was for the total purchases for January.

Fig. 33-5. Cash budget.

Lark Company Pro forma Income Statement For Quarter Ended March 31, 19–	Jan.	Feb.	Mar.	Total
Sales	$5,000	$6,100	$7,200	$18,300
Cost of Goods Sold:				
Beginning Inventory	3,345	4,080	4,815	3,345
Add: Purchases	3,885	4,620	4,815	13,320
Goods Available	7,230	8,700	9,630	16,665
Less: Ending Inventory	4,080	4,815	5,010	5,010
Cost of Goods Sold	3,150	3,885	4,620	11,655
Gross Profit	1,850	2,215	2,580	6,645
Operating Expenses:				
Depreciation	100	100	100	300
Sales Salaries	500	610	720	1,830
Supplies	250	305	360	915
Administrative Salaries	800	800	800	2,400
Advertising	25	25	25	75
Total Expenses	1,675	1,840	2,005	5,520
Net Income	$ 175	$ 375	$ 575	$ 1,125

Fig. 33-6. Pro forma income statement.

Preparing Budgeted Financial Statements

Once all of the budgets are complete, budgeted financial statements can be prepared. These are sometimes called *pro forma statements.* This is because they are prepared before the expected financial events occur. The pro forma income statement for the Lark Company is shown in figure 33-6. Note that it is based on the figures developed in the previously discussed budgets.

When the pro forma financial statements are completed, management must decide if they are a realistic plan for the firm. If a higher income is desired, the budgeting process must begin all over again. Thus, a firm must start preparing its budget as far in advance as possible in case it becomes necessary to make revisions on the initial plan. Most large firms begin preparing budgets for the next calendar year in September.

The entire sequence of the budgeting process is shown in figure 33-7.

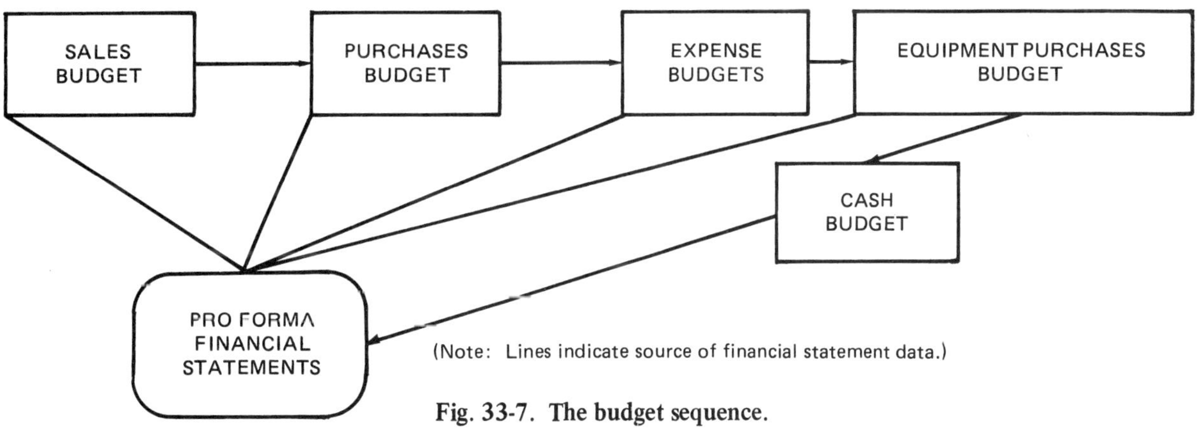

Fig. 33-7. The budget sequence.

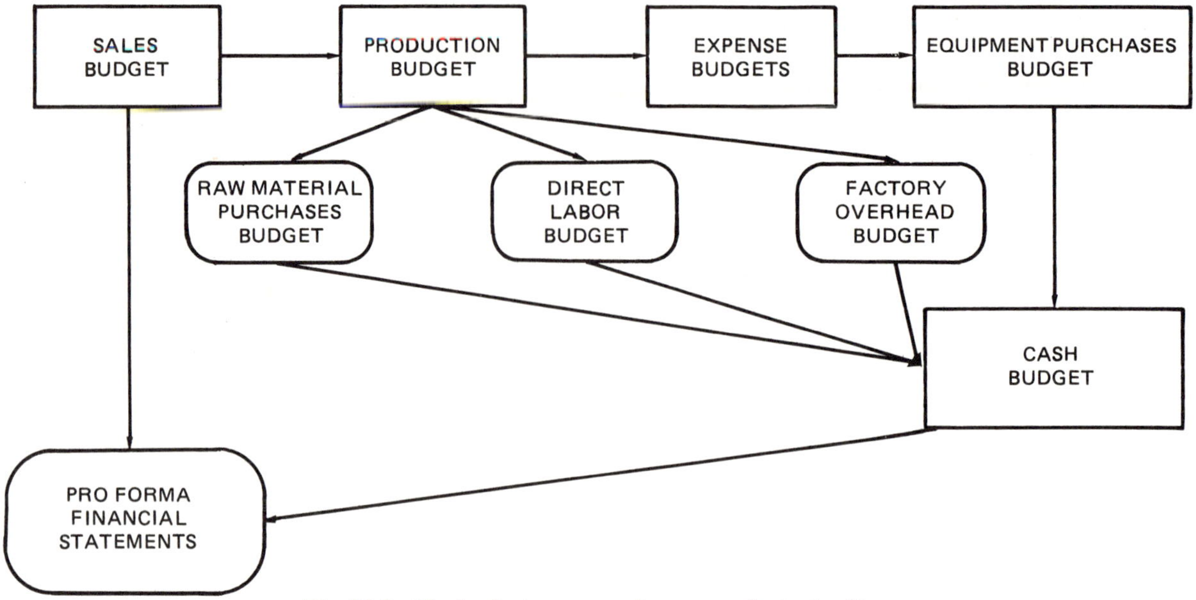

Fig. 33-8. The budget sequence for a manufacturing firm.

BUDGETING FOR A MANUFACTURING FIRM

The budget for a manufacturing firm is slightly more complicated than the budget of a merchandising firm. An extra step is involved in a manufacturing budget. Instead of going directly from the sales budget to the purchases budget, manufacturing firms must first prepare a production budget. The production budget shows the firm's plan for producing goods. It is stated in units per a specific period rather than in dollars.

The completed production budget is used to prepare three other budgets. These additional budgets are the raw materials purchases budget, the direct labor budget, and the factory overhead budget. The raw materials purchases budget resembles the purchases budget of a merchandising firm. The factory overhead budget is similar to an expense budget. Figure 33-8 shows the budget sequence for a manufacturing firm.

FLEXIBLE BUDGETS

Thus far, only fixed budgets (or static budgets) have been discussed. A *fixed budget* is based on only one level of sales. A fixed budget loses its usefulness if the expected level of sales is not reached.

For example, assume that a firm budgets sales at $5,000 and supplies expense at $250. What can be said about the efficiency of management if supplies expense is only $240, and sales are only $4,600? This question cannot be answered because the firm does not have a budget for a $4,600 level of sales. This is where a flexible budget is helpful. A flexible budget is useful when the expected sales levels are not met exactly (which, in reality, is most of the time).

A flexible budget is actually a series of budgets that are prepared by a firm. It is a combination of fixed budgets for many levels of sales. Figure 33-9 shows a fixed factory overhead budget for a department, assuming that 8,000 units of a product are produced during the month.

Production in Units	8,000
Factory Rent	$ 2,000
Depreciation of Machinery	4,000
Supervision	2,000
Total Fixed Costs	8,000
Indirect Labor	2,000
Supplies Used	4,000
Electricity	2,000
Total Variable Costs	8,000
TOTAL BUDGETED OVERHEAD	$16,000

Fig. 33-9. A fixed budget.

The main problem with this fixed budget is that usually, the expected production level is not met exactly. For example, the budget in figure 33-9 assumes that production will be 8,000 units and total costs $16,000. How efficient has the firm been if the total factory overhead was only $9,000, but only 1,000 units of production were manufactured? Obviously, a fixed budget is not very useful in this situation. What is needed is a budget for every possible level of production. This is accomplished by preparing a flexible budget. Figure 33-10 shows a flexible budget for the same department.

When using a flexible budget, the firm can compare actual costs to the appropriate column in the budget at the end of the month. If the actual production level for the month is some level for which there is no column, then a new column can be quickly made by means of interpolation or extrapolation. For example, using the budget shown in figure 33-10, it can be found that the budgeted factory overhead at a production level of 7,000 units would be $15,000. This is calculated as follows: since 7,000 units is one-half the distance between 6,000 and 8,000 units, then the cost for 7,000 units should be one-half the distance between $14,000 and $16,000.

BUDGET REPORTS

Follow-up reports of budgets are very important. A budget serves no purpose if it is prepared and then forgotten. For good control, the

Production in Units	6,000	8,000	10,000
Factory Rent	$ 2,000	$ 2,000	$ 2,000
Depreciation of Machinery	4,000	4,000	4,000
Supervision	2,000	2,000	2,000
Total Fixed Costs	8,000	8,000	8,000
Indirect Labor	1,500	2,000	2,500
Supplies Used	3,000	4,000	5,000
Electricity	1,500	2,000	2,500
Total Variable Costs	6,000	8,000	10,000
TOTAL BUDGETED OVERHEAD	$14,000	$16,000	$18,000

Fig. 33-10. A flexible budget.

FACTORY OVERHEAD COSTS ACTUAL PRODUCTION LEVEL – 7,000 UNITS	Budget	Actual	Variance	
Factory Rent	$ 2,000	$ 2,000	– 0 –	
Depreciation of Machinery	4,000	4,000	– 0 –	
Supervision	2,000	2,100	100	Unfavorable
Total Fixed Costs	8,000	8,100	100	Unfavorable
Indirect Labor	1,750	1,725	25	Favorable
Materials & Supplies	3,500	3,400	100	Favorable
Electricity	1,750	1,760	10	Unfavorable
Total Variable Costs	7,000	6,885	115	Favorable
TOTAL OVERHEAD	$15,000	$14,985	15	Favorable

Fig. 33-11. A budget report based upon production of 7,000 units.

firm must regularly compare the budgeted costs to the actual costs incurred. This is done by means of a budget report. A budget report consists of a column for budgeted costs, a column for the actual costs incurred, and a difference column. The difference column is sometimes called a *variance column.* A *variance* is defined as the difference between the budgeted costs and the actual costs. If the actual costs are higher than the budgeted costs, then the difference is called an *unfavorable variance.* If the actual costs are less than the budget, then the difference is called a *favorable variance.* Figure 33-11 shows a budget report based on the flexible budget shown in figure 33-10. The report assumes that actual production was 7,000 units.

The department supervisor uses the budget report to discover what caused the unfavorable variances. The reasons may be easy to find. For example, the unfavorable variance in supervision may be the result of the supervisors receiving a raise since the budget was prepared. Other variances may be harder to explain. For instance, the unfavorable electricity variance may be caused by higher utility rates, or extra cold weather, or a window left open at night. Whatever the causes of the variances, it is the supervisor's job to discover them.

SUMMARY

A firm's budget is its plan for the future. It sets the financial goals of the firm. It is one of the strongest tools possessed by management. The budget serves four purposes. It is used in planning, controlling, motivating, and communicating.

The complete budget for a firm is called the master budget. The master budget of a firm is made up of many small budgets. The sales budget is prepared first. It must be ready several months prior to the period for which it is to be used. The purchases budget or the production budget is prepared based on the sales budget. Next, expense budgets are prepared for each department of the firm. The last few steps of the budget preparation process include a cash budget and pro forma financial statements.

A budget should be followed up at the end of each month for control purposes. This is done by comparing budgeted costs with actual costs on a budget report.

REVIEW

1. Why do firms use a budget system?
2. Describe how a budget is used as a planning tool.
3. Explain how a budget can be used as a motivation tool.
4. Explain how a budget is used as a control tool.
5. Explain how a budget is used as a communications tool.
6. Why must the sales budget be prepared first?
7. Under what circumstances might a firm want to prepare its production budget first?
8. Why is a budget report prepared?
9. What is a budget variance?
10. What is an unfavorable variance?
11. What is a favorable variance?
12. Describe a fixed budget.
13. What is a flexible budget?

EXERCISES

1. The Trek Company sells widgets at a price of $3 per unit and fidgets at $4 per unit. During last January and February Trek sold 1,000 widgets each month. Trek sold 1,500 fidgets last January and 1,600 in February. Sales are expected to be 10% higher next year. Prepare a sales budget for January and February of next year.
2. Using the data from exercise 1, prepare a purchases budget for January and February. The firm likes to begin each month with enough inventory to cover that month's sales plus have a safety stock equal to 25% of the month's sales. The sales for March are budgeted at 800 widgets and 1,400 fidgets.

PROBLEMS

1. The Mesa Corporation has prepared the following flexible budget for the month of January.

Mesa Corporation
Expense Budget
For Month of January

Sales	$10,000	$12,000	$14,000
Sales Salaries	1,500	1,700	1,900
Officers Salaries	2,000	2,000	2,000
Rent Expense	400	400	400
Supplies Expense	200	220	240
Depreciation Expense	300	300	300
	$ 4,400	$ 4,620	$ 4,840

Actual sales were $10,500. Actual costs were:

Sales Salaries	$1,600
Officers Salaries	2,000
Rent Expense	400
Supplies Expense	170
Depreciation Expense	300
	$4,470

a. Prepare a budget report for the month. Be sure to state whether variances are favorable or unfavorable.

b. Assume that actual sales were only $9,000 for the month and actual costs were the same as those listed above ($4,470). Prepare a budget report for the $9,000 sales level.

2. New Farm Supply is forecasting its cash balance for June through August to determine whether it needs to borrow. Sales are expected to be $16,000 in April; $25,000 in May; $20,000 in June; $28,000 in July; and $20,000 in August. The firm wants to maintain a $5,000 minimum cash balance at the bank. At the beginning of June, New Farm has $2,000 on deposit at the bank. Seventy percent of the sales proceeds are collected in the month following sales, the remainder during the following month. Salaries are on a commission basis, representing 20% of sales, and are paid in the same month in which the sales are made. New Farm acquires its products in the month preceding the sales and pays for them in the same month that it sells the goods. The products cost 70% of the subsequent sales price. Prepare a cash budget for June, July, and August.

3. Juno Company has budgeted sales at $10,000 in January; $15,000 in February; $30,000 in both March and April; and $10,000 in May. The firm wants to have a $4,000 minimum cash balance. The firm has a $6,000 beginning cash balance. All sales revenue is collected in the month after sales are made. Wages and purchases of merchandise are paid for in the month preceding a given month's sales. Merchandise purchases and wages are 90% of the subsequent month's sales. Prepare a cash budget covering the four months, beginning in January. Assume that collections in January are $16,000. Show necessary loans and repayments. (Note: For this problem, ignore interest expense.)

4. Tamek Company has forecast next year's total sales. Thirty percent of sales are paid for during the month the goods are sold, the remaining 70% within the second month. Purchases are equal to 80% of sales. Purchases are made during the month preceding the sales. Cash should not fall below $3,000. If cash does fall below $3,000, assume that the firm borrows from the bank in the amount necessary to bring cash up to $3,000.

Prepare a cash budget for the months of February, March, April, and May based on the information given and the sales forecasted below.

January	$10,000	April	$24,000
February	8,000	May	9,000
March	22,000	June	6,000

Beginning cash balance for February is $7,000.
Other payments:

Wages		Taxes	
February	$ 800	March	$2,000
March	1,500		
April	1,500		
May	850		

5. State Company is planning to request a loan from its bank. The following sales forecast has been made for next year.

May	$ 60,000
June	60,000
July	120,000
August	180,000
September	240,000
October	120,000
November	120,000

Collection estimates are as follows: cash sales, 5%; collected the month following the sale, 80%; collected the second month following the sale, 15%. Payments for labor and raw materials are typically made during the month following the month in which these costs are incurred. Total labor and raw materials costs are estimated for each month as follows (payments are made the following month):

May	$ 30,000
June	30,000
July	42,000
August	294,000
September	102,000
October	78,000
November	54,000

General and administrative salaries are approximately $9,000 a month; lease payments under long-term lease contracts are $3,000 a month; depreciation charges are $19,000 per month; miscellaneous expenses will be $900 a month; income tax payments of $21,000 will be due in both September and December; and a payment of $60,000 on a new building must be paid in October. Cash on hand on July 1 will be $45,000, and a minimum cash balance of $30,000 should be maintained throughout the cash budget period.

Prepare a cash budget for July, August, September, and October. Show the necessary loans and repayments.

6. a. Using the following information, prepare a cash budget for Lisa stores for the period July 1 through September 30.

   (1) All sales are on credit. Payment for 10% of the sales is received during the month in which the sales are made; 60% in the month following; and 30% in the second month following.

   (2) Purchases during each month equal 75% of the following month's sales. Payment for purchases is made in the month following the purchase.

   (3) Inventory equals a base stock of $8,000 plus purchases for the following month.

   (4) The firm's minimum level of cash is $5,000. Cash is $6,000 as of July 1.

   (5) The gross profit margin is 25%.

   (6) Sales data and wages are as follows:

	Sales	Wages
May	$20,000	$2,000
June	20,000	2,000
July	30,000	2,500
August	50,000	3,000
September	50,000	3,000
October	60,000	3,500
November	30,000	3,000

   (7) Rent is $500 per month, depreciation is $400 per month, and other cash expenses are 2% of sales.

   b. What does the cash budget indicate?

7. Fine Products, Inc. is in the process of preparing its cash budget and purchases budget for the months of January, February, and March. The following information is available:

   (1) Ten percent of all sales are made on a cash basis.

   (2) Fifty percent of all credit sales are normally collected within ten days since the company offers its customers the opportunity to take a discount of 2% if they are paid within ten days.

   (3) The remaining 50% of credit sales are collected in the month following the sale and are not entitled to a discount.

   (4) The sales for each month occur fairly evenly throughout the month. For convenience, assume that all months have thirty days.

   (5) Estimated sales figures for the various months are as follows:

November	$100,000	February	90,000
December	100,000	March	120,000
January	80,000	April	120,000

(6) Inventories should always be equal to 25% of the following month's estimated sales.

(7) All purchases of inventory are paid for on the basis of terms of *net 30*.

(8) The company sells its product at a price of $10 per unit. The product is purchased at a price of $6 per unit.

(9) Salaries and wages amount to $5,000 per month plus 10% of sales.

(10) Rent and other fixed expenditures amount to $3,000 per month.

(11) Fine Products, Inc. expects to have a cash balance of $1,000 on January 1.

(12) All salaries, wages, rent, and other fixed expenditures are paid in the same month in which the costs are incurred.

(13) If the company experiences a cash shortage problem, it can borrow the necessary funds from National Bank for forty-five days at an interest rate of 12% per annum. All loans are in multiples of $1,000.

(14) The company feels that it must always maintain a balance of at least $1,000 in its cash account.

(15) The only equipment owned by the firm is the selling racks, displays and shelving. Depreciation is computed on a units-of-output basis at the rate of $1 per unit of sales.

---

a. Based on the above information, prepare a purchases budget for the months of January, February, and March. Assume that the January 1 beginning inventory is of the proper size.

b. Prepare a cash budget for the months of January, February, and March.

c. What conclusions should the management of Fine Products arrive at after seeing the cash budget?

34
Determining the Need for a Financial Audit

OBJECTIVES After studying this chapter, the student will be able to:

- Explain the purpose of an audit and describe the auditing process.
- Give the reasons for an annual financial audit.
- Explain the advantages of an audit.
- List and describe the twelve basic accounting principles.
- Explain the need for generally accepted accounting principles.

Many firms, both large and small, schedule annual financial audits. An *audit* is a check or review of the accounting records to determine that the records are accurate. In an annual audit, a CPA checks the firm's accounts at the end of each year to determine if the financial statements are correct. Upon completion of the audit, an audit report is issued. A typical audit report for a firm whose statements are found to be correct reads as follows:

> To the Stockholders
> FSR Industries, Inc.
>
> We have examined the balance sheet of FSR Industries, Inc. as of December 31, 1980, and the related statements of income and retained earnings and changes in financial position for the year then ended. Our examination was made in accordance with generally accepted auditing standards and accordingly included such tests of the accounting records and such other auditing procedures as we considered necessary in the circumstances.
>
> In our opinion, the financial statements referred to above present fairly the financial position of FSR Industries, Inc. as of December 31, 1980, and the results of its operations and the changes in its financial position for the year then ended, in conformity with generally accepted accounting principles applied on a basis consistent with that of the preceding year.

The language of this report has been standardized. The same basic form is almost always used. When outsiders, such as bankers or creditors, read this audit report, it increases their trust in the firm's financial statements. The existence of this report indicates that an independent person, the CPA, has certified that the statements are reasonably accurate. This can be very important to bankers who want to be sure that the assets on the firm's balance sheet actually exist. Since the auditor is an independent person, the bank knows there is no reason for the balance sheet to be misstated.

Most firms that have their records audited each year do so because some outside organization requires it. For example, a large corporation that is listed on the New York Stock Exchange must be audited each year. The Securities and Exchange Commission (SEC) of the federal government requires that thousands of medium to large firms undergo annual audits. Banks serving many small firms require a yearly audit by a CPA.

An audit is often required before a bank will loan money to a firm. In addition, after a loan is granted, the bank may require an audit every year until the loan is repaid. Banks require audits so that they can anticipate any problems that the borrower may have in the future.

Owners of small firms also find financial audits useful. It is helpful to have a public accountant come in each year to check the work of the private accountant who keeps the firm's books. The public accountant often finds errors made by the private accountant. In addition, the public accountant can check to be sure that the private accountant is not embezzling money from the firm, although there is no guarantee that fraud will always be detected.

In addition to the financial auditing service, auditors also provide managerial advisory services. Since public accountants work for many different firms, they are familiar with all types of accounting and production systems. Thus, the auditor may be able to suggest ways in which the firm can save money. This advice from an expert is one of the fringe benefits of an audit. Another benefit is that employees have been found to make less errors when they know their work will be audited at the end of the year.

Although audits are beneficial in many ways, they are quite expensive and may take two or three weeks of work by a CPA. Therefore, most firms do not have their records audited unless an outsider (such as a bank) requires it.

Because of the benefits of an independent review and opinion, it may be wise for a firm to hire a CPA for several days. The check made in this short time is not a complete financial audit. It is referred to as a *management audit* or *operations audit.* In an audit of this kind, the auditor does not audit the financial records. Instead, he or she tries to determine the efficiency of the firm's management and operating systems. The audit report for this type of audit consists of a list of ways in which the firm can cut costs or increase sales. Although all firms can benefit from management or operations audits, they need not be performed every year.

GENERALLY ACCEPTED ACCOUNTING PRINCIPLES

The audit report of the financial audit illustrated earlier in this chapter stated that the financial statements were prepared "in conformity with generally accepted accounting principles." A principle is a guide to be followed in completing a certain process. Thus, the phrase in the report means that the statements were prepared in the same manner as the statements of all other firms.

Accountants follow twelve basic principles when preparing financial statements. These principles have been mentioned throughout this text and are restated here. It should be remembered that these principles must be followed whenever the financial statements will be audited by a CPA.

The twelve principles, or guides, followed by accountants are:

1. Entity.
2. Going concern (business continuity).
3. Time period (periodic).
4. Monetary (unit-of-measure).
5. Cost.
6. Objectivity.
7. Matching.
8. Full disclosure.
9. Conservatism.
10. Consistency.
11. Materiality.
12. Revenue recognition.

Entity

The *entity principle* of accounting states that the affairs of a business must be kept separate from the personal affairs of the owners of the business. This means that the personal expenses of the owner have no effect on the expenses of the business. Every business is separate from its owner. Thus, the accounting records of a business firm should show only the firm's transactions and not the personal transactions of the owner.

Going Concern

The *going concern principle* assumes that a firm will remain in business indefinitely. In other words, it is assumed that the business is a *going concern.* This is sometimes referred to as the *continuity principle* since the firm is expected to continue operating for a long period of time. This principle allows an accountant to disregard the market value of assets as long as they are owned by the firm.

For example, if the R Company purchases a truck for $5,000 and depreciates it on a five-year life, the book value after one year is $4,000. In this situation, the market value of the truck is not important. Regardless of the market value, the truck is still shown at the $4,000 book value on the balance sheet. The market value will be significant only if R Company decides to sell the truck. Until then, it is the value the firm receives from using the truck that is important. Here, the going concern principle means that the firm does not plan to sell its assets.

Time Period

The *time period* or *periodic principle* states that the life of a business is divided into many short periods to simplify the keeping of accounting records. As a result of this procedure, some estimates are necessary.

In reality, an accountant cannot prepare an accurate set of financial statements for a firm until after the firm has gone out of business. Since a firm may operate for many years, it is impractical to wait until the firm ends to prepare the financial statements. Instead, the time period principle is followed, and the statements are prepared for short periods in the life of the firm.

Accountants recognize, however, that these short-term financial statements are not totally accurate. Some estimates are needed to prepare these statements. Depreciation and bad debts are examples of these estimates. Although an accountant never knows exactly how much a machine depreciates in a year, an estimate is made so that the statements can be prepared.

Monetary

The fourth principle is the *monetary* or *unit-of-measure principle.* It requires that accounting records be kept in terms of money. In the United States, this means that records are expressed in the form of dollars and cents. This principle assumes that money (the dollar) is a standard unit of measure. In other words, a dollar received in 1972 is worth exactly the same as a dollar received in 1982. Thus, inflation is not considered in accounting.

For example, if a firm bought land in 1950 for $1,000, and bought more land in 1978 for $1,000, the balance sheet for 1978 would show $2,000 worth of land. Although the land bought in 1950 may be much more valuable, the increase in value is not shown.

Using the monetary principle, accounting records merely show the number of dollars spent. The value of those dollars in different years is not expressed. Because it ignores inflation, the monetary principle is the most criticized of all of the accounting principles. Since inflation is a very real aspect of the economy, many accountants feel that the monetary principle should be changed.

Many accountants separate these first four principles from the remaining eight. It is felt that these first four principles define the type of firm for which the records are kept. For example, the firm is a separate entity and is a going concern. The life of the firm is divided into short time periods for accounting purposes, and records are kept in terms of money. Thus, these four principles identify the firm for which the financial statements are to be prepared. The remaining eight principles tell how the statements are to be prepared.

Cost

The *cost principle* requires that all transactions be recorded at cost. It is sometimes called the *historical cost principle.* Cost is considered to be the most objective way to determine value. Assets are always recorded at their cost even though they might be currently appraised at a much higher value. If ten different people were to appraise an asset, they might come up with ten different values. Thus, appraisals are not used in accounting because they are too arbitrary. Cost is the most objective measure of an asset's worth. The cost of an asset is a value agreed upon by two parties (the buyer and seller).

Objectivity

The *objectivity principle* requires that, as much as possible, statements be based on objective evidence. It states that amounts should never be based on opinion. In most cases, the most objective evidence is cost. When cost is not known, or cannot be used, then some other form of objective evidence should be used.

Matching

The *matching principle* says that revenues and expenses should be matched to the period to which they apply. This means that adjusting entries must sometimes be made to record the revenues and expenses in the proper period. Note that the need for the matching principle is caused by the existence of the time period principle. If the life of a firm was not divided into short periods of time, then there would be no need for the matching principle. Adjusting entries are necessary because accountants follow the matching principle.

Full Disclosure

It is assumed that financial statements tell (disclose) all of the information that statement users need to know. All facts that might influence the decision of a statement user are to be included in the financial statements. No attempt should be made to mislead the reader by omission of information.

Sometimes, footnotes are used to disclose information that is not normally part of the statement but is of importance in describing the firm's operations. An item often disclosed by a footnote is the method of inventory that is used. A firm might use FIFO, LIFO, or weighted average. All three are acceptable methods. However, a footnote should appear on the balance sheet stating which method is used, since the reader must know the inventory method to properly interpret the statements.

Conservatism

Although once an important concept, the *principle of conservatism* is not highly regarded by today's accountants. Basically, this principle says that the accountant should show as low a figure as possible for assets and revenues, and as high a figure as possible for liabilities and expenses. The idea behind this principle is that the accountant should never attempt to make a firm's financial position appear to be better than it actually is. Currently, most accountants object to the use of this principle. They feel that financial statements should not be overstated or understated. Instead, they should be correct.

The principle of conservatism, as applied to the balance sheet, was the most important principle prior to World War II. It was important because bankers wanted the balance sheet to show as low a figure as possible for assets. Thus, if the bank foreclosed on the assets, the assets could be sold for more than they were supposed to be worth. Today, banks do not wish to foreclose on a firm's assets, and making a profit on the sale of foreclosed assets is not important. Instead, banks desire to earn interest by granting loans. Therefore, the conservatism principle is no longer of great importance.

Consistency

The *consistency principle* requires that firms use the same accounting methods from one period to the next. For instance, a firm may use straight-line depreciation, double-declining-balance, sum-of-the-years'-digits, or units-of-output. However, the same method must be used every year. The firm cannot change frequently from one method to another. The purpose of this principle is to insure comparability from one year to the next. It would be impossible to compare the net income of 1977 to the net income of 1978 if straight-line depreciation was used in 1977 and sum-of-the-years'-digits method in 1978. Thus, when several methods are acceptable (such as for recording depreciation and inventories), the firm must use the same method every year.

Materiality

The *materiality principle* states that adherence to any other principle is not required if the cost of following that principle is too great. This means that other principles may be ignored if the financial statements are not materially affected by the decision. For example, assume that a firm buys a wastebasket for $3.00. The wastebasket is expected to have a life of twenty years. Following the matching principle, the wastebasket should be recorded as an asset and depreciated over twenty years. If the straight-line method were used, the expense would be $.15 per year ($3.00 ÷ 20 years). However, it would cost more than that to hire someone to write down the entry each year. Thus, in this situation, the materiality principle overrules the matching principle. The materiality principle permits the firm to record the $3.00 wastebasket as an expense immediately. Even though expensing the whole $3.00 in the first year is technically wrong, it is acceptable because it is such a small amount.

Revenue Recognition

The *revenue recognition principle* states that revenue should be recorded when it is earned. Revenue is said to be earned when the most important event in the earning of the revenue has occurred. This may be determined to be any one of the following three points in the sale of merchandise:

- At the time of the sale.
- At the time cash is received.
- At the time the goods are produced.

Time of Sale. Most firms record revenue at the time the sale is made. This is the method used in this text. Usually, persuading the customer to buy is the most important event in earning a revenue. Both collecting the cash and producing the product are easier tasks. Thus, the journal entry is usually recorded when the sale is made even though no cash is collected.

Time Cash is Received. For some types of firms, making the sale is not the most important event. Some stores, especially in low income neighborhoods, have a policy of selling to anyone on credit. These firms thus have a high percent of bad debts – sometimes as high as 50%. Since these firms are never sure that they will collect their money, they do not record a revenue until the cash is collected. This method is known as the *cash basis* of accounting. Many medical doctors also use a cash basis of accounting. If a patient is near death, he or she is quite willing to buy the doctor's services. However, after recovering, the patient may not have the money to pay the bill. Thus, the doctor is never sure of earning a revenue until the cash is collected.

Time Goods are Produced. There are also a few types of firms where neither making the sale nor collecting the cash are important events. In these firms, the major event is the production of the product. A gold mine is an example of a company that could use the production basis for determining when revenue is earned. There is a dependable market for gold since the government will buy all that is produced. Also, there is no problem in collecting the cash. What is difficult, though, is getting the gold out of the ground. Thus, the most important event in earning a revenue is the production of the gold, and a revenue can be recorded as soon as it is produced.

Another type of firm that can use the production basis is a construction contractor who works on long-term contracts. Assume that a firm has a $3,000,000 contract to build a bridge. It will take three years to build the bridge, and the firm will not receive its money until the bridge is completed. If the firm were to use either the sales basis or the cash basis, its revenues would be recorded as follows:

	Sales Basis	Cash Basis
Year 1	0	0
Year 2	0	0
Year 3	3,000,000	3,000,000

Since title to the bridge does not pass and cash is not collected until the third year, all revenues would be recorded in Year 3. However, this is unrealistic. Since the firm worked full time all three years, the revenues should be about the same each year. Therefore, long-term contractors may choose to record revenues on the production basis because it gives a more reasonable picture of the firm's operation. In the above example, if one-third of the work is done each year, $1,000,000 of revenue can be recorded in each of the three years. Contractors sometimes call the production basis the *percentage-of-completion method.*

In summary, note that the cash basis and the production basis are very rarely used. Almost all firms record revenues at the time the sale is made.

These twelve accounting principles are the rules that accountants follow when preparing financial statements. Some are more important than others, but they all must be considered when a firm is to be audited. These guidelines help all firms to follow the same set of rules when preparing financial statements.

SUMMARY

A financial audit by a CPA is necessary for many firms. However, since audits are expensive, the firm should be sure that it needs one before having it performed. If an audit is not required of a firm, it may still be advisable to hire a CPA to spend several days reviewing the firm's financial affairs. The results of this management audit can help a firm operate more efficiently.

When an audit is performed, the auditor must make sure that the firm's financial statements are prepared in accordance with the twelve generally accepted accounting principles: entity, going concern, time period, monetary, cost, objectivity, matching, full disclosure, conservatism, consistency, materiality, and revenue recognition.

The value of accounting and the basic principles on which it relies are summarized by the following points.

- All firms need accounting records. Although keeping detailed accounting records may be expensive, it will ultimately save the firm money.
- A good accounting system is a valuable management tool. If all accountants follow the generally accepted principles, the financial statements are even more useful.
- The existence of these principles means that all firms are following the same set of rules in preparing financial statements. Thus, a person who knows the rules can easily interpret the statements of any firm.

REVIEW

1. Who performs audits?
2. Define auditing.
3. Are audits required of all firms?
4. List three organizations that require audits.
5. What are some of the advantages of an audit?
6. Why are generally accepted accounting principles needed?
7. Which accounting principle permits a firm to violate other principles?

8. Which principle calls for footnotes to the financial statements?
9. Which principle requires a firm to use the same inventory method from one year to the next?
10. When do most firms record revenue?
11. What principle assumes that a firm will remain in business indefinitely?
12. Which principle states that assets should be recorded at the lowest possible value?
13. Which is the least important of the twelve principles?
14. Which principle prohibits including the personal transactions of the owners on the firm's books?
15. Give an example of a firm that might use a production basis to record revenue.
16. Give an example of a firm that might use a cash basis to record revenue.
17. Which of the basic accounting principles is threatened by the existence of high inflation?
18. The comparability of financial statements is the main objective of what principle?
19. What type of firm might use the percentage-of-completion method of recording revenue?
20. If a firm overstates its ending finished goods inventory, what will be the effect on Cost of Goods Manufactured?
21. If a firm overstates its ending goods in process inventory, what will be the effect on Cost of Goods Manufactured?

EXERCISES

1. Which accounting principle is violated in the following situation: The Ace Company bought a new delivery truck with a ten year life and debited Delivery Expense.

2. Which accounting principle is violated in the following situation: The Farr Company used straight-line depreciation last year because it wanted its expenses to be low. This year the firm used double-declining-balance because it wanted its net income to be low.

3. A small building contractor has a contract to build a new building at a contract price of $200,000. Title to the building will not pass until the building is completed. No cash will be received until title passes. The firm has the building 60% completed by the end of Year A. The work is finished in Year B.
   a. How much revenue will the firm record each year if the sales basis is used?
   b. If the cash basis is used?
   c. If the percentage-of-completion basis is used?

PROBLEMS

1. Select the number of the item which best describes each of the following principles (a-h).

    a. The Monetary Principle
    b. The Going Concern Principle
    c. The Business Entity Principle
    d. Cost Principle
    e. Full Disclosure Principle
    f. Materiality Principle
    g. Consistency Principle
    h. Time Period Principle

    (1) Accounting records are kept in terms of dollars.
    (2) Total assets of a firm.
    (3) The liabilities of a firm.
    (4) The custom of dividing the life of a business into short accounting periods of equal length.
    (5) Each firm is considered separate from the affairs of its owners.
    (6) Accounting reports are prepared on the assumption that the business firm for which they are prepared will continue to operate indefinitely on a successful basis.
    (7) To insure a high degree of comparability a firm must use the same acceptable accounting methods year after year.
    (8) Accounting should be accurate yet practical.
    (9) Everything needed for a true picture of a firm's financial position should be shown on its statements.
    (10) Assets are recorded at their liquidation value, not at their cost.
    (11) One of the major objectives of accounting is to properly determine periodic income by matching appropriate costs against revenue.
    (12) An intangible factor.
    (13) Everything is recorded at its cash equivalent value.

2. State the number of the accounting principle from the following list which was violated in each of the lettered situations. (If no principle was violated, indicate number *10.*)

    (1) Business Entity
    (2) Monetary
    (3) Periodic
    (4) Cost
    (5) Matching
    (6) Materiality
    (7) Full Disclosure
    (8) Consistency
    (9) Business Continuity
    (10) No principle was violated.

    a. The Colt Company bought a piece of equipment at an auction for $300. The auctioneer later told the proprietor of Colt Company that he had made a very good deal, since the equipment was really worth $1,000. Therefore, Colt Company recorded the asset on the books at $1,000.

b. A new president took control of the Century Company. He said all the fixed assets should be written up on the company's books since an appraisal showed them to be worth more than what the assets were being shown on the company's records. He claimed that the appraisal was objective evidence and the accountant agreed.
c. A new president took control of the Sharpes Corporation. She insisted that some assets should be decreased in value on the books, since they would be worth only scrap value if the company were to go bankrupt.
d. The first year that the Wesset Company was in business, it failed to make any adjusting entries.
e. The Mundy Company closed its books on December 31 and during the next three months prepared, printed, and sent out its annual report. The union in the company had gone on strike on Jan. 4 and, thus, there had been no production since that time. The annual report mentioned nothing about the strike since it did not affect the December 31 statements.
f. Harry Jones is the sole proprietor of a grocery store. To show a greater value for his firm on the financial statements, he included his personal residence as an asset of the business.
g. The Winchester Company switched from double-declining-balance to straight-line depreciation calculations. The change materially affected net income. The company did have a legitimate reason for changing to a different method. No further accounting action was taken.
h. The Ester Company bought a new desk lamp for the office at a cost of $8. It was expected to have a useful life of ten years. Its cost was debited to an expense account.
i. The Internal Revenue Service audited the tax returns of DX Company. The IRS claimed to have found some errors which would result in DX having to pay several thousand dollars additional taxes. DX claims that the tax returns are correct and now the situation has gone to tax court. No accounting action was taken as a result of this situation.
j. The Reming Company sells primarily on a cash basis. Only about 1% of their yearly sales are on credit. However, they go to considerable time and expense each year to determine what amount should be added to the Allowance for Bad Debts account.

Glossary

Accelerated depreciation – Depreciation methods that result in most of an asset's expense being recorded in the first half of its life; depreciation charges are speeded up as compared to straight-line depreciation.

Account – A record in which increases and decreases in a particular asset, liability, owner's equity, revenue or expense item are summarized.

Accounting – The language of business; the process of keeping records of business transactions.

Accounts payable – A liability account arising from the normal operations of a business; used to record the firm's credit purchases.

Accounts payable ledger – A subsidiary ledger for accounts with creditors.

Accounts receivable – An asset account representing amounts due from credit customers.

Accounts receivable ledger – A subsidiary ledger for accounts with credit customers.

Accrued expenses – An expense that has been incurred, but not paid.

Accrued revenue – A revenue that has been earned, but not received.

Accumulated depreciation – A contra-asset account used to show the depreciation that has already been recorded on a plant asset.

Adjusted trial balance – A trial balance prepared after the adjusting entries are made.

Adjusting entries – Entries made at the end of each period to bring the accounts up to date before financial statements are prepared; needed because some account balances are incorrect due to the passage of time.

Aging the accounts receivable – A method of estimating bad debt expense in which the receivables are grouped by age. A different percentage is applied to each age group, with a higher percentage being used for the older receivables since they are more apt to be uncollectible.

Allowance for bad debts – A contra-asset account that appears as a subtraction from accounts receivable; shows the amount of receivables that are estimated to be uncollectible.

American Institute of Certified Public Accountants (AICPA) – The national organization of CPA's which is comparable to the American Bar Association and the American Medical Association.

Amortization – The periodic write-off of an intangible asset.

Asset – An economic resource purchased by a firm that is expected to provide future economic benefits.

Asset account – A ledger account for an asset; normally has a debit balance.

Audit – A check of accounting records by an independent person to assure their fairness.

Audit opinion – An opinion by an auditor as to whether financial statements fairly present the results of a firm's activities.

Bad debt expense – An expense resulting from an uncollectible account.

Balance sheet – The financial statement that shows a firm's assets, liabilities, and owner's equity at a specific point in time; can be thought of as a photograph of a business at a specific moment.

Bank reconciliation – A statement showing the differences between a depositor's books and the bank's records of the same checking account.

Bank statement – A statement received from the bank showing all checking account transactions that took place during the previous month.

Basic accounting equation – The statement expressed by:

Assets = Liabilities + Owner's Equity.

Book Value – In reference to assets, cost minus accumulated depreciation, or the value of a plant asset on a firm's books. In reference to stock, the value of one share of stock on a corporation's books.

Books – The accounting records of a business.

Budget – A written financial plan for the future with dollar values; its preparation begins with the sales budget and ends with estimated financial statements.

CPA certificate – A certificate issued to those who have experience in public accounting and have passed the required examination.

Capital expenditure – An expenditure that is expected to benefit more than one period; recorded as an asset.

Cash budget – A forecast of cash flow for a future period.

Cash discount – A discount on the invoice price; given for paying an invoice earlier than normally required.

Cash flow statement – A statement showing a firm's sources and uses of cash during a period of time.

Cash payments journal – A journal (book of original entry) used to record all credits to cash.

Cash receipts journal – A journal (book of original entry) used to record all debits to cash.

Cash short and over – An account used to record the difference between the amount in a petty cash box and the amount that should be in the box; may be either an expense account or a revenue account, depending upon whether it has a debit or a credit balance.

Certificate in Management Accounting (CMA) – A certificate issued to those who have experience in management accounting and have passed a five-part examination.

Certified Public Accountant (CPA) – An accountant who has experience in public accounting and has passed the CPA examination.

Closing entries – The last entries made each period to close the temporary owner's equity accounts. Also used to transfer the results of operations from the temporary accounts to the permanent capital account.

Common-size financial statement – Statement which shows all amounts as percentages. Total assets equals 100% on the balance sheet and net sales equals 100% on the income statement.

Common stock – The class of stock that represents residual ownership in a corporation; first type of stock that a corporation issues.

Comparative statements – Two or more financial statements placed side by side; often accompanied by a percentage change calculation.

Conservatism principle – Rule stating that when alternative accounting principles or procedures are acceptable, the method that is most conservative should be used; results in showing the lowest income and the least amount of assets.

Consistency principle – The principle that insures comparability of financial statements from one period to the next. Whenever alternative accounting procedures are acceptable (LIFO, FIFO, etc.) a firm must be consistent from one period to the next.

Contra account – An account which appears on the financial statements as a subtraction from some other account; sometimes called a valuation account since it helps to show a truer value for the other account.

Control account – A general ledger account having a balance that represents many subsidiary ledger accounts.

Copyright – A government granted right to be the only publisher of a written work; an intangible asset.

Corporation – A firm organized as a separate legal entity and chartered under state or federal laws. Ownership is represented by shares of stock.

Cost of goods manufactured – The cost of producing a product in a manufacturing firm; the bottom line on a manufacturing statement. The three elements of cost are raw materials, direct labor, and factory overhead.

Cost principle – All transactions are to be recorded at cost, since cost is the most objective value.

Credit – The right side of an account.

Credit balance – The difference between the debits and credits in an account in which the credits exceed the debits.

Credit memorandum – A business paper that tells creditors or customers that their account payable or account receivable has been credited by the issuer of the memorandum; it usually results from a return of merchandise or correction of an error.

Creditor – A person or firm to whom a liability is owed.

Crossfooting – The process of adding across a multi-column special journal to be sure that the debits equal the credits.

Cumulative preferred stock – Preferred stock on which dividends accumulate until paid. If dividends are not paid in a given year, then it is said that there are *dividends in arrears*.

Current assets – Assets that will be turned into cash or used up within one year or the normal operating cycle, whichever is longer.

Current liabilities – Debts that must be paid within one year or the normal operating cycle, whichever is longer.

Current ratio – Current assets divided by current liabilities.

Date of record – The date between the declaration date and the date of payment which determines a specific shareholder's right to receive a dividend.

Debit – The left side of an account.

Debit balance – The difference between the debits and credits in an account in which the debits exceed the credits.

Debit memorandum – A business paper that informs creditors or customers that their account payable or account receivable has been debited by the issuer of the memorandum; used when neither an invoice nor cash is used.

Declaration date – The date on which a dividend is declared by a corporation's board of directors.

Deficit – Negative retained earnings (debit balance) in a corporation.

Depletion – The write-off of a natural resource.

Deposit in transit – A deposit which has been mailed to the bank, or placed in a bank's night depository, and thus is not received by the bank on the same day that the deposit is recorded by the depositor. A deposit in transit is added to the balance per bank statement on a bank reconciliation.

Depreciable cost – The cost of a plant asset minus the estimated scrap value.

Depreciation – The allocation of an asset's cost over its useful life.

Direct labor – The wages of those workers who work directly on the product being produced.

Direct write-off method – A method of writing off a bad debt to expense when it is discovered that the account is uncollectible. The direct write-off method usually violates the matching principle of accounting.

Discount on common (preferred) stock – A stockholder's equity account of a corporation; a contra-paid-in-capital account used when stock is sold for less than par value. Has a debit balance.

Dividend – A distribution of corporate assets to the stockholders.

Double-declining-balance method – An accelerated method of depreciation. A constant percentage (at twice the straight-line rate) is multipled times the remaining book value of a plant asset.

Drawing – Cash or other assets withdrawn from a business by the owner.

Entity principle – A principle that states that the affairs of a business are separate from the personal affairs of its owner or owners.

Exemptions – Deductions from gross income that a taxpayer is allowed on the federal income tax return. One exemption is allowed for the taxpayer, the taxpayer's spouse, and each dependent, with an additional one for each taxpayer or spouse who is blind or over the age of sixty-five.

Expense – A decrease in owner's equity resulting from the normal operations of a business.

Expense account – A temporary owner's equity account that shows the decreases in owner's equity resulting from the normal operations of the business; has debit balance and appears on the income statement.

Extraordinary items – Gains and losses resulting from non-recurring transactions; not a part of normal operations.

Extraordinary repairs – Large repairs that either lengthen the life of a plant asset or make the asset more productive; viewed as capital expenditures and debited to Accumulated Depreciation, since it is assumed that the repairs erase some of the depreciation that has already been recorded.

Factory overhead – All production (factory) costs other than raw materials and direct labor.

Federal unemployment tax – A tax imposed on the employer.

FICA tax (Federal Insurance Contributions Act) – Better known as social security; paid partially by the employee and partially by the employer.

FIFO – See *first-in, first-out*.

Financial Accounting Standards Board (FASB) – An independent group which establishes the procedures to be used in preparing financial statements.

Finished goods inventory – A current asset account representing those goods that are ready to be sold to customers. It is used in a manufacturing firm and is identical to the merchandise inventory account of a merchandising firm.

First-in, first-out – An inventory valuation method which assumes that the first goods received are the first ones sold; thus, the ending inventory consists of the most recent purchases.

Fiscal year – Any twelve-month period for which financial statements are prepared.

Fixed assets – Plant assets.

Fixed costs – Costs that are fixed (do not change) at all levels of production.

Flexible budget – A series of budgets for several different levels of sales.

FOB destination – Freight term that means title to goods passes when the goods reach their destination. Thus, seller owns goods while they are in transit, therefore, pays the freight charges.

FOB shipping point (FOB factory) – Freight term that means title to goods passes the moment they leave their shipping point. The buyer owns the goods while they are in transit and must pay the freight charges.

Footing – The process of adding a column of figures.

Form 941 – Employer's quarterly federal tax return. Shows wages paid and taxes withheld during the previous three months.

Form W-2 – A form given by the employer to the employee each January; shows the amount of wages earned during the previous year and the amount of taxes withheld from those wages.

Form W-4 – A form that is given by the employee to the employer stating how many exemptions the employee is claiming for tax purposes.

Full disclosure principle – All financial information that a user needs to know is included in the financial statements; may require the use of footnotes to include all necessary information.

Funds – Usually defined as working capital (current assets minus current liabilities).

General journal – A book of original entry.

General ledger – See *ledger*.

Generally accepted accounting principles – Accounting principles that have received substantial authoritative support from the major accounting organizations.

Going concern principle (business continuity) – Assumption that a firm will continue operating indefinitely.

Goodwill – An intangible asset which can only be bought when an entire business is purchased. It is the difference between the amount paid for a new business and the value of the identifiable assets received.

Gross profit – The difference between sales and cost of goods sold. It is the difference between the retail selling price and the wholesale cost of the goods sold.

Gross profit method – A method of estimating inventory values used when the inventory has been destroyed or on interim financial statements; requires that gross profit be estimated.

Income statement – The financial statement that shows a firm's revenues, costs, and expenses for a certain period of time.

Income summary account – Temporary account used only for closing entries; does not appear on any financial statement.

Indirect labor – The labor cost of those factory employees who do not work directly on the product; considered as a part of factory overhead. (Examples: wages of janitors and supervisors.)

Intangible assets – Assets that have no physical substance, but are expected to provide future economic benefits to the firm.

Interest – A charge made by a lender for the use of money. Computed as follows:

$$\text{Interest} = \text{Principle} \times \text{Interest Rate} \times \text{Time.}$$

Internal Revenue Service (IRS) – The federal government agency that collects income taxes.

Itemized deductions – Deductions that may be taken on the federal income tax return – the alternative to standard deduction. (Examples: medical expenses, state and county taxes, interest, contributions, and other miscellaneous costs.)

Journal – A book of original entry; the first place that a transaction is recorded.

Last-in, first-out – An inventory valuation method in which it is assumed that the last goods received are the first ones sold; the ending inventory consists of the earliest goods bought (advantageous for tax purposes during periods of inflation).

Ledger – A group of accounts, or a book of accounts; sometimes called a book of final entry.

Liability account – An account in the ledger for a liability; normally has a credit balance.

LIFO – See *last-in, first-out.*

Limited liability – One of the advantages of the corporate form of business; the owners (stockholders) are not personally liable for the firm's debts. Their liability is limited to their original investment.

Liquidation – The process of ending a partnership.

Lower-of-cost-or-market – A method of valuing inventory in which items are valued at the lower of cost or replacement cost.

Manufacturing statement – Supplement to the income statement in which the cost of goods manufactured is computed.

Manufacturing summary account – A temporary account used only to close out the accounts which appear on the manufacturing statement.

Market – When valuing inventories, refers to replacement cost.

Marketable securities – Investments that are classified as current assets.

Matching principle – A principle that states that revenues and expenses should be matched to the period to which they apply.

Materiality principle – The principle that permits violation of any other principle as long as the effect on the financial statements is immaterial.

Merchandising inventory – An asset account that represents the cost of goods being held for sale to customers.

Monetary principle – Accounting records are kept in terms of money; in the United States the dollar is the standard unit of measure.

Mutual agency – The right of each partner to act as an agent for a partnership; thus, any individual partner may bind the firm to a contract.

Net income – A situation in which revenues are greater than costs and expenses; shown as the bottom line on an income statement.

Net loss – A situation in which revenues are less than costs and expenses; the bottom line on an income statement when a firm has not been profitable.

No-par stock – Corporate stock that has not been assigned a par value.

NSF check (nonsufficient funds) – A check in payment for a firm's services for which there was no money in the customer's account; deposited in bank by firm. In this case the check is returned to the depositor.

Notes payable – A liability evidenced by a formal, written document signed by the debtor; usually involves an interest charge.

Objectivity principle – The rule stating all accounting evidence must be objective.

Operating cycle – The period of time required for a firm to obtain cash, buy inventory, sell the goods on credit, and collect the accounts receivable. The cycle begins with cash and ends with cash.

Organization costs – The costs of starting up a corporation including lawyer fees, state charter fee, and the cost of printing stock certificates; an intangible asset.

Outstanding checks – Those checks which have been written but have not yet cleared the depositor's bank; deducted from the balance per bank statement on a reconciliation.

Owner's drawing account – A temporary owner's equity account that shows the amount of assets that have been withdrawn from the business by the owner during the current period; has a debit balance.

Owner's equity – The owner's investment in a firm; is equal to assets minus liabilities.

Owner's equity account – An account in the ledger representing an owner's investment in a business, normally has a credit balance.

Paid-in capital – Capital acquired from the shareholders of a corporation.

Par value – An arbitrary value placed on corporate stock; the amount which is used in the accounting records.

Participating preferred stock – Preferred stock that may participate along with common in above-average earnings.

Partnership – A firm owned by two or more persons.

Patent – A government-granted right to be the only producer of a product during a seventeen-year period; an intangible asset.

Payment date – The date on which a dividend is paid.

Periodic inventory system – A method of accounting for inventory in which the amount of inventory on hand is known only for the balance sheet date and is determined by a physical count. Thus, the inventory account is only correct periodically.

Perpetual inventory system – A method of accounting for inventory that provides a continuous (perpetual) record of goods on hand.

Petty cash fund – A small amount of cash set aside to pay for minor expenses (such as stamps) for which it would be impractical to write a check.

Petty cash voucher – A receipt signed by a person who has received money from a petty cash fund.

Physical inventory – The process of physically counting the goods that are on hand on a specific date.

Plant assets – Assets which are used in the business and have a life of more than one year.

Post-closing trial balance – A trial balance that is prepared after the closing entries have been posted to assure that debits still equal credits.

Posting – The process of transferring amounts from the journals to the ledger accounts.

Preferred stock – The stock of a corporation that has certain preferences over common stock. Preferences include first right to dividends when declared and first right to any assets at liquidation.

Premium on stock – A stockholders' equity account of a corporation. It is a paid-in capital account used when stock is sold for more than par value.

Prepaid expenses – Expenses for which cash has already been paid, but which should be matched against future periods; classified as current assets.

Price-earnings ratio – The market price of one share of a corporation's stock divided by earnings per share.

Principal – The face amount of a note.

Principle – A guideline to aid in the preparation of financial statements.

Proprietorship – A business owned by one person; also used to refer to the owner's equity of a proprietor.

Proxy – A written authorization by a stockholder to permit someone else to vote his or her shares at a stockholders' meeting.

Purchases – An account for recording purchases of merchandise for resale in a firm with a periodic inventory system; has a debit balance and is classified as a cost account.

Purchases journal – A journal (book of original entry) that is used only to record credit purchases of merchandise to be sold.

Purchases returns – An account that is used to record returns of merchandise to suppliers; a contra-account to purchases.

Quick assets – Assets quickly convertible into cash such as cash, marketable securities, and accounts receivable.

Quick ratio – A measure of current debt-paying ability; computed by dividing quick assets by current liabilities.

Raw materials inventory – An asset account representing those materials that will eventually become a part of a manufacturing firm's finished product.

Retail method – A method of estimating inventory value in a retail store (such as a grocery or department store). Inventory is first priced at retail and then converted to cost.

Retained earnings – A stockholders' equity account in a corporation. It is the account to which the income summary account is closed; normally has a credit balance.

Retained earnings statement – A statement showing the changes in a corporation's retained earnings account during a period of time.

Revenue – An increase in owner's equity resulting from the normal operations of a business.

Revenue account – A temporary owner's equity account that shows the increases in owner's equity resulting from the normal operations of the business; has credit balance and appears on the income statement.

Revenue expenditure – An expenditure that is expected to benefit only the current period; recorded as an expense.

Revenue recognition principle – The principle stating that revenue should be recorded when it is realized. Revenue is realized when the most important event in earning a revenue has occurred; this could be at the time of the sale, at the time cash is received, or at the time of production.

Sales – A revenue account.

Sales journal – A journal (book of original entry) that is used only to record sales of merchandise on credit.

Sales returns and allowances – An account that is used to record returns of merchandise by customers; a contra-account to sales.

Schedule of accounts payable – A listing of all of the account balances in a subsidiary accounts payable ledger. The total of the schedule should be identical to the balance of the Accounts Payable Control account in the general ledger.

Schedule of accounts receivable – A listing of all of the account balances in a subsidiary accounts receivable ledger. The total of the schedule should be identical to the balance of the Accounts Receivable Control account.

Scrap value – The estimated value of a plant asset when it is no longer of any use to the firm.

Social security tax – See *FICA tax*.

Securities and Exchange Commission (SEC) – A federal government agency that was given authority by the Securities Acts of 1933 and 1934 to establish accounting principles. Works closely with the accounting profession.

Special journal – Journal that is used only for a specific type of transaction; saves labor since totals can be posted rather than individual amounts.

Specific identification method – A method of valuing inventory by identifying each item of inventory with a specific purchase invoice.

Standard deduction – The deduction that a taxpayer is allowed on the federal tax return; the alternative to itemized deductions.

State unemployment tax – A tax imposed on the employer.

Statement of changes in financial position – The third basic financial statement; shows the sources and uses of either cash or working capital.

Stock certificate – A sheet of paper that represents ownership in a corporation.

Stock dividend – A dividend paid (distributed) in the form of a corporation's own stock.

Stock split – An increase in the number of corporate shares outstanding; accompanied by a decrease in par value.

Straight-line depreciation – A depreciation method in which the depreciable cost (cost minus scrap value) is allocated over the useful life, in years, of the plant asset; results in an identical expense each year.

Subsidiary ledger – A supplementary ledger that is used when a firm has many accounts of a similar type; provides a detailed record of the balance of a control account in the general ledger. The total of the accounts in the subsidiary ledger equals the balance of the control account.

Sum-of-the-years'-digits depreciation – An accelerated method of depreciation in which the depreciable cost of a plant asset is multiplied by a fraction that declines each year.

Temporary owner equity accounts – The owner's drawing account, revenue accounts, and expense accounts.

Time period principle – The practice of dividing the life of a business into short periods for accounting convenience; results in the use of estimates to make accounts as accurate as possible.

Transaction – Business event that should be recorded in the accounting records.

Treasury stock – A corporation's own stock that it has reacquired.

Trial balance – A listing of all account balances designed to check whether the debits equal the credits. The debit balances are put in one column and the credit balances in another column.

Unearned revenue – Revenue that has been received, but not yet earned; considered a liability.

Units-of-output (production) depreciation – A depreciation method in which the depreciable cost (cost minus scrap value) is allocated over the useful life of the plant asset. The useful life is measured in terms of units expected to be produced.

Unlimited liability – Situation in which each owner is liable for all debts of the firm; one of the disadvantages of the partnership and proprietorship forms of business.

Valuation account – See *contra account.*

Variable costs – Costs that vary directly with volume.

Withdrawals – See *drawing.*

Work-in-process inventory – A current asset account representing the cost of those products that have been started but are not yet complete at the end of a period.

Work sheet – A large work paper used to assemble data needed to prepare the financial statements.

Working capital – Current assets minus current liabilities.

Acknowledgments

Sponsoring Editor: William W. Sprague

Editor: Mary L. Wright

Technical Editor: Esther B. Grant, Hillsborough Community College

Technical Reviewers: Thomas R. Fredericks, Waukesha County Technical Institute
Lawrence L. Kogut, Hillsborough Community College
Thomas J. Garrison, Times Mirror Magazines

Consulting Editor, Accounting Series: Edward G. Blum

Material for this text was classroom tested at Appalachian State University, Boone, NC; Broome Community College, Binghamton, NY; Hillsborough Community College, Tampa, FL; and the University of Mississippi, Oxford, MS.

Contributions of Content and Illustration:

Burns Photography, Schenectady, NY – Section Intro 1, 2, and 3
Decorators Workroom, Albany, NY – Section Intro 3, 14-1
McBee Systems, Albany, NY – Section Intro 4, 22-2 through 22-8, 23-1
Photo Workshop, Kingston, NY – 1-2, 14-4, Section Intro 4, 22-2 through 22-8, 23-8, 27-1
Nick Pignatelli, Troy, NY – 1-1
Joseph Tardi Associates, Troy, NY – 14-1, Section Intro 6 and 7
Small Business Administration, Washington, DC – 14-4, 23-8
T.R. Weed & Sons, New Paltz, NY – 27-1
Workingman's Florist, Albany, NY – Section Intro 1, 25-1

The authors express appreciation to their colleagues and students at both the University of Mississippi and Appalachian State University, and particularly to the following individuals:

Kim Pruitt, University of Mississippi
Doug Merritt, Lowes Hardware, Wilkesboro, NC
Brenda Merrit, Wilkes Community College, Wilkesboro, NC
R. Joseph Barnes, Appalachian State University, Boone, NC
Nancy Mullins, Arthur Anderson & Co., Milwaukee, WI
Barbara Weeks, University of Mississippi

Index

B

D

E

F

Q

R

T

U

V

W

Z